Studies in Celtic History XII

IRELAND, WALES, AND ENGLAND IN THE ELEVENTH CENTURY

STUDIES IN CELTIC HISTORY
General editor   David Dumville
ISSN 0261-9865

Already published
I · THE SAINTS OF GWYNEDD
Molly Miller

II · CELTIC BRITAIN IN THE EARLY MIDDLE AGES
Kathleen Hughes

III · THE INSULAR LATIN GRAMMARIANS
Vivien Law

IV · CHRONICLES AND ANNALS OF MEDIAEVAL IRELAND AND WALES
Kathryn Grabowski & David Dumville

V · GILDAS: NEW APPROACHES
M. Lapidge & D. Dumville (edd.)

VI · SAINT GERMANUS OF AUXERRE AND THE END OF ROMAN BRITAIN
E. A. Thompson

VII · FROM KINGS TO WARLORDS
Katharine Simms

VIII · THE CHURCH AND THE WELSH BORDER
IN THE CENTRAL MIDDLE AGES
C. N. L. Brooke

IX · THE LITURGY AND RITUAL OF THE CELTIC CHURCH
F. E. Warren (2nd edn, by Jane Stevenson)

X · THE MONKS OF REDON
Caroline Brett (ed. & transl.)

XI · EARLY MONASTERIES IN CORNWALL
Lynette Olson

Forthcoming
XIII · UNDERSTANDING THE UNIVERSE IN SEVENTH-CENTURY IRELAND
Marina Smyth

In preparation
GILDAS IN THE MIDDLE AGES
David Dumville (ed.)

COLUMBANUS: THE LATIN WRITINGS
Michael Lapidge (ed.)

NAVIGATIO SANCTI BRENDANI
Giovanni Orlandi

IRELAND, WALES, AND ENGLAND IN THE ELEVENTH CENTURY

K.L. MAUND

THE BOYDELL PRESS

First published 1991 by The Boydell Press, Woodbridge

The Boydell Press is an imprint of Boydell & Brewer Ltd
PO Box 9, Woodbridge, Suffolk IP12 3DF
and of Boydell & Brewer Inc.
PO Box 41026, Rochester, NY 14604, USA

ISBN 0 85115 533 2

British Library Cataloguing in Publication Data
Maund, K. L.
  Ireland, Wales and England in the eleventh century. –
  (Studies in Celtic history ; 0261–9865, 12).
  1. Wales, history
  I. Title II. Series
  942.9
  ISBN 0–85115–533–2

Library of Congress Cataloging-in-Publication Data
Maund, K. L., 1962–
  Ireland, Wales, and England in the eleventh century / K.L. Maund.
    p.   cm. – (Studies in Celtic history, ISSN 0261–9865 ; 12)
  Revision of thesis (Ph. D.)–University of Cambridge, 1987.
  Includes bibliographical references and index.
  ISBN 0–85115–533–2 (alk. paper)
  1. Wales–History–To 1536. 2. Wales–Relations–Ireland.
  3. Wales–Relations–England. 4. Eleventh century. I. Title.
  II. Series.
  DA715.M33   1991
  942.01'8–dc20   90–19312

This publication is printed on acid-free paper

Printed in Great Britain by
St Edmundsbury Press Ltd, Bury St Edmunds, Suffolk

202678

CONTENTS

For
Irene Maund

GENERAL EDITOR'S FOREWORD

The twelfth volume of *Studies in Celtic History* gives a central place to the political life of Wales in the eleventh century, here generously defined. By prosopographical study, involving close analysis of both genealogical and chronicling texts (not to mention some difficult documents from *Liber Landauensis*), Dr Maund has identified the principal families and factions who bore rule or influenced political events in that century. This is in itself a considerable achievement, for the period has often seemed a dark maze to those who would attempt to understand it.

The period to which Dr Maund has devoted her study is also, for Wales, the Second Viking Age. The involvement of Hiberno-Scandinavian warbands in Welsh politics is another theme of her book and (again) brings light to a formerly confusing area of the history of the late tenth and eleventh centuries. Increasingly, too, the eleventh century saw the resumption of routinely hostile relationships across the Anglo-Welsh border, in contrast to the relative quiet which had prevailed between the two peoples during the period of alliance from *ca* 885 to 1016. Once again, however, there are new patterns of political interaction and Dr Maund elucidates these by close study of sources from both cultures. After 1066 the Normans were to become involved in Welsh history, bringing a new era and with it new forms of aggression to cross-border relationships. Some early stages of that process are traced in this book. It is hoped, therefore, that students of Welsh, Irish, Scandinavian, and English history will find much here to interest them.

July 1990

David Dumville
Girton College
Cambridge

PREFACE

This book is intended to be primarily an examination of the Welsh context of eleventh-century politics, both within Wales itself and within the wider sphere of the British Isles. I have sought to identify and analyse patterns of political behaviour, and to chart their growth and development during the century. In this process the mid-eleventh-century king, Gruffudd ap Llywelyn, emerges as central, and the effects of his reign proved long lasting both inside and outside Wales. The second chapter is devoted to internal Welsh affairs, including a prosopography on a scale not previously attempted. In the third chapter I examine Anglo-Welsh relations before, during, and immediately after the Norman conquest of England, and demonstrate the changes wrought in those relations not simply by English events (as in most previous studies) but also by developments within Wales itself. The fourth chapter is concerned with the hitherto little-charted territory of Welsh relations with the Hiberno-Scandinavians, and the effects which these groups had one upon the other. In the fifth chapter I turn to the charters contained in that problematic source, the twelfth-century *Liber Landauensis*, and consider their validity as evidence for eleventh-century affairs. In this book Wales is placed centre-stage: the evidence demonstrates that at no time in the period under study should this area be considered a mere subsidiary or dependant of the more prominent neighbouring kingdoms.

This volume originated from the core of a dissertation accepted in 1987 for the Ph.D. degree of the University of Cambridge. I wish to acknowledge the stimulus provided by the Department of Anglo-Saxon, Norse and Celtic during my student years and the critical yet benevolent interest of the examiners of the dissertation, Dr David Kirby and Dr Martin Brett. I should also like to thank Dr D. N. Dumville for his continuing support and advice, Dr P. Sims-Williams for help with Welsh poetry, and Roger Dearnaley for many hours spent in computer-type-setting and designing the diagrams.

March 1990

K.L. Maund
School of Celtic Studies,
Dublin Institute for Advanced Studies

ABBREVIATIONS

ABT	The Welsh genealogical tract *Achau Brenhinoedd a Thywysogion Cymru*
AC (B)	The B-text of *Annales Cambriae*
AC (C)	The C-text of *Annales Cambriae*
AClon	Annals of Clonmacnoise
AFM	Annals of the Four Masters
AI	Annals of Inisfallen
ALC	Annals of Loch Cé
ASC (C)	The C-text of the Anglo-Saxon Chronicle
ASC (D)	The D-text of the Anglo-Saxon Chronicle
ASC (E)	The E-text of the Anglo-Saxon Chronicle
ASC (F)	The F-text of the Anglo-Saxon Chronicle
ASC (F Lat)	The Latin annals in the F-text of the Anglo-Saxon Chronicle
AT	Annals of Tigernach
AU	Annals of Ulster
ByS	*Brenhinedd y Saesson*
ByT (Pen. 20)	*Brut y Tywysogion* (MS. Peniarth 20 version)
ByT (RB)	*Brut y Tywysogion* (Red Book of Hergest version)
CS	*Chronicum Scottorum*
HGK	*Historia Gruffud vab Kenan*
HH	Henry of Huntingdon, *Historia Anglorum*
HL	The Welsh genealogical tract *Hen Lwythau Gwynedd a'r Mars*
HR^2	*Historia Regum Anglorum*, Part two, attributed to Symeon of Durham
JC	The Welsh genealogies in Oxford, Jesus College, MS. 20
JW	John of Worcester
LL	*Liber Landauensis*
MG	The Welsh genealogies in Aberystwyth, National Library of Wales, MS. Mostyn 117
MP	The miscellaneous Welsh pedigrees edited by Bartrum, *Tracts*, pp. 121–2 and 158

I

INTRODUCTION

The eleventh century was a time of political change for the British Isles, with such occurrences as the rise of the Uí Briain kings in Ireland, conquests in England first by Danes and later by Normans, and the absorption of the Hiberno-Scandinavian kingdom of Dublin into the wider Irish polity. This era of change was perhaps nowhere more apparent than in Wales. In addition to the external forces represented by the English, Hiberno-Scandinavians and Normans, the eleventh century saw many internal political factors operating within Wales itself, leading to the emergence of Gruffudd ap Llywelyn, and the creation by him (for the first and only time) of a kingdom of all Wales, an event which was to have important consequences, not only for Wales but for her neighbours also. Wales in the eleventh century provides a fascinating and important arena for the study of political behaviour, for that country's central geographical position meant that major changes and upheavals in neighbouring kingdoms were reflected within the Welsh polity.

The purpose of my book is to examine the relationship of Wales to England and the Hiberno-Scandinavians of Ireland in this important century, and to investigate the way in which Wales was affected by and involved in the political activities of its neighbours. No such study could be complete, however, without an initial examination of the nature of Welsh internal politics, and the complex network of alliance and kinship by which the native Welsh rulers were bound. I have therefore begun by looking at the internal events and personalities of Wales in the eleventh century, by considering the ways in which rulers of the various Welsh kingdoms were related to one another within the Welsh polity, and by examining the changes which occurred. From this, I have moved on to analyse Welsh reactions to the England and to the Hiberno-Scandinavians, and to show how the Welsh exploited and responded to the political circumstances of their neighbours. In this, one particular ruler stands out as significant: the mid-eleventh-century king, Gruffudd ap Llywelyn, who, initially king of Gwynedd, extended his power across all Wales, and influenced English politics also.

Was the Welsh response to internal and external change wholly random, or can patterns be identified? I have argued that the latter was the case, that we may find paradigms for political behaviour in Wales. In particular, the rise of Gruffudd ap Llywelyn marks a change in Welsh response to external forces, an awareness, perhaps, of an ability to intervene in and influence politics in other areas. I argue for a developing recognition by the Welsh of new modes of political behaviour in the eleventh century, growing out of the rapidly changing conditions of this turbulent period. In their dealings with threats presented by English, vikings, and

1

Normans, the Welsh learnt to exploit their enemies, turning some of them into allies, and using these to thwart other groups, both Welsh and otherwise. The Hiberno-Scandinavians, from being marauders, became a resource employed by kings and exiles to re-assert themselves, and ultimately, in the person of the half-viking Gruffudd ap Cynan, they came to rule in north Wales. The English also changed from enemies to allies – more reliable perhaps than the vikings, but also more dangerous, for entering an alliance with an English nobleman could carry with it the danger of acquiring the enmity of another English lord, no more so than during the time of Gruffudd ap Llywelyn and Edward the Confessor. The new threat of the Normans was severe, but not so great that Welsh rulers could not make use of the resources and rivalries of these invaders, playing them off against each other and against native rivals. Clear patterns of political behaviour emerge as the events of the period are studied: the intention of this book is to chart the development and progress of these patterns.

Many sources have been used in order to do this. In particular, these include the Welsh chronicles – two versions of *Annales Cambriae*, and three *Brutiau* – the Anglo-Saxon Chronicle, a variety of Irish chronicles – the Annals of Ulster, the Annals of Inisfallen, the Annals of Tigernach, and others. Some texts by Anglo-Norman authors have also been used, including the works of John of Worcester, William of Malmesbury, Orderic Vitalis, and Walter Map. In addition to the chronicles, I have also made extensive use of Welsh genealogical material. Attention has been given to charter-evidence, and in particular to the documents contained within the controversial *Liber Landauensis*, which are examined in some detail in the fifth chapter. Not all the sources are contemporary, not all of them are reliable, and many display biases, be they regional, political, or ecclesiastical. Many of the sources are dependent upon and related to each other. In matters of chronology, in particular, they are often in disagreement, and it is not always easy to reconcile their statements. I have endeavoured to draw together their evidence, and to reassemble from it as many pieces as possible of the jigsaw of eleventh-century Welsh politics.

The dating adopted in the text is in general that supplied by the editors of the primary sources and accepted by modern scholars, in particular, J. E. Lloyd, Frank Barlow, and R. R. Davies. There are exceptions to this, however, where a source lacks dates, or where those supplied by its editor are suspect. This is particularly the case with *Annales Cambriae*: dates cited here from the B- and C-texts of these chronicles have been achieved by an examination of the manuscripts and are placed in square brackets to show their somewhat tentative nature. The dates as given in the primary sources, where these differ from the generally accepted dates, are given in the footnotes.

II

THE ELEVENTH-CENTURY RULERS OF WALES:
THEIR POLITICAL AND
GENEALOGICAL RELATIONSHIPS

In the Welsh chronicles, in the period *ca* 975–*ca* 1110 there are eighty-five names all told of Welsh lay individuals, as opposed to Englishmen, vikings, Normans, Welsh ecclesiastics (this latter group is very small – a few bishops and one monk), Irishmen, and a few other foreigners (Malcolm III of Scotland, for instance). Within this total of eighty-five names, I include all names otherwise unqualified by a reference to their owners' origin and position: I concede the possibility that several of them may actually have been clerics, although this is no longer provable.

Of these eighty-five names, sixty-six are found in all or almost all the Welsh annalistic sources. These are the Latin texts known as *Annales Cambriae*[1] (versions B and C); and the vernacular chronicles known as *Brut y Tywysogion* (Peniarth MS 20 version[2] and Red Book of Hergest version[3]) and *Brenhinedd y Saesson*.[4] A handful of names seems to be found in only one version of *Annales Cambriae*, but I draw no conclusions from this, as it is entirely possible that the apparent absence is due to the shortcomings of Williams's edition. One name, Gwrmid, occurs in *Brut y Tywysogion* (Pen. 20) only, *s.a.* 977; this person may, however, have been Irish or Hiberno-Scandinavian rather than Welsh.

Not all the persons mentioned are identifiable. Some, while themselves of uncertain origin, become the first known members of notable families or descent-groups; others are probably the final members of fading dynasties; yet others are completely obscure. My purpose here is to endeavour to disentangle, clarify, and elaborate upon the figures of eleventh-century Wales, and to seek to reveal and explain their relationships, both personal and political. In doing so, I have largely omitted twelfth-century descendants of eleventh-century rulers: these will be referred to, but not discussed in great detail.

I intend in the main to use the evidence of the native Welsh sources, although reference will be made to English, Irish, and Anglo-Norman texts. However, since much of the material involved is genealogical, I consider it better to work

---

1 AC: *Annales Cambriae*, ed. Williams (ab Ithel); for the period 1035–1093, see also Lloyd, 'Wales and the coming'.
2 ByT (Pen. 20): *Brut y Tywysogion, Peniarth MS 20*, ed. Jones; *Brut y Tywysogion, Peniarth MS 20*, transl. Jones.
3 ByT (RB): *Brut y Tywysogion, Red Book of Hergest Version*, ed. & transl. Jones.
4 ByS: *Brenhinedd y Saesson*, ed. & transl. Jones.

within a mainly Welsh context, as the genealogical tradition within mediaeval Wales (and indeed later) seems not to have been changed in a major degree by outside influence. Hence it seems more appropriate to me to concentrate here upon native Welsh sources for the eleventh-century rulers and their actions, and to use the evidence of non-Welsh chroniclers as a supplement and check upon the Welsh texts.

It hardly needs to be said that the source-material is fraught with problems, complexities, and difficulties. In many cases, the date of a text is uncertain. Interrelationships between sources are not always clear. Modern editions, also, are not always as helpful as they might be. The eleventh century in Wales is better documented than the preceding centuries, but the evidence cannot always be treated as reliable or definitive. Much – indeed, most – of it is retrospective: almost all of it possesses a political or dynastic bias. Furthermore, it is of a heterogeneous character, and frequently self contradictory. Clearly, great care is necessary in attempting to draw even the most tentative conclusions. This is particularly true of the genealogical material; I shall approach it with scepticism in many cases, and occasionally with incredulity.

The eleventh century was a period of change and transition. Not only did it see the reign of the first 'king of all Wales', Gruffudd ap Llywelyn, but it was the century of the Norman conquest of England. Wales was not wholly annexed by the Normans in the eleventh century, but it was nevertheless a period of incursions, erosions, and gradual Norman expansion into territory formerly Welsh. The implications of this are especially great if one considers that for much of the time preceding the Norman conquest, the Welsh had been confronted by an England whose stability and solidarity was by no means always certain. The English raided, and were raided; the English kings claimed an overlordship over those of Wales, but not even the actions in the 1060s of Harold Godwinesson presented a threat on the scale of that posed by the Normans. Clearly, Norman activity worked to alter the Welsh polity, affecting internal Welsh relationships as well as Welsh attitudes to non-Welsh groups. The matter of post-Conquest Welsh 'foreign policy' will be discussed later. It is however hoped to give attention within this section to the way in which external stresses, pre- and post-Conquest, can be seen affecting Welsh activity within Wales.

Not all of the eighty-five persons named will be discussed. In general, I shall tend to omit those whose main period of activity occurred before 975 or after 1100. Others may also receive little attention: those whose identities are more or less obscure, those whose activities are minor or peripheral to the major political action of the century, and those who may only be identified retrospectively (the sons of Rhys Sais for instance).[5]

Although not all of the eighty-five persons mentioned were kings, a considerable proportion of them wielded power or influence on a local level. It is not always possible to identify the territory of a given person, however. There were persons who seem to have held some kind of joint rule. Some seem to have been local nobility. Others held sway over large areas. Of the eighty-five names, only three are female, occurring together in a retrospective discussion in the vernacular chronicles of the relationship between Owain ap Cadwgan ap Bleddyn and

---

5   *ByT* (Pen. 20) *s.a.* 1079 (*recte* 1081); *ByT* (RB) *s.a.* [1081]; *ByS s.a.* 1079 (*recte* 1081).

Nest ferch Rhys ap Tewdwr.[6] None of the three named is mentioned in the Latin annals. There is also the reference *s.a.* 1039 to the unnamed wife of Hywel ab Edwin.[7]

The eighty-five names in order of appearance are as follows.

Idwallon ab Owain – *AC* (B and C), *ByT* (Pen. 20), *ByT* (RB), *ByS*.
Einion ab Owain – *AC* (B and C), *ByT* (Pen. 20), *ByT* (RB), *ByS*.
Gwrmid – *ByT* (Pen. 20) only.
Hywel ab Ieuaf (ab Idwal Foel) – *AC* (B and C – B consistently refers to the sons of Ieuaf ab Idwal as 'the sons of Idwal'), *ByT* (Pen. 20), *ByT* (RB), *ByS*.
Iago ab Idwal Foel – *AC* (B and C), *ByT* (Pen. 20), *ByT* (RB), *ByS*.
Idwal Fychan ab Idwal Foel – *AC* (B and C), *ByT* (Pen. 20), *ByT* (RB), *ByS*.
Custennin ab Iago – *ByT* (Pen. 20), *ByT* (RB), *ByS*.
Maredudd ab Owain ap Hywel Dda – *AC* (B and C), *ByT* (Pen. 20), *ByT* (RB), *ByS*.
Cadwallon ab Ieuaf – *AC* (B and C). *ByT* (Pen. 20), *ByT* (RB), *ByS*.
Ionafal ap Meurig – *ByT* (Pen. 20), *ByT* (RB), *ByS*.
Ieuaf ab Idwal – possibly identical with Idwal Fychan ab Idwal Foel. The name in this form occurs *AC* (C), *ByT* (Pen. 20), *ByT* (RB), *ByS*. *AC* (B) has 'Idwal filius Idwal'.
Owain ap Hywel – *AC* (B and C), *ByT* (Pen. 20), *ByT* (RB), *ByS*.
Owain ap Dyfnwal – *AC* (B only), *ByT* (Pen. 20), *ByT* (RB), *ByS*.
Edwin ab Einion – *AC* (B 'Guyn filius Eynaun', C 'Owein filius Eyniaun'), *ByT* (Pen. 20), *ByT* (RB), *ByS*.
The sons of Meurig including Idwal ap Meurig – *AC* (B and C), *ByT* (Pen. 20), *ByT* (RB), *ByS*.
Tewdwr ab Einion – *AC* (B and C), *ByT* (Pen. 20), *ByT* (RB), *ByS*.
Cadwallon ap Maredudd – *ByT* (Pen. 20), *ByT* (RB), *ByS*.
Cynan ap Hywel – *AC* (B and C), *ByT* (Pen. 20), *ByT* (RB), *ByS*.
Mor ap Gwyn – *ByT* (Pen. 20), *ByT* (RB), *ByS*.
Gwlfach and Ubiad – *ByT* (Pen. 20), *ByT* (RB), *ByS*.
Aeddan ap Blegywryd and his four sons – *AC* (B and C), *ByT* (Pen. 20), *ByT* (RB), *ByS*.
Llywelyn ap Seisyll – *AC* (B and C), *ByT* (Pen. 20), *ByT* (RB), *ByS*.
Meurig ap Arthfael – *AC* (B and C), *ByT* (Pen. 20), *ByT* (RB), *ByS*.
Rhydderch ap Iestyn – *AC* (B and C), *ByT* (Pen. 20), *ByT* (RB), *ByS*.
Cynan ap Seisyll – *AC* (B and C), *ByT* (Pen. 20), *ByT* (RB), *ByS*.
Iago ab Idwal – *AC* (B and C), *ByT* (Pen. 20), *ByT* (RB), *ByS*.
Maredudd ab Edwin – *AC* (B and C), *ByT* (Pen. 20), *ByT* (RB), *ByS*.
Hywel ab Edwin – *AC* (B and C), *ByT* (Pen. 20), *ByT* (RB), *ByS*.
The sons of Cynan – *AC* (B and C), *ByT* (Pen. 20), *ByT* (RB), *ByS*.
Caradog ap Rhydderch – *AC* (B and C), *ByT* (Pen. 20), *ByT* (RB), *ByS*.
Meurig ap Hywel – *AC* (B and C), *ByT* (Pen. 20), *ByT* (RB), *ByS*.
Gruffudd ap Llywelyn – *AC* (B and C), *ByT* (Pen. 20), *ByT* (RB), *ByS*.

6 *ByT* (Pen. 20) *s.a.* 1106 (*recte* 1109); *ByT* (RB) *s.a.* 1105 (*recte* 1109); *ByS s.a.* 1106 (*recte* 1109).
7 *ByT* (Pen. 20) *s.a.* 1039 (*recte* 1041); *ByT* (RB) *s.a.* [1041]; *ByS s.a.* 1039 (*recte* 1041).

Hywel ab Owain – *AC* (B and C), *ByT* (Pen. 20), *ByT* (RB), *ByS*.
Gruffudd ap Rhydderch – *AC* (B and C), *ByT* (Pen. 20), *ByT* (RB), *ByS*.
Rhys ap Rhydderch – *ByT* (Pen. 20), *ByT* (RB), *ByS*.
Owain ap Gruffudd – *AC* (B and C), *ByT* (Pen. 20), *ByT* (RB), *ByS*.
Bleddyn ap Cynfyn – *AC* (B and C), *ByT* (Pen. 20), *ByT* (RB), *ByS*.
Rhiwallon ap Cynfyn – *AC* (B and C), *ByT* (Pen. 20), *ByT* (RB), *ByS*.
Maredudd ap Gruffudd – *AC* (B and C), *ByT* (Pen. 20), *ByT* (RB), *ByS*.
Ithel ap Gruffudd – *AC* (B and C), *ByT* (Pen. 20), *ByT* (RB), *ByS*.
Maredudd ab Owain ab Edwin – *AC* (B and C), *ByT* (Pen. 20), *ByT* (RB), *ByS*.
Caradog ap Gruffudd – *AC* (B and C), *ByT* (Pen. 20), *ByT* (RB), *ByS*.
Rhys ab Owain – *AC* (B and C), *ByT* (Pen. 20), *ByT* (RB), *ByS*.
Trahaearn ap Caradog – *AC* (B and C), *ByT* (Pen. 20), *ByT* (RB), *ByS*.
Rhydderch ap Caradog – *AC* (B and C), *ByT* (Pen. 20), *ByT* (RB), *ByS*.
Cynwrig ap Rhiwallon – *ByT* (Pen. 20), *ByT* (RB), *ByS*.
Goronwy and Llywelyn sons of Cadwgan – *AC* (C only – 'filios Cadugaun'), *ByT*
    (Pen. 20), *ByT* (RB), *ByS*.
Meirchion ap Rhys – *AC* (B and C), *ByT* (Pen. 20), *ByT* (RB), *ByS*.
Hywel ab Owain ab Edwin – *AC* (B and C), *ByT* (Pen. 20), *ByT* (RB), *ByS*.
Rhys ap Tewdwr – *AC* (B and C), *ByT* (Pen. 20), *ByT* (RB), *ByS*.
Meilir ap Rhiwallon – *AC* (B and C), *ByT* (Pen. 20), *ByS*.
Gwrgeneu ap Seisyll – *AC* (B and C), *ByT* (Pen. 20), *ByT* (RB), *ByS*.
The sons of Rhys Sais – *ByT* (Pen. 20), *ByT* (RB), *ByS*.
Madog ap Bleddyn – *AC* (B and C), *ByT* (Pen. 20), *ByT* (RB), *ByS*.
Cadwgan ap Bleddyn – *AC* (B and C), *ByT* (Pen. 20), *ByT* (RB), *ByS*.
Rhirid ap Bleddyn – *AC* (B and C), *ByT* (Pen. 20), *ByT* (RB), *ByS*.
Cedifor ap Gollwyn – *AC* (B and C), *ByT* (Pen. 20), *ByT* (RB), *ByS*.
Llywelyn ap Cedifor and brothers – *AC* (B and C), *ByT* (Pen. 20), *ByT* (RB), *ByS*.
Gruffudd ap Maredudd – *AC* (B and C), *ByT* (Pen. 20), *ByT* (RB), *ByS*.
Gruffudd ap Idnerth – *AC* (B and C), *ByT* (Pen. 20), *ByT* (RB), *ByS*.
Ifor ap Idnerth – *AC* (B and C), *ByT* (Pen. 20), *ByT* (RB), *ByS*.
Uchdryd ab Edwin – *AC* (B and C), *ByT* (Pen. 20), *ByT* (RB), *ByS*.
Hywel ap Goronwy – *AC* (B and C), *ByT* (Pen. 20), *ByT* (RB), *ByS*.
Owain ab Edwin – *ByT* (Pen. 20), *ByT* (RB), *ByS*.
Hywel ab Ithel – *AC* (B and C), *ByT* (Pen. 20), *ByT* (RB), *ByS*.
Gwyn ap Gruffudd – *ByT* (Pen. 20), *ByT* (RB), *ByS*.
Maredudd ap Bleddyn – *AC* (B and C), *ByT* (Pen. 20), *ByT* (RB), *ByS*.
Goronwy ap Rhys – *ByT* (Pen. 20), *ByT* (RB), *ByS*.
Gwgan ap Meurig – *AC* (B and C), *ByT* (Pen. 20), *ByT* (RB), *ByS*.
Meurig ap Trahaearn – *AC* (B and C), *ByT* (Pen. 20), *ByT* (RB), *ByS*.
Gruffudd ap Trahaearn – *AC* (B and C), *ByT* (Pen. 20), *ByT* (RB), *ByS*.
Owain ap Cadwgan – *AC* (B and C), *ByT* (Pen. 20), *ByT* (RB), *ByS*.
Nest ferch Rhys – *ByT* (Pen. 20), *ByT* (RB), *ByS*.
Gwladus ferch Rhiwallon – *ByT* (Pen. 20), *ByT* (RB), *ByS*.
Angharad ferch Maredudd – *ByT* (Pen. 20), *ByT* (RB), *ByS*.
Madog ap Rhirid – *ByT* (Pen. 20), *ByT* (RB), *ByS*
Ithel ap Rhirid – *ByT* (Pen. 20), *ByT* (RB), *ByS*.
Llywarch ap Trahaearn – *ByT* (Pen. 20), *ByT* (RB), *ByS*.
Maredudd ap Rhydderch – *ByT* (Pen. 20) *ByT* (RB), *ByS*.

6

Henry ap Cadwgan – *ByT* (Pen. 20), *ByT* (RB), *ByS*.
The sons of Uchdryd – *ByT* (Pen. 20), *ByT* (RB), *ByS*.

Some of these had careers recorded with reasonable detail; some are known only by one or two actions; some are named solely in obits. Not all find mention in all the chronicle-texts and, although most are mentioned in all the native Welsh sources, *Annales Cambriae* frequently lack details found in the *Brutiau*. A few are mentioned also in English, Irish, or Anglo-Norman sources. Many of them are noted in the genealogical material, though not all; and, indeed, the genealogies add a number of 'contemporaries' who are untraceable in the annals. There are a few historical persons, such as Cadwgan ap Meurig ap Hywel, who are mentioned in neither the chronicles nor the genealogies, but who occur in *Liber Landauensis*.[8] Such, then, is the raw material. I hope, by examining these persons, their careers, and their (reputed) descent, to build up a picture of eleventh-century Welsh internal political history. The shortcomings of the sources make it impossible for such a picture to be complete, but I intend to make the account as full as possible.

THE TRADITIONAL APPROACH TO ELEVENTH-CENTURY WELSH POLITICS

What is noteworthy in the period now reached is the success of men who were out of the direct line of succession from Rhodri the Great in seizing royal authority in Gwynedd and Deheubarth.[9]

It has become almost inescapable to think of the succession to power in early mediaeval Wales in terms of the dynasty of Rhodri Mawr. The fortunes of this family seemingly dominated the political scene throughout most of Wales in the tenth century, and there has been a tendency on the part of historians to view the eleventh century also within this framework. There has thus grown up the idea that this dynasty had a 'right to rule'. Writers from Giraldus Cambrensis onwards have subscribed to the legend of the attribution of various areas of Wales to the various sons of Rhodri Mawr. This in turn has given rise to the notion of the natural primacy of the descendants of these sons over the areas thus allotted. Descendants of Cadell ap Rhodri are supposed to rule in the South, and descendants of Anarawd ap Rhodri in the North. To some degree, this is the situation that prevailed in the tenth century. The eleventh century, however, cannot be said to fit into this model. Attempts to analyse the century in these terms have continued, nevertheless, thus giving rise to the picture of the century as a period of so-called 'intrusive rulers' displacing 'legitimate' scions of the dynasty of Rhodri Mawr. The result has been a distortion of the political events of the time. Such eminent writers as Sir John Lloyd have believed firmly in legitimate right to rule being conferred by membership of the family of Rhodri Mawr. It has to be said that

8   *The Text*, edd. Evans & Rhys.
9   Lloyd, *A History*, I.346. On the Second Dynasty of Gwynedd and its historiography see Dumville, 'The "six" sons' and 'Brittany'.

7

there is no good evidence to suggest that the Welsh of the period saw kingship in quite these terms. A re-assessment is overdue.

To what degree did the dynasty of Rhodri Mawr maintain prominence in the eleventh century? Certainly members of the dynasty continue to be mentioned throughout the period. Descendants of Einion ab Owain of the Southern branch made attempts to gain or to keep power in the South, most notably in the persons of Hywel ab Edwin (1033–1044) and Rhys ab Owain (1075–1078). Gruffudd ap Cynan, whose biographer in the twelfth century was so concerned to emphasise his hero's descent from Rhodri, achieved possession of Anglesey, though not the entirety of Gwynedd, towards the end of the century. However, the only area which seems to have remained consistently under the sway of its 'traditional' dynasty during this time is Glamorgan.

A considerable number of the prominent men of the Welsh eleventh century were either persons of uncertain background – Bleddyn ap Cynfyn or Trahaearn ap Caradog for instance, whose direct forebears are little more than names in pedigrees – or else they were linked to the dynasty of Rhodri Mawr, but in what might be considered an indirect fashion. Thus Gruffudd ap Llywelyn, who ruled Gwynedd 1039–1063, was connected to the dynasty through his mother, and possibly through his paternal grandmother also. At least two of the 'intrusive' rulers themselves became founders of important lines: the descendants of Rhydderch ab Iestyn (ruler of Deheubarth 1023–1033) were to play a prominent role in south Wales throughout the eleventh century; and the later eleventh century and the twelfth century positively abound with descendants of Bleddyn ap Cynfyn (ruler of Gwynedd 1063–1075), who, moreover, is recurrent in the pedigree-material, both royal and of the *uchelwyr*. Owain Cyfeiliog, for example, was a great-grandson of Bleddyn in the direct male line, and Owain's son Gwenwynwyn was connected through his mother to Trahaearn ap Caradog (see figures 1 and 2).

Clearly Lloyd's 'intrusive rulers' were capable of founding dynasties, and certainly by the time of composition of the genealogical material called *Hanesyn Hen*[10] a descent from Bleddyn or Trahaearn was as noteworthy as one from Rhodri Mawr. It is interesting, furthermore, that while various writers and compilers of pedigrees showed an interest in Bleddyn's line throughout succeeding centuries there is one branch of the family of Rhodri Mawr, attested in the chronicles, which failed to find mention in the genealogical material. The descendants of Edwin ab Einion ab Owain of the 'Southern Branch' seem, despite their recorded historical actions, to have left no important mark, and no one in later years seems to have cared to note their pedigree. Yet this group included the important ruler Hywel ab Edwin, and also Rhys ab Owain, the slayer of Bleddyn.

A re-examination is needed of those things which went to make a Welsh ruler in the eleventh century. It is possible that the notion of legitimacy through a descent, preferably direct, from a specific group is to some degree anachronistic, for it assumes a narrowness which might not have been a consideration in early mediaeval Wales and which may restrict our interpretation of events. The importance of membership of the dynasty of Rhodri Mawr may be a later concept which

---

10 For *Hanesyn Hen*, see Bartrum, *Tracts*, pp. 75–120.

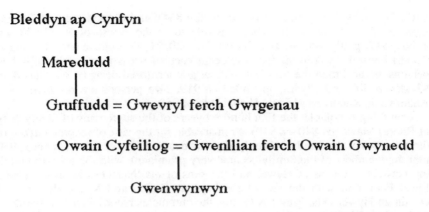

Bleddyn ap Cynfyn
|
Maredudd
|
Gruffudd = Gwevryl ferch Gwrgenau
|
Owain Cyfeiliog = Gwenllian ferch Owain Gwynedd
|
Gwenwynwyn

ABT 8g

Figure 1

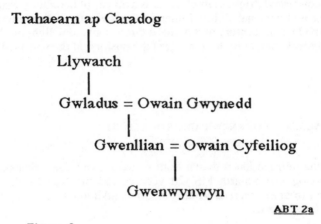

Trahaearn ap Caradog
|
Llywarch
|
Gwladus = Owain Gwynedd
|
Gwenllian = Owain Cyfeiliog
|
Gwenwynwyn

ABT 2a

Figure 2

has been projected backwards onto the politics of the eleventh century, unbalanc-ing our view of it. I propose to begin by making a brief survey of the apparent tenures of the various and sundry descendants of Rhodri Mawr.

Most noteworthy is the lack of territorial attributions of kings in the early mediaeval period. Individuals from various families are called 'king', but actual regions are almost never mentioned outside the context of invasion. Between *ca* 840 and *ca* 960 I have noted only three instances of the 'X, king of Y' type, and not one of these was a member of the dynasty of Rhodri Mawr. In general, it seems (from the annalistic evidence at least) that it is easier to be clear as to where a king did not rule than where he did.

The three kings whose kingdoms are named in the chronicles are Ithel of

9

Gwent (*ca* 848); Cyngen, king of Powys (*ca* 854); and Gwgon, king of Ceredigion (*ca* 871). None of the three was related to the House of Rhodri Mawr, although Gwgon's sister Angharad is said (JC 20, 21, 42) to have been married to Rhodri himself. In point of fact, the occurrence of *rex* is pretty sparing. A few persons are accorded the title, but without any territorial designation; Cadell ap Rhodri *ca* 909 and Clydog ap Cadell *ca* 919. Two persons are *rex Brittonum*: Anarawd ap Rhodri *ca* 915 and Hywel Dda *ca* 950.

One thing is notable: the first hundred years of the supremacy of the dynasty of Rhodri Mawr (*ca* 840–*ca* 940) is remarkable for the lack of recorded detail of the activities of the family. It is only after the death of Hywel Dda in or about 950 that the members of the family became very prominent, with the apparent feuding between the sons of Hywel and the sons of his 'Northern Branch' cousin, Idwal Foel, and with the rise of the brothers Einion and Maredudd, sons of Owain ap Hywel Dda. Previous to this, the chronicles record as many members of the older Welsh dynasties as descendants of Rhodri. The sources are difficult, admittedly, but in this period there is no apparent sign of any strong sense of the inherent legitimacy of this family.

Information is not in general supplied by the annalists as to who was ruling where, let alone the basis of their power. It could be that, as far as tenth-century Wales was concerned ,'right to rule' was less a matter of hereditary issues than of *force majeur* and personal ability. I intend to examine the events and characters of the Welsh eleventh century and perhaps throw some new light on the validity of this framework, and to try to reinterpret the position of the so-called 'intrusive rulers'.

A HISTORICAL SURVEY OF KNOWN AREAS OF ACTIVITY

The following information is drawn from *Annales Cambriae*, versions B and C, *Brut y Tywysogion* (Peniarth MS. 20 version and the Red Book of Hergest version), and from *Brenhinedd y Saesson*. Some additional information is drawn from *Liber Landauensis*.

(1) Deheubarth

(i) 'Southern Britons/kingdom of the South'
    1023 the kingdom of the South held by Rhydderch ab Iestyn.
    1033 the kingdom of the South held by Maredudd and Hywel, sons of Edwin.
    1039 Hywel ab Edwin driven from the South by Gruffudd ap Llywelyn.
    1069 Maredudd ab Owain ab Edwin held the kingdom of the South.
    1075 Rhys ab Owain and Rhydderch ap Caradog held the South.
    1093 Rhys ap Tewdwr described as king of the South on his death.

(ii) Dyfed
    952 Dyfed ravaged twice by Iago and Ieuaf, sons of Idwal Foel.

992 Edwin ab Einion and Edylfi the Englishman ravaged all the territory of Maredudd ab Owain in Deheubarth, viz Ceredigion, Dyfed, Gower, and Cydweli.

1042 the battle of Pwlldyfach, in Dyfed, at which Hywel ab Edwin defeated the vikings who had been ravaging the territory.

1047 Dyfed and Ystrad Tywi ravaged by Gruffudd ap Llywelyn.

1091 (and again at 1116) On the death of a leading man of Dyfed, Cedifor ap Gollwyn, his sons invited Gruffudd ap Maredudd into the area. He was however killed by Rhys ap Tewdwr at Llandudoch.

1093 On the death of Rhys ap Tewdwr, Dyfed plundered by Cadwgan ap Bleddyn. Shortly afterwards, together with Ceredigion, Dyfed was over-run by the Normans.

1096 Pembroke castle ravaged by Uchdryd ab Edwin, Hywel ap Goronwy, the warband of Cadwgan ap Bleddyn, and others.

1102 One half of Dyfed given to Iorwerth ap Bleddyn by Henry I, together with Powys, Ceredigion, Ystrad Tywi, Cydweli, and Gower. However, later in the same year, Henry revoked this grant and gave Dyfed to a knight named Saer. In 1105, it was again re-granted, this time to Gerald of Windsor.

(iii) Ceredigion

991 ravaged by Edwin ab Einion and Edylfi the Saxon, being part of Maredudd ab Owain's territory in Deheubarth.

1044 A battle at the mouth of the Tywi between Hywel ab Edwin and Gruffudd ap Llywelyn. Hywel was slain.

1099 A portion of Powys and Ceredigion bestowed on Cadwgan ap Bleddyn after he made peace with the Normans.

1102 Ceredigion included in Henry I's gift to Iorwerth ap Bleddyn, who gave it to his brother Cadwgan.

(iv) Brycheiniog

983 Brycheiniog and all the lands of Einion ab Owain ravaged. According to *Annales Cambriae*, the ravagers were the English, plus Hywel ab Ieuaf. According to the *Brutiau* the ravagers were the English, who were defeated by Hywel ab Ieuaf and Einion ab Owain.

1093 Rhys ap Tewdwr slain by the Normans who were inhabiting Brycheiniog.

1096 Brycheiniog raided by Normans who were promptly slain by Gruffudd and Ifor, sons of Idnerth ap Cadwgan at Aberllech.

1099 Llywelyn ap Cadwgan slain by the men of Brycheiniog.

(v) Ystrad Tywi

1041 The battle of Pencadair in Ystrad Tywi, between Gruffudd ap Llywelyn and Hywel ab Edwin (who lost).

1047 Seven score of the men of the warband of Gruffudd ap Llywelyn slain through the treachery of the men of Ystrad Tywi. In vengeance, Gruffudd ravaged Dyfed and Ystrad Tywi.

1102 included in Henry I's gift, later revoked, to Iorwerth ap Bleddyn and subsequently given to Hywel ap Goronwy.

11

(vi) Cydweli
991 ravaged by Edwin ab Einion and Edylfi the Englishman as part of the territory in Deheubarth of Maredudd ab Owain.
1102 part of Henry I's gift, later revoked, to Iorwerth ap Bleddyn and subsequently given to Hywel ap Goronwy.

(vii) Gower
970 ravaged by Einion ab Owain.
977 ravaged a second time by Einion ab Owain.
991 ravaged by Edwin ab Einion and Edylfi the Englishman as part of the territory in Deheubarth of Maredudd ab Owain.
1102 part of Henry I's gift, later revoked, to Iorwerth ap Bleddyn and subsequently given to Hywel ap Goronwy.

(2) Gwynedd

(i) Anglesey
984 ravaged (together with Lleyn) by Custennin ab Iago and Godfrey Haraldsson.
986 Maredudd ab Owain slew Cadwallon ab Ieuaf and took his territory. According to *Brut y Tywysogion* (RB), which appears to be mistaken, Cadwallon gained said territory in this year. According to *Brenhinedd y Saesson*, Maig ab Ieuaf, slain in the same year, was associated with Cadwallon in holding the territory.
987 ravaged by vikings, and many captives taken. As a result Maredudd ab Owain took the remaining inhabitants to Ceredigion and Dyfed.
1075 Gruffudd ap Cynan besieged and/or took possession of Anglesey.
1099 granted to Gruffudd ap Cynan by the Normans.

(ii) Gwynedd (in general)
1000 held by Cynan ap Hywel.
1022 Llywelyn ap Seisyll described as 'king of Gwynedd.'
1033 held by Iago ab Idwal after the death of Llywelyn ap Seisyll.
1039 held by Gruffudd ap Llywelyn after the death of Iago ab Idwal.
1069 held by Bleddyn ap Cynfyn.
1075 held by Trahaearn ap Caradog.

(iii) Lleyn
978 ravaged by Gwrmid, or possibly by Hywel ab Ieuaf and the English.
980 ravaged by Custennin ab Iago and Godfrey Haraldsson.

(iv) Clynnog Fawr
978 ravaged by Hywel ab Ieuaf and the English.

(3) Powys

(i) Powys
1069 ruled by Bleddyn ap Cynfyn – *Brut y Tywysogion* (RB) only.
1099 Part of Powys granted to Cadwgan ap Bleddyn by the Normans.

12

1102 given to Iorwerth ap Bleddyn by Henry I, and conferred by Iorwerth on his brother Cadwgan.

(ii) Meirionydd

986 Meirionydd gained by cunning by Cadwgan ab Ieuaf *Brut y Tywysogion* (RB) only. Thomas Jones considered this to be a mistake for Maredudd ab Owain, as it is grouped with the territories which Maredudd took from Cadwgan in that year.[11]

(4) Morgawnng

Most of the following information is taken from *Liber Landauensis*. Dates are as given by Wendy Davies.[12]

(i) Glamorgan/Morgannwg

992 ravaged by Maredudd ab Owain with a Hiberno-Scandinavian mercenary force.

Liber Landauensis charter 253 (*ca* 1025)   Rhydderch ab Iestyn referred to as king of Morgannwg.

LL 253   a reference to Hywel (ab Owain) as king of Morgannwg, *ca* 1025.

LL 265a   reference to Gruffudd ap Rhydderch as king of Morgannwg, *ca* 1030.

LL 255, 249a, 259   references to Meurig ap Hywel as king of Glamorgan, *ca* 1035.

LL 261, 263   references to Meurig as king of Morgannwg, *ca* 1040 and *ca* 1045.

LL 267   Cadwgan ap Meurig referred to as king of Morgannwg, *ca* 1070.

LL 272   Caradog ap Gruffudd referred to as king of Morgannwg, *ca* 1072.

Is it possible to unravel these events, and to attempt an assessment of the motives behind them? I propose to make a prosopography of the persons involved, their relationships to one another, both familial and political, and to attempt to clarify the happenings of the period. I shall do this region by region.

Deheubarth

The persons of Welsh origin mentioned in the chronicles as having been active somewhere within Deheubarth at one time or another in the eleventh century, and a little before, are as follows, in chronological order of appearance.

Iago and Ieuaf, sons of Idwal
Einion ab Owain
Hywel ab Ieuaf
Edwin ab Einion

[11] *ByT* (RB), p. 279, n. 17.20–3.
[12] Davies, *The Llandaff Charters*, pp. 126–9.

13

Maredudd ab Owain ap Hywel Dda
Rhydderch ab Iestyn
Maredudd ab Edwin
Hywel ab Edwin
Gruffudd ap Llywelyn
Maredudd ab Owain ab Edwin
Rhys ab Owain
Rhydderch ap Caradog
Caradog ap Gruffudd
Cedifor ap Gollwyn
Gruffudd ap Maredudd
Rhys ap Tewdwr
Cadwgan ap Bleddyn
Gruffudd and Ifor, sons of Idnerth ap Cadwgan
Llywelyn ap Cadwgan
Uchdryd ab Edwin
Hywel ap Goronwy
Iorwerth ap Bleddyn

Not all twenty-four are said to have held kingship in Deheubarth, or in parts of Deheubarth. Several can be seen active in the region as aggressors rather than defenders or rulers. As the century ends, a new element enters the picture, as increasingly large areas of south Wales fell under Norman control. Many of the persons active in the 1090s in these areas were involved in attacks on Norman settlers, or else were receiving land from the gift of these Normans. I deal first with those twelve who are seen to bear rule.

(1) Einion ab Owain

Einion is mentioned in *Annales Cambriae* (B and C), both versions of *Brut y Tywysogion*, and *Brenhinedd y Saesson*. In addition to having his lands ('Brycheiniog and all the lands of Einion ab Owain') ravaged in 983 by the English led by Ælfhere, Einion himself ravaged Gower in 970 and in 977, which possibly suggests that it was not part of his territory. He was killed in 984 by the men of Gwent.

It is relatively easy to establish his identity. His patronymic is given by all the chronicle-texts, and one of the copies of *Brenhinedd y Saesson* – that in Aberystwyth, National Library of Wales, MS. 7006 – describes him as 'Eynion vab Oweyn vab Howel Dda vab Kadell ap Rodri', *s.a.* 968.

Einion is a significant figure for the politics of the eleventh century; for, although he died well before its start, he is the ancestor of no fewer than six of the explicitly named rulers/claimants of the South, in the direct male line. There is, however, an oddity about this, in that in the genealogical material he appears only in his function as ancestor of Rhys ap Tewdwr and the latter's descendants, or as a descendant of Hywel Dda. The remaining five of his historically important descendants are all omitted from the extant pedigrees, and can therefore be identified only from the annalistic evidence.

Early genealogical texts mentioning Einion are: Mostyn (MG), probably of

14

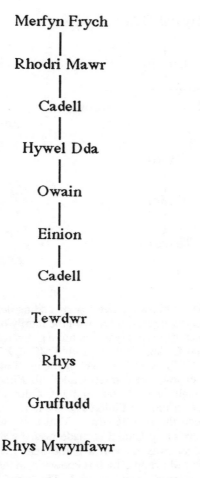

Merfyn Frych
|
Rhodri Mawr
|
Cadell
|
Hywel Dda
|
Owain
|
Einion
|
Cadell
|
Tewdwr
|
Rhys
|
Gruffudd
|
Rhys Mwynfawr

MG 2

Figure 3

the second half of the thirteenth century, item two;[13] Jesus College (JC), of the latter part of the fourteenth century, item 24;[14] and *Achau Brenhinoedd a Thywy-sogion Cymru (ABT)*,[15] of unclear but late mediaeval date, item 7 (*Bonedd Tywy-sogion Kymru/Bellach yr ysbyswn o Vonedd Tywysogion Kymry*) sections j and m, and item ten (*Gwehelyth Deheubarth*). The agreement between these texts as to Einion's ancestry and descendants is high, and their main interest seems to have been to express the pedigrees of Rhys Gryg, or of his father Rhys mwynfawr. All take the line back to Rhodri Mawr; MG 2 takes it to Merfyn Frych (see figure 3). JC 24 has the same line of descent as MG 2, but omitting Merfyn and adding

13 Bartrum, *Tracts*, p. 39.
14 *Ibid.*, p. 47.
15 *Ibid.*, pp. 101–2 and 104.

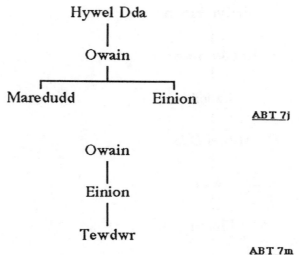

Figure 4

Rhys Gryg. *ABT* 7j extends the known genealogy by adding detail as to Einion's brother – *ABT* 7 is a large pedigree concerned with the family of Rhodri Mawr in an elaborated form, and so tends to supply information as to brothers and cousins (see figure 4). *ABT* 7m omits Cadell, who is found in MG 2, JC 24, and *ABT* 10; further, MSS. CFGHJ of *ABT* 7m give Tewdwr's name as 'Tewdwr Mawr', thus confusing him with his nephew Tewdwr ap Cadell ab Einion, the father of Rhys.[16] The text moves straight on to the descendants of this younger Tewdwr – hence omitting the entire generation of Einion's sons and revealing confusion in all versions of *ABT* between the two Tewdwrs. That there was a Tewdwr ab Einion as distinct from Tewdwr ap Cadell is made clear by the annalistic evidence that Tewdwr ab Einion was slain in a battle near Llangwm.[17] Neither Cadell ab Einion nor Tewdwr Mawr ap Cadell is known from the chronicles: they find mention only in the genealogical material. This confusion of the two Tewdwrs by the compiler or in the source of *ABT* is perpetuated in *ABT* 10, a pedigree (of Rhys mwynfawr extending back to Rhodri Mawr) essentially the same as MG 2 and JC 24, save for the omission of Cadell ab Einion, and thus jumping straight from Einion to Tewdwr father of Rhys. It has additional matter relating to the mother of Rhys mwynfawr and the wife of Rhys ap Tewdwr.

Given that the compiler of *ABT* was probably simply confused by the two Tewdwrs, the evidence of the pedigree-material and of the chronicles seem to support a view of Einion having both a son and a grandson of that name. The pedigrees attest also the existence of Cadell.

The chronicles refer to a third son, Edwin, active in the late tenth century, who occurs in 992, ravaging the lands of Maredudd ab Owain ap Hywel Dda together

16 *Ibid.*, p. 104.
17 *AC* (B) *s.a.* [994]; *ByT* (Pen. 20) *s.a.* 993 (*recte* 994); *ByT* (RB) *s.a.* [994]; *ByS s.a.* 993 (*recte* 994).

16

with Edylfi the Englishman and in the same year ravaging St Davids. The name Edwin presents a slight problem: the *Brutiau* all give Edwin, but *Annales Cambriae* (B) read 'Guyn filius Eynaun', and C 'Owein filius Eyniaun'. Lloyd pointed out however that 'Guin' could easily be an error for 'Etguin' (a misreading – 'et guin').[18] Lloyd was referring to a similar difficulty with *Annales Cambriae* (B) over Edwin ap Hywel but, as Thomas Jones indicated, the argument is equally applicable here.[19]

The significance of this son Edwin is considerable, as it is through him that Einion's five other important descendants may be traced. The five are: Maredudd and Hywel, sons of Edwin; Rhys and Maredudd, sons of Owain; and Gruffudd ap Maredudd. To these should be added Hywel ab Owain, who is never said to have ruled or claimed to rule in the South, but who was killed in 1078 with his brother Rhys by Caradog ap Gruffudd.

None of these is mentioned in the genealogies, but the annalistic material is sufficient to reconstruct their relationship. The succession of patronyms plus the consistent emphasis on the connexion of these men to south Wales is such as to make their kinship to each other clear. It might be objected that no 'Owain ab Edwin' is known from the chronicles: however, on the first occurrence of Maredudd ab Owain in 1069, he is referred to as 'Maredudd ab Owain ab Edwin' in the *Brutiau*.

The relationship can therefore be tabulated as in figure 5. The relationship between these men has been accepted by Lloyd and others since him, and I can see no very good reason for disputing it. The omission of this group from the pedigrees is presumably explicable by the lack of any important descendants in the twelfth century and later: it seems possible that this particular branch of the family of Rhodri Mawr may have died out with Gruffudd ap Maredudd in 1091.

A full tabulation of the eleventh-century descendants of Einion ab Owain is given in figure 6. Mr Bartrum has supplied Einion with a fourth son Idwallon, *ob.* 975.[20] This, however, appears to be a misconception based upon *Brut y Tywysogion* (Red Book of Hergest version), *s.a.* 975, which refers to an Idwallon ab Einion dying in that year. Since *Annales Cambriae* (B and C), *Brut y Tywysogion* (Peniarth 20 version), and *Brenhinedd y Saesson* all agree on Idwallon ab Owain, it seems reasonable to suppose that *ByT* (RB) is in error here.

(2) Maredudd ab Owain ap Hywel Dda

The career of Maredudd ab Owain is well documented both in *Annales Cambriae* (B and C) and the *Brutiau*. He first occurs in 986, when he slew Cadwallon ab Ieuaf and took the latter's territory, named as 'Wenedocia' in *Annales Cambriae* (B), and as Gwynedd and Anglesey by *Brut y Tywysogion* (Pen. 20) and *Brenhinedd y Saesson* (*Annales Cambriae* [C] omits to name the territory; *Brut y Tywysogion* [RB] lacks the reference altogether). *Brenhinedd y Saesson* also attributes to Maredudd the killing of Maig ab Ieuaf on the same occasion. This

18 Lloyd, *A History*, I.337, n. 61.
19 *ByT* (Pen. 20), transl. Jones, p. 142, n. 7.23, and p. 146, n. 10.14.
20 Bartrum, *Welsh Genealogies*, I.42.

17

conquest of the North may suggest that Maredudd had already acquired prominence in the South, perhaps after the death of his brother Einion.

While it is not proposed to discuss the career of Maredudd ab Owain in detail here, it is worth noting in passing that his hold over Gwynedd would seem to have been shortlived, as under the following year all the chronicle-texts record him leaving Anglesey in the wake of a viking-attack and carrying off with him to Dyfed and Ceredigion all those men who had not been seized in the raid. Henceforth, his activity, in so far as it can be located, seems to occur in the South – in 991 he ravaged Maes Hyfaidd, apparently in English hands at this time. His lands are named as 'Demetiam et Keredigiaun, Guhir et Kedweli' in the B-version of *Annales Cambriae*, a list found also in the two versions of *Brut y Tywysogion* and in *Brenhinedd y Saesson*. (The reading of *Annales Cambriae* [C] is not certain to me: Williams' text appears to imply that C does not name the lands, but the difficulty of using this edition makes this omission by no means certain.) These territories were ravaged in 991 by Edwin ab Einion, Maredudd's nephew, and the English. In 994, Maredudd fought with the sons of Meurig near Llangwm. Lloyd viewed this battle as an attempt by the 'Northern Branch' to recover Gwynedd from Maredudd.[21] I do not see that this is necessarily the case. 'Llangwm' occurs twice in *Liber Landauensis* (173; 274) – the two are not apparently the same place, but even so both are in the South. In Melville Richards's *Welsh Administrative and Territorial Units*[22] there are four entries for this name: Llangwm Dinmael in Denbigh; Llangwm in the manor of Llanycefn, Pembrokeshire; Llangwm in Rhos, Pembrokeshire; Llangwm in Monmouthshire (including the Llangwm Isaf of *LL* 274). It does not seem immediately obvious why a battle for possession of Gwynedd should occur in Pembrokeshire or Monmouth. The Llangwm Dinmael in Denbigh might conceivably be the site of the conflict, but the reference to the battle follows straight on from a note of a pestilence in Maredudd's lands, given in the preceding annal as Ceredigion, Dyfed, Gower, and Cydweli. Also, Tewdwr ab Einion ab Owain, another of Maredudd's nephews, seems to have been killed in this battle, and there is no evidence for either him or his father having been active in the North.

Maredudd ab Owain died in 999, earning him, in the *Brutiau*, the distinction of being called 'most praiseworthy king of the Britons'. Like his brother Einion, Maredudd stands in a significant position dynastically vis à vis the eleventh-century rulers. In the genealogies he seems chiefly to have been remembered through his daughter Angharad, mother of Gruffudd ap Llywelyn and of Bleddyn ap Cynfyn, and ancestress to the enormous progeny which the writers of pedigrees attributed to Bleddyn. Maredudd also had a son, Cadwallon, who died in 992. Early genealogical references to him are found in JC 20 and *ABT*. There is agreement between these as to his descent from Hywel Dda, although JC does not take his ancestry any further back than that. *ABT* does, tracing Bleddyn ap Cynfyn via Maredudd to Elidir Lydanwyn (*ABT* le).[23] Elsewhere, however, *ABT*

21 Lloyd, *A History*, I.346.
22 p. 129.
23 Bartrum, *Tracts*, p. 96.

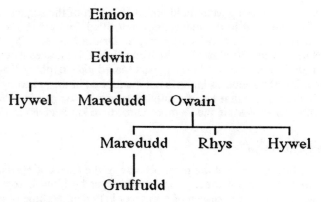

Figure 5

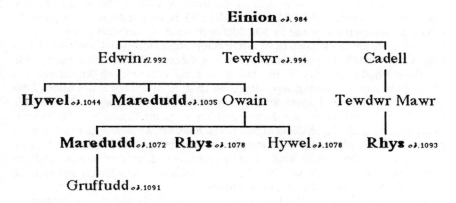

Bold Face indicates an association with rule of the South, or part of the South.

Figure 6

is content to take the line back only to Rhodri Mawr. JC 31 mentions a second daughter, Lleucu.[24]

Clearly, the main importance of Maredudd in the pedigrees was in relation to his daughter Angharad and her descendants, especially Bleddyn ap Cynfyn. Surprisingly little mention is made of Bleddyn's brother Rhiwallon, and there is a fair amount given to their sister Iwerydd, who though a child of Cynfyn was quite possibly not a daughter of Angharad ferch Maredudd.

---

[24] *Ibid.*, p. 48.

19

The pedigrees involving Maredudd are: JC 27, part of the sequence *Ach Rhys Gryg*;[25] JC 31, unnamed in the manuscript, but titled *Gwehelyth Buellt* by Bartrum; *ABT* 1e, part of *Ach Llywelyn ap Iorwerth Drwyndwn*; *ABT* 2f, *Plant Ywein Gwynedd*;[26] *ABT* 7j and 7k, *Plant Rhodri Mawr*.[27] *ABT* 7m makes it clear also that the Tewdwr ab Einion slain at Llangwm was Maredudd's nephew. The Edwin ab Einion who raided Maredudd's lands is not mentioned in the genealogies, but the chronicles make it clear that he was another nephew (see above, *sub* Einion ab Owain). A tabulation of Maredudd's more immediate kin is given in figure 7.

(3) Rhydderch ab Iestyn

Rhydderch ab Iestyn is one of the most obscure of the rulers of eleventh-century Wales. His historical significance is undeniable, yet he himself remains essentially mysterious. All that is known of his career is that at the time of the death of Llywelyn ap Seisyll in 1023 Rhydderch was holding 'regnum dextralium Britonum' and that in 1033 he was slain by the Irish. In addition, he occurs in *Liber Landauensis* charters 253, 264a, and 264b. 253 is very dubious. It purports to record a confirmation (made by Rhydderch as king) to Llandaff of all its lands and churches, with support from Archbishop Æthelnoth (of Canterbury) and King Cnut. Wendy Davies has assigned it a theoretical date of *ca* 1025. 264a mentions Rhydderch only as the father of King Gruffudd ap Rhydderch (*ca* 1030).[28] He appears as king and witness to 264b *ca* 1025, but is not himself the grantor. None of the charters reveals very much about him, although 253 calls him 'Riderch filius Iestin rex Morcannuc immo totius Gualie excepta tantum insula Euonie quam iacob filius Idgual per se tenebat', a claim which might have surprised Hywel ab Owain of Glamorgan, among others. How Rhydderch came to be ruling in the South, what (if any) opposition there was to him, and the factors on which his rule was based, are all unknown. Rhydderch can thus be considered to be one of the so-called intrusive rulers.

Beyond the patronym 'ab Iestyn' nothing is really known of his ancestry – and, interestingly enough, there is little evidence of attempts by genealogists to discover it. Yet he was the first of a line which was to recur throughout the eleventh century, three of whose members were prominent enough to attract English attention as well as Welsh (his sons Rhys and Gruffudd, and his grandson Caradog ap Gruffudd). That his origin was obscure is made plain by the one mediaeval pedigree which does mention him. *ABT* 17,[29] *Gwehelyth Gwent*, in MSS. FHJ[30] calls him 'Rhydderch ab Iestyn ap Gwrgan', a clear error – and the compiler of MS. H realised it, for the name Gwrgan is crossed out in the manuscript. There was a Iestyn ap Gwrgan active in the eleventh century, but he cannot have been the father of Rhydderch, for he appears in *Liber Landauensis*

---

25 *Ibid.*, p. 47.
26 *Ibid.*, p. 97.
27 *Ibid.*, p. 101.
28 On the dating of this charter, see chapter 5, *sub* Charters of Bishop Joseph.
29 Bartrum, *Tracts*, p. 105.
30 *Ibid.*

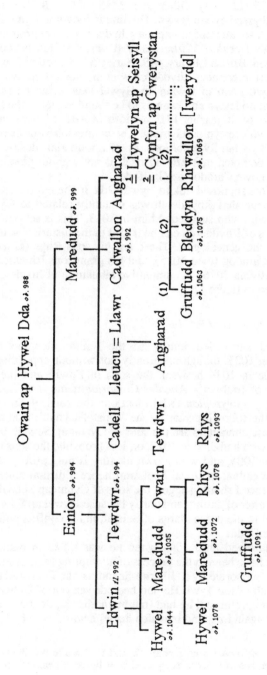

Figure 7

making a grant in 1075 (*LL* 271). Other than MSS. FHJ, *ABT* 17 makes no attempt to trace the pedigree beyond Iestyn. The line is shown in figure 8.

There is however a later attempt to explain Rhydderch's background. This is found in Lewys Dwnn's *Heraldic Visitations of Wales*,[31] written between 1586 and 1613, and in London, British Library, MS. Harley 5835, section 7, written *ca* 1610. These two purport to connect Rhydderch with the main dynasty of Rhodri Mawr by making Iestyn a son of Owain ap Hywel Dda. I see no reason for placing any faith in this; no Iestyn ab Owain is to be found in any of the historical sources, and the writers of the earlier FHJ versions of *ABT* 17 were capable of making the confusion with Iestyn ap Gwrgan. The connexion is probably spurious, perhaps the result of family-ambitions, or of antiquarian desire to 'tidy' loose ends.[32] It should be noted that *ABT* 17 itself is not without problems, as it omits the historically known Caradog ap Gruffudd.

Figure 9 represents the supposed link to Hywel Dda. In the remote case of this being true, it would mean that Rhydderch was distantly related to Hywel and Maredudd, sons of Edwin, who succeeded him in 1033. This is set out in figure 10. Several descendants of Rhydderch can be traced in the historical sources, bur they are not found in the genealogies. These are his sons Rhys (killed by the English in 1053) and Caradog (died 1035), and his grandsons Rhydderch (died 1076) and Meirchion (living 1076). A cumulative tabulation of his descendants, including these, is given in figure 11.

(4) Hywel and Maredudd, sons of Edwin

Hywel and Maredudd succeeded jointly to the South after the death of Rhydderch ab Iestyn in 1033, though apparently not without opposition, as the *Brutiau* record a battle in 1034 between the sons of Edwin and the sons of Rhydderch (the battle of Irathwy – *Annales Cambriae* name it without giving participants, and *Brut y Tywysogion* [RB] mentions the sons of Edwin only). Maredudd was killed the following year by the 'sons of Cynan': I do not know for certain whether these characters are the sons of Cynan ap Seisyll, brother of the famous Llywelyn, who had died in 1027, or, less probably, the sons of Cynan ap Hywel, who died in 1005, and whose own identity is not entirely clear – he was conceivably a descendant of Idwal Foel, and hence a distant cousin of the sons of Edwin. On balance I should suggest the sons of Cynan ap Seisyll as more probable, partly as a matter of dating, and partly because Hywel ap Edwin was to prove a long-term rival to the descendants of Seisyll, in his conflict with Llywelyn ap Seisyll's son Gruffudd.

Hywel ab Edwin survived until 1044 when he was killed in battle against Gruffudd. He seems to have been in the process of attempting to reinstate himself in the South, as he was supported by a Hiberno-Scandinavian fleet, and the battle was fought at the mouth of the Tywi. He had been driven out of Deheubarth by Gruffudd in 1039; having returned, he had fought another battle there, at Pencadair in 1041, which he again lost (and in which his wife was seized by Gruffudd).

---

[31] Cited by Bartrum, *Welsh Genealogies*, I, chart 42, and V.72 *sub* Iestyn ab Owain.
[32] R. R. Davies, however, seems to have accepted this pedigree: *Conquest*, pp. 58–9 and 61.

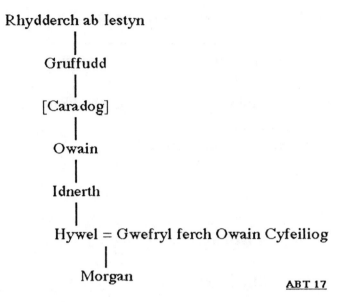

Rhydderch ab Iestyn
|
Gruffudd
|
[Caradog]
|
Owain
|
Idnerth
|
Hywel = Gwefryl ferch Owain Cyfeiliog
|
Morgan   ABT 17

Figure 8

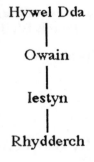

Hywel Dda
|
Owain
|
Iestyn
|
Rhydderch

Figure 9

But he seems to have retained his rule, for in 1042 he drove out the Hiberno-Scandinavians who had been harassing Dyfed. He is one of the better documented kings of eleventh-century Wales, and also one of the more interesting. On his ancestry, see above, *sub* Einion ab Owain.

Hywel's relationship to his enemy, Gruffudd ap Llywelyn, is fairly remote – in kinship-terms they would have been distant cousins (figure 12) via their grandfathers. The relationship might be greater if the pedigrees which connect Llywelyn ap Seisyll with the Northern branch of the family of Rhodri Mawr are accepted as embodying some validity. However, the degree to which kinship through the female line was significant in Wales in the eleventh century is not

23

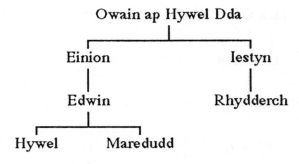

Figure 10

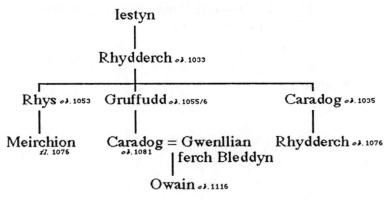

Figure 11

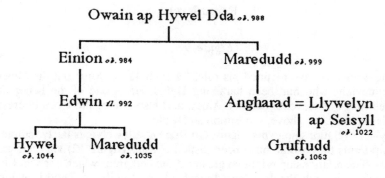

Figure 12

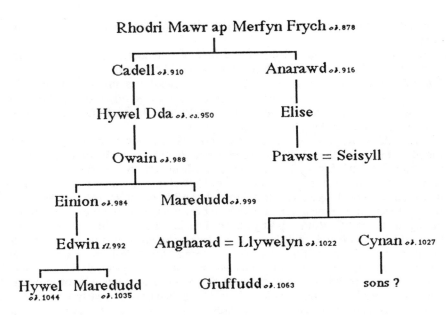

Rhodri Mawr ap Merfyn Frych *ob.*878

Cadell *ob.*910

Anarawd *ob.*916

Hywel Dda *ob. ca.*950

Elise

Owain *ob.*988

Prawst = Seisyll

Einion *ob.*984

Maredudd *ob.*999

Angharad = Llywelyn *ob.*1022

Cynan *ob.*1027

Edwin *fl.*992

Hywel *ob.*1044

Maredudd *ob.*1035

Gruffudd *ob.*1063

sons ?

Figure 13

known for sure, and it is possible that Hywel and Gruffudd did not consider themselves as kin; in general it seems to have been kin in the male line who were the important group. The sons of Cynan who slew Maredudd, if they were the sons of Cynan ap Seisyll, would stand in a slightly more remote cousinship still if the link through Prawst is accepted (figure 13). If this link is rejected, there is no relationship at all. Hywel ab Edwin is not mentioned by any of the extant early pedigrees.

(5) Gruffudd and Rhys, sons of Rhydderch

Gruffudd ap Rhydderch enjoys an interesting distinction: he is one of the few Welsh kings to have found mention in English records. And it is fortunate that he did, for Welsh texts are remarkably laconic about him. It is from the Anglo-Saxon Chronicle (version D) and John of Worcester that we know he was a king of the South. *Annales Cambriae* and the *Brutiau* do not include this information.

The information on his career as given in the Welsh chronicles is very sparse. *Annales Cambriae* (B) mention him only once, in the very garbled entry *s.a.* 1055: 'Grifinus filius Rederch occidit et Herfordiam uastauit'. *Annales Cambriae* (C) are slightly more helpful, recording a *seditio magna* between Gruffudd ap Rhydderch and Gruffudd ap Llywelyn *s.a.* 1046, and giving a more comprehensive obit ('Grifud filius Lewelin Grifud filium Rederch interfecit'). The *Brutiau* are almost as scanty in their information: but they do mention the sons of Rhydderch as fighting in the battle of Irathwy against the sons of Edwin in 1034, and they add to the name of Gruffudd ap Rhydderch that of his brother Rhys as involved in the great treachery of 1045. Gruffudd's death is given *s.a.* 1054,

25

although it seems more probable from the English sources that he died in 1055 or 1056.

It seems to be characteristic of the line of Rhydderch ab Iestyn that its members are elusive in the Welsh sources. Gruffudd can additionally be found in *Liber Landauensis* 264a as *rex Morcannuc*, witnessing a grant made by one Seisyll ap Gistlerth, *ca* 1030. The date is that given by Wendy Davies,[33] but I do not feel certain that Gruffudd could be considered as king of anywhere at this date, even as as a sub-king of his father.

Gruffudd ap Rhydderch was accorded considerable prominence by Sir John Lloyd, a state of affairs which may be partly explicable by the latter's distaste for the other Gruffudd. Lloyd certainly envisaged Gruffudd ap Rhydderch as having represented a major threat to Gruffudd ap Llywelyn – more so than the better documented Hywel ab Edwin. But Gruffudd ap Llywelyn appears to have suffered setbacks from time to time throughout his career, and no more so than usual during the time of Gruffudd ap Rhydderch. This is not to deny the competence of Gruffudd ap Rhydderch, but the seeming lack of interest in him by the Welsh annalists is itself interesting: why omit a 'great' king? Political bias towards Gruffudd ap Llywelyn? Yet the annalists do not omit Hywel ab Edwin. Bias against the line of Rhydderch in general? Yet they provide quite a lot of information about Gruffudd's son Caradog. Gruffudd ap Rhydderch clearly was prominent in his own time; certainly he drew English notice. However, Lloyd's comment,[34] 'Gruffudd ap Rhydderch . . . found means of stirring up on his own behalf the provincial feeling of Deheubarth and organised a formidable movement against the intruder from North Wales' is perhaps overstating the case. Gruffudd ap Llywelyn had been threatening the South for eleven years before ever Gruffudd ap Rhydderch had come to power there, and anyway the Northern king in several respects had better dynastic claims by Lloyd's own framework of descent from Rhodri Mawr than had Gruffudd ap Rhydderch. (Gruffudd ap Llywelyn was a grandson of Maredudd ab Owain of the Southern branch through the female line: Gruffudd ap Rhydderch was not related to Rhodri's dynasty at all.)

The English evidence on Gruffudd ap Rhydderch is mainly to be found in the D-text of the Anglo-Saxon Chronicle[35] and in the Chronicle of John of Worcester,[36] although the Anglo-Saxon Chronicle (C)[37] has a reference to the death of Rhys ap Rhydderch. The English material is as follows.

Anglo-Saxon Chronicle (C) *s.a.* 1052: 'Eac man ofsloh Hris þæs welscan cynges broþer.'

Anglo-Saxon Chronicle (D) *s.a.* 1050: 'On þam ilcan geare, comon upp on Wylisc Axa of Yrlande .xxxvi. scypa and þærabuton hearmas dydon mid Gryfines fultume þæs wæliscan cynges'. (John of Worcester also mentions this raid, *s.a.* 1049, and the evidence of his text makes it clear that the Gruffudd in question was Gruffudd ap Rhydderch.)

---

33 *The Llandaff Charters*, p. 128.
34 Lloyd, *A History*, II.361.
35 ASC (D): *An Anglo-Saxon Chronicle*, edd. Classen & Harmer.
36 JW: John of Worcester's Chronicle, ed. Howard, *Florentius Wigornensis*.
37 *The C-text*, ed. Rositzke.

Anglo-Saxon Chronicle (D) *s.a.* 1053: 'And man rædde þæt man sloh Ris þæs wyliscean cynges broþor for ðy he hearmas dyde: and man brohte his heafod to Glewcestre on Twelftan æfan'.

JW *s.a.* 1049: 'Eadem anno mense Augusto, Hibernienses pirate .xxxvi. nauibus ostium, intrantes Sabrinae fluminis in loco qui dicitur Wilcsceaxan appulerunt et cum adiutorio Griffini regis Australium Britonum, circa loca illa praedam agentis, nonnulla mala fecerit'.

JW *s.a.* 1053: 'Griffini regis Australium Walensium frater, Rhesus nomine, propter frequentes praedas quas agebat in loco qui Buledun dicitur, iussu regis Eadward occiditur, et Glaworna caput eius ad regem in uigilia Epiphaniae Domini est allatum'.

John of Worcester also mentions a raid by a 'King Griffin' *s.a.* 1052, but I take this to be Gruffudd ap Llywelyn, since John always refers to him as *rex Walensium*, but always specifies *rex Australium Walensium* when speaking of Gruffudd ap Rhydderch.

While it is outside my purpose here to speculate on why the Anglo-Saxon Chronicle (D) and John of Worcester display this interest in the happenings of Wales in the mid-eleventh century, their entries are of undeniable value. They provide extra light on Gruffudd ap Rhydderch as a ruler capable of not simply retaining his rule but of making his presence felt in England. It is interesting to wonder whether it was not in part the activity of Gruffudd ap Rhydderch on the borders which led Swegn Godwinesson, then earl in Hereford, to ally himself with the other Gruffudd in 1052: a joint punitive expedition?

It is difficult to assess Gruffudd ap Rhydderch: Lloyd[38] commented that 'If he had not been overshadowed and ultimately overwhelmed by a prince of the calibre of Gruffydd ap Llywelyn, Gruffydd of South Wales might have played no mean part in the history of his country'. Indeed, he succeeded in doing this despite Gruffudd ap Llywelyn, though perhaps no more so than his predecessor Hywel ap Edwin, or his father Rhydderch ab Iestyn.

Little more can be discovered of Gruffudd ap Rhydderch in the genealogies than is known of his father. He is included in the *Gwehelyth Gwent* of *ABT* 17,[39] and Lloyd seems to have thought that the family was associated with Ergyng and Gwent Uchaf, on the evidence of *Liber Landauensis*. This is doubtless possible, but *Liber Landauensis* can no further illuminate their ancestry than any other source: the line of Rhydderch ab Iestyn does seem to have quite literally come from nowhere.

Finally, Rhys ap Rhydderch, Gruffudd's brother, has achieved a mention in the work of William of Malmesbury, albeit an erroneous one.[40] William stated that Harold Godwinesson slew two brothers, kings of the Welsh, Rhys and Gruffudd. The Gruffudd to whom he refers was actually Gruffudd ap Llywelyn; Rhys was indeed slain by the English, but that Harold was the killer is probably an invention of William's.

---

[38] Lloyd, *A History*, II.362.
[39] Bartrum, *Tracts*, p. 105.
[40] William of Malmesbury, *De Gestis Regum Anglorum*, I.xxx: ed. Stubbs, I.237.

(6) Gruffudd ap Llywelyn

See below, under Gwynedd.

(7) Maredudd ab Owain ab Edwin

Maredudd ab Owain ab Edwin was a brother of the more famous Rhys ab Owain
and a nephew of Hywel ab Edwin. *Annales Cambriae* (B and C) record nothing
of him save his death in 1072 at the hands of the Normans, and possibly (C only)
at those of Caradog ap Gruffudd ap Rhydderch.

The *Brutiau* add to what is known of him, noting that in 1069, in the wake of
the battle of Mechain (in which Bleddyn ap Cynfyn established himself in the
North), Maredudd ab Owain – referred to as 'Maredudd ab Owain ab Edwin' –
held the kingdom of the South. The *Brutiau* give the date 1070 for Maredudd's
death; Thomas Jones amended this in his edition to 1072, on the basis of the
death of Diarmait mac Maíl na mBó, a notice of which accompanies Maredudd's
obit.

Maredudd's rule in the South is interesting. That it is recorded in the same
annal as Bleddyn's victory may suggest a settling-down throughout Wales after a
period of disorder on the death of Gruffudd ap Llywelyn. Certainly the Welsh
chronicles are remarkably lacking in comment for the years 1064–8. *Annales
Cambriae* note only the death of Joseph, bishop of St Davids, and the English
events of 1066. The *Brutiau* are much the same, adding the pilgrimage to Rome
of Donnchad Ua Briain and a note of the first *decemnouenalis*. The Anglo-Saxon
Chronicle presents the events of 1063/4 as though Bleddyn simply took over on
his half-brother's death, and there is some suggestion in Anglo-Norman sources
that in the post-Conquest years Bleddyn to some degree supported the rebellion
of Eadwine and Morcar, the English earls, against William the Conqueror. But
there is nevertheless a strong possibility that the situation in Wales itself was not
entirely straightforward. The succession of Maredudd ab Owain in the South is
particularly interesting in that it represents a return to the old line of Einion ab
Owain ap Hywel Dda, despite a period of twenty-five years of rule by newer lines
(Gruffudd ap Rhydderch 1044–1055/6; Gruffudd ap Llywelyn 1055/6–1063); nor
had the family of Rhydderch ab Iestyn disappeared from the South, for Gruffudd
ap Rhydderch's son Caradog had been in a position to harass Harold Godwinesson at Portskewet (Gwent) in 1065 (Anglo-Saxon Chronicle [C and D], and
John of Worcester).

This is the Caradog ap Gruffudd whom *Annales Cambriae* (C) associate with
the killing of Maredudd in 1072, and in this association the C-text has the
agreement of the *Brutiau*. The involvement is not at all improbable, given that
they were rival claimants to the South, Maredudd by virtue of his kinship with
Hywel ab Edwin and Einion ab Owain, Caradog through his father and grandfather, the successful 'usurpers' – note also that when in 1075 Rhys ab Owain,
the brother of Maredudd ab Owain, took the South, he did so in association with
Rhydderch ap Caradog, the first cousin of Caradog ap Gruffudd, and that Rhys
himself was killed by Caradog ap Gruffudd.

Maredudd ab Owain ab Edwin does not feature in any of the early genealogies, nor, seemingly, in any of the late ones. For his ancestry, see above, *sub*

Einion ab Owain. He is however mentioned in two Anglo-Norman sources, the *Historia Ecclesiastica* of Orderic Vitalis, and Domesday Book for Herefordshire. In Orderic's account Maredudd is probably to be identified with the 'King Maria-doth' whom William FitzOsbern laid low.[41] In Domesday Book, Maredudd features as the recipient of a grant of an estate at Kenchester from Earl William FitzOsbern, although by the time of Domesday Book itself the land was held by Maredudd's son Gruffudd.[42]

(8) Rhys and Hywel, sons of Owain

They were brothers of Maredudd, above. Rhys held the South, on the evidence of *Annales Cambriae* (C) and the *Brutiau*, after the death of Bleddyn ap Cynfyn in 1075 – no ruler is named for the intervening period 1072–75; it seems most likely that no one person was supreme, but rather that there was a struggle between the sons of Owain and Caradog ap Gruffudd of the rival line of Rhydderch ab Iestyn. *S.A.* 1075 in both *Annales Cambriae* (C) and the *Brutiau*, Rhys is said to have held joint rule in the South with Rhydderch ap Caradog, another member of the house of Rhydderch ab Iestyn. While Maredudd ab Owain ab Edwin is not said to have shared his rule, it is entirely possible that he too had a co-ruler (and an inimical one at that), most probably in that case Caradog ap Gruffudd.

The career of Rhys ab Owain is quite well documented, especially when its shortness (three years) is considered. He was a participant in the conspiracy of Ystrad Tywi against Bleddyn in 1075, and is said to have been the actual killer of the latter (*Annales Cambriae* [B and C]; *Brut y Tywysogion* [Pen. 20 and RB]; *Brenhinedd y Saesson*). He was involved in the battle of Camddwr against the sons of Cadwgan ab Elystan Glodrydd in the same year, which he seems to have won (although *Brut y Tywysogion* [Pen. 20], makes the error of saying he was killed in this battle, and then again in 1078); he fought the same people again in 1077 at the battle of Gweunytwl and won; he fought Trahaearn ap Caradog at the battle of Pwllgwdig and was defeated, and was slain later in the same year (1078), together with his brother Hywel, by Caradog ap Gruffudd.

The battle of Camddwr deserves a brief aside, since it is one of the most confused events of eleventh-century Wales. It appears to have been fought between the sons of Cadwgan ap Elystan on the one side, and Rhys ab Owain and Rhydderch ap Caradog on the other. The *Brutiau* add Caradog ap Gruffudd also, seemingly on the side of the sons of Cadwgan, although this is not immediately obvious from the punctuation of the edited texts. The chronicle-texts are complex in their accounts of it, moreover, and reconstruction requires a certain amount of care. *Annales Cambriae* (B) omit the battle altogether. The C-text reads 'Grifud autem nepos Iacob non obsedit bellum Camdubr inter filios Kadugaun et inter Res at Rederch, qui uictores fuerunt'. It is clear that this is in fact a conflation of two events, combined with a textual error: the text can be corrected to read 'Grifud autem nepos Iacob Mon obsedit. Bellum Camdubr inter filios Kadugaun . . .', etc.. This emendation makes sense of the annal, since Gruffudd ap Cynan is

41 Orderic Vitalis, *Historia Ecclesiastica*, Book IV: ed. & transl. Chibnall, II.260.
42 *Domesday Book*, Herefordshire, fos 187ra and 187va.

known to have been active in Mon (Anglesey), at this time; the emendation was suggested by Lloyd[43] and Thomas Jones.[44] *Brut y Tywysogion* (Pen. 20) states that the battle took place between Goronwy and Llywelyn, sons of Cadwgan, and Rhys ab Owain and Rhydderch ap Caradog and Caradog ap Gruffudd 'who fell there together'. The end of this statement is clearly wrong, for all of the participants are to be found in subsequent annals. *Brut y Tywysogion* (RB) reads[45]

Ac yna y bu y vrwydwr yg Kamdwr rwg Goronw a Llywelyn meibion Kadwgawn, a Charadawc vab Gruffud gytac wynt, a Rys vab ywein a Ryderch vab Caradawc y gyt a rei hyny.

And then was the battle in the Camddwr between Goronwy and Llywelyn sons of Cadwgan, and Caradog ap Gruffudd along with them, and Rhys ab Owain and Rhydderch ap Caradog along with them.

This is the unamended text, as opposed to the text as it stands in Jones's edition, in which he has supplied the information as to the victors (in square brackets). *Brut y Tywysogion* (RB) does not actually state the outcome of the battle, although it does make clear which side Caradog ap Gruffudd was fighting on.

Brenhinedd y Saesson has a less garbled account, reading[46]

Yn y vlwydyn honno y bu ymlad Camdwr y rwng meibion Cadwgavn, nyt amgen, Goronw a Llywelyn, gyt a Caradauc vab Grufud o'r neill parth, a Rys vab Oweyn a Ryderch vab Caradauc o'r parth arall, y rei a oruuwyt arnadunt.

In that year the battle of the Camddwr took place between the sons of Cadwgan, namely Goronwy and Llywelyn, together with Caradog ap Gruffudd, on the one side, and Rhys ab Owain and Rhydderch, on the other side, who were defeated.

The apparent defeat of Rhys and Rhydderch would seem to be a product of the complicated syntax and large number of subordinate clauses present in the entry, rather than representing an alternative idea as to who lost the battle. On balance, what seems to have happened is that Rhys and Rhydderch won: this is based both on the evidence of *Annales Cambriae* (C), and on *Annales Cambriae* (B) which in their account of the battle of Gweunotyll two years later, between the sons of Cadwgan and Rhys, state that Rhys won for the second time. *Brut y Tywysogion* (RB) also says this. *Brut y Tywysogion* (Pen. 20) and *Brenhinedd y Saesson* seem to imply that the sons of Cadwgan won, although again their syntax is not of the clearest.

All three of the sons of Owain were killed by Caradog ap Gruffudd – Maredudd in 1072, Rhys and Hywel togther in 1078. This is not surprising, since they were presumably his main rivals for rule in the South, especially after the removal in 1076 of Rhydderch ap Caradog by yet another scion of the line of Rhydderch ab Iestyn, Meirchion ap Rhys. However, the slaying by Caradog of Rhys and Hywel follows a thorough defeat of the brothers at the hands of the

---

43 'Wales and the coming', p. 154, n. 2.
44 *ByT* (Pen. 20), transl. Jones, p. 153, n. 16.23–4.
45 *ByT* (RB), ed. & transl. Jones, pp. 28–9.
46 *ByS*, ed. & transl. Jones, pp. 78–9.

then ruler of Gwynedd, Trahaearn ap Caradog; so Rhys's power was already broken.

Rhys was not quite the last of the descendants of Edwin ab Einion ab Owain to aspire to rule in the South, but he was the last to do so successfully (although Einion's line through Cadell ab Einion was to succeed in the person of Rhys ap Tewdwr). Rhys ab Owain is treated as a villain by the *Brutiau* (the entry *s.a.* 1076 in *Brut y Tywysogion* [Pen. 20] is a clear example of this).[47] Yet unlike most of the eleventh-century kings, he seems never to have feuded with his own kin. His enemies were all outside his own family – the descendants of Rhydderch ap Caradog and the associates of Bleddyn. He does not feature in any of the early genealogies. On his descent see *sub* Einion ab Owain.

(9) Rhydderch ap Caradog

Rhydderch was co-ruler in the South with Rhys ab Owain in 1075 according to the *Brutiau*, and involved in the same year in the battle of Camddwr. He was killed in 1076 by his cousin Meirchion: *Annales Cambriae* (B) simply give the killing without naming the killer; *Annales Cambriae* (C) give the name Meirchion without any patronym; *Brut y Tywysogion* (Pen. 20 and RB) and *Brenhinedd y Saesson* give the patronym 'ap Rhys ap Rhydderch'. *Brut y Tywysogion* (RB) further makes him a participant in the battle of Gweunotyll in 1077, but this is clearly an error and appears to represent a duplication of the names of the participants in the earlier battle of Camddwr.

Rhydderch was a member of the family of Rhydderch ab Iestyn, being a son of Caradog ap Rhydderch ab Iestyn, who is recorded in *Annales Cambriae* (B and C) and in the *Brutiau* as having been killed by the English in 1035, which is itself interesting in that another brother, Rhys ap Rhydderch, was also killed by the English, in 1053. Meirchion, Rhydderch's slayer, was a son of this Rhys.

None of these individuals features in the early genealogies. According to Bartrum,[48] however, Caradog ap Rhydderch occurs in Lewys Dwnn's *Heraldic Visitations* (I.143, 144, 274) and in London, British Library, MS. Harley 2300, part 2 (Fos. 100r–193v), a south Welsh manuscript of *ca* 1625, probably by Walter Hopkin. Rhydderch ap Caradog occurs in Dwnn, (I.143 and 274), and in London, British Library, MS. Harley 5835, a south Welsh manuscript of *ca* 1610. (See figure 14.)

Bartrum has also attributed to Meirchion ap Rhys a daughter, Elen, who married into the Perrot family of Iestynton. The family is further complicated by the existence of two members bearing the name 'Owain ap Caradog'. One of these is evidenced in *ABT* 17 – Owain ap Caradog ap Gruffudd – and also in the *Brutiau s.a.* 1113 (*recte* 1116). The second Owain, Owain ap Caradog ap Rhydderch, is evidenced in this annal only. One of them died in that year (Bartrum has assumed that they both did so), but which died is not immediately clear, for the annal in question is extremely long and complicated and furthermore deals with two more Owains (Owain ab Edwin and Owain ap Cadwgan) as well as the two of the line of Rhydderch ab Iestyn. Owain ap Caradog ap

---

47 *ByT* (Pen. 20), transl. Jones, p. 17.
48 *Welsh Genealogies*, V.95.

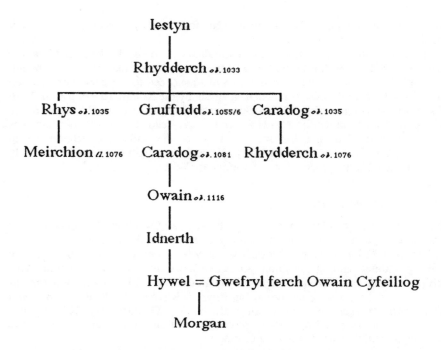

Iestyn
|
Rhydderch *o.s. 1033*

Rhys *o.s. 1035*　　Gruffudd *o.s. 1055/6*　Caradog *o.s. 1035*
|　　　　　　　　　|　　　　　　　　　　|
Meirchion *fl. 1076*　Caradog *o.s. 1081*　Rhydderch *o.s. 1076*
　　　　　　　　　　|
　　　　　　　　　Owain *o.s. 1116*
　　　　　　　　　　|
　　　　　　　　　Idnerth
　　　　　　　　　　|
　　　Hywel = Gwefryl ferch Owain Cyfeiliog
　　　　　　　　　　|
　　　　　　　　　Morgan

The line from Iestyn to Morgan is from **ABT 17**.

Figure 14

Rhydderch is said in this annal (and referred to by this long form of name), in the context of a list of leaders summoned by the French against Gruffudd ap Rhys ap Tewdwr, to be holding part of Cantref Mawr. He is not said to have died. The same list includes 'Owain son of Caradog by Gwenllian daughter of that same king Bleddyn' – this presumably being Owain ap Caradog ap Gruffudd, since it would have been impossible for Caradog ap Rhydderch ab Iestyn, who died in 1035, to have married a daughter of Bleddyn ap Cynfyn, whose known period of activity is 1063–1075. It is this later Owain who seems to have been killed in 1116, defending Carmarthen against Gruffudd ap Rhys. The annal also mentions a Maredudd ap Rhydderch ap Caradog holding Cantref Bychan under Richard FitzPons. This Maredudd would seem to have beeen a son of Rhydderch ap Caradog. The descendants of Rhydderch ap Caradog and Meirchion ap Rhys, as given by Bartrum and as discoverable from the chronicles, are given in figure 15. The main genealogical authority seems to be Lewys Dwnn.

The association of the descendants of Rhydderch ab Iestyn in the twelfth century with Cantref Mawr and Cantref Bychan is interesting, especially when it is remembered that the family is connected with Gwent in *ABT* 17. This would seem to indicate that the family had wide territorial interests, perhaps as a result of their successes in the eleventh century.

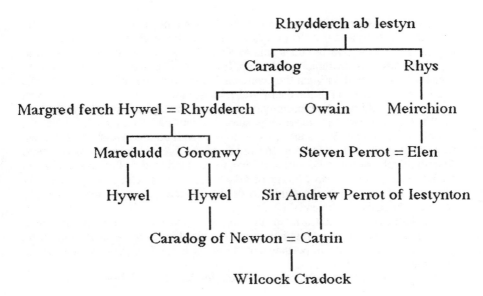

Figure 15

(10) Rhys ap Tewdwr

Rhys ap Tewdwr is said by the chronicle-texts to have begun to rule in 1079. No area is specified but, as this date makes him contemporary with Trahaearn ap Caradog, who is known to have been ruling in the North, it is probable that he was active in the South. He was moreover a member of the so-called Southern Branch of the dynasty of Rhodri Mawr, and the *Historia Gruffud vab Kenan* associates him with the South.[49] His later career makes the Southern connexion plain. He was a participant in the battle of Mynydd Carn, in 1081 (*Annales Cambriae* [B and C]; *Brut y Tywysogion* [Pen. 20 and RB]; *Brenhinedd y Saesson*). In 1088, however, he suffered a reverse, being expelled by the sons of Bleddyn ap Cynfyn. Rhys fled to Ireland, but returned with a fleet of Hiberno-Scandinavians with whose aid he defeated the sons of Bleddyn at Llech-y-Crau and paid off his fleet (*Annales Cambriae* [B and C] and the *Brutiau*). In 1091 he repelled an attempted takeover by Gruffudd ap Maredudd, whom he slew (*Annales Cambriae* [B and C]; *Brut y Tywysogion* [Pen. 20 and RB]; *Brenhinedd y Saesson*) – *Brenhinedd y Saesson* adds to this that Rhys defeated not only Gruffudd but also the summoners of Gruffudd, the sons of Cedifor ap Gollwyn, and that Gruffudd had been summoned specifically against Rhys. He was killed in 1093 by the Normans of Brycheiniog (according to all the source-texts). The *Brutiau* call his death 'the fall of the kingdom of the Britons', and specify that he was king of the South.

---

[49] ed. Evans, pp. 13–14. For an English translation, it is still necessary to use *The History of Gruffudd ap Cynan*, ed. & transl. Jones.

Rhys ap Tewdwr is also noted in two Anglo-Norman sources, Domesday Book for Herefordshire, and the *Historia Ecclesiastica* of Orderic Vitalis. The Domesday reference concerns the dues paid to King William by 'Riset of Wales', who from the dating is presumably Rhys ap Tewdwr.[50] The dues amounted to forty pounds. It is not said for what they were paid, however. The reference by Orderic Vitalis is in the context of the list of Welsh kings laid low by William FitzOsbern and his men.[51] Although no patronyms are given, this again is probably meant to be Rhys ap Tewdwr, but impossibly, since William had died *ca* 1071. The list, 'Risen et Caducan et Mariadoth', seems to represent notable Welsh kings known to Orderic, who had suffered at the hands of the French. In point of fact both Maredudd (ab Owain ab Edwin) and Rhys were killed by the Normans. Cadwgan I take to be Cadwgan ap Meurig of Glamorgan, whose career is unfortuately obscure, but who from the evidence of the Llandaff charters seems to have ceased to be active in the early 1070s.

The battle of Mynydd Carn was in some ways a turning point in the history of the later eleventh century. It is however a confused event as far as the annalistic record goes. Given its importance, it deserves a brief digression in order to illuminate it somewhat.

The evidence of the chronicle-texts about the battle is as follows.

Annales Cambriae (B): 'Annus. Bellum Montis Carn, in quo Traharn filius Caradauci et Caradauc filius Grifini et Meiler filius Ruallan a Reso filio Teudur et a Grifino filio Conani occisi sunt'.[52]

('*Annus.* The battle of Mynydd Carn in which Trahaearn ap Caradog and Caradog ap Gruffudd and Meilir ap Rhiwallon were killed by Rhys ap Tewdwr and Gruffudd ap Cynan.')

Annales Cambriae (C): 'Annus Bellum Montis Carn in quo Traharn filius Cradauc et Cradauc filius Grifud et Meilir filius Ruallaun et Res filius Teudur et Grifud filius Eynnaun filius Iacob occiduntur'.[53]

('*Annus.* The battle of Mynydd Carn in which Trahaearn ap Caradog and Caradog ap Gruffudd and Meilir ap Rhiwallon and Rhys ap Tewdwr and Gruffudd ab Einion ab Iago were killed.')

Brut y Tywysogion (Pen. 20): 'Blwydyn wedy hyny y bu ymlad Mynyd karn ac yno y llas Trahayarn ap Karadawc, a Charadawc a Gruffud a Meilyr meibyon Riwallawn a Rys vab Tewdwr ac yny ol ynteu y doeth Gruffud wyr y Yago as Ysgottyeid yn borth idaw'.[54]

('A year after that was the battle of Mynydd Carn. And there Trahaearn ap Caradog and Caradog and Gruffudd and Meilyr sons of Rhiwallon and Rhys ap Tewdwr were slain. And after him came Gruffudd, grandson of Iago, together with Irish, to help him.')[55]

---

50 *Domesday Book*, Herefordshire, fo. 179rb.
51 Orderic Vitalis, *Historia Ecclesiastica*, Book IV: ed. & transl. Chibnall, II.260.
52 *AC* (B), ed. Lloyd, 'Wales and the coming', p. 176.
53 *AC* (C), ed. Lloyd, 'Wales and the coming', p. 177.
54 *ByT* (Pen. 20), ed. Jones, p. 23.
55 *ByT* (Pen. 20), transl. Jones, p. 23.

Brut y Tywysogion (RB): 'Ac yna y bu vrwydyr yMynyd Carn. Ac yna y llas Trahaern ab Caradawc a Chradawc vab Gruffud wyr Iago ac Yscotteit gyt ac ef, yn ganhorthwy idaw'.

('And then there was a battle on Mynydd Carn. And then were slain Trahaearn ap Caradog and Caradog ap Gruffudd, grandson of Iago, and Irish along with him to help him.')[56]

Brenhinedd y Saesson: 'Anno Domini .M.LXXIX. y bu ymlad Mynyd Carn. Ac yno y llas Trahaearn vab Caradauc a meibion Riwallawn, Caradauc a Grufyd a Meilir, y gan Rys vab Teudwr; canys Grufud, nei Iago, ac Yscottieit llidiauc a doeth yn borth idav.'

('*Anno Domini* .M.LXXIX. the battle of Mynydd Carn took place. And there Trahaearn ap Caradog and the sons of Rhiwallon, Caradog and Gruffudd and Meilir, were slain by Rhys ap Tewdwr; for Gruffudd, nephew of Iago, and fierce Irish came to his aid.')[57]

The implications of these various readings for the text-history of this section of the sources are endless. *Brut y Tywysogion* (RB) appears to have lost a line, jumping from the 'Gruffudd' of Caradog ap Gruffudd to the information which should have followed on from the second Gruffudd (grandson of Iago). *Brut y Tywysogion* (Pen. 20) and *Brenhinedd y Saesson* (and hence presumably their lost Latin source) have the same error – Caradog and Gruffudd and Meilir sons of Rhiwallon for Caradog ap Gruffudd and Meilir ap Rhiwallon; and *Brenhinedd y Saesson* has seemingly mistranslated *nepos* as nephew rather than grandson.[58] *Annales Cambriae* in both versions are relatively clear, although this is in part due to the superior readings of B supplied by Lloyd – the annal as printed by Williams has the names distorted almost beyond recognition, a state of affairs apparently due more to the editor than to the manuscript.[59] *Annales Cambriae* (C) and *Brut y Tywysogion* (Pen. 20) both claim that Rhys ap Tewdwr was a casualty of the battle, which he palpably was not.

The participants would seem to have been Trahaearn ap Caradog, Caradog ap Gruffudd, and Meilir ap Rhiwallon on the one hand, and Rhys ap Tewdwr and Gruffudd ap Cynan on the other. All of Trahaearn's group apparently fell in the battle. Trahaearn himself had been the main ruler in the North except possibly for Anglesey; Caradog ap Gruffudd was probably dominant in the South, although Rhys had been a serious rival to him since about 1079. Gruffudd ap Cynan may have acquired Anglesey after the death of Bleddyn ap Cynfyn in 1075, although the chronicles by no means agree on this, and the evidence of the *Historia Gruffud vab Kenan* suggests that he may have held it only briefly.[60] This text is however an unreliable source, given its panegyric nature, and its account of Mynydd Carn should be treated with considerable caution, particularly as it views Rhys as being a subordinate protegé of Gruffudd ap Cynan. Such a state of affairs seems improbable, given that at this date Rhys would appear to have enjoyed a rather more secure position than Gruffudd.

---

56 *ByT* (RB), ed. & transl. Jones, p. 30. Jones in his text supplied the involvement of Meilir and Rhys in square brackets, together with the name 'Gruffudd', but I have omitted his emendation.
57 *ByS*, ed. & transl. Jones, pp. 80–1.
58 *ByS*, ed. & transl. Jones, p. 297, n. 81.29–30.
59 *AC*, ed. Williams, p. 27.
60 ed. Evans, pp. 6–16.

Trahaearn ap Caradog was a cousin (of some kind) to Bleddyn ap Cynfyn, and no relation at all to Rhys ap Tewdwr or indeed any of the participants in the battle, with the possible exception of Meilir ap Rhiwallon. Caradog ap Gruffudd was the son of Gruffudd ap Rhydderch, and the last of that family to play any major role in the political life of the eleventh century. Meilir's father, Rhiwallon, was the brother of Bleddyn ap Cynfyn and, according to the *Brutiau s.a.* 1106, Meilir's sister Gwladus was the wife of Rhys ap Tewdwr (*ABT* 10 also gives this statement). Rhys ap Tewdwr and Gruffudd ap Cynan were both descendants of Rhodri Mawr, Gruffudd being a member of the 'Northern Branch', and Rhys a member of the 'Southern Branch'. Both were near the beginning of their careers at this time, and possibly somewhat at a disadvantage against the established Trahaearn and Caradog: the alliance between Rhys and Gruffudd may therefore have been one based on practical necessity. Gruffudd would have had a claim of sorts on the North through his grandfather, Iago ab Idwal (ruled 1033–1039), while Rhys would have had one on the South, through his great-grandfather, Einion ab Owain, his great uncle Edwin ab Einion, and his cousins, Hywel and Maredudd, sons of Edwin, and Rhys, Hywel, and Maredudd, sons of Owain. Mynydd Carn, resulting as it did in a victory for Rhys and Gruffudd, could be seen as the return of the 'old' order, with the resurgence (albeit shortlived) of rulers descended in a direct male line from Rhodri Mawr, despite the flourishing 'intrusive' lines.

As regards the later career of Rhys ap Tewdwr, the source of his conflict in 1088 with the sons of Bleddyn ap Cynfyn is not immediately clear, given that the line of Bleddyn was mainly associated with Powys rather than the South. One reason which suggests itself is that Rhys's authority may have extended into the North – or at least into Powys – as well as the South: one must note that Gruffudd ap Cynan does not become prominent in the eleventh century at all (spending much of the 1080s in prison), for his main career was in the twelfth century; and in his absence, the main power in the North would have been these very sons of Bleddyn. Alternatively, the sons of Bleddyn may have been seeking to avenge their kinsmen Trahaearn and Meilir, or to re-establish the wider influence enjoyed by Gruffudd ap Llywelyn, their uncle, and possibly by their father Bleddyn. It is also worth noting that upon Rhys's death Cadwgan ap Bleddyn plundered Dyfed, which region, together with Ceredigion, was then seized by the Normans (which is doubtless part of the reason why the *Brutiau* refer to Rhys's death as the 'fall of the kingdom of the Britons'.[61] Formulae like 'king of the Britons' seem in the Welsh chronicles to have been applied only to such kings as can be said to have had influence (or direct authority) over much of Wales at some time in their lives. The similar reference to the 'kingdom of the Britons' in connexion with Rhys may suggest that he possessed (or was later thought to have possessed) some similar influence.

The family of Bleddyn does appear to have been largely Powys-based, although the increasing influence of the Normans did make some difference in this – Iorwerth ap Bleddyn was granted considerable amounts of land in south Wales by Henry I. Bleddyn himself does not seem to have held the South, but did take an interest in it. Of the two battles between the sons of Bleddyn and Rhys, only

---

[61] *ByT* (Pen. 20) *s.a.* 1091 (*recte* 1093).

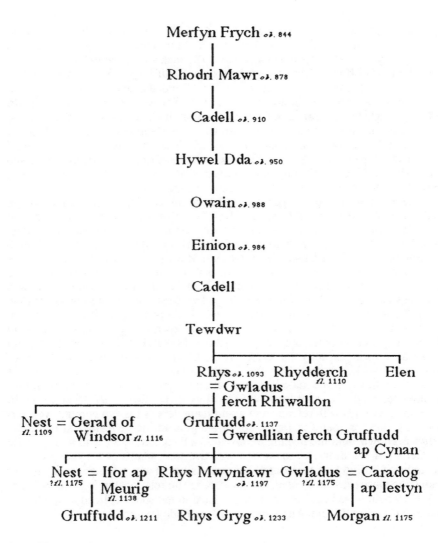

Merfyn Frych *ob.* 844
|
Rhodri Mawr *ob.* 878
|
Cadell *ob.* 910
|
Hywel Dda *ob.* 950
|
Owain *ob.* 988
|
Einion *ob.* 984
|
Cadell
|
Tewdwr
|
Rhys *ob.* 1093   Rhydderch   Elen
= Gwladus   *fl.* 1110
ferch Rhiwallon

Nest = Gerald of   Gruffudd *ob.* 1137
fl. 1109   Windsor *fl.* 1116   = Gwenllian ferch Gruffudd
ap Cynan

Nest = Ifor ap   Rhys Mwynfawr   Gwladus = Caradog
?fl. 1175   Meurig   *ob.* 1197   *?fl.* 1175   ap Iestyn
fl. 1138

Gruffudd *ob.* 1211   Rhys Gryg *ob.* 1233   Morgan *fl.* 1175

Figure 16

Llech-y-Crau, which Rhys won (thereby re-establishing himself) is known by name. The other, earlier, battle, as a result of which he was expelled to Ireland, is unnamed and therefore unlocatable. Lloyd simply assumed that the family of Bleddyn was Powys-based and belligerent.[62] It is most likely that a mixture of these motives lay behind their action.

About 1091, Rhys faced another challenge in the shape of one Gruffudd ap Maredudd. Gruffudd was in fact related to Rhys, being the son of Maredudd ab

62 Lloyd, *A History*, II.398.

Owain ab Edwin, ruling in the south 1069–72, and the nephew of Rhys ab Owain (1075/8). As the son of a former king, Gruffudd probably had a better claim on the territory than Rhys ap Tewdwr himself. The men who seem to have begun the rebellion in Gruffudd's favour were the sons of Cedifor ap Gollwyn, described by the *Brutiau* as 'the leading man of Dyfed',[63] and the revolt may represent a preference for Edwin ab Einion's branch of the Southern descendants of Rhodri Mawr, as against the branch of Cadell ab Einion. It is, however, equally possible that Gruffudd was in some way sponsored by the Normans; after the death of William I, Rhys's position became increasingly insecure, a point to which I shall return in chapter three. Rhys ap Tewdwr was by no means a readily accepted king. He was killed in 1093 by the Normans of Brycheiniog. His slaying seems to have been preparatory to their expansion into Dyfed and Ceredigion.

There is a fair amount of genealogical material relating to Rhys. He occurs in MG 2, JC 24, *ABT* 7n, *ABT* 8a, *ABT* 10 (*Gwehelyth Deheubarth*), *ABT* 15, and *ABT* 16. Several of these are concerned with links to him through the female line. The MG and JC pedigrees both correctly list him as Rhys ap Tewdwr ap Cadell ab Einion.[64] *ABT* 7n, the part of *Plant Rhodri Mawr* concerning this branch, gives the names of the children of Tewdwr but, as this immediately follows a list of the children of Einion, it seems clear that *ABT* 7n has confused Tewdwr ab Einion and Tewdwr ap Cadell ab Einion, and its pedigree for Rhys is thus one generation short;[65] *ABT* 10 has the same mistake.[66] MG 2 is a pedigree of Rhys mwynfawr, extending back to Merfyn Frych. JC 24 goes down one generation further, to Rhys Gryg, but is carried only as far as Rhodri Mawr. *ABT* 8a mentions Rhys not in an ancestorial capacity, but rather as the killer of Madog and Rhirid sons of Bleddyn, as is also known from the Welsh chronicles.[67] *ABT* 10 is a pedigree of Rhys mwynfawr, in the male line, but with the names of his mother and grand-mother supplied (the latter being wife to Rhys ap Tewdwr). *ABT* 15 and *ABT* 16 both include Rhys with reference to grand-daughters of his.[68] A cumulative chart showing these is found in figure 16. In addition to the genealogical evidence, Rhys is known from the *Brutiau* to have had a daughter, Nest, who was the wife of Gerald of Windsor. His connexion with the descendants of Edwin ap Einion, including Gruffudd ap Maredudd, his rival, is not given in the genealogies, but can be reconstructed from annalistic evidence. The relationship is given in figure 17. He would have been very distantly related to the sons of Bleddyn ap Cynfyn (and to his wife) through Angharad ferch Maredudd (figure 18).

(11) Cedifor ap Gollwyn

Nothing is known of the career of Cedifor ap Gollwyn. His death is noted in both *Annales Cambriae* and the *Brutiau* as occuring in 1091, subsequent to which his sons (named as 'Llywelyn and the others') invited Gruffudd ap Maredudd into

63 *ByT* (Pen. 20) *s.a.* 1113 (*recte* 1116); *ByT* (RB) *s.a.* 1113 (*recte* 1116); *ByS s.a.* 1113 (*recte* 1116).
64 Bartrum, *Tracts*, pp. 39 and 47.
65 Bartrum, *Tracts*, p. 101.
66 *Ibid.*, p. 104.
67 *Ibid.*, p. 102.
68 *Ibid.*, p. 105.

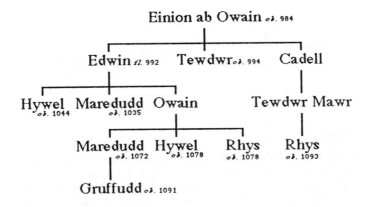

Figure 17

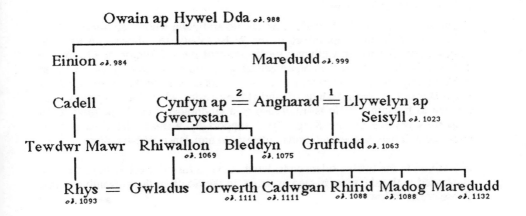

Figure 18

Dyfed, in opposition to Rhys ap Tewdwr. Cedifor is mentioned posthumously in the vernacular texts *s.a.* 1113, in a paragraph dealing with the brothers of Owain ap Cadwgan ap Bleddyn and their various mothers. Cedifor's daughter Ellylw is said to have been the mother of Morgan ap Cadwgan; Cedifor himself is described as 'the man who had been lord over all Dyfed'.[69] Although nothing more is known of him, the fact that his sons were in a position to invite Gruffudd ap Maredudd suggests that the family was influential in southern Wales.

In addition to his inclusion in the list of brothers of Owain ap Cadwgan in the

69 See note 63.

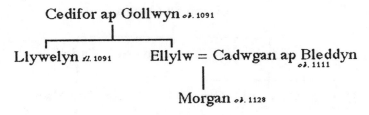

Cedifor ap Gollwyn *ob.* 1091

Llywelyn *fl.* 1091   Ellylw = Cadwgan ap Bleddyn *ob.* 1111

Morgan *ob.* 1128

Figure 19

Brutiau, Cedifor occurs also in *ABT* 18b (*Gwehelieth Dyfet*),[70] a pedigree of one Rikert ap Maredudd extending back to 'Kyndeyrn Vendigait'. This Rikert would appear to have been a great-great-grandson of Cedifor. Of this line, only Cedifor himself is traceable in the annalistic texts. It is worth noting, however, that Cedifor became an important figure in the later genealogical material.[71] Cedifor's kin as known from the chronicles is shown in figure 19, while the line as given by *ABT* 18b is shown in figure 20.

(12) Gruffudd ap Maredudd

Gruffudd was son of the Maredudd ab Owain ab Edwin who ruled briefly 1069–1072. For Gruffudd's appearance in the Welsh polity, see above, *sub* Rhys ap Tewdwr and Cedifor ap Collwyn; for his descent see *sub* Einion ab Owain. He does not figure in any of the known genealogical material. He is, however, noted in Domesday Book for Herefordshire. He occurs first in the list of the lands of Hugh Donkey as holding a hide of land at Kenchester, which had originally been granted to his father.[72] He is listed also as a landholder himself, holding seven properties granted by the King.[73] This support by William the Conqueror is interesting: it may suggest a Norman attempt to unbalance Welsh politics.

In addition to the twelve rulers considered above, a further twelve, not explicitly associated with rule, were named as active in the South in the eleventh century. These are as follows:

(1) Iago and Ieuaf, sons of Idwal, and
    Hywel ab Ieuaf;
(2) Edwin ab Einion;
(3) Caradog ap Gruffudd;
(4) Cadwgan and Iorwerth, sons of Bleddyn;
(5) Gruffudd and Ifor, sons of Idnerth ap Cadwgan, and
    Llywelyn ap Cadwgan;
(6) Uchdryd ab Edwin;
(7) Hywel ap Goronwy.

---

70 Bartrum, *Tracts*, p. 106.
71 Bartrum, *Welsh Genealogies*, I.47.
72 *Domesday Book*, Herefordshire, fo 187ra.
73 *Ibid.*

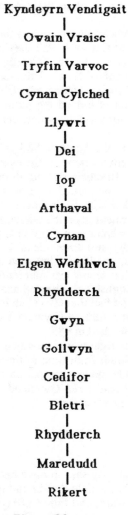

Kyndeyrn Vendigait
|
Ovain Vraisc
|
Tryfin Varvoc
|
Cynan Cylched
|
Llyvri
|
Dei
|
Iop
|
Arthaval
|
Cynan
|
Elgen Weflhvch
|
Rhydderch
|
Gvyn
|
Gollvyn
|
Cedifor
|
Bletri
|
Rhydderch
|
Maredudd
|
Rikert

Figure 20

The first half of the list above comprises largely individuals who were concerned with intra-Welsh political issues and strife; the latter were mostly active as opponents of the Normans.

(1) Iago and Ieuaf, sons of Idwal, and Hywel ab Ieuaf

These three were all members of the 'Northern Branch' of the dynasty of Rhodri Mawr. As Hywel's main sphere of action was the North, I postpone further discussion of his career until later: I do not propose to devote more than a cursory

41

examination to the sons of Idwal Foel, as their main activities were well before the eleventh century.

The sons of Idwal appear in a Southern context three times: in 949 they fought the sons of Hywel Dda at Nant Carno; in 952 they ravaged Dyfed twice; in 954 they fought the sons of Hywel and ravaged Ceredigion. The attack in 949 may have been a response to the death of Hywel Dda, recorded for the same year, an event which would have had long-reaching effects throughout Wales, given the extent of his sphere of influence; indeed the strife which followed can be explained in terms of a struggle for supremacy between the Northern and Southern dynasties.

Hywel ab Ieuaf appeared in the South in 983. The Latin and the vernacular chronicles give slightly different accounts of the event in question – according to *Annales Cambriae* (B and C), Brycheiniog and all the lands of Einion ab Owain were ravaged by the English accompanied by Hywel ab Ieuaf. The *Brutiau* imply that Hywel ab Ieuaf was allied with Einion against the English; however, this interpretation is entirely dependent upon the punctuation of the entry as supplied by Thomas Jones; by moving a comma, it is possible to give the account of *Brut y Tywysogion* (Pen. 20 and RB) and *Brenhinedd y Saesson* the same sense as *Annales Cambriae*. Moreover, an alliance between the predominantly Northern Hywel and the Southern Einion seems less inherently likely than an alliance of the Northern ruler with the English and directed against his Southern rival. This is made even more likely by the fact that Hywel ab Ieuaf had been allied with the English previously, in 978, in a raid on Clynnog Fawr. Interestingly enough, it was through the English that he died in 985.

The influence of these three figures was mostly in the North, but they seem to have made attempts on the South from time to time, just as their cousin Maredudd ab Owain ap Hywel Dda made attempts on the North. For genealogical detail on Hywel ab Ieuaf, see below *sub* Gwynedd. His relationship to his rival Einion ab Owain is, however, given in figure 21.

(2) Edwin ab Einion

Edwin ab Einion is never explicitly said to have held rule over the South, or in any area therein, although it is possible that he did in fact exercise some power. He was a son of Einion ab Owain, and father of Hywel and Maredudd, sons of Edwin, who were ruling in the South in 1033. Only one of his actions is known, although the incident is recorded in both the Latin and the vernacular chronicles: this is his ravaging of all the territory of Maredudd ab Owain in 992, with the help of the English. Edwin was clearly a contender for rule (supreme rule?) and therefore it is not especially surprising to find the English involved with him, since it would have been very much to the advantage of the English to promote strife between Welsh leaders. Edwin's expedition seems to have been successful to some degree: he is said to have taken hostages. In the same year, Maredudd ab Owain ravaged Glamorgan, which may suggest that Glamorgan was involved on Edwin's side.

Maredudd and Edwin were uncle and nephew, Maredudd being the brother of Edwin's father Einion. Edwin does not, however, occur in any of the early

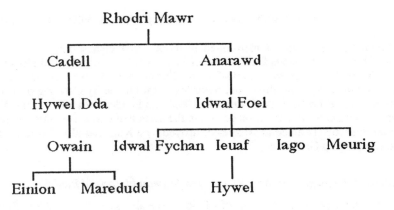

                          Rhodri Mawr

        Cadell   Anarawd

      Hywel Dda   Idwal Foel

    Owain   Idwal Fychan Ieuaf   Iago   Meurig

  Einion   Maredudd   Hywel

Figure 21

genealogical material. For his pedigree, which can be reconstructed from the chronicles, see above, *sub* Einion ab Owain.

(3) Caradog ap Gruffudd

Although Caradog is not explicitly said to have held rule within the South, he almost certainly did. He is found consistently opposing those named in the sources as ruling in the South. In 1072, he killed Maredudd ab Owain ab Edwin who had been ruling since 1069. In 1075 he fought with Rhys ab Owain and his own cousin Rhydderch ap Caradog (these two being said earlier in the same annal to have gained rule in the South) at the battle of Camddwr. In 1078, Caradog slew Rhys and his brother Hywel. He lost his own life in 1081, fighting yet another rival contender for the South, Rhys ap Tewdwr, in the battle of Mynydd Carn. His ally in this battle was the ruler of Gwynedd, Trahaearn ap Caradog, who was also slain. Rhys ap Tewdwr had as his ally Trahaearn's rival Gruffudd ap Cynan: in some measure the battle can be viewed as the downfall of the new order at the hands of the old.

It is worth noting that, although the 1070s were a contentious era, at no point is Caradog found in conflict with Trahaearn – indeed the two would seem to have been allies; it was the defeat inflicted upon Rhys ab Owain by Trahaearn at Pwllgwdig in 1078 which laid Rhys open to his death at Caradog's hands later in the same year. Indeed, it is possible that the connexion might have begun with Trahaearn's predecessor, Bleddyn ap Cynfyn, since Caradog is said to have married Gwenllian ferch Bleddyn.[74]

Caradog is mentioned in one mediaeval genealogical source, *ABT* 17,[75] for which see above *sub* Rhydderch ab Iestyn, and in one later one, London, British Library, MS. Harley 2414, a south Welsh manuscript of *ca* 1615, by Llywelyn

---

74 *ByT* (RB) *s.a.* 1113 (*recte* 1116); *ByT* (Pen. 20) *s.a.* 1113 (*recte* 1116); *ByS s.a.* 1113 (*recte* 1116).
75 Bartrum, *Tracts*, p. 105.

Sion. He was the father of the Owain ap Caradog who was killed at Carmarthen in 1116.

Caradog ap Gruffudd is mentioned in three non-Welsh sources: the Anglo-Saxon Chronicle (versions CDE), John of Worcester's Chronicle, and Domesday Book. The entries in the Anglo-Saxon Chronicle and John of Worcester's Chronicle are essentially the same, recording a raid made by Caradog on Harold Godwinesson at Portskewet (Gwent) in 1065 – an incident unknown from Welsh sources. The Domesday mention occurs in the survey of Gloucestershire, where a passing reference is made to villages destroyed by a King Caradog[76] whom I take to be Caradog ap Gruffudd.

(4) Iorweth, Cadwgan, Madog, Rhirid, and Maredudd, sons of Bleddyn

For the main activites of the sons of Bleddyn, see also *sub* Gwynedd and Powys. Their Southern activities were as follows.

1088 The sons of Bleddyn – named as Cadwgan, Madog, and Rhirid – expelled Rhys ap Tewdwr from his territory. Madog and Rhirid were killed in a second battle, on Rhys's return later in the same year.

1093 On the death of Rhys ap Tewdwr, Dyfed was plundered by Cadwgan.

1096 The warband of Cadwgan was involved in the despoiling of Pembroke castle.

1099 Cadwgan, on returning from exile in Ireland, made peace with the Normans and was given Ceredigion and a portion of Powys.

1102 Cadwgan, Maredudd, and Iorwerth supported the rebellion of Robert de Bellême. Iorwerth, however, was suborned by Henry I and rewarded with Ceredigion, Ystrad Tywi, Powys, Cydweli, Gower, and half of Dyfed. He made peace with his brothers and gave Ceredigion and half of Powys to Cadwgan, but seized and imprisoned Maredudd. Henry I later in the same year reneged and gave Dyfed to a knight named Saer, and Ystrad Tywi, Cydweli, and Gower to Hywel ap Goronwy.

Much of the activity of these brothers was aimed at the Normans and this trend can be seen in their actions in other parts of Wales also. It is possible that Cadwgan's raid on Dyfed after the death of Rhys was an anti-Norman move (Rhys having died at Norman hands, his lands were vulnerable to Norman incursion), but it is more likely that he was trying to expand his own influence, having failed to do so in 1088. Cadwgan himself was a thorn in the side of the Normans for most of his life. His brother Iorwerth was imprisoned by Henry I in 1103. The strife with Rhys ap Tewdwr may have had its roots in Rhys's slaying of Trahaearn ap Caradog, who was a cousin (of some sort) to the family of Bleddyn, and who may have been protector of the sons of Bleddyn after the death of Bleddyn himself (although this can only be a speculation). Alternatively, Cadwgan may have been looking to expand his power. The careers of these men will be considered in greater detail later.

---

[76] *Domesday Book*, Gloucestershire, fo 162ra.

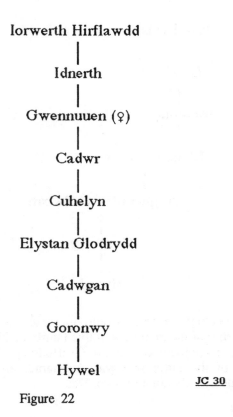

Iorwerth Hirflawdd
|
Idnerth
|
Gwennuuen (♀)
|
Cadwr
|
Cuhelyn
|
Elystan Glodrydd
|
Cadwgan
|
Goronwy
|
Hywel

JC 30

Figure 22

(5) The sons of Idnerth ap Cadwgan ap Elystan Glodrydd

This is essentially the next generation down of the family who, in the persons of Goronwy and Llywelyn, sons of Cadwgon, opposed Rhys ab Owain in the battles of Camddwr (1075) and Gweunotyll (1077). However, as their patronym shows, Gruffudd and Ifor, sons of Idnerth ap Cadwgan, are the nephews of the earlier pair. Llywelyn ap Cadwgan was killed by the men of Brycheiniog in 1099, and Goronwy died in 1101.

Gruffudd and Ifor occur only once, and their first names are given only in the *Brutiau, Annales Cambriae* referring simply to the sons of Idnerth ap Cadwgan (the same is not true of the sons of Cadwgan: first names are given in all the Welsh annalistic sources, Latin and vernacular). The sons of Idnerth are recorded as having achieved a victory over the Normans of Brycheiniog at Aberllech in 1096.

The family of Elystan Glodrydd was a significant group. at least as far as the genealogical material is concerned. The evidence of their genealogies in JC, §§30–34,[77] seems to link the family to Buellt, which if true may go a long way to

---

77 Bartrum, *Tracts*, p. 48.

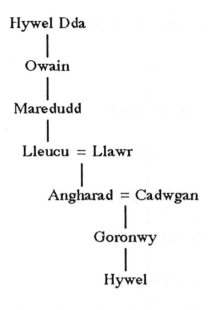

$$\begin{array}{c}
\text{Hywel Dda} \\
| \\
\text{Owain} \\
| \\
\text{Maredudd} \\
| \\
\text{Lleucu} = \text{Llawr} \\
| \\
\text{Angharad} = \text{Cadwgan} \\
| \\
\text{Goronwy} \\
| \\
\text{Hywel}
\end{array}$$

JC 31

This genealogy, if true, would increase the closeness of the relationship of the members of this family to Bleddyn ap Cynfyn, and also make them kinsmen of Gruffudd ap Llywelyn, since the mother of the latter two was Angharad, another daughter of Marredudd ab Owain ap Hywel Dda.

Figure 23

explaining their strife with Rhys ap Tewdwr and with the Normans. JC 30–31 are concerned with Hywel ap Goronwy (*ob.* 1106), reaching back to Iorwerth Hirflawdd in one case, and to Hywel Dda in the other. Hywel was the son of Goronwy ap Cadwgan. §32 is a list of the sons of Seisyll ap Llywelyn ap Cadwgan, and extends back only as far as Elystan. §33 is the pedigree of Llywelyn's wife Ellelw back to Gwgon 'Keneu menrud', and §34 continues this latter line back to Coel Hen. In §33, Llywelyn is referred to as 'Llewelyn o Vuellt'. This pedigree is however defective, for it states that Gwgon 'Keneu menrud' was killed at Abergwili by Llywelyn ap Seisyll, which would have been chronologically impossible, since if this figure ever lived he could not have been a contemporary of Llywelyn ap Seisyll (*ob.* 1023). Bartrum has dated Gwgon to the later ninth century.[78] The attempt to connect the family with Hywel Dda is interesting; it seems to have been done for the benefit of Hywel ap Goronwy, who was slain by treachery on behalf of the Normans in 1106, despite having received large land-grants from Henry I in 1102. The pedigrees from JC (except §34) are given in figures 22–25. None of the children of Llywelyn ap Cadwgon named in §32 is known from the annalistic texts.

[78] *Ibid.*, p. 141.

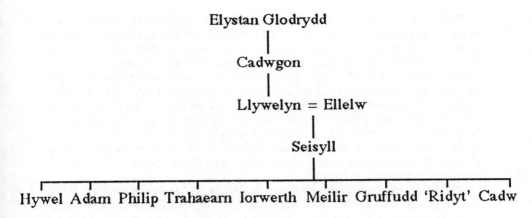

Figure 24

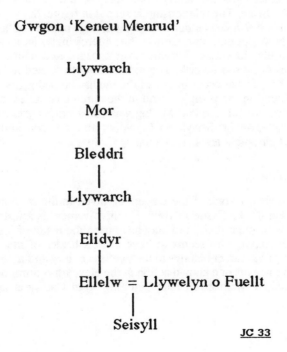

JC 33

Figure 25

47

Trahaearn ap Caradog can also be traced back to Iorwerth Hirflawdd, which might make him a very distant kinsman of the family of Elystan. The line back to Iorwerth is found in MG 4[79] and *ABT* 11 (*Gwehelyth Gwerthyrnion*)[80] as well as JC 30. It is, however, unstable: MG (which goes back even further, to Gwineu Deufreuddwyd) and *ABT* both give a larger number of generations between Elystan and Iorwerth. Both also lack a female Gwennuuen, and instead offer a Cadwr gwenwyn. MG 4 has two Kadwrs, *ABT* 11 only one. The pedigrees are set out in parallel form in figure 26, together with an emended version as suggested by Bartrum.[81] It is worth noting that MG 4 includes Tegonwy ap Teon, the father of Iorwerth Hirflawdd, who was also claimed as an ancestor by Bleddyn ap Cynfyn, thus making the sons and grandsons very distant cousins of their contemporaries, the sons of Bleddyn.

The family of Elystan appears as well in *ABT* 14 (*Gwehelyth Kydewain*),[82] in a female branch, via Dyddgu ferch Madog ap Idnerth. This is a pedigree of Maredudd ap Robert ap Llywarch ap Trahaearn – Dyddgu is said to have been the mother of Maredudd, and she is traced back to Elystan. Another female member of the family, Euron ferch Hoedlyw ap Cadwgon, occurs in the *Brutiau*, *s.a.* 1113, as a wife of Cadwgon ap Bleddyn ap Cynfyn and mother of his son Maredudd. Ieuaf ap Cadwgon is known from *ABT* 8g,[83] a pedigree of Gwenwynwyn. Ieuaf is given in the line of Gwenwynwyn's mother, Gwenllian ferch Owain Cyfeiliog. A cumulative pedigree is given in figure 27. If the connexion with Hywel Dda given in JC 31 is accepted, the family would have been fairly closely related to its enemy Rhys ab Owain. The relationship is set out in figure 28.

Bartrum in his *Welsh Genealogies* has cited a large number of later genealogical manuscripts mentioning this family. But, interestingly, its members are not easily traced in the chronicles. Elystan never appears, and neither does his son Cadwgon or his grandson Idnerth. The sons of Idnerth named in the chronicles, Gruffudd and Ifor, do not occur in any of the mediaeval pedigrees, while Madog ab Idnerth is found in the pedigrees and in the chronicles, as are his sons (from their death-dates, we can see that Madog was considerably younger than Gruffudd and Ifor). However, Seisyll ap Llywelyn ap Cadwgon and his sons are absent from the chronicle-texts, as is Ieuaf ap Cadwgon.

(6) Uchdryd ab Edwin

Uchdryd ab Edwin was one of the leaders involved in the raid on the Norman stronghold of Pembroke Castle in 1096. His involvement is attested in both the Latin and the vernacular texts, and may have been the result of his kinship with Cadwgon ap Bleddyn, who seems to have been a leader of the rebellion. Although the rest of his career belongs to the twelfth century and to the North, he is discussed here since his one known action in the eleventh century occurred in the South. He received Meirionydd and Cyfeiliog from Cadwgon ap Bleddyn in

[79] *Ibid.*, p. 39.
[80] *Ibid.*, p. 104.
[81] *Ibid.*, p. 137.
[82] *Ibid.*, p. 105.
[83] *Ibid.*, p. 102.

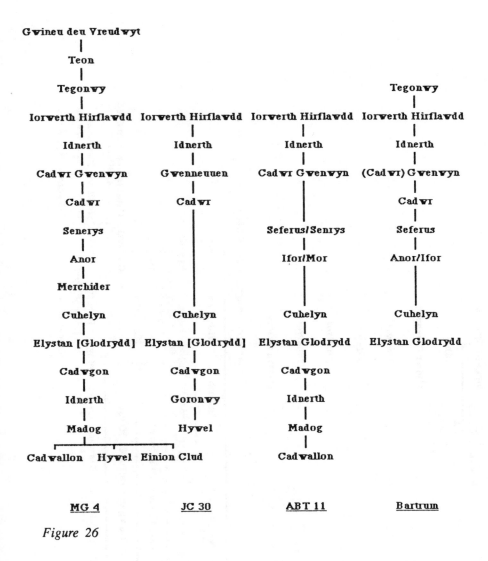

Gvineu deu Vreudvyt
|
Teon
|
Tegonvy .... Tegonvy
| |
Iorverth Hirflavdd   Iorverth Hirflavdd   Iorverth Hirflavdd   Iorverth Hirflavdd
| | | |
Idnerth   Idnerth   Idnerth   Idnerth
| | | |
Cadvr Gvenvyn   Gvenneuuen   Cadvr Gvenvyn   (Cadvr) Gvenvyn
| | |
Cadvr   Cadvr   Cadvr
| |
Senerys   Seferus/Senrys   Seferus
| |
Anor   Ifor/Mor   Anor/Ifor
|
Merchider
| |
Cuhelyn   Cuhelyn   Cuhelyn   Cuhelyn
| | | |
Elystan [Glodrydd]   Elystan [Glodrydd]   Elystan Glodrydd   Elystan Glodrydd
| | |
Cadvgon   Cadvgon   Cadvgon
| | |
Idnerth   Goronvy   Idnerth
| | |
Madog   Hyvel   Madog
| |
Cadvallon Hyvel Einion Clud   Cadvallon

MG 4   JC 30   ABT 11   Bartrum

Figure 26

1116, according to the *Brutiau*, on condition that he held friendship with Cadwgon and his sons. In the same year, he nevertheless allied with the sons of
Trahaearn ap Caradog against Cadwgon. The annal further supplies a certain
amount of information on his family-background: he is said to have been first
cousin to Maredudd ap Bleddyn, since he was the son of Bleddyn's sister Iwerydd (she and Bleddyn were half-siblings, having the same father but different
mothers). Uchdryd's brother Owain seems to have been the Owain ab Edwin who
aided the French in 1098, and later rebelled. Owain's sons were allied with
Uchdryd in 1118 against the sons of Cadwgon. Owain died in 1105. Uchdryd's
death is not recorded. This split between Bleddyn's offspring and those of his

49

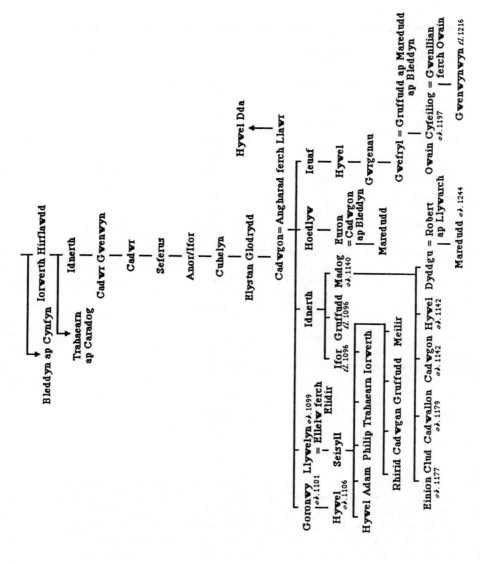

Figure 27

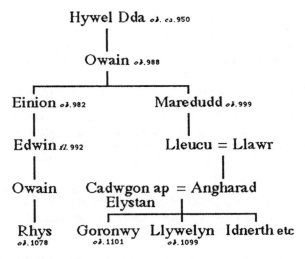

Hywel Dda *ob. ca.950*

|

Owain *ob.988*

Einion *ob.982*   Maredudd *ob.999*

| |

Edwin *fl.992*   Lleucu = Llawr

Owain   Cadwgon ap = Angharad
        Elystan

Rhys   Goronwy Llywelyn Idnerth etc
ob.1078 *ob.1101* *ob.1099*

Figure 28

sister is interesting; it seems to have been notorious since *Brut y Tywysogion* refers to it explicitly,[84] and Uchdryd is referred to as a man of wiles and deviousness. The enmity appears to have had its origins in the dispute resultant upon the abduction of Nest, wife of Gerald of Windsor, by Owain ap Cadwgon, which occurred in 1109. Uchdryd, acting with Madog and Ithel, sons of Rhirid ap Bleddyn, was involved in the attempt to drive out Owain and Cadwgon, although even then he seems to have been an unreliable ally. The general tenor of references to him in the *Brutiau* is such as to suggest a man of evil reputation.

Uchdryd's pedigree is not known from any of the mediaeval genealogical sources, but it can be reconstructed from the chronicles. This information is set out in figure 29. His father is named as Edwin ap Goronwy *s.a.* 1115 in the *Brutiau*, but nothing is known of him beyond this. Some later genealogical manuscripts mention Uchdryd, however. These are:

National Library of Wales, MS. Peniarth 131, pp. 71–138 and 177–188, by Gutun Owain, *ca* 1480
NLW MS. Peniarth 129, pp. 4–134, *ca* 1500
NLW MS. Peniarth 128 ('Llyfr Edward ap Roger'), p. 718b, before 1582.

(7) Hywel ap Goronwy

A member of the family of Elystan Glodrydd, Hywel ap Goronwy was one of the leaders of the raid in 1096 on Pembroke Castle. In 1102 he received Ystrad Tywi, Gŵyr, and Cydweli from Henry I, but was expelled from his holdings (named as Ystrad Tywi, Rhyd-y-Gors, and their bounds) in 1105, in revenge for which he ravaged and slew many of the Normans and re-occupied the territory. He was

---

[84] *ByT* (Pen. 20) *s.a.* 1113 (*recte* 1116).

51

killed in 1106 through the treachery of his son's foster-father, Gwgan ap Meurig, who was aided by the Normans of Rhyd-y-Gors. *Annales Cambriae* (B and C) further give the name of his expellor in 1105 as Richard FitzBaldwin. The *Brutiau* give no name, but do mention this same Richard in the same annal as repairing the castle at Rhyd-y-Gors.

Hywel is reasonably prominent in the mediaeval genealogies also. He is the subject of JC 30–31,[85] which give his ancestry on the male side, and also through his paternal grandmother. The male line goes back to Iorwerth Hirflawdd, and the female to Hywel Dda. His great-grandmother is said to have been a daughter of Maredudd ab Owain ap Hywel Dda, thus making him a kinsman of the family of Bleddyn. However, Uchdryd ab Edwin, with whom he raided Pembroke, would not have been related to him, since, even if Lleucu ferch Maredudd existed, Uchdryd as a son of Iwerydd ferch Cynfyn was probably not descended from Angharad ferch Maredudd. (For a detailed discussion of the pedigrees involved and their problems, see above, under the sons of Idnerth ap Cadwgan, and also figures 22 and 23.)

From the remarks above, it can be seen that there was a considerable difference between the political scene of the tenth century in Deheubarth and that in the eleventh. The later tenth century in the South does seem to show a pattern of domination by the family of Rhodri Mawr, and a tendency for there to be confrontations between the so-called Northern and Southern branches of that line. In addition, there was internal friction within the Southern branch. The section of the Southern branch represented by Maredudd ab Owain ap Hywel Dda died out in the male line, to re-emerge in the female line in both north and south Wales, in the person of Gruffudd ap Llywelyn. The segment represented by the descendants of Einion ab Owain ap Hywel Dda ultimately divided into two lines, the descendants of Edwin ab Einion and the descendants of Cadell ab Einion. This section of the Southern branch continued to have some influence in the South until 1093, and on into the twelfth century in the person of Gruffudd ap Rhys ap Tewdwr. Members of this family held Deheubarth for considerable portions of the eleventh century: Hywel ab Edwin ab Einion, 1033–1044; Maredudd ab Owain ab Edwin, 1069–1072; (in part) Rhys ab Owain, 1075–78; Rhys ap Tewdwr, 1079–1093. It is also likely that some members of the family held parts of the South at various times, but without their possession being noted in the surviving sources. There is, for instance, no real indication of who was influential in the territories of the South between the death of Maredudd (I) ab Owain (999) and the appearance of Rhydderch ab Iestyn (1023). An Irish impostor, Rhain, had tried to take the South in 1022, only to be expelled by the king of Gwynedd, Llywelyn ap Seisyll – this Rhain claiming to be a son of Maredudd ab Owain ap Hywel Dda. That he was expelled leads one to wonder what was the extent was of the power and influence of Llywelyn. Before 1022 very little is known, but it seems entirely possible that such men as Edwin ab Einion (father of the later ruler Hywel), his brother Cadell, and the latter's son Tewdwr Mawr (ancestor of Rhys ap Tewdwr) were active and influential in the South in this period. *Liber Landauensis* affords little indication of Southern kings in this

---

[85] Bartrum, *Tracts*, p. 48.

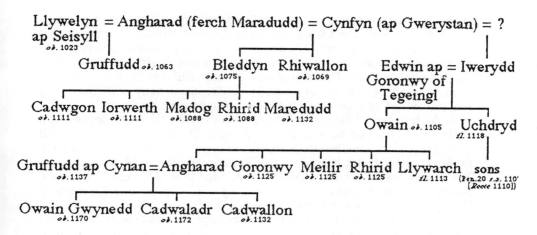

Llywelyn = Angharad (ferch Maradudd) = Cynfyn (ap Gwerystan) = ?
ap Seisyll
ob. 1023

Gruffudd *ob.* 1063   Bleddyn Rhiwallon   Edwin ap = Iwerydd
                 ob. 1075   *ob.* 1069   Goronwy of
                                              Tegeingl

Cadwgon Iorwerth Madog Rhirid Maredudd
ob. 1111   *ob.* 1111   *ob.* 1088   *ob.* 1088   *ob.* 1132   Owain *ob.* 1105   Uchdryd
                                                          fl. 1118

Gruffudd ap Cynan = Angharad Goronwy Meilir Rhirid Llywarch   sons
ob. 1137   *ob.* 1125   *ob.* 1125   *ob.* 1125   *fl.* 1113   (*Pen.*20 *r.s.* 110'
                                                                [*Reece* 1110])

Owain Gwynedd Cadwaladr Cadwallon
ob. 1170   *ob.* 1172   *ob.* 1132

Figure 29

period[86] – other than the local dynasties in Glamorgan, represented in the early eleventh century by Hywel ab Owain (*ob.* 1043) and the shadowy Edwin ap Gwriad.

In the eleventh century, the two main dynasties vying for supremacy in south Wales were the descendants of Einion ab Owain, of the Southern branch of the family of Rhodri Mawr, and the new dynasty of Rhydderch ab Iestyn. The rivalry between the two can be traced through much of the century. Only once is there any explicit 'alliance' between members of the two families. This was in 1075/6, when Rhys ab Owain of the family of Einion and Rhydderch ap Caradog of the family of Rhydderch are found sharing rule. Against them stood the important figure of Caradog ap Gruffudd, Rhydderch's cousin, who was also a rival to Rhys ap Tewdwr, and who died in battle against the latter in 1081.

The documentation for Deheubarth in the early eleventh century is scanty – the apparent 'gap' between Maredudd ab Owain ap Hywel Dda and Rhydderch ab Iestyn has already been mentioned. Rhydderch seems to have been succeeded by Maredudd's great-nephews, Hywel and Maredudd, sons of Edwin, and Hywel was succeeded by Rhydderch's son Gruffudd. Was this a succession to a kingdom or to an overlordship? The latter seems more likely, especially given that Glamorgan seems to continue to be ruled by local dynasties, although these seem to have acknowledged the power of at least the line of Rhydderch. The alternation was disturbed in the period 1056–1063 by Gruffudd ap Llywelyn of Gwynedd, who ruled in the South after slaying Gruffudd ap Rhydderch. It is possible, also, that his father Llywelyn ap Seisyll had enjoyed some influence in the South, in the early eleventh century. 1063–1069 appears to have been a time of chaos throughout Wales and, apart from the activities of Caradog ap Gruffudd in 1064, little is known of the South. The period 1069–1079 was marked by a struggle between the sons of Owain ab Edwin, of the line of Einion ab Owain, on the one hand, and Caradog ap Gruffudd on the other. To this succeeded the

---

86 *LL* charters 249a, 249b, 255, 257, 259, 260, 261, 267, and 272.

relatively lasting influence of Rhys ap Tewdwr (1079–1093). This Rhys was a descendant of Einion ab Owain, but not in the same direct line as those other descendants of Einion who had ruled in the eleventh century. This latter line made one last attempt to regain the Southern kingdom, in 1091, in the person of Gruffudd ap Maredudd. The attempt was not successful, and Gruffudd was slain. After the death of Caradog ap Gruffudd in 1081, the dynasty of Rhydderch ap Iestyn faded out, and this family did not return to power in the South.

In the later part of the century, the family of Elystan Glodrydd, apparently a noble kindred from Buellt, began to be important. The prominence in this period of hitherto 'minor' families was doubtless due in part to the massive disruption of the South caused by the Normans, especially after the death of Rhys ap Tewdwr. The descendants of Elystan Glodrydd are referred to as defenders of the South, and at least one of them (Hywel ap Goronwy) – or possibly two (Llywelyn ap Cadwgan also) – was slain by the Normans.

In south Wales in the late eleventh century large areas had been seized by the Normans. Others were in the Normans' gift, and were controlled by different Welshmen at different times according to royal favour. Some of these belonged to families with little previous connexion with the South: Iorwerth ap Bleddyn, for instance. The 1090s display the breakdown of the old Deheubarth under the power and influence of the Normans. The old dynasties disappeared, and were replaced by Norman lords or previously less prominent Welsh families. However, the Norman incursions into the South seem to have been regarded as more than just a local problem: those found harassing the Normans were by no means all local men – the Powysian family of Bleddyn ap Cynfyn being especially prominent. The Normans were clearly recognised as a threat to all of Wales, not only the beleagured South.

GWYNEDD

While there is a reasonable amount of information about Gwynedd, the documentation is in general far less specific as to particular areas within the kingdom than it is for the South. As with the South, there is a noticeable decrease in recorded events coincident with the reign of Gruffudd ap Llywelyn.

Persons explicitly mentioned as active in the North in this period are as follows:

(1) Hywel ab Ieuaf;
(2) Custennin ab Iago;
(3) Maredudd ab Owain ap Hywel Dda;
(4) Cadwallon ab Ieuaf and Maig ab Ieuaf;
(5) Cynan ap Hywel;
(6) the sons of Meurig;
(7) Llywelyn ap Seisyll;
(8) Iago ab Idwal;
(9) Gruffudd ap Llywelyn;
(10) Bleddyn ap Cynfyn and Rhiwallon ap Cynfyn;
(11) Trahaearn ap Caradog;
(12) Gruffudd ap Cynan.

In addition, the following should probably be noted:

(1) Aeddan ab Blegywryd;
(2) Cynan ap Seisyll and the sons of Cynan;
(3) Maredudd and Ithel, sons of Gruffudd (ap Llywelyn);
(4) Cynwrig ap Rhiwallon;
(5) Meilir ap Rhiwallon;
(6) Gwrgenau ap Seisyll;
(7) Cadwgan ap Bleddyn;
(8) Owain ab Edwin.

While not all of these were rulers, they were all active in some way in the North in that period. As with Deheubarth, towards the end of the eleventh century Norman incursions had a major effect on the politics of the region: however, the effects were not as long-lasting as in the South, and native rulers of known hereditary connexion with the region continue to be recognisable well into the twelfth century.

(1) Hywel ab Ieuaf

Hywel ab Ieuaf was a grandson of the Northern ruler Idwal Foel ab Anarawd ap Rhodri Mawr, one of several grandsons active in the late tenth century. The annalistic evidence is fairly detailed as to his career, although it should be noted that the B-text of *Annales Cambriae* consistently refers to the sons of Ieuaf ab Idwal as sons of Idwal, either by confusion with Ieuaf's father Idwal Foel, or by confusion with his brother Idwal Fychan.[87] The C-text of *Annales Cambriae* in one place omits the name 'Hywel', though supplying the correct patronymic.

Hywel first appears in 974, when he expelled his uncle Iago ab Idwal Foel from the latter's kingdom, Gwynedd. The *Brutiau* directly, and the B-text of *Annales Cambriae* indirectly, credit Hywel with the actual expulsion. *Annales Cambriae* (C) record this expulsion and the beginning of Hywel's rule, but do not explicitly connect the two. In 978 Hywel ravaged Clynnog Fawr together with the English (*Brut y Tywysogion* [Pen. 20], *Brenhinedd y Saesson*) and possibly Lleyn (*Brut y Tywysogion* [RB]). (*Brut y Tywysogion* [Pen. 20] and *Brenhinedd y Saesson* record the ravaging of Lleyn but attribute it to one Gwrmid.) In 979 Hywel is again said to be holding Iago's kingdom, the latter having been captured by Hiberno-Scandinavians in the same year.[88] The *Brutiau* imply that Hywel had been in possession of the kingdom for some time. *Annales Cambriae* are too sparse to offer such an implication, and, indeed, tend to give the impression that Hywel acquired the kingdom as a result of this capture. In 980 (the *Brutiau*, not *Annales Cambriae*) Hywel is said to have slain Custennin ab Iago at Gwaith Hirbarwch, the latter having just ravaged Lleyn and Anglesey in the company of Godfrey Haraldsson. In 983, Hywel was involved in the ravaging by the English of the lands of his distant cousin, Einion ab Owain of Deheubarth. The nature of

---

87 *AC* (B) *s.a.* [979], [983], [985], and [986].
88 *ByS s.a.* 977 (*recte* 978) reads 'seized by the men of Hywel ab Ieuaf'. Jones explained this as a misreading of *gentiles* as *gentes* (*ByT* [Pen. 20], transl. Jones, p. 144, n. 9.6–8).

his involvement is somewhat unclear – according to *Annales Cambriae* (C), Hywel was on the side of the English, while the *Brutiau* apparently say that he was acting with Einion (*Annales Cambriae* [B], while noticing the raid, do not mention Hywel). However, given Hywel's previous involvement with the English (in 978), and given the relatively hostile relations existing between Gwynedd and Deheubarth at this time, it seem more probable that he was on the attacking, and not the defending, side. The phrasing of the *Brutiau* is such as to admit of this meaning, although the alternative meaning, as given by Thomas Jones, is the more natural way of reading the Welsh. However, it is interesting that the manuscript punctuation of *Brut y Tywysogion* (Pen. 20) is such as to make the reading agree with *Annales Cambriae* (C) in placing Hywel on the side of the English. Given this, and the historical context, and the probable primacy of *Annales Cambriae* (C), it would seem reasonable to accept that Hywel was aiding the English rather than Einion on this occasion.[89] Einion had risen to considerable power in southern Wales, and it is possible that his raid was an attempt by the English and North Welsh alike to curb his strength and reduce the extent to which he was a threat on their borders. Hywel's death is recorded in 985. He is said to have been killed by the English, through treachery.

There is a modest amount of genealogical material available about Hywel ab Ieuaf. He occurs in *ABT* 7,[90] the long account of the descendants of Rhodri Mawr. It is worth noticing, however, that all his known Welsh opponents were members of his own family, the most distantly related being Einion ab Owain. The Custennin ab Iago whom he slew in 980 was his first cousin, the son of his father's brother Iago whom Hywel had driven out of Gwynedd in 994. This was in a way simply a continuation of family-tradition, since the descendants of Idwal Foel seemingly delighted in imprisoning, mutilating, overthrowing, and killing each other (and also their Southern-branch cousins when possible). Hence Iago ab Idwal imprisoned his brother Ieuaf, father of this Hywel, in 969. Meurig ab Idwal was blinded in 974, the same year in which Hywel drove Iago from Gwynedd, and indeed Hywel may have had some responsibility for the blinding. Hywel's kinship with his rivals Iago ab Idwal, Custennin ab Iago, and Einion ab Owain is shown in figure 30.

According to the Welsh chronicles, Hywel had a son Cynan who ruled in Gwynedd from 1000 to his death in 1003. This Cynan presents a slight problem as far as the pedigree-material is concerned. No Cynan ab Hywel is known from the early genealogies, but a Cynan ab Ieuaf ab Ieuaf ('Cynan y Cwn') is mentioned in *ABT* 7d. Ieuaf ab Ieuaf is not recorded in the chronicles but, without speculating on his possible existence, I should suggest that *ABT* 7d is in error here, and that the Cynan to whom it refers is the Cynan ab Hywel of the chronicles, save that his paternity has been wrongly ascribed. It is not unreasonable thus to correct *ABT* 7: it contains a number of errors (for instance it omits Cadwallon ab Ieuaf, and its pedigree for Rhys ap Tewdwr is a generation too short, having confused his father Tewdwr ap Cadell with his great-uncle, Tewdwr ab Einion). Given the level of unreliability in this particular pedigree, I can see no very good reason for assuming that both Hywel ab Ieuaf and his supposed

89 This view was also taken by Lloyd, *A History*, I.350.
90 Bartrum, *Tracts*, p. 101.

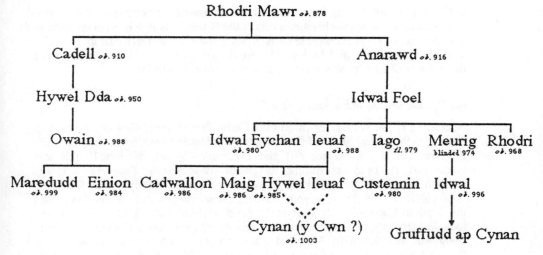

Figure 30

brother Ieuaf should have had sons named Cynan. In this I differ from Mr Bartrum.[91]

(2) Custennin ab Iago

Together with Godfrey Haraldsson, Custennin ab Iago ravaged Lleyn and Anglesey in 980, and was slain in the same year, as a consequence of this raid, by his first cousin Hywel ab Ieuaf at Gwaith Hirbarwch (*Brutiau* only). His activities can almost certainly be explained by the fact that Hywel had driven Custennin's father Iago ab Idwal from the kingship of Gwynedd in 974, and these territories were part of that kingdom. As far as the pedigree-material is concerned, he is named in *ABT* 7e which gives him the epithet *Du* ('the black') and refers to his death in the aforementioned battle (see figure 30).[92]

(3) Maredudd ab Owain ap Hywel Dda

For a full discussion of his career, see above, *sub* Deheubarth. Maredudd's involvement in Northern affairs was apparently only brief. In 986, the year after the death of Hywel ab Ieuaf (and two years after the death of his brother, Einion ab Owain, also a powerful ruler in the South), he invaded, and slew Hywel's brother Cadwallon ab Ieuaf, and possibly also Maig ab Ieuaf, and took Cadwallon's territory, named as Gwynedd (*Annales Cambriae* [B]) or as Gwynedd and Anglesey (the *Brutiau*). The following year, Godfrey Haraldsson ravaged Anglesey and took two thousand captives: Maredudd took the remaining men with him

91 Bartrum, *Welsh Genealogies*, I.41.
92 Bartrum, *Tracts*, p. 101.

to Ceredigion and Dyfed. He seems to have ransomed the captives in 989. There is no further evidence for his direct rule in the North, although it is not inconceivable that he may have been able to maintain some kind of overlordship.

Cadwallon, Maig, and Maredudd were distant cousins, all being members of the dynasty of Rhodri Mawr. For details, see above, *sub* Deheubarth.

(4) Cadwallon and Maig sons of Ieuaf

According to the vernacular chronicles, Cadwallon ab Ieuaf slew one Ionafal ap Meurig in 985. Maig ab Ieuaf first occurs the following year, 986, where his obit is given. *Annales Cambriae* (B) give the name 'Meurig ab Idwal'; this text consistently refers to sons of Ieuaf as sons of Idwal. *Annales Cambriae* (C) have no mention of Maig at all. *Brut y Tywysogion* (Pen. 20 only) gives the name 'Maig ab Ieuaf'. In the same year, *Annales Cambriae* (B) and the *Brutiau* record the death of Cadwallon ab Ieuaf at the hands of Maredudd ab Owain, who then took his territory of Gwynedd and Anglesey. *Brenhinedd y Saesson* says that Maig was also killed by Maredudd, and that the territory was his as well as Cadwallon's, a state of affairs which seems possible, given that the two were brothers. *Brut y Tywysogion* (RB) has fallen into error, describing the subjugation of Gwynedd as by Cadwallon, rather than by Maredudd ab Owain. It also omits the death of Maig.

The 'Meurig ab Idwal' of *Annales Cambriae* (B) is most probably a mistake, as was indicated above. There was a Meurig ab Idwal at this time; he was the uncle of Maig, and had been blinded, perhaps by Maig's brother Hywel, in 974. It is possible that the obit in *Annales Cambriae* (B) refers to him – nothing is known of him in after his blinding. If this is the case, then Maig ab Ieuaf is evidenced in the vernacular texts only.

Cadwallon is not mentioned in any of the mediaeval genealogical material. *ABT* 7 has omitted him from its list of the sons of Ieuaf ab Idwal. Maig however is mentioned, in *ABT* 7d, together with Hywel.[93] They were distantly related to their enemy Maredudd ab Owain (see figure 30). No descendants are recorded for either of them.

(5) Cynan ap Hywel

Cynan ap Hywel held Gwynedd from the year 1000, until he was slain in 1003. It is not known who was responsible for his death. He was very probably the son of Hywel ab Ieuaf. For his pedigree, and the complications thereof, see above, *sub* Hywel ab Ieuaf.

(6) The Sons of Meurig

According to the *Brutiau*, hostages from among the sons of Meurig were in Gwynedd in 993. They were involved in a battle with Maredudd ab Owain ap Hywel Dda of south Wales near Llangwm, in which they were victorious, in 994.

---

93 *Ibid.*

In 996 Idwal ap Meurig was slain. Such is the extent of the annalistic record for the sons of Meurig ab Idwal Foel. Like the various sons of Ieuaf ab Idwal who have already been discussed, they were members of the Northern branch of the dynasty of Rhodri Mawr, though a seemingly less succesful offshoot – their father Meurig had been blinded in 974. None of them seems to be recorded by name, other than Idwal.

This Idwal was the great-grandfather of the notable late eleventh- early twelfth-century ruler of Gwynedd, Gruffudd ap Cynan. He is noted as such in the first pedigree in *Historia Gruffud vab Kenan*;[94] in JC 26,[95] a pedigree of Rhys Gryg; *ABT* 1,[96] a pedigree of Llywelyn ab Iorwerth; and *ABT* 7g,[97] *Plant Rhodri Mawr*. He is not mentioned in MG 1, the pedigree of Llywelyn the Great, however, as might be expected: this text has conflated Idwal ap Meurig with his grandfather Idwal Foel ab Anarawd.[98] Idwal is the only son of Meurig to appear in the mediaeval genealogies.

Maredudd ab Owain ap Hywel Dda would have been their distant cousin. Their battle with him probably indicates a struggle for supremacy in the North. The chronicles do not make it clear who was ruling in the North in the period 985–1000 but, given Maredudd's exodus in 986 and the accession in 1000 of Hywel ab Ieuaf's son Cynan, it seems probable that the family of Idwal Foel had retained some degree of power there. Lloyd was of the opinion that Maredudd held Gwynedd until his death in 999:[99] it is not impossible that he may have held an overlordship of sorts, but it appears most likely that the family of Idwal Foel continued as local kings. These sons of Meurig may have held this position for at least some of the last fifteen years of the tenth century.

(7) Llywelyn ap Seisyll

Llywelyn ap Seisyll is the first of Lloyd's 'intrusive rulers' whose rule can actually be demonstrated. Not much is known about him but, such as it is, it is more than is known of his near-contemporary, the Southern ruler Rhydderch ab Iestyn. He is known from both *Annales Cambriae* and the *Brutiau*, and both record all three of his known actions. In addition, his death is noticed in some Irish texts (the Annals of Tigernach,[100] the Annals of Loch Cé,[101] the Annals of Clonmacnoise,[102] the Annals of Ulster,[103] and *Chronicum Scottorum*,[104] although it should be remembered that these texts are by no means all independent of one another).

In 1018, Llywelyn slew Aeddan ab Blegywryd and his four sons. Lloyd took it

---

94 ed. Evans, pp. 1–2, and Bartrum, *Tracts*, p. 36.
95 *Ibid.*, p. 47.
96 *Ibid.*, pp. 95–6.
97 *Ibid.*, p. 101.
98 *Ibid.*, pp. 38–9.
99 *A History*, I.345–6.
100 AT *s.a.* 1023.
101 ALC *s.a.* 1023.
102 AClon *s.a.* 1023.
103 AU *s.a.* 1023.
104 CS *s.a.* 1021.

that Aeddan was at that time king of Gwynedd and that Llywelyn overthrew him.[105] However, other than in his manner of death, Aeddan is totally obscure, and I do not feel able completely to accept Lloyd's view on this issue. Rather than his being the king, it seems entirely possible that Aeddan may have been a local nobleman of standing within Gwynedd, whom Llywelyn may have had to defeat in order to establish himself securely or perhaps in order to maintain himself in power. In 1022 Llywelyn opposed and slew one Rhain, an Irishman who had managed to establish himself in Deheubarth, claiming that he was a son of Mareddudd ab Owain ap Hywel Dda. Llywelyn, in both *Annales Cambriae* and the *Brutiau*, is referred to as 'king of Gwynedd'. His action against Rhain therefore argues for his influence in the South as well as the North. It is interesting that no Southern ruler is mentioned as being in opposition to Rhain at this time: this may reflect a state of confusion or conflict within Deheubarth at this time. Llywelyn died the following year, 1023, and it may be of significance that the entry dealing with the kingship in Deheubarth of Rhydderch ab Iestyn follows this obit. Is it possible that Llywelyn had gained some supremacy in the South as well as in the North? The succession to Gwynedd is recorded in the *Brutiau*, but not under the year of Llywelyn's death: it occurs instead in the year of the death of Rhydderch ab Iestyn. However, the statement reads that Iago ab Idwal (ap Meurig) held the kingdom of Gwynedd after Llywelyn, not after Rhydderch. It thus seems likely that Rhydderch was not direct ruler in the North. It does however seem possible that the two kingships were connected in some way in this period – the strongest ruler may have had a claim to overlordship over the territory of his weaker colleague, or at least the annalists may have viewed matters in this way.

There is surprisingly little genealogical evidence about Llywelyn. He is mentioned in passing as the father of Gruffudd ap Llywelyn in JC 27, though without his patronym.[106] This pedigree is concerned with Rhys Gryg, who was a descendant of Gruffudd ap Llywelyn's maternal half-brother Bleddyn ap Cynfyn. It is very corrupt, confusing Bleddyn with his father Cynfyn, and listing Trahaearn ap Caradog as another brother of Gruffudd and Bleddyn (he was probably a cousin of some kind to Bleddyn). Llywelyn is also mentioned in JC 33, again in a corrupt context.[107] This is a pedigree of Ellelw, wife of Llywelyn ap Cadwgon of Buellt, and is one of four dealing ultimately with Hywel ap Goronwy (§§30–34). The pedigree itself seems reasonably sound; the context mentioning Llywelyn is not, as he is named as the slayer, at Abergwili (the battle with Rhain), of Ellelw's ancestor Gwgon 'Keneu Menrud' who, if he existed, would, according to Bartrum,[108] have lived in the late ninth century, and who therefore could not reasonably be supposed to have died at Llywelyn's hand.

ABT 7, sections f and k,[109] is more interesting, and if true may throw some more light on at least one reason behind Llywelyn's rule in the North, as well as on his ancestry. This is part of the pedigree dealing with descendants of Rhodri

105 *A History*, I.346–7.
106 Bartrum, *Tracts*, p. 47.
107 *Ibid.*, p. 48.
108 *Ibid.*, p. 141.
109 *Ibid.*, p. 101.

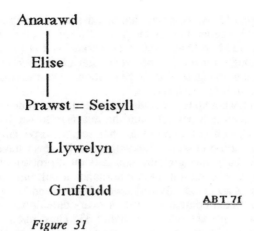

Figure 31

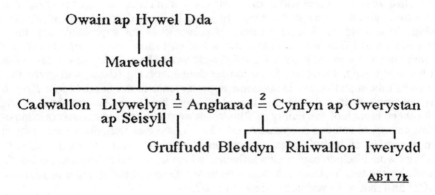

Figure 32

Mawr, and Llywelyn is connected with it by two links in the female line, via his mother and his wife. This may in itself be suspect – links through the female line were all too often fabricated – but the marriage of Llywelyn to Angharad ferch Maredudd ab Owain ap Hywel Dda seems well enough known from a variety of sources, including the *Brutiau*,[110] to be reasonably credible. Llywelyn's father Seisyll is not even given a patronym, and appears to have been entirely obscure. *ABT* 7f makes Llywelyn the son of Prawst, daughter of Elise ab Anarawd, two people who are not evidenced outside the genealogies. However, such parentage, be it true or fabricated, would have the effect of connecting him with the Northern Branch of the dynasty of Rhodri Mawr, in the eyes of at least the genealogists. It is impossible to say whether any such claim was made for, or by, Llywelyn

---

110 *ByT* (Pen. 20) *s.a.* 1113 (*recte* 1116); *ByT* (RB) *s.a.* 1113 (*recte* 1116); *ByS s.a.* 1113 (*recte* 1116).

in his lifetime. It should also be noted that this descent from Prawst would place Llywelyn in the same generation as the sons of Ieuaf ab Idwal Foel, and as his father-in-law Maredudd ab Owain, none of whom lived beyond the end of the tenth century, although it is not inconceivable that Elise or Prawst or both might have been among the youngest of their generations. The information from these pedigrees is set out in figures 31 and 32.

If Maredudd ab Owain ap Hywel Dda did indeed have some form of overlord-ship in the North, then it is possible that the marriage to Angharad might have provided Llywelyn with some claim to that region, especially as Maredudd apparently left no surviving sons. This would not however have been likely to have been a particularly strong claim, and it is most probable that the bulk of Llywelyn's power was based not upon inheritance at all, but upon charisma. If the link via Prawst is accepted, Llywelyn would have been kin to a considerable number of his significant contemporaries, or near-contemporaries, including his wife. These relationships are set out in figure 33. Thus, his successor, Iago ab Idwal ap Meurig, would have been his cousin via Anarawd ap Rhodri, as would have been his last definitely known predecessor, Cynan ap Hywel ab Ieuaf. It is not clear who was ruling within the South (or within certain areas of the South) at this time, and therefore it is not easy to judge Llywelyn's genealogical relation-ships (if any) to the Southern rulers. However, it is not improbable that these rulers included Edwin ab Einion (who is known to have been living in the late tenth century) and his brother Cadell. These would have been close relatives of Llywelyn's wife. However, given the incident involving Rhain, and given that sons of Edwin ab Einion did not come to prominence in the South before 1033, it is not unlikely that during this period at least there were no members of the Southern branch of the family of Rhodri Mawr who were old enough or compe-tent enough to achieve supremacy in the South, and that Deheubarth was subject to a number of 'petty' kings, without any one clear overlord. Such a state of affairs would help to explain the influence which Llywelyn enjoyed in the South, and also the two 'usurpations' which occurred there at this time, that of Rhain in 1022 and that of Rhydderch ab Iestyn in 1023.

(8) Iago ab Idwal

Known from the C-version of *Annales Cambriae* and from the *Brutiau*, Iago ab Idwal was the successor of Llywelyn ap Seisyll in Gwynedd. Beyond his succes-sion in 1023 and his death in 1039, very little is known about him. The circum-stances of his death are not entirely clear. *Annales Cambriae* (C) and *Brut y Tywysogion* (Pen. 20 and RB) say that he was killed, and that after him Gwynedd was held by Gruffudd ap Llywelyn.[111] *Brenhinedd y Saesson* attributes his death to Gruffudd ap Llywelyn, but this is by far the least reliable of the vernacular Welsh chronicles, and it does not seem to me that there is any good reason for accepting its testimony here as against *Annales Cambriae* and *Brut y Tywsogion*; indeed, the attribution to Gruffudd looks remarkably like a piece of scribal

---

111 *ByT* (Pen. 20) is corrupt, referring to Gruffudd as 'Llywelyn his (Iago's) son'. On the death of Iago, see also Maund, 'Cynan ab Iago'.

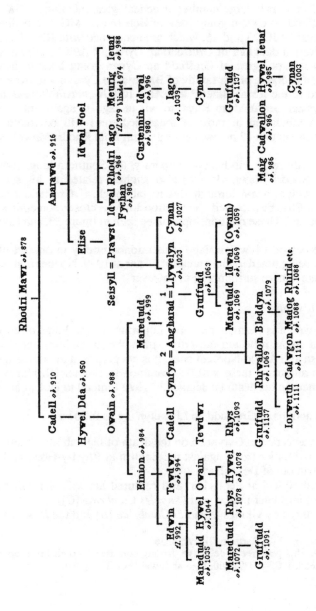

Figure 33

'tidying'. Iago is also mentioned in the Welsh chronicles in 1075 and 1081 in connexion with Gruffudd ap Cynan, who is here defined as 'grandson of Iago'.

The relationship between Iago and Gruffudd ap Cynan has resulted in Iago being mentioned in a fairly large number of genealogies, including *HGK* 1,[112] a pedigree of Gruffudd ap Cynan going back to Beli Mawr; MG 1, a pedigree of Llywelyn the Great;[113] JC 25 and 26, which are concerned with Rhys Gryg who was descended from a daughter of Gruffudd ap Cynan;[114] *ABT* 7g (*Plant Rhodri Mawr*),[115] which is a pedigree of Gruffudd ap Cynan going back to Idwal ap Meurig; *ABT* 8g, a pedigree of the family of Bleddyn ap Cynfyn with which Iago is here connected in the female line;[116] and *ABT* 10 (*Gwehelyth Deheubarth*), a pedigree of Rhys ap Gruffudd ap Rhys, to whom Iago is again linked in the female line.[117] A tabulation of most of these pedigrees will be found under Gruffudd ap Cynan, section 12 below. Iago's descent from Rhodri Mawr is shown in figure 34.

Iago was distantly related to his contemporary, the Southern king, Hywel ab Edwin, through Rhodri Mawr. He was also slightly related to his successor Gruffudd ap Llywelyn, again through Rhodri, although, if Gruffudd's descent from Prawst ferch Elise be accepted, the relationship was closer, something in the range of third cousins. These relationships can be seen in figure 33, *sub* Llywelyn ap Seisyll.

Like his predecessor, Llywelyn, Iago is mentioned briefly in one set of Irish annals, his death being noted in the Annals of Ulster at 1039. No mention is made there of the circumstances surrounding it, however.

(9) Gruffudd ap Llywelyn

Gruffudd ap Llywelyn is perhaps the most important of the kings of eleventh-century Wales, a status reflected not only within Welsh sources, but also in a number of English and Anglo-Norman ones. It is not proposed to discuss in detail here his English alliances: these will be examined in chapter III. Nor will the English involvement in his death be detailed.[118] Here I intend to look at his Welsh activities.

The recorded actions of Gruffudd ap Llywelyn are as follows.

1039: Gruffudd succeeded in Gwynedd on the death of Iago ab Idwal, and in the same year won a major battle against the English at Rhyd-y-Gors, and drove Hywel ab Edwin out of Deheubarth.

1041: he defeated Hywel at Pencadair, and captured his wife; he was himself captured by vikings later in that year (*Annales Cambriae* [C]).

1044: he was captured by vikings (*Annales Cambriae* [B] and the *Brutiau*).

112 *HGK*, ed. Evans, pp. 1–2; Bartrum, *Tracts*, p. 36.
113 *Ibid.*, pp. 38–9. This pedigree is defective, having confused Iago ab Idwal ap Meurig (king of Gwynedd, 1023–1039) with Iago ab Idwal Foel (living 979).
114 *Ibid.*, p. 47.
115 *Ibid.*, p. 101.
116 *Ibid.*, p. 102.
117 *Ibid.*, p. 104.
118 See Maund, 'Cynan ab Iago'. On his English alliances see also Maund, 'The Welsh alliances'.

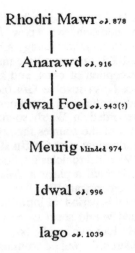

Rhodri Mawr *ob.* 878

|

Anarawd *ob.* 916

|

Idwal Foel *ob.* 943(?)

|

Meurig blinded 974

|

Idwal *ob.* 996

|

Iago *ob.* 1039

Figure 34

1044: he met with Hywel ab Edwin, who had hired a Hiberno-Scandinavian fleet, at the mouth of the River Tywi, and defeated and killed him.

1045: he was involved in a great dispute with the new Southern leaders, Gruffudd and Rhys, sons of Rhydderch.

1047: seven score of his warband were slain in Ystrad Tywi, and in revenge Gruffudd ravaged Dyfed and Ystrad Tywi.

1056: he slew Gruffudd ap Rhydderch. In the same year he lead an army against the English, and sacked Hereford.

1058: he ravaged England in the company of Magnus Haraldsson.

1063: he was slain by his own men. In the *Brutiau* the notice of his death is accompanied by a short panegyric.

1075: he is mentioned in the *Brutiau* as the brother of Bleddyn ap Cynfyn.

1115: he is mentioned in the *Brutiau*, in a genealogical discussion, as the brother of Bleddyn and the son of Angharad ferch Maredudd.

This is the evidence of the Welsh chronicles only. Gruffudd is also noted in the Anglo-Saxon Chronicle, in the *Chronicarum Chronica* of John of Worcester, the *Historia Ecclesiastica* of Orderic Vitalis, the *Gesta Regum Anglorum* of Willam of Malmesbury, *De Nugis Curialium* by Walter Map, and several of the Irish annalistic collections. This clearly demonstrates the extraordinary standing and influence of Gruffudd: no other Welsh ruler of his time attracted such attention from non-Welsh writers. He was the first and only Welsh ruler ever to succeed in dominating all of Wales, even as far as Glamorgan.[119] Yet he still had time to spare for involving himself in English politics. The raids noted in the Welsh chronicles in 1056 and 1058 are also recorded in the Anglo-Saxon Chronicle which further informs us that on these occasions Gruffudd was acting together with the Mercian nobleman, Earl Ælfgar, who on both these occasions was

[119] *LL* charter 269.

seeking reinstatement in his lands after being banished by the English king, Edward the Confessor.[120] In addition, we know from Orderic Vitalis that Gruffudd was married to Ælfgar's daughter Ealdgyth.[121] It is worth noting that in the period of his reign (1039–1063), almost all the major events recorded in the Welsh chronicles (with the exception of obits, and a couple of entries dealing with Hiberno-Scandinavian activity) involve Gruffudd. He is by far the best documented of all the eleventh-century rulers, although it should be pointed out that nearly all his actions recorded in Welsh sources occur in south Wales, reflecting the geographical bias of the sources themselves. To say that the mid eleventh century in Wales was dominated by Gruffudd ap Llywelyn is perhaps an understatement: as far as the Welsh chronicles go, he almost *is* the mid-eleventh century. He also seems to have held a place in folk-history, as the anecdotes related of him by Walter Map demonstrate.[122]

The apparent absence, from this period, of intra-Welsh struggle which did not in some way involve Gruffudd would seem to be a tribute to his ability, his ambition, and his standing. He had two rivals, both Southern kings, Hywel ab Edwin and Gruffudd ap Rhydderch. Hywel he seemingly more or less dominated from his (Gruffudd's) accession in 1039 to Hywel's death in battle in 1044 – Hywel was expelled twice by Gruffudd. Gruffudd ap Rhydderch resisted him with rather more success, and was probably responsible for the destruction of his rival's warband in 1047. However, neither seems to have been able to challenge Gruffudd ap Llywelyn in his own Northern territory. For the five years after the latter's death, the Welsh chronicles record no Welsh events at all and, although we know from the Anglo-Saxon Chronicle that he was succeeded by his half-brother Bleddyn,[123] it nevertheless appears probable that chaos ensued in Wales, with struggles for power going on in the North between Gruffudd's sons and his two half-brothers, and in the South between the sons of Owain ab Edwin and the various offshoots of the family of Rhydderch ab Iestyn.

Gruffudd was quite closely related to his enemy Hywel ab Edwin: Gruffudd's mother Angharad ferch Maredudd and Hywel's father Edwin ab Einion were first cousins, and the Gruffudd–Hywel strife can be seen as a continuation of the existing tenth-century pattern of hostility between North and South. He was not related to Gruffudd ap Rhydderch in any way – unless the latter's improbable descent from the supposed Iestyn ab Owain ap Hywel Dda be accepted. It is interesting, however, that the strife between the family/successors of Llywelyn ap Seisyll and the family of Rhydderch ab Iestyn appears to have been restricted to the two Gruffudds, for, while nothing is known of Bleddyn ap Cynfyn's relationship with his Southern contemporaries of the line of Rhydderch, it seems that Bleddyn's cousin and successor, Trahaearn ap Caradog, was allied with Gruffudd ap Rhydderch's son, Caradog.

The reign of Gruffudd ap Llywelyn is extraordinary, and even more so when it is realised that he had several extremely competent contemporaries, including Gruffudd ap Rhydderch and the English earl, Harold Godwinesson. It is a

120 ASC (CDE) *s.a.* 1056; ASC (D) *s.a.* 1058.
121 Orderic Vitalis, *Historia Ecclesiastica,* Book III: ed. & transl. Chibnall, II.138.
122 *De Nugis Curialium,* edd. & transl. James *et al.,* pp. 186–96.
123 ASC (D) *s.a.* 1063.

measure of Gruffudd ap Llywelyn's ability that he co-existed with such individuals, yet continued to shine. It is an even greater measure that he is remembered in English, Irish, and Anglo-Norman sources, as well as Welsh. During his reign, particularly after his acquisition of the South, his power is made plain by the lack of internal strife – as far as we can tell, between 1056 and his death in 1063 Wales enjoyed peace.

Gruffudd ap Llywelyn left few descendants, and none who distinguished himself in any way. In none of the genealogical material is he said to have left sons. *Annales Cambriae* and the *Brutiau*, however, mention Maredudd and Ithel, sons of Gruffudd, who fell in battle against Bleddyn in 1069. Although the chronicles do not specify these men's father, it seems reasonable to suppose that the two were sons of Gruffudd ap Llywelyn, not of Gruffudd ap Rhydderch. The Owain ap Gruffudd who died in 1059 may also be another son of Gruffudd ap Llywelyn. Where Grufffudd himself is mentioned in the pedigree-material, it is as the son of Angharad ferch Maredudd, and of Llywelyn ap Seisyll, with one exception. This is JC 27,[124] a pedigree of Rhys Gryg, which reads as follows.

Rees gryc mab merch Madawc m. Meredud m. Bledynt <m.> Kynwyn m. Gwedylstan m. Kynvin. Y Kynvin hwnnw, a Gruffud vab Llewelyn, a Thrahayarn m. Cradawc, tri broder oedynt, meibion y Hagharat merch Maredud mab Ewein m. Howel da.

Rhys Gryg the son of the daughter of Madog son of Maredudd <son of> Bleddyn son of Cynfyn son of Gwedylstan son of Cynfyn. That Cynfyn, and Gruffudd son of Llywelyn, and Trahaearn son of Caradog, were three brothers, sons of Angharad daughter of Maredudd son of Owain son of Hywel Dda.

This text is clearly corrupt, confusing Bleddyn with his father Cynfyn, and claiming that Trahaearn ap Caradog was a son of Angharad ferch Maredudd. However, it seems equally clear from this that Gruffudd ap Llywelyn was considered to be someone worth mentioning if at all possible – Rhys Gryg was barely related to him, but the compiler of JC 27 nevertheless appears to have felt that Gruffudd should be included.

Gruffudd is also mentioned in JC 33[125] (see above, *sub* Llywelyn ap Seisyll). It is possible that Gruffudd was included in order to define the importance of his father Llywelyn who features as the reputed slayer of an ancestor of Hywel ap Goronwy. He is also found in *ABT* 7f, ostensibly a pedigree of his father,[126] and in *ABT* 7k, which gives his descent from Angharad ferch Maredudd.[127] He also features in *Hen Lwythau Gwynedd a'r Mars* 1 (*Bonedd Llwyth Kelling Meibion Uchelwyr*), a set of interrelated genealogies of people descended in some way from Maelog Dda.[128] Gruffudd is said to have married Ceinfryd ferch Rhirid Mawr, by whom he had a son, Cynan. This Ceinfryd is said to have also had a son by Trahaearn ap Maelog Dda, which provides the reason for the inclusion of Gruffudd in this pedigree. However, no Cynan ap Gruffudd is known from the chronicles, and no descendants are recorded for him in the mediaeval genea-

---

[124] Bartrum, *Tracts*, p. 47.
[125] *Ibid.*, p. 48.
[126] *Ibid.*, p. 101.
[127] *Ibid.*
[128] *Ibid.*, p. 111.

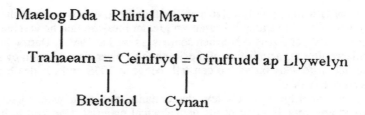

Figure 35

logies. It is impossible to say whether there is any truth in the liaison with Ceinfryd: Gruffudd is known to have had at least two wives (if that is the correct term), the nameless wife of Hywel ab Edwin, whom he abducted and took for his own in 1041, and Ealdgyth, daughter of Earl Ælfgar, whom he probably married after 1056. The mothers of his sons Owain, Maredudd, and Ithel are not known. However, it was not uncommon for rulers to have several wives at this time (Gruffudd ap Cynan had two, and Cadwgan ab Bleddyn reputedly had five). The marriage to Ceinfryd is tabulated in figure 35. His relationship to Rhodri Mawr and to the other eleventh-century members of this line is shown in figure 36. Figure 37 shows the spurious kinship with Gruffudd ap Rhydderch.

Finally, John of Worcester and Giraldus Cambrensis[129] both mention one other descendant, Nest, grand-daughter of Gruffudd and Ealdgyth, who married Bernard of Neufmarché.

(10) Bleddyn and Rhiwallon sons of Cynfyn

The maternal half-brothers of Gruffudd ap Llywelyn, Bleddyn and Rhiwallon, sons of Cynfyn came to power in north Wales after Gruffudd's death. They first occur in Welsh sources in 1069 when they fought the battle of Mechain against Gruffudd's sons Maredudd and Ithel, both of whom were slain, as was Rhiwallon. According to the Welsh chronicles, Bleddyn ruled the North after this victory (there is, however, considerable evidence in non-Welsh sources to show that he had been reigning for some time before this). Bleddyn himself was slain in 1075 by the treachery of the men of Ystrad Tywi, and by implication the south-Welsh ruler Rhys ab Owain. His death in these circumstances suggests that he may have tried to perpetuate his half-brother's influence in the South. In the *Brutiau*, his obit is accompanied by a short panegyric, including a reference to his kinship with Gruffudd. He was succeeded in Gwynedd by his cousin Trahaearn ap Caradog, who in 1078 killed Rhys ab Owain, an act which the *Brutiau* interpret as avenging Bleddyn, and which they accompany with another panegyric on Bleddyn. Bleddyn is also mentioned in the *Brutiau* in two digressions on genealogy, *s.a.* 1106 and *s.a.* 1113, concerned with his children and with his descent from Angharad ferch Maredudd.

Bleddyn ap Cynfyn also finds a mention in several non-Welsh sources, some of which relate actions of his prior to 1069, though always in an English context. He is noticed in the Anglo-Saxon Chronicle, by John of Worcester, by Orderic

---

[129] *Giraldi Cambrensis Opera*, edd. Brewer, *et al.*, IV.28–9.

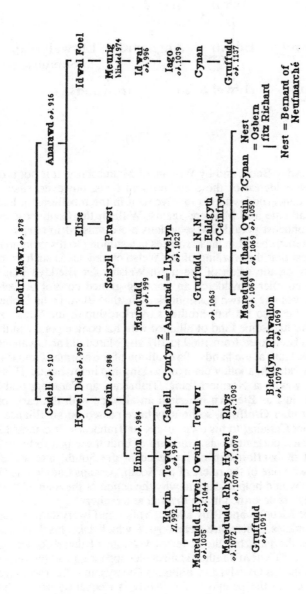

Figure 36

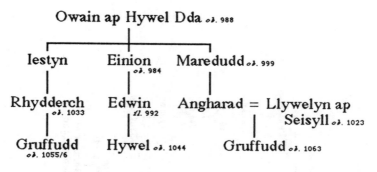

Figure 37

Vitalis, in Domesday Book, and by William of Malmesbury. It is not proposed to discuss here the evidence of these authors and texts, however, since they are almost entirely concerned with his involvement in the rebellions of Eadric *Cild* and of Earls Eadwine and Morkere against William the Conqueror in the immediate post-Conquest period. These actions are discussed in chapter II. However, that he is remembered in these sources is testimony to his prominence.

It is of interest that the wording of the Welsh chronicles is such as to suggest that it was only on the death of the north-Welsh ruler Bleddyn that Rhys ab Owain and his co-ruler Rhydderch ap Caradog gained control of Deheubarth. This situation gives rise to two possiblities: first, that Bleddyn had inherited not only Gwynedd, but also his half-brother's overlordship of the South; secondly, that he may have had some kind of alliance with his contemporary in the South. Deheubarth had been ruled from 1069 to 1072 by Maredudd ab Owain ab Edwin, who had met his death at the hands of a coalition of the Normans and Caradog ap Gruffudd ap Rhydderch, another claimant to kingship in the South. This Caradog was later to ally with a Northern king, Trahaearn ap Caradog, and it is not impossible that, just as Bleddyn inherited an alliance with the earls of Mercia from his half-brother Gruffudd, so he may have passed on an alliance with the south-Welsh ruler Caradog to his own successor Trahaearn. It is most likely that the situation which pertained was a mixture of both these possibilities: Bleddyn had some kind of overlordship or influence in the South, and some kind of understanding with one of the rulers of the South, perhaps Caradog ap Gruffudd. Such a situation would help to explain why the action of the men of Ystrad Tywi in killing Bleddyn is described in the *Brutiau* as treachery.

The father of Bleddyn and Rhiwallon, Cynfyn ap Gwerystan, is unknown in the Welsh chronicles. There are genealogies which take his line back many generations into the past, but the different versions of these do not agree, and indeed the name of Cynfyn's father is unstable, appearing as Gwerystan, Gwerstan, and sometimes as Gwedylstan, although Gwerystan is the form given by the annalistic sources. In the pedigrees the family is frequently said to have been connected with Powys, and certainly in the twelfth century Powys was the main sphere of action for the sons and grandsons of Bleddyn. It is not possible to know how ancient this connexion is; nor is there any particular reason for supposing

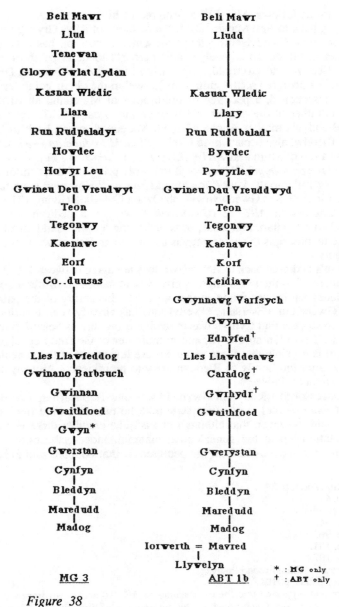

```
        Beli Mawr                        Beli Mawr
           |                                |
         Llud                             Lludd
           |                                |
        Tenevan                             |
           |                                |
    Gloyw Gwlat Lydan                       |
           |                                |
     Kasnar Wledic                    Kasuar Wledic
           |                                |
         Llara                            Llary
           |                                |
    Run Rudpaladyr                   Run Ruddbaladr
           |                                |
        Howdec                           Bywdec
           |                                |
       Howyr Leu                        Pywyrlew
           |                                |
   Gwineu Deu Vreudwyt           Gwineu Dau Vreuddwyd
           |                                |
         Teon                             Teon
           |                                |
        Tegonwy                          Tegonwy
           |                                |
        Kaenawc                          Kaenawc
           |                                |
         Eorf                             Korf
           |                                |
       Co..duusas                        Keidiaw
           |                                |
           |                       Gwynnawg Varfsych
           |                                |
           |                             Gwynan
           |                                |
           |                           Ednyfed[†]
           |                                |
    Lles Llawfeddog               Lles Llawddeawg
           |                                |
   Gwinano Barbsuch                   Caradog[†]
           |                                |
        Gwinnan                         Gwrhydr[†]
           |                                |
       Gwaithfoed                       Gwaithfoed
           |                                |
         Gwyn[*]                            |
           |                                |
        Gwerstan                         Gwerystan
           |                                |
        Cynfyn                           Cynfyn
           |                                |
        Bleddyn                          Bleddyn
           |                                |
       Maredudd                         Maredudd
           |                                |
        Madog                            Madog
                                            |
                               Iorwerth  =  Mawred
                                            |
                                        Llywelyn        * : MG only
           MG 3                           ABT 1b         † : ABT only
```

Figure 38

that it is untrue, although the family may not have risen to prominence before the eleventh century.

There is a large amount of material in the early pedigrees relating to Bleddyn, and a reasonable amount relating to Rhiwallon. Their sister, or half-sister, Iwerydd, is also found in several pedigrees. Mediaeval genealogies mentioning

71

Bleddyn are as follows: MG 3,[130] a pedigree of his grandson Madog ap Maredudd, going back to Beli Mawr; JC 27,[131] a pedigree of Rhys Gryg, going back to Gwerystan (here Gwedylstan) – this text, which is corrupt, has been described above, *sub* Gruffudd ap Llywelyn, and purports to describe the relationship between Bleddyn and Gruffudd; ABT 1 (*Ach Llewelyn ap Iorwerth Drwyndwn*) section b,[132] a pedigree of the mother of Llywelyn the Great going back to Beli Mawr, and section d, a pedigree of the mother of Maredudd ab Bleddyn (the great-grandfather of the mother of Llywelyn the Great).[133] ABT 1e[134] is a pedigree of Bleddyn's mother Angharad ferch Maredudd, going back to Elidir Lydanwyn. Bleddyn also occurs in ABT 7k[135] (*Plant Maredudd ap Ewein*), where he is listed as a son of Angharad. ABT 8 (*Llyma Iach Vathraval Tywysogion Pywys* or *Plant Bleddyn ap Kynfyn*),[136] is devoted to his offspring and their children. In this respect it is similar to the later *Rhandiroedd Powys*.[137] However, the latest person mentioned in ABT 8 is Gwenwynwyn ab Owain Cyfeiliog (living 1216). Finally, Bleddyn appears in ABT 12 (*Gwehelyth Powys*),[138] a pedigree of Gruffudd Maelor, Owain Fychan, and Elise, sons of Madog ap Maredudd ab Bleddyn. In two of the manuscripts this genealogy is taken back to Beli mawr, in the others to Cynfyn only.

Bleddyn's pedigree back to Beli Mawr does not agree between MG 3 and ABT 1b (see figure 38) – the two pedigrees give certain names in a different order, and each includes names not found in the other. The instability of the patronym of Cynfyn (Gwerystan, Gwerstan, Gwedylstan) has already been mentioned. This leads me to suspect that Cynfyn was in reality as obscure as Seisyll, father of the earlier ruler Llywelyn ap Seisyll, and grandfather of Gruffudd ap Llywelyn. In this case, it is possible that these pedigrees are inventions of the genealogists, at some time after the family of Bleddyn grew to prominence. Anyway, it is clear that they are not reliable.[139]

The successor to Bleddyn in Gwynedd was one Trahaearn ap Caradog. Both *Annales Cambriae* and the *Brutiau* state that the two men were first cousins. It has to be said, however, that although this is quite credible there is no trace of such a relationship in the genealogical material. Indeed, the only connexion between them discoverable from the pedigrees is that both are said to have been

130 Bartrum, *Tracts*, p. 39.
131 *Ibid.*, p. 47.
132 *Ibid.*, pp. 95–6.
133 *Ibid.*, p. 96.
134 *Ibid.*, p. 96.
135 *Ibid.*, p. 101.
136 *Ibid.*, p. 102.
137 ed. Bartrum, 'Rhandiroedd Powys'.
138 Bartrum, *Tracts*, p. 104.
139 Bartrum has suggested that the extra names in ABT 1b are drawn from a pedigree of another Gwaithfoed, Gwaithfoed ap Gwrdyr ancestor of Ednywain Bendew. He would also drop 'Gwyn' from MG 1. His suggested pedigree for Bleddyn would thus read: 'Bleddyn ap Cynfyn ap Gwer(y)stan ap Gwaithfoed ap Gwynnan ap Gwynnawg farfsych ap Lles llawddeawg (or llawfeddawg ?) ap Ceidio ap Corf ap Caenawg ap Tegonwy' (*Tracts*, p. 137). This however does not explain the reversed order of Lles, Gwynnawg, and Gwynnan in ABT 1b, and seems to me to indicate further the unreliable and unstable nature of this pedigree.

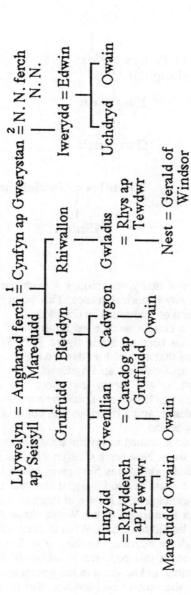

Figure 39

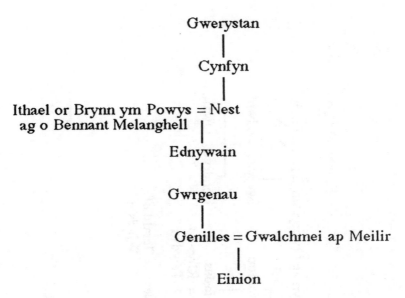

Figure 40

descended – at a distance of many generations – from one Tegonwy ap Teon, who is not mentioned in any historical source. This point will be examined in more detail in the discussion of Trahaearn ap Caradog.

The *Brutiau* preserve a certain amount of information about the family of Bleddyn ap Cynfyn: this has been set out in figure 39.[140] While this evidence is not entirely clear, it seems that one of Bleddyn's daughters was married to the Southern king, Caradog ap Gruffudd ap Rhydderch. This is of interest, for it might be seen as support for the theory that there was an alliance of sorts between Bleddyn and Caradog. However, it must be admitted that this by itself is a very small piece of evidence, and a marriage was not necessarily indicative of any lasting alliance in this period.

Bleddyn's sister Iwerydd is named in several texts. However, the pedigree *HL* 2c[141] gives him a second sister, Nest ferch Cynfyn. *HL* 2 is a pedigree of Einion ap Gwalchmai, and the inclusion of this Nest gives him a link to the important family of Bleddyn, which may in itself suggest that the connexion and Nest herself are fabrications. Nothing else is known of this sister, and her so-called son Ednywain ab Ithael is not mentioned in the Welsh chronicles (although this in itself does not prove that he did not exist). What is interesting is that the family into which Nest is said to have married, like the line of Bleddyn, is from Powys. The information contained in this pedigree is shown in figure 40. Figure 41 shows Bleddyn's descendants, as known from the genealogies in *ABT*.

Rhiwallon ap Cynfyn, the brother of Bleddyn, also occcurs in a number of

140 *ByT* (Pen. 20) *s.a.* 1113 (*recte* 1116); *ByT* (RB) *s.a.* 1113 (*recte* 1116); *ByS s.a.* 1113 (*recte* 1116).
141 Bartrum, *Tracts*, pp. 112–13.

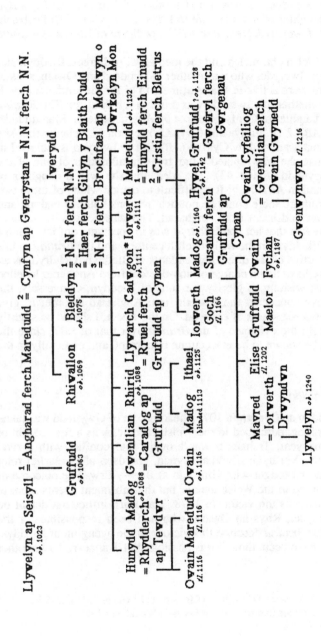

Figure 41

* Various offspring: see sub Cadwgon ap Bleddyn.

pedigrees. Although he died in 1069, Rhiwallon appears to have been fairly well known – in the non-Welsh sources, he is associated with his brother's anti-Norman activities. Like Bleddyn, he was a half-brother of Gruffudd ap Llywelyn (*ABT* 7k);[142] and a daughter of his was wife to Rhys ap Tewdwr of Deheubarth, according to *ABT* 10 (*Gwehelyth Deheubarth*),[143] a pedigree of Rhys ap Gruffudd (see figure 42).

According to the Welsh chronicles and the mediaeval pedigrees, Bleddyn and Rhiwallon had a sister, Iwerydd, who was mother to Uchdryd and Owain, sons of Edwin, both of whom were active in Wales at the end of the eleventh century. It is not entirely clear whether this Iwerydd was a full or a half-sister. The *Brutiau* state that she was a daughter of Cynfyn, but not by Angharad ferch Maredudd.[144] On the other hand, *ABT* 2 (*Plant Owain Gwynedd*) section f,[145] claims that she was a daughter of Angharad, and by Cynfyn (*ABT* 2e).[146] Iwerydd is included in this genealogy because she was reputedly the great-grandmother of one of the wives of Owain Gwynedd (figure 43). The idea that she was a daughter of Angharad is also found in *ABT* 7k.[147] It is difficult to decide which of these two claims is the more truthful: there could be political reasons both for making and for rebutting the claim to descent from Angharad. The statement in the *Brutiau* may be a result of the fact that her son Uchdryd was in constant conflict with his cousins, the sons of Bleddyn, in the early twelfth century, and the *Brutiau* in this period are very supportive of the direct descendants of Bleddyn. Uchdryd, as an enemy, may therefore have had a charge of non-descent from Angharad levelled at him by an annalist wishing to glorify the sons of Bleddyn. Conversely, the genealogists may have concocted the descent from Angharad in order to give more prestige to later descendants of Iwerydd. On the whole, I should be slightly more inclined to accept the evidence of the *Brutiau* over that of *ABT*, since the latter frequently can be shown to be inacccurate or corrupt, and especially in the case of *ABT* 7.

(11) Trahaearn ap Caradog

On the death of Bleddyn ap Cynfyn in 1075, the kingdom of Gwynedd was taken by Trahaearn ap Caradog, described in the Welsh chronicles as a first cousin of Bleddyn. In the same year, Trahaearn was brought into conflict with a rival claimant for rule in the North, Gruffudd ap Cynan, grandson of the earlier ruler Iago ab Idwal. Trahaearn fought with Gruffudd at Bron-y-Erw. The outcome of this battle is not recorded in the Welsh annals, but the subsquent events seem to suggest that Trahaearn was the victor. In 1078, Trahaearn inflicted a defeat on the Southern Welsh ruler, Rhys ab Owain, who had been responsible for the death of Bleddyn. The *Brutiau* describe this victory as the avenging of Bleddyn, which indeed it may have been, though it is possible that Trahaearn had another

142 *Ibid.*, pp. 101–2.
143 *Ibid.*, p. 104.
144 *ByT* (Pen. 20) *s.a.* 1113 (*recte* 1116); *ByT* (RB) *s.a.* 1113 (*recte* 1116); *ByS s.a.* 1113 (*recte* 1116). This last text is in error, calling Iwerydd 'daughter of Edwin'.
145 Bartrum, *Tracts*, pp. 97–8.
146 *Ibid.*
147 *Ibid.*, pp. 101–2.

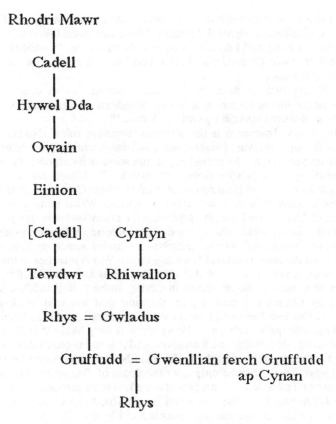

Rhodri Mawr
|
Cadell
|
Hywel Dda
|
Owain
|
Einion
|
[Cadell]   Cynfyn
| |
Tewdwr   Rhiwallon
| |
Rhys = Gwladus
|
Gruffudd = Gwenllian ferch Gruffudd
| ap Cynan
Rhys

Figure 42

motive also. In 1081, he came into conflict with Gruffudd ap Cynan again. The latter had leagued himself with a south Welsh king, Rhys ap Tewdwr, and Gruffudd and Rhys marched against Trahaearn and his ally, another south Welsh king, Caradog ap Gruffudd. Together with these two was one Meilir ap Rhiwallon, apparently a son of Rhiwallon ap Cynfyn, the brother of Bleddyn. A battle took place, known as the battle of Mynydd Carn, and Trahaearn, Caradog and Meilir were all slain.

Such is the evidence of the Welsh chronicles. The biography of Trahaearn's rival, Gruffudd ap Cynan, the *Historia Gruffud vab Kenan* does include some additional information, for instance describing a battle prior to that of Bron-y-Erw, called Gwaet-Erw, which Gruffudd is supposed to have won. But while Gruffudd is known to have been active in north Wales in 1075, before Bron-y-Erw, there is no certain evidence outside the *Historia Gruffud vab Kenan* for this battle, and even if Gruffudd be supposed to have won a victory (other than his possible taking of Anglesey) in 1075, there is no very good reason for supposing that it was against Trahaearn. The picture of Trahaearn as given in *Historia*

77

Gruffud vab Kenan is one-sided; he is the usurper, the coward, the illegitimate pretender to Gruffudd's 'rightful' heritage. I have discussed this text's account of Trahaearn elsewhere, and I do not propose to detail it here.[148] suffice to say that I do not find *Historia Gruffud vab Kenan* reliable as a source for the career of Trahaearn ap Caradog.

There is very little evidence for Trahaearn outside Welsh sources, the only reference being his inclusion in a list of Welsh rulers defeated by Robert of Rhuddlan, in Robert's epitaph by Orderic Vitalis.[149]

In many ways, Trahaearn is the ultimate 'intrusive ruler'. No one seems to know exactly who he was. Nevertheless, he was seemingly an effective ruler during his six year reign. The period of his rule was a difficult one in north Wales, with increasing Norman incursions, yet outside the biased pages of *Historia Gruffud vab Kenan*, there is no record of trouble within Gwynedd, and Trahaearn was secure enough to be able to intervene in south Welsh affairs. On the other hand, it must be admitted that the reporting for north Wales in this period is far less detailed than for south Wales, and there is Orderic's reference to account for. The *Historia Gruffud vab Kenan* describes a massive attack on Trahaearn by a coalition of all the most powerful Normans on the Welsh marches at the time. Yet no other source, not even the Welsh chronicles, has any trace of this (and it is surprising that such a major action involving Robert of Rhuddlan should go unnoticed by Orderic). I cannot help thinking that the raid as described by *Historia Gruffud vab Kenan* has been over-exaggerated, and that Trahaearn was not attacked with quite such force. However, it is very likely that he had one or more skirmishes with Robert of Rhuddlan, and it is to his credit that he seems to have survived reasonably unscathed. The main Norman incursions into Gwynedd appear to have been achieved only after the death of Trahaearn. In spite of this, Lloyd wrote of Trahaearn '. . . his power rested on most insecure foundations . . . consistently menaced, on the one hand by Gruffudd [ap Cynan], who did not cease harassing him at sea, and on the other hand by the Normans . . .'.[150] In fact, the only evidence for Gruffudd's activities in this period comes again from *Historia Gruffud vab Kenan*; none of them are so much as hinted at in the Welsh chronicles, and none of them are inherently very credible, at least as they are presented in this text. I would argue that as they stand, the Welsh chronicles for this period, and especially *Annales Cambriae*, represent an earlier layer of recording than *Historia Gruffud vab Kenan*, and that where they can be checked, they are more accurate.[151] These annals, far from noting any actions of Gruffudd 1076–1081, are not even entirely certain of his identity, referring to him not as 'Gruffudd ap Cynan', but as 'Gruffudd grandson of Iago'. This indicates not only that his father was obscure, but that the entries for the years in question were probably made more or less contemporaneously with the events described. Any later annalist would have been familiar with Gruffudd as Gruffudd ap Cynan, and would not have needed to define him and his claim to rule by reference to his long-dead grandfather. The view taken by Lloyd seems to reflect not only his

---

148 See Maund, 'Trahaearn'.
149 Orderic Vitalis, *Historia Ecclesiastica*, Book VIII: ed. & transl. Chibnall, VI.144.
150 *A History*, II.383.
151 See Maund, 'Trahaearn'.

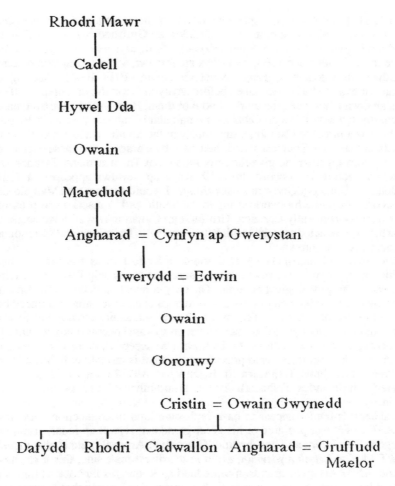

Rhodri Mawr
|
Cadell
|
Hywel Dda
|
Owain
|
Maredudd
|
Angharad = Cynfyn ap Gwerystan
|
Iwerydd = Edwin
|
Owain
|
Goronwy
|
Cristin = Owain Gwynedd

Dafydd   Rhodri   Cadwallon   Angharad = Gruffudd
                                                   Maelor

Figure 43

dependence on *Historia Gruffud vab Kenan* as a reliable and truthful witness to Trahaearn's activities, but also his tendency to see the politics of eleventh-century Wales in terms of 'legitimate' claimants to rule descended from Rhodri Mawr, and 'illegitimate' usurpers wrongfully displacing them.

Gruffudd's ultimate defeat of Trahaearn was not as easy as Lloyd has made it out to be. Gruffudd was able to overthrow Trahaearn only after having allied himself with Rhys ap Tewdwr, who by that time was ruling in Deheubarth, and was thus possessed of a reasonable power-base (unlike Gruffudd). Indeed, as the annals stand, the battle of Mynydd Carn was between Trahaearn and Caradog ap Gruffudd on the one hand, and Rhys on the other, with Gruffudd arriving with an Irish fleet to help him. Moreover, the battle is far better understood in a Southern rather than a Northern context.

In 1081, Deheubarth was split effectively by the presence of two individuals with a strong claim to supremacy – Caradog ap Gruffudd, son of Gruffudd ap Rhydderch (overlord in the South 1044–1055/6), and who had himself been active in the south since 1064; and Rhys ap Tewdwr, a great-grandson of Einion ab Edwin, and cousin to King Hywel ab Edwin (1033–1044). Caradog and Trahaearn seem to have been allies before Mynydd Carn: the downfall in 1078 of Rhys ab Owain had been the work of both of them. Both would have had reasons for enmity towards Rhys ab Owain – he had slain Trahaearn's cousin Bleddyn, and he was a threat to Caradog's supremacy in the South. In 1078, this Rhys was heavily defeated by Trahaearn, and then slain by Caradog, and these two events, coming close together, do give the impression that Trahaearn and Caradog were knowingly acting in concord. In 1079, Rhys ap Tewdwr appeared, a further challenge to Caradog. Given this background, I would suggest that Mynydd Carn was in origin a battle for overlordship in the South, and Trahaearn was present in order to support his ally Caradog. Gruffudd ap Cynan may well have seized the opportunity, and acted together with Rhys, hoping to benefit should Caradog and Trahaearn be overthrown.

Who was Trahaearn? The Welsh annals refer to him as the first cousin of Bleddyn ap Cynfyn.[152] However, the origin of this cousinship is revealed neither there nor in the genealogical material. The only connection between Bleddyn and Trahaearn that can be seen in the early pedigrees is that they are both traced back to the same remote ancestor, Tegonwy ap Teon. But, as has already been shown, the pedigree of Bleddyn going back to Tegonwy (and beyond) is very unstable, and hence, even if the pedigree of Trahaearn be accepted, there is no guarantee that the relationship it seems to provide to Bleddyn is reliable or believable. The pedigree which links Trahaearn to Tegonwy is *ABT* 2a, part of *Plant Owain Gwynedd*; it includes Trahaearn as the grandfather of one of the wives of Owain.[153]

Trahaearn's family appear to have had some kind of connection with Arwystli: *ABT* 13d[154] is a pedigree of his great-grandson, Hywel ap Ieuaf, going back to Tegonwy ap Teon, and has the title 'Gwehelyth Arwystli'. He is also included in *ABT* 14, *Gwehelyth Kydewain*, again in the direct male line; this text sets out the ancestry of his great-grandson Maredudd ap Robert, as far back as Ednywain ap Bleddyn in the line of Tegonwy.[155] It is interesting to note that his numerous family spent the early years of the twelfth century slaughtering one another – and that some of his sons and grandsons are known only from the account of this found in the *Brutiau*. The two descendants featured in *ABT* 13 and 14 are known historical personages. Trahaearn is also claimed as an ancestor of Gwenwynwyn ap Owain Cyfeiliog, through the female line,[156] and of Llywelyn the Great, also in the female line, by extention from the above, in *ABT* 2a.[157] These various descendants, plus the possible link to Bleddyn ap Cynfyn are shown in figure 44.

---

152 *AC* (C) 'consobrinus'; *ByT* (RB) 'y gefyndero'. On these terms, see Charles-Edwards, 'Some Celtic Kinship Terms'.
153 Bartrum, *Tracts*, pp. 96–7.
154 *Ibid.*, p. 104.
155 *Ibid.*, p. 105.
156 *Ibid.*, pp. 96–7.
157 *ABT* 2a ends with three children of Owain Gwynedd, Maelgwn, Gwenllian, and

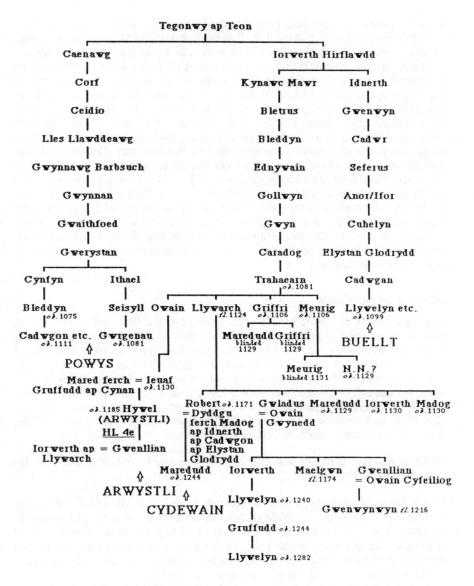

Tegonwy ap Teon

Caenawg — Iorwerth Hirflawdd

Corf — Kynawc Mawr / Idnerth

Ceidio — Bletrus / Gwenwyn

Lles Llawddeawg — Bleddyn / Cadwr

Gwynnawg Barbsuch — Ednywain / Seferus

Gwynnan — Gollwyn / Anor/Ifor

Gwaithfoed — Gwyn / Cuhelyn

Gwerystan — Caradog / Elystan Glodrydd

Cynfyn | Ithael — Trahaearn *ob.1081* | Cadwgan

Bleddyn *ob.1075* | Seisyll | Owain | Llywarch *fl.1124* | Griffri *ob.1106* | Meurig *ob.1106* | Llywelyn etc. *ob.1099*

Cadwgon etc. *ob.1111* | Gwrgenau *ob.1081*

POWYS

Maredudd *blinded 1129* | Griffri *blinded 1129*

BUELLT

Meurig *blinded 1131* | N.N.? *ob.1129*

Mared ferch = Ieuaf
Gruffudd ap Cynan | *ob.1130*

ob.1185 Hywel
(ARWYSTLI)

HL 4e

Iorwerth ap = Gwenllian
Llywarch

Robert *ob.1171* | Gwladus | Maredudd *ob.1129* | Iorwerth *ob.1130* | Madog *ob.1130*
= Dyddgu | = Owain
ferch Madog | Gwynedd
ap Idnerth
ap Cadwgon
ap Elystan
Glodrydd

ARWYSTLI

Maredudd *ob.1244* | Iorwerth | Maelgwn *fl.1174* | Gwenllian
= Owain Cyfeiliog

CYDEWAIN

Llywelyn *ob.1240* | Gwenwynwyn *fl.1216*

Gruffudd *ob.1244*

Llywelyn *ob.1282*

Note that Trahearn's descent from Tegonwy is one generation shorter than those of Bleddyn and Llywelyn ap Cadwgon, his contemporaries.

Figure 44

81

Trahaearn may also have been related to the family of Elystan Glodrydd, through Iorwerth hirvlawd ap Tegonwy. This family were associated with Buellt. It must be said, however, that the pedigree of Elystan is as unstable as that of Bleddyn.

It has already been said that the exact nature of Trahaearn's cousinship with Bleddyn is unknown. But that he was a kinsman, and a closer one than the line via Tegonwy would make him, seems clear, both from the annalistic evidence and from the corrupt pedigree JC 27,[158] the text of which has already been given, *sub* Gruffudd ap Llywelyn. This pedigree, although inaccurate, calling Cynfyn (in error for Bleddyn) and Gruffudd an Llywelyn, and Trahaearn three sons of Angharad ferch Maredudd, does seem to bear witness that Bleddyn and Trahaearn were close kin of some kind – not brothers, though. It is unlikely that Trahaearn can have been a son of Angharad; if he had been one would expect the annals to have commented on it, as they are very well informed on Bleddyn and his family. Bartrum has attempted to account for the relationship by suggesting that the mother of Trahaearn was a sister of Cynfyn.[159] This is possible: it is also possible, given JC 27, that the relationship was somehow through Angharad – via her sister, or half-sister, or cousin, or some such? However, it is not possible to prove either speculation.

(12) Gruffudd ap Cynan

The main career of Gruffudd ap Cynan belongs to the first half of the twelfth century. However it is proposed to consider here only his eleventh-century activities. The evidence of the Welsh chronicles will be given primacy over that of *Historia Gruffud vab Kenan* (which, it must be said is thin as far as the eleventh century is concerned). Gruffudd is first noticed in the Welsh chronicles in 1075 when he was active in some way in Anglesey. *Brut y Tywysogion* (Pen. 20) says that Gruffudd gained possession of it after the death of Bleddyn; *Brut y Tywysogion* (RB) and *Brenhinedd y Saesson* say that he besieged it.[160] *Annales Cambriae* (C) is extremely confused, reading:[161]

Grifud autem nepos Iacob non obsedit bellum Candubr inter filios Kadugaun et inter Res et Rederch, qui victores fuerunt

This is obviously an error, and what seems to have happened is that a scribe, by writing 'non' for 'Mon' (Anglesey), has run an account of Gruffudd besieging Anglesey into one of the battle of Camddwr. Gruffudd is absent from the record of *Annales Cambriae* (B) in this year. It is interesting that only one of these texts seems to imply that Gruffudd had any success in this siege, and that the earlier account of *Annales Cambriae* (C) mentions only the siege.

In the same year, the *Brutiau* record that Gruffudd fought a battle with Trahaearn ap Caradog at Bron-y-Erw, which he seemingly lost. The account

Iorwerth. This Iorwerth was the father of Llywelyn the Great: see *ABT* 1a, Bartrum, *Tracts*, p. 95.
158 Bartrum, *Tracts*, p. 47.
159 Bartrum, *Welsh Genealogies*, I.46.
160 *ByS* has him besieging the Isle of Man, 'Manaw', rather than Anglesey, 'Mon'.
161 *AC* (C) *s.a.* [1082].

given for this year (or what appears to be meant to be this year) in *Historia Gruffud vab Kenan*, is, as one might expect, more elaborate, claiming that Gruffudd won victories in both Anglesey and Gwynedd, defeating and killing Cynwrig ap Rhiwallon in the former and defeating Trahaearn in the latter. While Cynwrig ap Rhiwallon was slain in 1075 by the men of Gwynedd, according to the *Brutiau*, there is no evidence outside *Historia Gruffud vab Kenan* for the involvement of Gruffudd, and even there he is said not to have actually taken part in the battle, but to have sent agents. As has been said above, *sub* Trahaearn ap Caradog, there is no evidence for the victory over Trahaearn either, and both *Historia Gruffud vab Kenan* and the Welsh chronicles show that in the same year, Gruffudd lost against Trahaearn (and returned to Ireland, according to *Historia Gruffud vab Kenan*). From the account in this text, it is tempting to speculate if its author had access to some collection of the Welsh chronicles for this period, and was simply making use of any event that could be fitted to his hero. At all events, I do not see that it adds anything reliable to our knowledge for Gruffudd's career in 1075, and it does admit what is already shown in the Welsh chronicles; that Gruffudd in this year made an attempt to gain Gwynedd and failed.[162]

In 1081, Gruffudd was a participant in the battle of Mynydd Carn, supporting Rhys ap Tewdwr of south Wales against Caradog ap Gruffudd (also of south Wales) and his own rival Trahaearn. *Annales Cambriae* (C) refer to him here as 'Grifud filius Eynaun filius Iacob'. The vernacular annals further say that Gruffudd was accompanied by a Hiberno-Scandinavian fleet, which he had brought to the assistance of Rhys. This latter phrasing in the *Brutiau* is further support for the contention that Mynydd Carn was essentially a battle with a Southern Welsh political context (see above, *sub* Rhys ap Tewdwr, Caradog ap Gruffudd and Trahaearn ap Caradog), and not a fight centred on Gruffudd (as *Historia Gruffud vab Kenan* naturally suggests).

In the annals' descriptions of all the above events, Gruffudd is named as 'grandson of Iago', rather than 'son of Cynan', which is a witness to the obscurity of Gruffudd and of his father Cynan, at least on his first appearance on the Welsh political scene. It is a great contrast to *Historia Gruffud vab Kenan*, which greatly emphasizes Gruffudd's descent from Rhodri Mawr, and gives the impression that the people of Gwynedd could hardly wait to replace the 'illegitimate' Trahaearn with the 'legitimate' Gruffudd. Reading this text, with its emphasis on Gruffudd's 'rightful' throne, it is not hard to see how Lloyd's model of the 'legitimate' descendants of Rhodri Mawr struggling with the illegitimate usurpers (Lylwelyn ap Seisyll, Gruffudd ap Llywelyn, Bleddyn ap Cynfyn, Trahaearn ap Caradog and so on) grew up, and became accepted. Needless to say, the Welsh chronicles give no real support to this notion, with their panegyrics of Gruffudd ap Llywelyn and Bleddyn, and their apparent uncertainty over the identity of Gruffudd ap Cynan upon his first arrival (see above, *sub* Trahaearn ap Caradog).

The next action of Gruffudd known from the Welsh annals is not until 1098, when he is said to have been a part of the Welsh force (together with Cadwgan ap Bleddyn) resisting the invasion of Earl Hugh of Chester and Earl Hugh of Shrewsbury. Fearing possible treachery amongst their own men, Gruffudd and

162 See Maund, 'Trahaearn'.

Cadwgan fled to Ireland. *Brenhinedd y Saesson*, however, attributes this flight to Gruffudd and Cadwgan having learnt that the Normans were being lead to Anglesey by Cadwgan's cousin, Owain ab Edwin. Cadwgan and Gruffudd returned to Wales in 1099, and made peace with the Normans. Each was granted territory; *Brut y Tywysogion* (RB) says they seized territory; the *Annales Cambriae* (both versions) state that Gruffudd was again besieging Anglesey in this year; with which *Brenhinedd y Saesson* is in agreement. *Brut y Tywysogion* (Pen. 20) says that Gruffudd was granted Anglesey by the Normans. However he acquired it, it is from 1099 that Gruffudd can be said to be really ruling in north Wales, and it is not until 1099 that he can be seen as having had any real success in gaining control over Gwynedd or any portion of Gwynedd. This is partly due to the presence of Trahaearn up until 1081, and partly due to the massive gains that the Normans made in north Wales in the late eleventh century (many of which they lost in the early twelfth century). Gruffudd was absent from the Welsh polity for much of the later eleventh century: soon after Mynydd Carn he was captured and imprisoned, either by Hugh of Chester, or by Robert of Rhuddlan, according to Orderic Vitalis[163] and to *Historia Gruffud vab Kenan*.[164] The length of this captivity is not certain – *Historia Gruffud vab Kenan* does not give a definite length.[165] Orderic makes reference to Gruffudd raiding the territory of Robert of Rhuddlan,[166] presumably after Mynydd Carn, which may have been what provoked his capture in the first place. However, it is not really possible to be sure of the dates of his captivity. Lloyd, relying on *Historia Gruffud vab Kenan*, thought that Gruffudd had escaped by 1094, and attributes the north Welsh success against the Normans in that year to the new heart put into them by the reapearance of Gruffudd. However, the Welsh chronicles make no mention of Gruffudd at all in this rebellion, attributing the leadership instead to Cadwgan ap Bleddyn. This is not to say that Gruffudd was not involved; only that his role may have been more minor than Lloyd and the author of *Historia Gruffud vab Kenan* would have us believe. It is noteworthy, indeed, that after relating the escape of Gruffudd, *Historia Gruffud vab Kenan* describes a long period of wandering. Its claim that he was prominent in the 1094 rising is also doubtful, given the panegyric nature of the text in question, and given the corresponding absence of Gruffudd from the Welsh chronicles. As far as the activity of Gruffudd ap Cynan in the last two decades of the eleventh century is concerned, probably all that can be said is that, after having defeated Trahaearn, he enjoyed some initial success in the North, harassing Robert of Rhuddlan, but was soon made captive, and did not escape from this captivity until some time in the mid- to late-1090s. The question of his imprisonment, and his possible involvement in the death of Robert of Rhuddlan will be discussed in chapter III.

This is not to deny the importance and ability of Gruffudd ap Cynan. In the twelfth century he was to prove himself a capable and effective ruler. However, I should like to raise the question of to what extent the significance accorded to

---

163 Orderic Vitalis, *Historia Ecclesiastica*, Book VIII: ed. & transl. Chibnall, IV.140–2, 144.
164 ed. Evans, pp. 16–17.
165 *Ibid.*, pp. 17–18.
166 Orderic Vitalis, *Historia Ecclesiastica*, Book VIII: ed. & transl. Chibnall, IV.134–6.

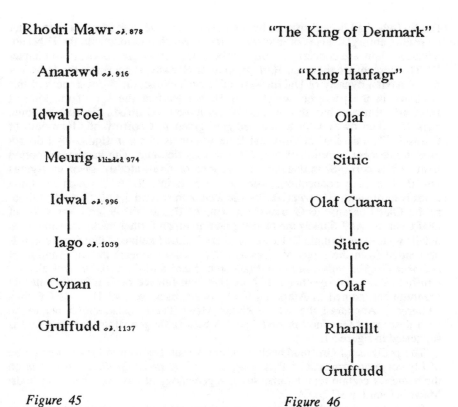

Rhodri Mawr *ob.* 878	"The King of Denmark"
Anarawd *ob.* 916	"King Harfagr"
Idwal Foel	Olaf
Meurig *blinded* 974	Sitric
Idwal *ob.* 996	Olaf Cuaran
Iago *ob.* 1039	Sitric
Cynan	Olaf
Gruffudd *ob.* 1137	Rhanillt
	Gruffudd

Figure 45   *Figure 46*

Gruffudd ap Cynan, and particularly as far as the late eleventh century is concerned, has been over-emphasized, in the light of the existence of *Historia Gruffud vab Kenan*.[167]

Genealogically, Gruffudd ap Cynan occupies a very major position – he had numerous notable descendants. Not surprisingly, *Historia Gruffud vab Kenan* incorporates a fair amount of pedigree material about him, giving his descent in the male line from Rhodri Mawr, and then back to Beli Mawr via Essyllt mother of Rhodri.[168] His descent from Merfyn, father of Rhodri, back to 'Adaf m. Duw' is also given. Through his mother, Rhanillt of Dublin, a Hiberno-Scandinavian 'princess', he is said to be descended from the kings of Dublin, the king of Norway, and the Irish kings of Leinster and Munster. He is also said to have been indirectly related to the kings of Mide, and to have been half-brother to two Ulster princes. The Irish material in particular in these pedigrees makes a lot of grandiose claims for Gruffudd, and their reliability is suspect. It does seem clear, however, that he was connected to the former Hiberno-Scandinavian rulers of

---

[167] This has been noted also by Davies, *Conquest, Coexistence and Change*, pp. 33 and 43–5.

[168] ed. Evans, pp. 1–2; Bartrum, *Tracts*, pp. 36–7.

Dublin (who had been displaced by the kings of Leinster and Munster in the later eleventh century). This is of interest, so far as Welsh relations with the Hiberno-Scandinavians are concerned, and will be discussed in greater detail in chapter IV. The descent from Harald Harfagr, king of Norway, is spurious: the Hiberno-Scandinavian dynasty of Dublin were of Danish extraction.[169] Awareness of this is shown in the pedigree, which calls Harald Harfagr the son of the king of Denmark. Bartrum has shown that the pedigree of Gruffudd via Rhodri going back to Adam owes a lot to the pedigree given in Geoffrey of Monmouth of Gurust.[170] The descent of Gruffudd from Rhodri is given in figure 45. I do not give the descent back to Adam, as it is mostly fictional. The various purported Irish and Hiberno-Scandinavian connections of Gruffudd are given in figures 46–50. The Irish connections were also stated in *ABT* 6,[171] which does not entirely agree with *Historia Gruffud vab Kenan* in several details (it reads 'Glina-ru' for Olaf Cuaran: this Gluniarn was king of Dublin 981–9, and was a son of Olaf Cuaran). *ABT* 6 takes the Norwegian line much further back, agreeing in its details with Heimskringla.[172] However, there is little likelihood that Gruffudd was descended from the kings of Norway. *ABT* 6 (d–h) repeats the information of *Historia Gruffud vab Kenan* on Mailcorce, Slani and Gormflaith, and also on Gruffudd's two half-brothers. *ABT* 6i gives the lineage of Gruffudd's paternal grandmother, named as Afandreg ferch Gwair, back to Koel Hen. *ABT* 6j is a pedigree of Angharad, the wife of Rhodri Mawr. There is also a reference to the Irish descent of Gruffudd in *ABT* 2p.[173] A believable genealogy for Gruffudd is suggested in figure 51.

The pedigree of Gruffudd back to Adam is found as well in MG 1, a pedigree of Llywelyn ap Iorwerth.[174] This disagrees with *Historia Gruffud vab Kenan* on the names of certain remoter ancestors. A genealogy of Gruffudd back to Rhodri Mawr is found in JC 26.[175]

Gruffudd seems to have had a large number of children, grandchildren and so on. A cumulative chart of all of these is found as figure 52. The relevant early pedigrees are as follows:

ByT a Gwenllian f. Gruffudd, a pedigree of Madog ap Cadwgan[176]
JC 25 Gwenllian f. Gruffudd, a pedigree of Rhys Gryg[177]
JC 28 Pedigree of Llywelyn ap Iorweth back to Gruffudd ap Cynan[178]
ABT 2 The descendants of Owain Gwynedd ap Gruffudd[179]
ABT 3 The descendants of Cadwaladr ap Gruffudd[180]

---

169 Bartrum, *Tracts*, pp. 135–6.
170 *Ibid.*, p. 134.
171 *Ibid.*, pp. 99–100.
172 *Ibid.*, p. 152.
173 *Ibid.*, p. 97.
174 *Ibid.*, pp. 38–9.
175 *Ibid.*, p. 47.
176 *Ibid.*, p. 40.
177 *Ibid.*, p. 47.
178 *Ibid.*
179 *Ibid.*, pp. 96–7.
180 *Ibid.*, p. 98.

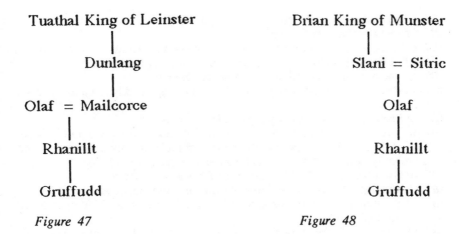

Tuathal King of Leinster

Dunlang

Olaf = Mailcorce

Rhanillt

Gruffudd

Figure 47

Brian King of Munster

Slani = Sitric

Olaf

Rhanillt

Gruffudd

Figure 48

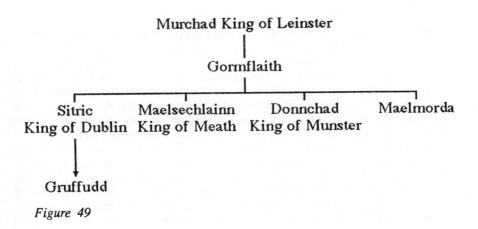

Murchad King of Leinster

Gormflaith

Sitric
King of Dublin

Maelsechlainn
King of Meath

Donnchad
King of Munster

Maelmorda

Gruffudd

Figure 49

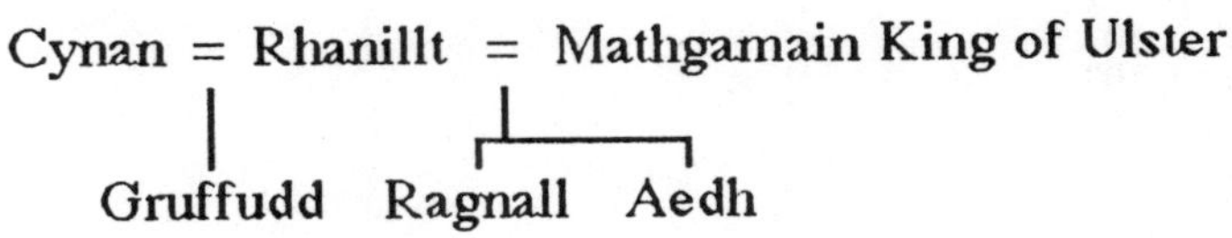

Cynan = Rhanillt = Mathgamain King of Ulster

Gruffudd   Ragnall   Aedh

Figure 50

87

ABT 4 The descendants of Cadwallon ap Gruffudd[181]

ABT 5 *Plant Gruffudd ap Cynan*[182]

ABT 6 Pedigree of Gruffudd himself, with elaborate details on the wives of Merfyn Frych, Rhodri Mawr and so on, as well as Irish material[183]

ABT 7g The descent of Gruffudd from Rhodri Mawr[184]

ABT 8d Rruel f. Gruffudd, a pedigree of Llywarch ap Bleddyn, whose wife she was[185]

ABT 8g Pedigree of Gwenwynwyn, including Gruffudd[186]

ABT 8i Gwenllian f. Gruffudd, a pedigree of Cadwallon ap Madog ap Cadwgan. The implication is that she was the mother of this Cadwallon; however, what is probably meant is that she was the mother of his father Madog[187]

ABT 10 Gwenllian f. Gruffudd, pedigree of Rhys ap Gruffudd[188]

ABT 11 Rhanillt f. Gruffudd, pedigree of Cadwallon ap madog ab Idnerth[189]

ABT 12 Susanna f. Gruffudd, pedigree of Gruffudd Maelor ap Madog ap Maredudd ap Bleddyn[190]

ABT 13 Mared f. Gruffudd, pedigree of Hywel ab Ieuaf ab Owain ap Trahaearn ap Caradog[191]

HL 5b Slani f. Gruffudd, pedigree of Hwfa ab Ithel velyn o Ial, whose wife she is said to have been[192]

HL 9g Rikart ap Cadwaladr ap Gruffudd, married into the family of Gollwyn ap Tangno[193]

Both Lloyd and Bartrum seem to have thought that Gruffudd had two daughters by the name of Gwenllian. However, given the pedigree evidence, I do not see that this is a necessary assumption: 'Gwenllian f. Gruffudd' is said to have been the mother of children by Cadwgan ap Bleddyn (*ob.* 1111) and by Gruffudd ap Rhys ap Tewdwr (*ob.* 1137). The long gap between these two *obits* would give time for one Gwenllian to have married both men serially. Alternatively, it is possible that she might have had non-marital liaisons with one or the other or both. To suppose the existence of two Gwenllians seems unnecessary.

Several of the children of Gruffudd who are named in the pedigrees do not appear to have left descendants. In some cases, also, they are named for 'ancestors' of Gruffudd; for instance Slani and Iago, named as full siblings in *ABT* 5b, Slani supposedly marrying into the line of Ithel velyn o Ial (*HL* 5b). Neither of these two are credited with any progeny. I would thus put a tentative questionmark by them, and also by Idwal, Agnes and Rruel. In the case of reputed

---

181 *Ibid.*
182 *Ibid.*, pp. 98–9.
183 *Ibid.*, pp. 99–100.
184 *Ibid.*, p. 101.
185 *Ibid.*, p. 102.
186 *Ibid.*, p. 102.
187 *Ibid.*, p. 103.
188 *Ibid.*, p. 104.
189 *Ibid.*
190 *Ibid.*
191 *Ibid.*
192 *Ibid.*, p. 115.
193 *Ibid.*, p. 118.

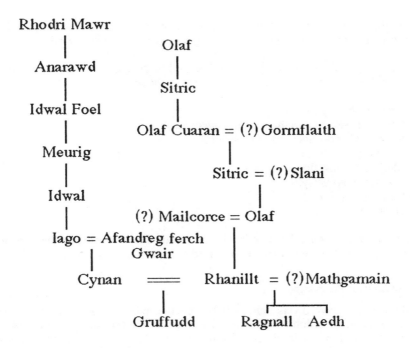

Figure 51

daughters of Gruffudd, including those with progeny, there may be grounds for some suspicion: fabrication of a daughter of a famous king was one of the ways in which families aggrandised themselves in their genealogies.

While some of the offspring of Gruffudd may have existed only in the minds of later generations, it is still true that Gruffudd had many notable, genuine descendants. These include his son Owain Gwynedd, his great-grandson Llywelyn the Great, Rhys Gryg, Gwenwynwyn ap Owain Cyfeiliog and many others. The name of Gruffudd ap Cynan is found in many of the early genealogies; it seems either that he was very prolific, or that claiming him as an ancestor conferred kudos upon the claimant, or, as appears most likely, a mixture of the two.

Gruffudd had allied with Rhys ap Tewdwr in 1081: Rhys's son Gruffudd later married Gwenllian ferch Gruffudd ap Cynan (this seems not, however, to have prevented Gruffudd ap Cynan from betraying Gruffudd ap Rhys to the Normans in 1115, although the link with Gwenllian may have been subsequent to this). Similarly, Gruffudd ap Cynan had acted together with Cadwgan ap Bleddyn in 1098. This Cadwgan also married Gwenllian, and Cadwgan's nephew, Madog ap Maredudd, is said to have married Susanna ferch Gruffudd. Another son of Bleddyn (albeit one unknown to the Welsh chronicles), Llywarch, was married to Rruel ferch Gruffudd. Gruffudd seems to have enjoyed reasonably friendly relations with the family of Bleddyn in the earlier twelfth century, but he refused to support Maredudd ap Bleddyn and the sons of Cadwgan against the Normans in

1121. He appears to have been a clever and able ruler, and he was undeniably a survivor; as an ally, however, he would appear to have been less reliable.

With Gruffudd ap Cynan, I come to the end of the explicitly named rulers of Gwynedd. However, attention should be paid to the following:

(1) Aeddan ab Blegywryd
(2) Cynan ap Seisyll and the sons of Cynan
(3) Maredudd and Ithel sons of Gruffudd
(4) Cynwrig ap Rhiwallon
(5) Meilir ap Rhiwallon
(6) Gwrgenau ap Seisyll
(7) Cadwgan ap Bleddyn
(8) Owain ab Edwin

All are known to have been active in the North, in some way, in the eleventh century, although none of them are referred to as having been rulers as such.

(1) Aeddan ab Blegywryd

Aeddan ab Blegywryd was slain in 1018, together with his four sons, by Llywe-lyn ap Seisyll, an action which is usually taken as marking the beginning of the reign of Llywelyn, the implication being that Aeddan was the previous ruler of Gwynedd. In point of fact, there is no real evidence for this latter assumption. Aeddan is completely obscure, apart from the manner of his death, and moreover is absent from all the mediaeval genealogical sources. It seems more probable that he was not a king, but a local noble of Gwynedd who was opposed to Llywelyn in the latter's rise to power, or who rebelled against him. The fact is that there is no explicitly named ruler of Gwynedd between the death of Cynan ap Hywel in 1003 and the Rhain episode of 1022 where Llywelyn ap Seisyll is accorded the status of king of Gwynedd by the Welsh chronicles. From this, it appears likely that in the early eleventh century there was no one overlord or supreme ruler in the North, but rather there were a number of minor, localised rulers, within different areas of Gwynedd. Aeddan was perhaps one such petty ruler, and Llywelyn ap Seisyll may have begun as another. The death of Aeddan in 1018 may mark the final stage of Llywelyn's acquisition of supremacy in the North.

It is interesting to note that not one of the known members of the Idwal Foel branch of the dynasty of Rhodri Mawr, which had been so successful in the later tenth century, remained. The last of the sons of Idwal Foel, Ieuaf, had died in 988. The sons of this Ieuaf were also all dead by the end of the 980s. Meurig ab Idwal Foel, who was blinded in 974, but whose death-date is unknown, had a son, Idwal, who died in 996. Cynan ap Hywel ab Ieuaf ab Idwal Foel had ruled Gwynedd for three years, before dying in 1003. The only other known member of the family was Iago ab Idwal ap Meurig, who succeeded to Gwynedd after the death of Llywelyn ap Seisyll in 1023. If the other sons of Ieuaf ab Idwal, Cadwallon and Maig, had left sons, these are now unknown.

Llywelyn ap Seisyll is first mentioned in the Welsh chronicles in 1018, in

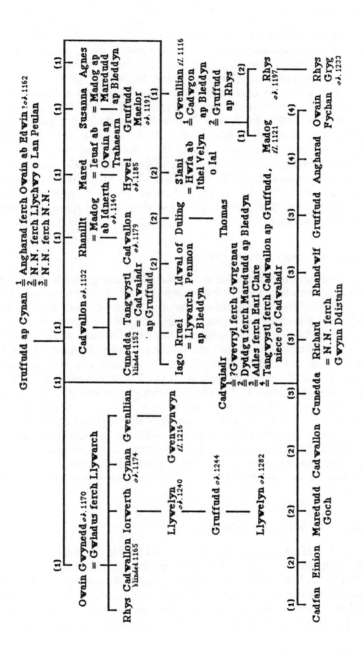

Figure 52

connexion with his slaying of Aeddan: he died in 1023. This would give him a reign of five years, supposing the death of Aeddan marked its commencement. However, it is entirely possible that his rule had begun before 1018, and that the latter date represents his achievement of the overlordship of Gwynedd.

Finally, *Liber Landauensis* mentions a 'Blegywryd son of Einion', a *vir famossimus*, who is usually thought to be meant to be the reputed counsellor of Hywel Dda, who is supposed to have been responsible for *Llyfr Blegywryd*.[194] Of the two documents in *Liber Landauensis* mentioning him, one is dated in the text to 955 (impossibly, as it claims Hywel Dda to be living), and the other has been assigned a date of *ca* 950 by Wendy Davies.[195] It might be suggested that this Blegywryd was the father of Aeddan – after all, the association of Aeddan with Gwynedd is simply an assumption arising from his fighting with Llywelyn ap Seisyll. Llywelyn did involve himself in the affairs of the South, challenging the Irish claimant to Deheubarth, Rhain, in 1022. It is thus barely possible that Aeddan was a south Welsh figure, and even a son of this Blegywryd. However, this is pure speculation, and there is no very obvious way of further illuminating our knowledge of Aeddan.

(2) Cynan ap Seisyll and the sons of Cynan

Cynan ap Seisyll is noted in the Welsh chronicles as having died in 1027. He was almost certainly a brother of Llywelyn ap Seisyll: *ABT* 7f, which recounts Llywelyn's descent from Prawst ferch Elise, includes Cynan as another of her sons. While nothing else is known of Cynan himself, the sons of Cynan are said in the chronicle-texts to have killed the south Welsh ruler Maredudd ab Edwin in 1035. While it is conceivable that these sons may have been offspring of Cynan ap Hywel rather than of Cynan ap Seisyll, the latter seems more likely, given the dates involved (Cynan ap Hywel died in 1003). This attack on a Southern ruler may suggest that the family of Llywelyn ap Seisyll continued to be significant after Llywelyn's death, maintaining an interest in events outside the North. While it cannot be proved, it is not impossible that Cynan himself held some power in Gwynedd after his brother's death: while the *Brutiau* state that Llywelyn was succeeded by Iago ab Idwal, this is not noted by them until 1033, which may suggest that before this date Iago was not sole ruler. (This would also argue for some influence over the North by the Southern king, Rhydderch ab Iestyn, in this period.)

(3) Maredudd and Ithel sons of Gruffudd

Maredudd and Ithel sons of Gruffudd were both killed in the battle of Mechain in 1069, fighting against Bleddyn and Rhiwallon sons of Cynfyn. Ithel and Rhiwallon both fell in the battle: Maredudd died of cold while fleeing. The wording of the *Annales Cambriae* does not give any information about the state of affairs in Gwynedd before this battle. *Brenhinedd y Saesson* claims that it was only after the battle that Bleddyn began to rule, a statement which the wording of *Brut y*

---

194 *LL*, charters 218 and 221.
195 Davies, *Llandaff Charters*, p. 120.

Tywysogion (Pen. 20 and RB) could be taken as supporting. This, however, is in conflict with the Anglo-Saxon Chronicle evidence that Bleddyn and Rhiwallon began to rule after the death of Gruffudd ap Llywelyn in 1063. It is possible that *Brenhinedd y Saesson* is referring to the start of Bleddyn's sole rule, without his brother Rhiwallon. Equally, it is possible that the text is in error: *Brenhinedd y Saesson* is in general the least reliable of the vernacular Welsh chronicles for this period.

Maredudd and Ithel are usually taken to be sons of Gruffudd ap Llywelyn, although this kinship is nowhere explicitly stated. However, there is no real reason to question that this is the case.

It is not known how old these sons were on the death of their father, nor is it known what they were doing 1063–1069. According to the evidence in non-Welsh sources, Bleddyn succeeded to his half-brother Gruffudd, and was in-volved in some of the English resistance to Willam I in the same period. It is thus a possibility that there may have been some instability within Gwynedd at this time, with a power struggle between Gruffudd's half-brothers, and his sons, with the latter being perhaps able to take advantage of circumstances attendant upon Bleddyn's being away with his English allies. Mechain would thus mark the end of the instability, and the beginning of the supremacy of Bleddyn.

(4) Cynwrig ap Rhiwallon

Cynwrig ap Rhiwallon is noticed in the vernacular annals only. He is said to have been slain in 1075 by the men of Gwynedd. *Historia Gruffud vab Kenan* claims that he had usurped Anglesey, and associates Gruffudd ap Cynan with his death.[196] There is no evidence in the annals to support this.

He does not seem to have been related to Rhiwallon ap Cynfyn, but rather may have been of the line of Tudur Trefor, a noble, not royal, family, according to *HL* 12.[197] He was a cousin of Rhys Sais (whose sons were responsible for the death of Gwrgenau ap Seisyll in 1081). This Rhys was supposedly associated with Maelor.

However, it should be noted that Cynwrig ap Rhiwallon ap Dingad of *HL* 12 may not be the Cynwrig ap Rhiwallon of the annals. *HL* 13[198] mentions a Cynwrig ap Rhiwallon of Maelor, and 'Cynwrig ap Rhiwallon ap Dingad' is included in *ABT* 9, a pedigree of Ednyfed Fychan.[199] Bartrum has assigned a date of *ca* 1090 to this Cynwrig ap Rhiwallon ap Dingad of *HL* 12 and *ABT* 9,[200] and *HL* 13 and suggests that this later Cynwrig has become confused with Cynwrig ap Rhiwallon of Maelor, whom he takes to be the Cynwrig who died in 1075. He seems to consider that this Cynwrig was also a member of the line of Tudur Trefor, and that the pedigrees have become corrupted in some way. This is possible, but the dangers of dating from pedigrees and generation lengths should be borne in mind.

196 ed. Evans, pp. 7–8.
197 Bartrum, *Tracts*, p. 119.
198 *Ibid.*
199 *Ibid.*, p. 103.
200 *Ibid.*, p. 153.

Why this Cynwrig was slain by the men of Gwynedd is not known. Perhaps he was unpopular, or becoming too powerful, or encroaching outside his own territory. But his position within the Welsh polity cannot really be reconstructed.

(5) Meilir ap Rhiwallon

Meilir ap Rhiwallon was a son of Rhiwallon ap Cynfyn, and hence a member of the family of Bleddyn, who was his paternal uncle. He was a participant in the battle of Mynydd Carn, fighting on the side of Trahaearn ap Caradog and Caradog ap Gruffudd. Like them, he was slain in the battle. His presence on the side of Trahaearn seems reasonable: Trahaearn was a first cousin of Bleddyn, and presumably therefore of Rhiwallon. He was thus a second cousin of Meilir. Meilir does not occur in the early genealogies.

(6) Gwrgenau ap Seisyll

According to the Welsh chronicles, Gwrgenau ap Seisyll was killed in 1081 by the sons of Rhys Sais. The *obit* is placed after the account of the battle of Mynydd Carn. Nothing else is known of him in the annals, but *Historia Gruffud vab Kenan* describes him as the ally of Trahaearn ap Caradog at the battle of Bron-y-Erw in 1075, and associates him with the 'usurping' activities of Trahaearn in Gwynedd, claiming that he came from a Powys family.[201] The reliability of this text is not certain, but this assertion is interesting nonetheless, especially in the light of the evidence of the early pedigree material. Trahaearn, Gwrgenau's supposed ally, was a first cousin of the former ruler of Gwynedd, Bleddyn ap Cynfyn. The pedigree *HL 8*, *Gwyr Arfon*, is concerned with a line into which Lleucu, daughter of Gwrgenau, married.[202] *HL* 8 section c reads as follows:

Lleuku ferch Wrgeneu ap Seissyllt ap Ithel ap Gwerystan ap Gwaithfoed oedd fam Iorwerth a Chynwric a Thrgyr

Lleucu daughter of Gwrgenau ap Seisyll ap Ithel ap Gwerystan ap Gwaithfoed was the mother of Iorwerth and Cynwrig and Trygyr

It is the name Gwerystan ap Gwaithfoed in this pedigree which is significant. This is the same name as that usually given for the grandfather of Bleddyn ap Cynfyn. If the two are identical, then Gwrgenau was a second cousin to Bleddyn, and possibly also a kinsman of Trahaearn. His possible relationship to Bleddyn is given in figure 53.

If Gwrgenau was indeed an ally of Trahaearn, then his death in 1081 can be seen as a consequence of Trahaearn's fall. If he had originated in Powys, then he might have been resented in Gwynedd, or he might have been thought to have been infringing on the rights of another family. There is no particular reason to suppose his death was arranged by Gruffudd ap Cynan, but it may have been an indirect result of the latter's coming to power (albeit briefly).

201 ed. Evans, pp. 10 and 13.
202 Bartrum, *Tracts*, p. 117.

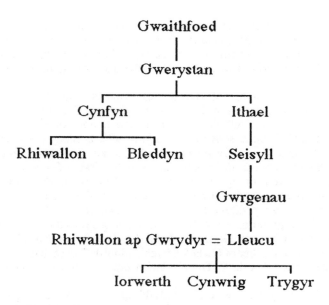

Figure 53

Other than the pedigree cited above, Gwrgenau does not feature in the medi-aeval genealogies.

(7) Cadwgan ap Bleddyn

A full discussion of Cadwgan ap Bleddyn will be found *sub* Powys. He was active, however, throughout most of Wales in the later eleventh century, mostly involved in conflicts with the Normans. As far as Gwynedd is concerned, Cadwgan was active there in 1094 (though only according to the *Brutiau*), meeting and defeating a Norman force at Coedysbys. In 1098, he was part of the Welsh force that was besieged on Anglesey by Hugh of Chester and Hugh of Shrewsbury. Cadwgan fled from the island with Gruffudd ap Cynan, and took refuge in Ireland. In 1099, he and Gruffudd returned to Wales. Cadwgan made peace with the Normans, and was able to gain possession of Ceredigion and part of Powys, possibly through Norman gift.

The interest that Cadwgan had in Gwynedd does not require a great deal of explanation. He was one of the leaders of anti-Norman action throughout Wales, although he later came to terms with them. Moreover, Gwynedd had formed part of the territory ruled by his father Bleddyn ap Cynfyn 1063–1075. His own main sphere of action was, however, Powys.

(8) Owain ab Edwin

Owain ab Edwin was a brother of Uchdryd ab Edwin, who was discussed *sub* Deheubarth, and a son of Iwerydd ferch Cynfyn, the (half) sister of Bleddyn and Rhiwallon, sons of Cynfyn. It was this Owain who lead the Normans to Anglesey

95

in 1098, but he then deserted them after the slaying of Earl Hugh of Shrewsbury, and led a rebellion himself. His activities in this year are recorded in the *Brutiau* only. His *obit* is found in both the *Brutiau* and *Annales Cambriae*, however; he died in 1105, apparently of natural causes (after a long illness, according to the *Brutiau*).

He appears in a number of genealogical sources, and also in one of the genealogical accounts found in the *Brutiau*, which notes that his daughter Angharad was a wife of Gruffudd ap Cynan, and mother of Owain Gwynedd, Cadwallon and Cadwaladr sons of Gruffudd as well as many unnamed daughters.[203] ABT 2, *Plant Owain Gwynedd*, includes Owain since his grand-daughter Cristin ferch Goronwy was the mother of several of Owain Gwynedd's children. His pedigree is given through Iwerydd back to Rhodri Mawr.[204] ABT 5, *Plant Gruffudd ap Cynan*, mentions Owain as the father of Angharad wife of Gruffudd but does not give her pedigree beyond Owain himself.[205] HL 4, *Llywth Bran*, includes him as a grandfather of Rhael, who married into the line of Bran and was a daughter of his son Goronwy.[206] HL 13, *Llywth Penllyn*, also mentions Owain, here as grandfather of Gwladus ferch Aldud ab Owain, but again does not take the line beyond Owain.[207] These relationships are shown in figures 54 and 55.

His daughter Angharad, wife of Gruffudd ap Cynan, is one of the very few women whose death is noticed by the Welsh chronicles, in the year 1162. Owain himself is an interesting figure: he is quite prominent in the pedigrees, which suggests that descent from him was worth mentioning. Yet little is known of his career, and he himself is relatively undocumented. Owain is thus a minor figure, but perhaps one who was more important in his own time than the records suggest.

It may thus be seen that, in Gwynedd in the tenth century there was a pattern of domination of the political scene by the dynasty of Rhodri Mawr, as was the case in Deheubarth. And, as in Deheubarth, this pattern broke down in the eleventh century, with the appearance of so-called 'intrusive' rulers. However, the situation in Gwynedd is made more complicated by the fact that several of its 'intrusive' rulers, such as Llywelyn ap Seisyll, Gruffudd ap Llywelyn and Bleddyn ap Cynfyn, were connected to the dynasty of Rhodri (although in an indirect way) through Angharad ferch Maredudd, and perhaps through Prawst ferch Elise. Prawst, if she existed, would have been a member of the Northern Branch of the dynasty; Angharad was part of the Southern Branch. It is tempting to speculate that the marriage of Angharad to Llywelyn was an attempt to ally North and South, or to improve the claim of Llywelyn and his progeny to all Wales, a policy used in the ninth century by Rhodri Mawr himself. Llywelyn ap Seisyll was active in both north and south Wales: his son Gruffudd succeeded in holding both

---

203 *ByT* (Pen. 20) *s.a.* 1122 (*recte* 1125) and 1161 (*recte* 1162); *ByT* (RB) *s.a.* 1122 (*recte* 1125) and 1160 (*recte* 1162); *ByS s.a.* 1122 (*recte* 1125) and 1161 (*recte* 1162).
204 Bartrum, *Tracts*, pp. 96–7.
205 *Ibid.*, pp. 98–9.
206 *Ibid.*, p. 115.
207 *Ibid.*, p. 119.

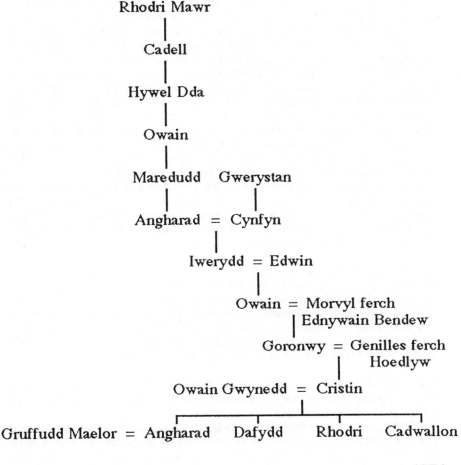

Rhodri Mawr
|
Cadell
|
Hywel Dda
|
Owain
|
Maredudd   Gwerystan
| |
Angharad = Cynfyn
          |
Iwerydd = Edwin
         |
Owain = Morvyl ferch
       | Ednywain Bendew
Goronwy = Genilles ferch
         | Hoedlyw
Owain Gwynedd = Cristin
              |
Gruffudd Maelor = Angharad   Dafydd   Rhodri   Cadwallon

ABT 2

Figure 54

under his control. Since Maredudd ab Owain ap Hywel Dda died in 999, and his son-in-law is first heard of in 1018, the date of the marriage is of some interest, although it cannot be known with any accuracy. It presumably predates Angharad's marriage to Cynfyn ap Gwerystan, since her son by Llywelyn, Gruffudd, was active from 1039 while her sons by Cynfyn, Bleddyn and Rhiwallon, are not active until 1063 in the extant records. Even by the most generous estimates, Gruffudd must have been in his mid-forties at the time of his death, and was probably older: Bleddyn may have been anything up to twenty years his junior. The death-dates of their respective sons are interesting in this context: one of Gruffudd's sons may have predeceased him, and it is fairly likely that this son was adult, as minors do not tend to feature in the early Welsh chronicles.

97

Gruffudd's other two sons are found contesting for Gwynedd in 1069, and are again presumably adult. However, on Gruffudd's death, the kingdom had been granted to his half-brothers rather than to any of his sons, which may suggest that they were relatively young. The sons of Bleddyn nearly all lived into the twelfth century, apart from two who were killed in battle in 1088. Two other sons died, again by violence, in 1111. Maredudd ap Bleddyn seems to have died of natural causes in 1132. It is a long stretch of time to be covered by three generations (Angharad, born no later than 999/1000; Bleddyn probably born after 1023, and possibly closer to 1039; Maredudd who was still active in the early twelfth century, and who may have been in his sixties or seventies at his death, so born perhaps 1065 × 1070). Even allowing for the fact that some of these sons were born late in their fathers' lives, it would seem that Angharad was married to Llywelyn by about 1020 at the latest, and probably before that.

Llywelyn ap Seisyll created not so much a dynasty as a network of staggered kinship, a strange phenomenon which successfully dominated north Wales for much of the eleventh century, and continued to be successful into the twelfth, in the persons of the sons of Bleddyn and their descendants. Members of this loose network are found ruling as follows:

?1018–1023 Llywelyn ap Seisyll
?1023–?1027 Cynan ap Seisyll, brother of the above
1039–1063 Gruffudd ap Llywelyn, son of Llywelyn ap Seisyll
1063–1069 Bleddyn and Rhiwallon sons of Cynfyn, half-brothers of the above,
    and probably in conflict with Gruffudd's sons Maredudd and Ithel
1069–1075 Bleddyn ap Cynfyn, half-brother of Gruffudd ap Llywelyn
1075–1081 Trahaearn ap Caradog, first cousin of Bleddyn

This is a total period of forty-seven years (fifty-one if Cynan is included): indeed, since it is probable that Llywelyn ap Seisyll began reigning before 1018, the total was probably rather more than fifty years.

Who was in power in the remaining parts of the century? It is not always clear. Certainly, the century opened with the North under the control of a scion of the Northern Branch of the dynasty of Rhodri Mawr, Cynan ap Hywel, who ruled 1000–1003. There is then a blank, until Llywelyn ap Seisyll first appears in 1018 (compare the blank in south Wales 999–1023). Attempts have been made to fill this gap by attributing rule to Aeddan ap Blegywryd, but as has been said above, there is no real evidence for this. However, the similar gap in the Southern record may indicate that there is a deficiency in the sources, which certainly have very few entries for the early eleventh century. Of this handful, a fair number are concerned with England and Ireland. Iago ab Idwal, of the line of Idwal Foel, seemingly ruled from Llywelyn's death in 1023 to 1039. However, he is not actually mentioned in the Welsh chronicles until 1033, and although the *Brutiau* claim that he ruled after Llywelyn, the period 1023–1033 is again very thinly documented (three short entries in all). One of these entries, for 1025 (*recte* 1027) records the death of Cynan ap Seisyll, the brother of Llywelyn. Could Iago and Cynan have been co-rulers 1023–1027? It is possible: and if this is the case, it adds four more years to the period of power of the kin network originating with Llywelyn ap Seisyll.

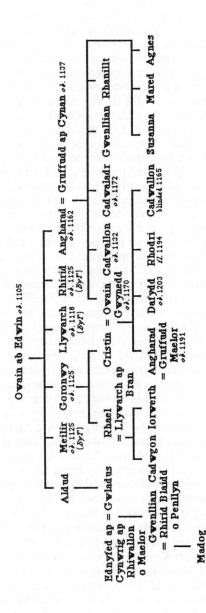

Figure 55

The period from 1081 to the end of the century is confusing. A great deal of this may be attributed to the activities of the Normans, who made large gains in north Wales at this time. Gruffudd ap Cynan was active from 1075, but initially does not seem to have held much territory, and that only intermittently, being a captive of the Normans for a period of uncertain length between 1081 and 1098. Who was ruling meantime? Rhys ap Tewdwr held the supremacy in the South until 1093, coming into conflict with the sons of Bleddyn ap Cynfyn in 1088. Cadwgan ap Bleddyn was apparently leading the Northern resistance in 1094. However, no one individual seems to have been predominant: there again seems to have been a number of locally powerful figures, but without any clear over-lord. These local leaders were probably such people as the sons of Bleddyn and Owain ab Edwin. The true rise to power of Gruffudd ap Cynan belongs to the twelfth century, and to the decrease of Norman power in Gwynedd.

It is necessary to point out, however, that almost none of the eleventh-century rulers of Gwynedd was really 'intrusive' (even if a link with the dynasty of Rhodri Mawr be supposed a necessity), with the possible exception of Trahaearn ap Caradog. Llywelyn ap Seisyll may have been a member indirectly of the Northern Branch of the dynasty of Rhodri Mawr, or this connection may have been fabricated in later times, but in his own time he seems to have been recognised as a rightful ruler, in so far as it is possible to tell from the Welsh chronicles, which do not tend to comment upon such things. Gruffudd ap Llywelyn may have inherited this link to the Northern Branch from his father, and certainly had one to the Southern Branch via his mother Angharad (whose father Maredudd ab Owain ap Hywel Dda had ruled Gwynedd briefly in the later tenth century). He also had the far more powerful claim of being the son of a former king. His status is probably reflected by the short panegyric upon his prowess found in the Welsh chronicles for the year 1039. Bleddyn ap Cynfyn was both a son of Angharad and a brother of Gruffudd – and it was not uncommon for a brother to succeed at this period (consider Hywel and Cadwallon, sons of Ieuaf in the late tenth century, or Maredudd and Rhys sons of Owain in the third quarter of the eleventh). Like Gruffudd, he was the subject of praise in the Welsh chronicles, and the fortunes of his sons and grandsons play a large part in the annalistic record of the following century. Cynan ap Hywel, Iago ab Idwal, and Gruffudd ap Cynan were all descendants of Idwal Foel, and if Llywelyn ap Seisyll was a son of Prawst ferch Elise, then he and his son Gruffudd were cousins of this group. These relationships appear in figure 56.

What is most noticeable about the loose kinship network that began with Llywelyn is that their relationships to one another are predominantly through female links. This is certainly the case with Gruffudd ap Llywelyn and Bleddyn, and very probably the case with Bleddyn and Trahaearn. Links through women could be important – the prominence accorded to Gruffudd ap Cynan's maternal Irish kin in *Historia Gruffud vab Kenan* as opposed to his paternal kin bears witness to this. The pattern of domination in north Wales in the eleventh century seems to suggest that such links could be – and were – used where politic, but nowhere do the Welsh chronicles seem to imply that such links were vital for a king to be recognised at this time. In the end it was probably personal ability and charisma that were significant in the maintenance of power and position.

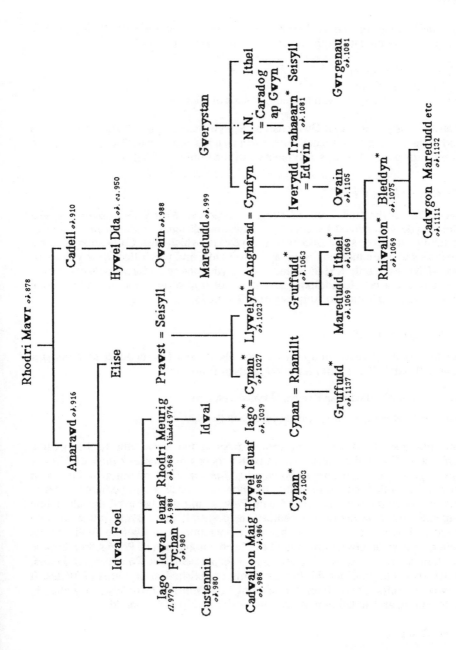

Individuals marked * had rule in North Wales in the eleventh century.

Figure 56

POWYS

The individuals named as having had some connection with Powys and/or Meirionydd in the late tenth and eleventh centuries are as follows:

(1) 'Cadwallon ab Ieuaf'
(2) Bleddyn ap Cynfyn
(3) Cadwgan, Iorwerth, and Maredudd, sons of Bleddyn

It also seems possible that Gwrgenau ap Seisyll was associated with Powys: he is said to have come from thence in *Historia Gruffud vab Kenan*[208] and his pedigree would indicate that he was a connection of the family of Bleddyn ap Cynfyn.

(1) 'Cadwallon ab Ieuaf'

According to the Red Book of Hergest version of *Brut y Tywysogion*, in 986 Meirionydd was gained by craft by Cadwallon ab Ieuaf.[209] The name is almost certainly an error, since 986 was the year in which this Cadwallon lost his territories to Maredudd ab Owain ap Hywel Dda, and was killed. *Brut y Tywysogion* (RB) is the only text to include Meirinydd amongst Maredudd's conquests, but it is a reasonable addition, and it is not improbable that Maredudd took Meirionydd in addition to Anglesey and Gwynedd.

(2) Bleddyn ap Cynfyn

For the career of Bleddyn ap Cynfyn see above, *sub* Gwynedd. *Brut y Tywysogion* (RB only), in the entry for 1069 reads as follows:[210]

Ac yna y kynhelis Bledyn ap Kynuyn Gwyned a Phowys

And then Bleddyn ap Cynfyn held Gwynedd and Powys.

This reference to Bleddyn acquiring Powys at the same time as he became supreme in Gwynedd is absent from both versions of *Annales Cambriae, Brut y Tywysogion* (Pen. 20) and *Brenhinedd y Saesson*. The mention of Powys in connection with Bleddyn is of interest, however, since in the pedigree material this family tends to be associated with Powys, and it is believed that their line originated there. In the twelfth century, the descendants of Bleddyn were mainly based in Powys. It is possible that the association began before Bleddyn: his father, Cynfyn ap Gwerystan, may have been a nobleman of Powys. In addition, the family are the subject of the later genealogical text *Rhandiroedd Powys*, which seems to consider the line as firmly established in that area of Wales. It may be, therefore, that rather than gaining Powys in 1069, Bleddyn may already have held it, and added to it in 1069 the overlordship of Gwynedd.

---

208 ed. Evans, p. 10.
209 *ByT* (RB), *s.a.* [986].
210 *ByT* (RB), ed. & transl. Jones, pp. 27–8.

(3) The sons of Bleddyn ap Cynfyn

Aspects of the careers of Iorwerth and Cadwagan sons of Bleddyn have already been discussed *sub* Gwynedd and Deheubarth. From this it can be seen that Cadwgan in particular was active throughout Wales, driving Rhys ap Tewdwr out of Deheubarth in 1088, ravaging Dyfed after Rhys's death in 1093, attacking and defeating the Normans at Coedysbys in Gwynedd in 1094. He was probably the main power in the North in the 1080s and earlier 1090s, and it is interesting that it was to the sons of Bleddyn that Robert de Bellême appealed in 1102 for assistance in his rebellion against Henry I, and not to Gruffudd ap Cynan. Cadwgan is said to have acquired Powys at least twice: in 1099 he received it, apparently by Norman grant, on his return from Ireland, and in 1102 he was given it by his brother Iorwerth. Iorwerth had been encouraged to desert Robert de Bellême by Henry I, and in return had received grants of Powys, Ceredigion (which had been part of the territory ascribed to Cadwgan in 1099), Ystrad Tywi, Cydweli, Gower and half of Dyfed. Given that in the vernacular annals the entry recording this transaction is prone to eulogise Iorwerth, it is possible that Ceredigion and Powys were included by the annalist to aggrandise Iorwerth – of all the lands he was given by Henry, only Ceredigion and Powys, which Iorwerth supposedly immediately gave to Cadwgan, were not revoked almost at once by the English king. Henry is said in the same year to have granted Dyfed to a knight named Saer, and Gower, Ystrad Tywi and Cydweli to Hywel ap Goronwy. (It is of course possible that Ceredigion and Powys, though held by Cadwgan, were offered to Iorwerth because Cadwgan was in rebellion, and Iorwerth did not wish to dispossess his brother.) It should be borne in mind that Powys, although greatly pressurised by the Normans at this time, was the probable homeland of the family of Bleddyn, and it is in this area that the line is found active in later years. The long text *Rhandiroedd Powys* is a witness to this association. The text survives in various manuscripts, and has been edited by Bartrum.[211] The earliest manuscript containing it is BL Additional Manuscript 14919 fos. 118r–121v, dated 1493 on fo. 118r, and possibly written by Gutun Owain. This is a very important text on the family of Bleddyn ap Cynfyn as it describes, or purports to describe, the division of Powys amongst Bleddyn's descendants. The title is found only in the later manuscripts. The early manuscripts containing it have been listed by Bartrum as follows:[212]

BL Additional MS 14919 fos. 118r–121v, 1493
BL Additional MS 14967 fos. 167v–168v, by Gutun Owain ?*ca* 1495
Ibid., fos. 168v–170v, by Edward ap Roger (*ob.* 1587)
Peniarth MS 127 pp. 231–238, by Syr Thomas ap Ieuan ap Deicws, *ca* 1510
Peniarth MS 130 pp. 80–92, first half of the sixteenth century
Peniarth MS 132 pp. 135–40, attributed by Robert Vaughan of Hengwrt to Lewys
    Morgannwg, but more probably by Lewys ab Edward (*fl. ca* 1560)

---

[211] 'Rhandiroedd Powys', ed. Bartrum.
[212] 'Rhandiroedd Powys', ed. Bartrum, pp. 231–2.

The text deals with the 'traditional' units of Powys Fadog and Powys Wenwynwyn, and as such is anachronistic in its early parts; these divisions did not apply in the eleventh century. The latest individuals mentioned in the line of Powys Fadog are Tudur, Elise and Gruffudd Fychan, sons of Gruffudd, who were all born probably around 1430. The latest individuals mentioned in the line of Powys Wenwynwyn are John and Elizabeth, children of Sir Richard Grey, who were born around 1460. Bartrum suggests that BL Add. 14919 may be the original of the text. He considers it of little significance because it makes few genealogical or territorial statements that are not known from any earlier source.[213] However, it seems to me that the bringing together of all this material into one text is significant in itself: possibly some branch of the family in the fifteenth century needed to prove its status and show the age of its line. It undeniably reinforces the idea that Bleddyn's family was associated with Powys. It repeats the possibly erroneous statement that Iwerydd ferch Cynfyn was a daughter of Angharad ferch Maredudd, in conflict with the *Brutiau*, which seems to have been a common belief, whose validity cannot be discovered with any certainty.

Interestingly, *Rhandiroedd Powys* attributes the rule of all Powys not to Cadwgan or to Iorwerth, but to a third brother, Maredudd, and the division of the territory is said to have occurred on his death, when the kingdom was split between his sons. This is understandable: Cadwgan and Iorwerth were both killed in 1111, Maredudd survived until 1132 and became quite powerful, although his earlier career was unedifying (he was imprisoned by Iorwerth 1102–1107, and is not heard of between his escape and his succession to Iorwerth in 1111). He was prominent from 1111, however. It would seem that land and power passed between the brothers – and was sometimes shared, as may have been the case with Cadwgan and Iorwerth. Transitions were not always smooth: it is worth noting that, although Cadwgan and Iorwerth both died in 1111, Iorwerth was slain first, and upon his death Henry I granted Powys to Cadwgan. (Cadwgan had been under a cloud owing to the activities of his son Owain, and in 1110 Henry had imprisoned him and given his lands to Gilbert FitzRichard.) Maredudd did not acquire the territory until after the death of Cadwgan. Powys seems to have been the family territory – Iorwerth and Cadwgan both fell victim to the ambition of their nephew Madog ap Rhirid, son of the Rhirid ap Bleddyn who was killed in 1088. The supremacy of this family in Powys can be seen in the early twelfth century at least, in the probable order Cadwgan, Iorwerth/Cadwgan, Cadwgan (Iorwerth was imprisoned 1102–1110), Iorwerth/Cadwgan, Maredudd. Before them, influence and control was probably wielded by their father Bleddyn, and their cousin Gwrgenau ap Seisyll.

The sons of Bleddyn were prolific, and feature in many genealogical sources. Early pedigrees including them are listed below.

(i) Cadwgan

 Brut y Tywysogion (Pen. 20 and RB) and *Brenhinedd y Saesson* in the entry for 1116 list the brothers of Owain ap Cadwgan and their mothers.

---

[213] *Ibid.*, p. 231.

ABT 8e *Llyma Iach Vathraval Tywysogion Powys/Plant Bleddyn ap Cynfyn*
lists Cadwgan as father of Owain and Madog 'gwelyth gwyr Nannau'.[214]
ABT 8i, a genealogy of his grandson Cadwallon ap Madog, son of Madog ap
Cadwgan and Gwenllian ferch Gruffudd ap Cynan.[215]

(ii) Madog and Rhirid sons of Bleddyn (both killed 1088 in battle with Rhys ap
Tewdwr)
ABT 8a Rhirid and Madog both said to have had the same mother.[216]

(iii) Iorwerth
ABT 8c gives the mother of Iorwerth.[217]

(iv) Maredudd
MG 3, a pedigree of Madog ap Maredudd, going back to Beli Mawr (see
above, *sub* Bleddyn ap Cynfyn).[218]
JC 27, a pedigree of Maredudd's great-gransdson, Rhys Gryg, to whom he
was related in the female line. This is the corrupt pedigree which records
the connexion of Trahaearn ap Caradog to this family by incorrectly
making him a son of Angharad ferch Maredudd.[219]
JC 29, a pedigree of Llywelyn ap Iorwerth through his mother, going back to
Maredudd.[220]
ABT 1b, a pedigree of the mother of Llywelyn ap Iorwerth, including Maredudd, and going back to Beli Mawr (see *sub* Bleddyn ap Cynfyn).[221]
ABT 1d the mother of Maredudd.[222]
ABT 3b Dyddgu ferch Maredudd given as the mother of Einion and Maredudd Goch and Cadwallon sons of Cadwaladr ap Gruffudd ap Cynan.[223]
ABT 8 section b his mother; section f his sons and their mother; section g the
descent of Gwenwynwyn from him, and beyond to Beli Mawr; section h
his grandson Iorwerth.[224]

The sons of Bleddyn and their descendants are shown in figures 57–59.

Powys is much more difficult to chart in the eleventh century than Gwynedd or
Deheubarth, and in the later part of the century, like much of the North, it
suffered at Norman hands. It seems possible that it formed part of the territory of
the Idwal Foel branch of the family of Rhodri Mawr in the late tenth century.
Thereafter there is no clear evidence, but it is likely that Powys was part of the

---

214 Bartrum, *Tracts*, p. 102.
215 *Ibid.*, p. 103.
216 *Ibid.*, p. 102.
217 *Ibid.*
218 *Ibid.*, p. 39.
219 *Ibid.*, p. 47.
220 *Ibid.*
221 *Ibid.*, pp. 95–6.
222 *Ibid.*, p. 96.
223 *Ibid.*, p. 98.
224 *Ibid.*, pp. 102–3.

territory of Gruffudd ap Llywelyn 1039–1063, and possibly of his father Llywelyn 1018–1023. The family of Bleddyn ap Cynfyn seem to have originated there, and were perhaps originally a local noble family. With the rise to power of Bleddyn, this family became more prominent, and Powys became their power base. It is interesting to speculate that Gruffudd ap Llywelyn may have placed his half-brothers Rhiwallon and Bleddyn as sub-kings in Powys before his death. If this were the case, then they would have already had strength and status at the death of Gruffudd, unlike his sons. This may have contributed to the success that Bleddyn enjoyed as king of north Wales.

It is also notable that the three families of Trahaearn ap Caradog, Bleddyn ap Cynfyn and Elystan Glodrydd – the noble lines of Arwystli, Powys, and Buellt respectively – are all claimed to be interlinked by both ancestry and intermarriage. Whether or not their common descent from Tegonwy ap Teon is accepted, it is clear that at some point these families were regarded as coming from a common stock. In the later years of the eleventh century, these families, from Powys and its neighbours, are increasingly prominent in the political scene. They seem to have been in the process of acquiring princely, if not royal, power, and their activities spread out across most of Wales, affecting far more than their own original regions. The sons of Bleddyn were perhaps the most successful at this. Their line continued to be important into the twelfth century and beyond, forming links with other, older, dynasties. In particular, they interbred with the family of Gruffudd ap Cynan: this was sound political sense in the troubled twelfth century when Gruffudd and his sons were dominant in north Wales. It has the interesting side effect that later figures such as Llywelyn the Great and Rhys Gryg, descendants of Gruffudd ap Cynan (Rhys in the female line) were also descendants of the family of Bleddyn ap Cynfyn of Powys.

MORGANNWG

It is difficult to trace activites within this area of Wales in the extant Welsh annals – in the early mediaeval period there is only one direct mention of Glamorgan, in 992. The kings of this area are barely noted in the annals: in the eleventh century there is a notice of the death of one king of the Glamorgan dynasty, and a notice of the capture by vikings of another. However, there is a certain amount of evidence to be gleaned from *Liber Landauensis*,[225] although information from this text should be treated with considerable care, as its reliability cannot always be guaranteed. The problems presented by the apparently eleventh century charters in this document are discussed in detail in chapter V.

From this text, and from the annals, a rough succession may be reconstructed for the area, although as with Gwynedd it is not always possible to be sure in which area within Morgannwg a given ruler held sway. Individuals to be considered are as follows:

[225] *LL*, charters 246, 249a, 249b, 251, 253, 255, 257, 258, 259, 260, 261, 262, 263, 264a, 264b, 267, 271, 272, and 274.

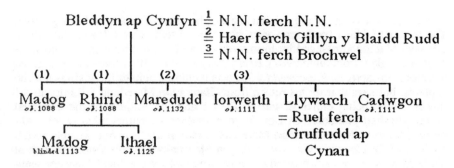

Figure 57

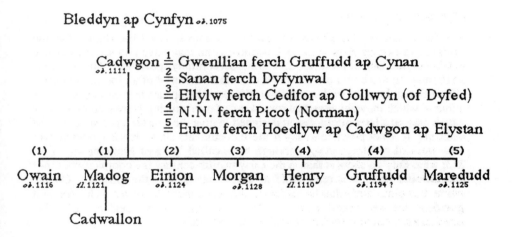

Figure 58

(1) Maredudd ab Owain ap Hywel Dda
(2) Rhydderch ab Iestyn
(3) Hywel ab Owain
(4) Meurig ap Hywel
(5) Gruffudd ap Rhydderch
(6) Cadwgan ap Meurig
(7) Caradog ap Gruffudd

(1) Maredudd ab Owain ap Hywel Dda

Maredudd ab Owain ap Hywel Dda invaded Morgannwg with a force of Hiberno-Scandinavians mercenaries in 992, and ravaged it. Since Maredudd's own lands had been raided by his nephew Edwin ab Einion and the English in the same year, this may have been either a punitive expedition (supposing that Edwin

107

had influence in Glamorgan, but this cannot be proved) or a search for plunder. The account of his expedition varies from text to text. *Brut y Tywysogion* (Pen. 20) says Maredudd ravaged by hiring vikings and ransoming captives (presumably those taken from him in 987). *Brut y Tywysogion* (RB) records the hiring, but mentions no captives. *Brenhinedd y Saesson* mentions neither the vikings nor the captives, but says that on his return from Glamorgan Maredudd fell into 'their' power, 'they' being either Edwin ab Einion and the English or the unnamed group who had plundered St Davids, in Maredudd's territory, also in 992. *Annales Cambriae* do not mention Maredudd's raid at all. It is not possible to tell from *Liber Landauensis* who was ruling in Morgannwg at this time, although at the beginning of the eleventh century representatives of two local dynasties seem to be ruling in parts of the area.[226]

(2) Rhydderch ab Iestyn

For the career of Rhydderch ab Iestyn, see above, *sub* Deheubarth. On the evidence of two charters in *Liber Landauensis* he may have had some influence in Glamorgan. One of these, *LL* 253, is almost certainly spurious.[227] The other, *LL* 264b, may be more reliable, although it contains material of a type conventional within the style of *Liber Landauensis*. Rhydderch appears in this text only as a witness, which may either reflect some kind of overlordship possessed by him, or which may be a later interpolation designed to give the charter a greater apparent authority. It is not possible to say if these documents show that Rhydderch ever was overlord of Morgannwg, although he is called 'king of Morgannwg' in *LL* 253; what they do show is that in the early twelfth century the compilers of *Liber Landauensis* thought it reasonable to claim that he had this position. On the whole it is quite likely that he had some influence there, however, as his son and grandson are also found active in this area, again on the evidence of *Liber Landauensis*, but also on that of the Welsh chronicles.

(3) Hywel ab Owain

The death of Hywel ab Owain is noted in the Welsh chronicles in 1043, in all texts with the exception of *Annales Cambriae* (C). In the *Brutiau* he is called king of Glamorgan, and is said to have died in extreme old age. He is found in two of the Llandaff charters,[228] in one of them in conjunction with his son Meurig, and would seem to have been active from quite early on in the eleventh century. In *LL* 255 it is his son Meurig who is called king, and it may be that Meurig was ruling in his father's lifetime, either as sub-king, or due to his father's age. *Liber*

---

221 *Ibid.*, pp. 95–6.
222 *Ibid.*, p. 96.
223 *Ibid.*, p. 98.
224 *Ibid.*, pp. 102–3.
225 *LL*, charters 246, 249a, 249b, 251, 253, 255, 257, 258, 259, 260, 261, 262, 263, 264a, 264b, 267, 271, 272, and 274.
226 *LL*, charters 246, 249b, 251, and 257.
227 Davies, *Llandaff Charters*, p. 126.
228 *LL*, charter 257 – Hywel called king; with Meurig, 255.

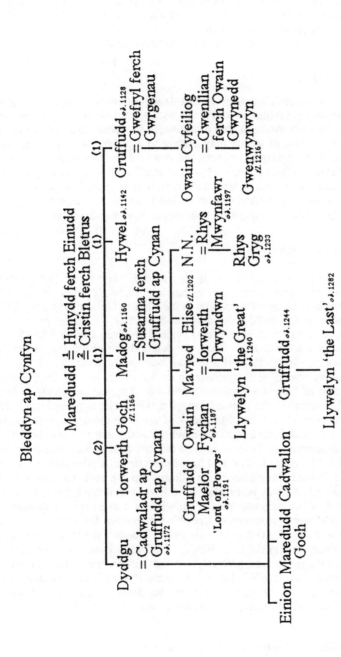

Figure 59

Landauensis also refers to Hywel as a sub-king of Rhydderch ab Iestyn,[229] a state of affairs which is not impossible, but which should not be regarded as proved on the testimony of *Liber Landauensis* alone.

There are no references to Hywel in any of the early pedigrees.

(4) Meurig ap Hywel

According to all the Welsh chronicles except *Annales Cambriae* (B), Meurig ap Hywel was captured by vikings in 1039. His escape and subsequent career are not noted, but he cannot have remained a captive, as he occurs in a number of the Llandaff charters, several of which may belong to a period subsequent to this. The core of most of them may be reliable, but it would be inadvisable to depend upon them for details of his career.[230] However, the fact that he occurs with his father in two of them, and without him in the rest, may suggest that at least some of them date from after his father's death in 1043, and hence after his capture. Again, Meurig is not noted in any of the mediaeval genealogical sources.

(5) Gruffudd ap Rhydderch

Gruffudd ap Rhydderch is found in one of the Llandaff charters, *LL* 264a, where he is described as 'rex morcannuc'. Davies has assigned to it a date of *ca* 1030, on grounds of the progression of witnesses in the Llandaff charters as a whole.[231] This would mean that Gruffudd was ruling in his father's lifetime, perhaps as another sub-king together with Hywel ab Owain. However, I have reservations about both the date and the charter. These are detailed elsewhere, but, in brief, I find the inclusion of Gruffudd in this charter somewhat unlikely. The entire charter has the air of having been rewritten in favour of Llandaff (perhaps at the time of compilation of *Liber Landauensis*), and would appear originally to have been a grant to Llangynfyl. The grantor, Seisyll ap Gistlerth, appeared in *LL* 259 as a man of Meurig ap Hywel, but like many of the individuals named in *Liber Landauensis* he may have been a local noble who was capable of acting both with and without royal permission. I would suggest that the charter has been tampered with at Llandaff, and Bishop Joseph and his immediate associates added into the record. Gruffudd himself may also be an addition to the text, to give it more authority; alternatively he may be original to it. However, if the latter is the case, I do not see that 1030 is a reasonable date, for while it is true that the witness list contains people who were associates of Joseph's predecessor Bleddri (d.*ca* 1022), there is also one witness who occurs in a charter of Joseph's successor, Herewald (consecrated at some time in the later 1050s). Gruffudd's own period of activity is 1044–1055/6, though he was probably around before that, although not of kingly status. Joseph died in 1045, but as it is likely that he is not original to the charter, this latter date is not a restriction on the dating of *LL* 264a. I would suggest a date of *ca* 1040–1055/6. (On this, see below, chapter V.)

---

229 *The Text of the Book of Llan Dâv*, edd. Evans & Rhys, p. 252.
230 *LL*, charters 249a, 255, 259, 261, and 263.
231 Davies, *Llandaff Charters*, p. 128.

110

From this document, it is not possible to say whether Gruffudd and his kin were rulers in Morgannwg. However, given that three generations of the family feature in *Liber Landauensis*, it seems probable.

(6) Cadwgan ap Meurig

Cadwgan ap Meurig, son of Meurig ap Hywel, is known only from *Liber Landauensis*. He occurs in *LL* 259, 260, 261, 263, 267. In 260 and 267 his brother Rhys is also named. Most of these charters may contain some reliable material (260 is spurious),[232] although they cannot be depended upon for details of Cadwgan's career. They do however bear witness to his reign, which probably ended around 1075. He does not occur in any early genealogical text.

(7) Caradog ap Gruffudd ap Rhydderch

For the main career of Caradog ap Gruffudd, see above, *sub* Deheubarth. One of the Llandaff charters was supposedly granted by him, *LL* 272. The charter seems to be fairly reliable, and it is likely that he had some influence in Morgannwg, where he might have had some kind of joint rule with Cadwgan ap Meurig. It was on its borders that he killed Maredudd ab Owain ab Edwin in 1072, according to the Welsh chronicles. In addition, the description of the churches subject to Llandaff in the time of Herewald[233] states that in the time of this bishop, while Cadwgan reigned in Glamorgan, Caradog reigned in Ystrad Tywi and Gwent Iscoed, and his cousin Rhydderch ap Caradog held Ewias and Gwent Uch Coed. This seems reasonable, and helps to explain the presence of both Caradog and Cadwgan as contemporaries and kings in *Liber Landauensis*.

Glamorgan had its own dynasty in the eleventh century, as represented by Hywel, Meurig and Cadwgan. After the latter's death (and probably before it) the region was under the Norman influence, although native rulers did survive, in the form of such persons as Iestyn ap Gwrgan, the grantor of *LL* 271. At least one of the Llandaff charters, *LL* 274, has the Norman earl of Hereford, Roger FitzWilliam, as guarantor (although the originality of this text – and of Roger's place in it – cannot be relied upon). The region probably acknowledged various overkings in the eleventh century, including Rhydderch ab Iestyn and his son Gruffudd. While Gruffudd ap Llywelyn is never called king of Morgannwg, it is extremely likely that he did have control over it. *LL* 269, a charter with a large amount of suspicious detail, purports to have been made by him (it is a confirmation charter), and he is associated with the consecration of Bishop Herewald. It is likely that he had influence in Glamorgan (as everywhere else) even if he did not directly rule there.

The native dynasty of eleventh-century Morgannwg is not mentioned in the pedigree texts. However, they may be reconstructed from the evidence of *Liber Landauensis*, and this is shown in figure 60. The dynasty is not found beyond Cadwgan in any source known to me.

232 *Ibid.*, p. 127.
233 *The Text of the Book of Llan Dâv*, edd. Evans & Rhys, pp. 278–9.

UNKNOWNS

There remains a number of people of uncertain provenance to consider. These are as follows:

(1) Idwallon ab Owain
(2) Ionafal ap Meurig
(3) Llywarch ab Owain
(4) Mor ap Gwyn
(5) Owain ap Dyfnwal
(6) Meurig ab Arthfael
(7) Hywel ab Ithel
(8) Gwyn ap Gruffudd
(9) Goronwy ap Rhys

(1) Idwallon ab Owain

The death of Idwallon ab Owain is recorded in the Welsh chronicles in 975. Nothing more is known of him, and he does not appear in any of the early pedigree material. It is possible that he may have been a son of Owain ap Hywel Dda, or, alternatively, a brother of Hywel ab Owain of Glamorgan; or he may belong to another family altogether.

(2) Ionafal ap Meurig

Ionafal ap Meurig was slain in 985 by Cadwallon ab Ieuaf of the line of Idwal Foel. He does not appear in the pedigrees, but it seems likely that he was another son of Meurig ab Idwal Foel. He would thus have been a cousin to his slayer Cadwallon, and his death would take its place amongst the kinslayings practised by that family in the later tenth century. If this was the case, then his sphere of action was probably Gwynedd.

(3) Llywarch ab Owain

Llywarch ab Owain was blinded in 987. It is not at all clear who he was – another son of Owain ap Hywel Dda? A brother of Hywel ab Owain? A brother of the aforementioned Idwallon ab Owain?

(4) Mor ap Gwyn

The death of Mor ap Gwyn is recorded in 1002. Unless he was a brother of Caradog ap Gwyn, the father of Trahaearn ap Caradog of Arwystli and Gwynedd, I cannot find an identity for him. To make him a brother of Caradog is tortuous (Caradog's son Trahaearn was active 1075–1081) and the dates barely allow it. It is most likely that he did not belong to this line, and must be regarded as completely obscure.

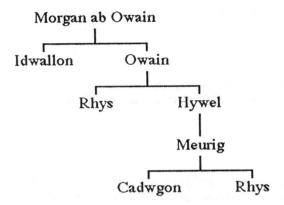

Figure 60

(5) Owain ap Dyfnwal

Owain ap Dyfnwal was slain in 1015. Beyond this, nothing is known about him.

(6) Meurig ab Arthfael

The death of Meurig ab Arhtfael is recorded in 1021. There was a ruler of the same name in Glamorgan in the 870s, but clearly they are not identical (unless his *obit* is severely misplaced in our annals). He is completely obscure.

(7) Hywel ab Ithel

Hywel ab Ithel is recorded as having gone to Ireland in 1099, and as holding Rhos and Rhufoniog in 1118. In the same year, he was killed in conflict with the sons of Owain ab Edwin. Lloyd considered that he achieved rule under the protection of the sons of Bleddyn[234] – he sought help from Maredudd ap Bleddyn against the sons of Owain in 1118, and also from Madog and Einion sons of Cadwgan ap Bleddyn, which may support Lloyd's view. He defeated the sons of Owain, but died later from the wounds he had sustained.

The pedigree of this Hywel is not known. He may have been a member of a local noble family, or he may have been a son of Ithel ap Gruffudd ap Llywelyn (*ob.* 1069), which might explain how he was able to achieve power in these areas.

(8) Gwyn ap Gruffudd

According to the vernacular annals, Gwyn ('Owain' Brut y Tywysogion [RB]) ap Gruffudd died in 1102. Bartrum[235] identifies him with the Gwyn ap Gruffudd of

234 Lloyd, *A History*, II.465.
235 Bartrum, *Tracts*, p. 155.

HL 2 (*Llywth Aelan*) section f.[236] This text, however, while supplying him with a long list of ancestors, gives no clues as to his career.

(9) Goronwy ap Rhys

Goronwy ap Rhys was imprisoned and died in 1102. Nothing else is known of him. He is probably to be taken as an obscure son of Rhys ap Tewdwr.

CONCLUSION

The eleventh century was a period of great change within Wales. There is a clear and obvious movement away from the pattern of dominance in both north and south Wales by the line of Rhodri Mawr. This pattern had been noticeable in the later tenth century, but breaks down in the eleventh. The direct line of Rhodri does not vanish completely, being represented in the South by Hywel and Maredudd, sons of Edwin, by Maredudd, Rhys, and Hywel, sons of Owain, and by Rhys ap Tewdwr; and in the North by Cynan ap Hywel, Iago ab Idwal and Gruffudd ap Cynan. But two new dynasties are very prominent: the family of Rhydderch ab Iestyn, a line totally unrelated to that of Rhodri Mawr, in south Wales; and the kin network begun by Llywelyn ap Seisyll, some of whom were descendants of Rhodri in the female line, in north Wales.

In addition to the times of power of these various groups, there are periods of confusion in the record of the eleventh century in Wales. The first is *ca* 1000–*ca* 1020, when there is no known Northern ruler between Cynan ap Hywel (*ob.* 1003) and Llywelyn ap Seisyll (reigning by 1018, and probably before then); in the South, there is no known ruler between Maredudd ab Owain ap Hywel Dda (*ob.* 999) and Rhydderch ab Iestyn (succeeded 1023). The second period is that following the death of Gruffudd ap Llywelyn in 1063 until 1069. Although non-Welsh sources indicate that Bleddyn ap Cynfyn had at least some power in this period, it is possible to infer from Welsh sources that he was not unchallenged in the North. In the South, no ruler is known until the rise of Maredudd ab Owain ab Edwin in 1069, although it is again clear that he had rivals, most notably Caradog ap Gruffudd. For both these periods, it is possible to make informed guesses about who may have held power, but corroborating evidence is lacking. In addition, these two periods are but thinly recorded in the Welsh annals. The third period is somewhat different: with increased Norman activity in Wales, and in particular after the death of Rhys ap Tewdwr in 1093, there are no individuals who can be definitely described as kings in north or south Wales, although there are prominent figures such as Cadwgan ap Bleddyn and Hywel ap Goronwy. This is the period, however, when Norman success in Wales (and especially north Wales) was at its height, and it is not surprising that the Welsh succession to the Welsh kingdoms should be disrupted at this time, and that so many Welsh leaders should owe their lands, at least in part, to Norman grant.

[236] *Ibid.*, pp. 112–13.

The sequence of rulers in north and south Wales can be reconstructed to some extent, from the chronicles and pedigrees, and by the use of a little guesswork. The order may have been somewhat as below.

(1) Deheubarth

999–1023 ?Edwin ab Einion, ?Cadell ab Einion, ?Tewdwr ap Cadell, either consecutively, or contemporaneously in different parts of the kingdom. It is also possible that Rhydderch ab Iestyn first came to importance at some point within this period.

1023–1033 Rhydderch ab Iestyn

1033–1044 Hywel ab Edwin (with his brother Maredudd 1033–1035)

1044–1055/6 Gruffudd ap Rhydderch. Gruffudd and his brothers had been active during the preceding reign, however; they fought with the sons of Edwin in 1034. He was probably powerful in some areas of the kingdom, and possibly also in some parts of Morgannwg.

1056–1063 Gruffudd ap Llywelyn

1063–1069 ?Caradog ap Gruffudd and his cousins; ?Maredudd ab Owain and his brothers.

1069–1072 Maredudd ab Owain ab Edwin

1072–1075 ?Caradog ap Gruffudd; ?Rhys and Hywel sons of Owain

1075–1076 Rhys ab Owain and Rhydderch ap Caradog, jointly.

1076–1078 Rhys ab Owain (?and his brother Hywel), Caradog ap Gruffudd

1078–1081 Rhys ap Tewdwr (from 1079), Caradog ap Gruffudd. If the evidence of *Liber Landauensis* can be believed, Caradog's main sphere of influence may have been Ystrad Tywi and Gwent Iscoed.

1081–1093 Rhys ap Tewdwr

(2) Gwynedd

1000–1003 Cynan ap Hywel

1003–*ca* 1015 ?the sons of Meurig ab Idwal Foel, ?Llywelyn ap Seisyll

ca 1015–1023 Llywelyn ap Seisyll

1023–1039 Iago ab Idwal (certainly 1033–1039; very probably before that, although he may have owed some allegiance to Rhydderch ab Iestyn of south Wales.) In the period 1023–1027, he may have shared his power with Cynan ap Seisyll

1039–1063 Gruffudd ap Llywelyn

1063–1069 Bleddyn and Rhiwallon sons of Cynfyn (the half-brothers of Gruffudd ap Llywelyn), ?the sons of Gruffudd ap Llywelyn

1069–1075 Bleddyn ap Cynfyn

1075–1081 Trahaearn ap Caradog, the first cousin of Bleddyn

1081–1099 various people at various times: probably no one person was ever supreme throughout the area. Gruffudd ap Cynan and the sons of Bleddyn (especially Cadwgan ap Bleddyn) should be included in this group. It may also have included Owain ab Edwin and his brother Uchdryd, sons of Bleddyn's sister Iwerydd.

The picture for Powys and Morgannwg is less clear: on the evidence of *Liber Landauensis*, Morgannwg continued to be under the influence of its own dynasty,

115

in the persons of Hywel ab Owain, Meurig ap Hyel and Cadwgan ap Meurig. However, their power cannot have been absolute: it seems very likely that this area fell under the sway of Rhydderch ab Iestyn in the period *ca* 1023–*ca* 1033, and it is not unlikely that his son Gruffudd also had some control there. It is also likely that the hegemony of Gruffudd ap Llywelyn extended to Morgannwg, although at what time this began would be hard to say. Caradog ap Gruffudd is found active in this area in the 1070s and may well have had a powerbase there. The history of Morgannwg in the later years of the eleventh century is very unclear: the area was probably beginning to fall to the Normans by the 1070s. There is barely any evidence about Powys in our sources (apart from the reference in *Brut y Tywysogion* [RB] to the rule there of Bleddyn, and the later acquisition of this territory by Cadwgan ap Bleddyn). It is not possible to make any definite statements about who ruled this area when, but given the close links that we see growing in the later eleventh century between the kings of Gwynedd and the noble lines of mid-Wales, it is probable that Powys owed allegiance to the rulers of Gwynedd.

Despite the troubles of the century, there is a considerable coherence to the rulers of the eleventh century. They no longer all belong to the dynasty of Rhodri Mawr in the direct male line. However, they are clearly interlinked by both kinship and alliance. Hence Gwynedd for much of the period was ruled by members of a group that cannot exactly be called a dynasty, but which had a kind of collateral cohesion. Llywelyn ap Seisyll was succeeded by Iago ab Idwal, who may have been his distant cousin. This Iago was followed by Gruffudd, the son of Llywelyn ap Seisyll, and his own distant cousin. Gruffudd was followed by his maternal half-brothers Bleddyn and Rhiwallon sons of Cynfyn; and Bleddyn by his first cousin Trahaearn ap Caradog. Even Trahaearn was related to some of his successors: the sons of Bleddyn would have been his cousins. Gruffudd ap Cynan was not related to Trahaearn as far as we know; however, he was the grandson of Iago ab Idwal and the distant cousin of Gruffudd ap Llywelyn and the sons of Cynfyn. This long network was bound by alliances also. At the end of the century, the two most prominent representatives of it, Gruffudd ap Cynan and Cadwgan ab Bleddyn, are found acting together. In his last battle Trahaearn was supported not only by his south Welsh ally Caradog ap Gruffudd, but by another cousin, Meilir ap Rhiwallon ap Cynfyn. The attack made on Rhys ap Tewdwr of south Wales in 1088 by the sons of Bleddyn may also be an indication of the cohesion that there was between at least some of the strands of this network. Rhys bore some of the responsibility for the death of Trahaearn in 1081; in driving him out of Deheubarth, the sons of Bleddyn may have been, in part, avenging Trahaearn. Some years before this, Traheaern himself had defeated Rhys ab Owain of the South, who was implicated in the death of Bleddyn; an action considered by the *Brutiau* to be the avenging of Bleddyn.

In south Wales, two distinct dynasties are recognisable. The first is a continuation of the Southern Branch of the dynasty of Rhodri Mawr, represented by the descendants of Einion ab Owain, through his sons Edwin and Cadell. The notable fact about the descendants of Edwin ab Einion is their internal cohesion: at no time are its members found in conflict with one another, not even in the person of the belligerent Rhys ab Owain. This is a contrast to the behaviour of the Southern Branch of the dynasty of Rhodri Mawr in the later tenth century. The descendants of Cadell ab Einion only became powerful at the expense of the line of Edwin. (Rhys ap Tewdwr, of the Cadell line, killed the last known member of the Edwin line, Gruffudd ap Maredudd, in 1091.) The line of Cadell was to enjoy prominence in the twelfth century and beyond, in the persons of Gruffudd ap Rhys, the Lord Rhys and Rhys Gryg.

The other dynasty found in the South in the eleventh century is that of Rhydderch ab Iestyn. Like the father of Llywelyn ap Seisyll, the parentage of Rhydderch ab Iestyn is obscure: the line came seemingly from nowhere, and enjoyed a meteoric success. It is noticeable that most of our information about this family comes from non-Welsh sources, and the Welsh texts themselves are remarkably reticent on the doings of the family, with the exception of Caradog ap Gruffudd. This is not the case with the other group of so-called 'usurpers' (Llywelyn ap Seisyll, Gruffudd ap Llywelyn, Bleddyn ap Cynfyn, Trahaearn ap Caradog) all of whom are fairly well noted in the Welsh chronicles. The silence about the Rhydderch line may reflect that they were regarded as usurpers, or, more probably, it may reflect a bias in the chronicles, which do seem to exhibit a preference for the kings of north Wales at this period.

Not all the lines that dominate the eleventh century survive into the twelfth. That of Rhydderch ap Iestyn is far less significant after the death of Caradog ap Gruffudd in 1081, and that of Edwin ends with Gruffudd ap Maredudd in 1091. Gruffudd ap Llywelyn is not claimed as direct ancestor in any early genealogy known to me, and unless Hywel ab Ithel of Rhos was his grandson, he has no direct male descendants in the twelfth century who are mentioned in the Welsh chronicles. The family of Trahaearn survived into the twelfth century, but largely tore itself apart in internal strugggles in the late 1120s and 1130s. The fate of the line of Cadell has already been noted. The real success in genealogical terms is the family of Bleddyn ap Cynfyn, which spread across north Wales, and re-mained powerful for many years: an extraordinary achievement for a line of 'usurpers', and comparable to that of the family of Rhodri Mawr in the ninth century. Gruffudd ap Cynan can be seen as continuing the success of this latter family, and it too had many prominent members in the twelfth and later centuries.

It is possible to identify three turning points for Wales in the eleventh century; the death of Gruffudd ap Llywelyn in 1063, the death of Bleddyn ap Cynfyn and the battle of Camddwr in 1075, and the battle of Mynydd Carn in 1081. These three events all had long-reaching effects, which were felt throughout all Wales. In all cases, the result was an almost complete change in the political structure of the time. Hence the death of Gruffudd encompassed the dissolution of his hegemony, and the re-emergence of the independent kingdom of Deheubarth. The battle of Camddwr and the fall of Bleddyn led to the emergence of the allies Rhydderch ap Caradog and Rhys ab Owain in the South, while the previously unknown Trahaearn began his reign in the North. The battle of Mynydd Carn essentially marked the end of the dynasty of Rhydderch ab Iestyn in the greater part of south Wales (although they stayed important in Morgannwg in the twelfth century), and the triumph of the old Southern Branch of the dynasty of Rhodri Mawr. It brought to an end the direct rule of the collaterals of Gruffudd ap Llywelyn – although the sons of Bleddyn continued to be important, none of them were actually kings of Gwynedd, and Gruffudd ap Cynan, although related

117

to Gruffudd ap Llywelyn, is more properly seen as a survival of the Northern Branch of the line of Rhodri Mawr.

Towards the end of the century, as the Norman threat became greater, an increasingly large number of 'minor' figures are noticed in the Welsh chronicles. Most notable are the various sons and grandsons of Elystan Glodrydd, who are particularly active in south Wales, although the family is associated with Buellt; Cedifor ap Gollwyn, the 'leading man of Dyfed', whose sons nearly succeeded in replacing Rhys ap Tewdwr with his kinsman Gruffudd ap Maredudd, and who may have represented the supporters of the Edwin line of the Southern Branch of the dynasty of Rhodri Mawr; Gwrgenau ap Seisyll, the ally and kinsman of Trahaearn, and a member of a Powys family; and the sons of Edwin of Tegeingl and Iwerydd ferch Cynfyn, Uchdryd and Owain. The prominence of these individuals is in part due to the disruption caused by the Normans, which allowed such groups to come to the fore as the ruling families were pressurized by the invaders. At the end of the eleventh century, many members of the ruling families were imprisoned or in exile: Gruffudd ap Cynan was captive for much of the 1080s and 1090s, and fled to Ireland with Cadwgan ap Bleddyn in 1098–1099. Iorwerth ap Bleddyn was captive 1102–1110, and Maredudd ap Bleddyn 1102–1107. Gruffudd ap Rhys ap Tewdwr was an exile in Ireland fronm the time of the death of his father until 1114. Many leading Welshmen were assassinated by the Normans, including Maredudd ab Owain ab Edwin, Rhys ap Tewdwr and Hywel ap Goronwy. The conditions were such to allow these previously minor families to grow in power.

The pattern of 'intrusive' rulers seen by Lloyd is difficult to sustain. With the exception of *Historia Grufffud vab Kenan*, our Welsh sources pass no judgements on the legitimacy of kings (the sole exception to this is Rhain in 1022). Indeed, if we were to take our opinion of the eleventh-century rulers of Wales solely from the Welsh chronicles, then the kings who would be seen as respected and admired would be Gruffudd ap Llywelyn, the 'head and shield and defender to the Britons',[237] and Bleddyn ap Cynfyn, who, far from being treated as the puppet king described by R. R. Davies,[238] was spoken of as 'terrible in war, beloved and meek in peace and a defence for all'.[239] As was noted above, it is possible to see biases in our sources, and the line of Rhydderch ab Iestyn in particular has suffered on account of this. But I cannot see that Lloyd's 'intrusive' rulers can definitely be recognised as such from the Welsh chronicles.

The eleventh century was an era of great change for Wales. It opened with a period in which the old dynasties were weak, and this gave a chance for the rise to power of new lines, such as those of Rhydderch ab Iestyn and Llywelyn ap Seisyll. It saw the first and only unification of all Wales under one ruler, Gruffudd ap Llywelyn, in the years 1056–1063. It saw too the arrival of the Normans, and the beginning of the erosion of independent Wales. To dismiss its political history as a procession of 'intrusive rulers' is to miss the complexity of

---

237 *ByT* (Pen. 20) *s.a.* 1061 (*recte* 1063).
238 Davies, *Conquest*, p. 24.
239 *ByT* (Pen. 20) *s.a.* 1076 (*recte* 1078).

the era, and to award its kings less than their due. The eleventh century for Wales was a time of dynamic change; by and large, whatever their dynastic background (or lack of it), the rulers who dominated the century were able to meet, overcome, and survive the challenges with which they were presented.

III

ANGLO-WELSH POLITICAL RELATIONS
IN THE ELEVENTH CENTURY

My purpose in this chapter will be to examine the political interrelationships of
the Welsh kingdoms with England throughout the eleventh century. In the wake
of the work of J. E. Lloyd,[1] L. H. Nelson,[2] and Christopher Lewis,[3] I do not
intend to attempt a new discussion of the Domesday material. For convenience,
given the length of the period involved, I shall divide my examination into three
parts: the early eleventh century until the beginning of the reign of Gruffudd ap
Llywelyn in 1039; the mid-eleventh century, encompassing the reigns of
Gruffudd ap Llywelyn and Edward the Confessor, and ending with the death of
Earl Eadwine and the captivity of Earl Morkere in 1071; and the later eleventh
century, 1072–1103 (the latter date being decided by the final Welsh repercus-
sions of the rebellion of Robert de Bellême). My choice of these divisions is in
part decided simply by the convenient breaks provided by the accession of the
Confessor, and the beginning of the Norman conquest of Wales; however, I hope
also to be able to show that the rise to power in Wales of Gruffudd ap Llywelyn
was accompanied by a change in the general nature of political relations between
England and Wales. It will be noticed, further, that I shall be looking at the
relationships predominantly from a Welsh standpoint, and analysing incidents
largely in terms of the effects upon, and place within, the Welsh context.

The background to the political attitudes prevailing between England and
Wales in the eleventh century is mainly one of strife, for much of the pre-
eleventh-century period is marked by border raids and conflicts between Welsh
and English, punctuated only by the uneasy allegiance imposed upon Welsh
rulers by Alfred and his successors in the late ninth century and the first half of
the tenth.[4] With increasing Scandinavian pressure in the later tenth century,
however, this allegiance was eroded, and by the opening of the eleventh century,
Welsh and English seem to have met mostly in conflict, although the occasional
alliance appears to have been made between individual Welsh rulers and Englishmen, usually in a context of internal Welsh strife.[5] However, it does not seem that

---

1 Lloyd, 'Wales and the Coming'.
2 Nelson, *The Normans in South Wales*.
3 Lewis, 'The Norman Settlement of Herefordshire under William I'.
4 See Lloyd, *A History*, I.335–337; Loyn, 'Wales and England in the Tenth Century: the
  Context of the Æthelstan Charters'; and Kirby, 'Hywel Dda – Anglophil?'.
5 Such as that which obtained between Hywel ab Ieuaf of Gwynedd and the English,
  possibly the men of Ælfhere of Mercia. Hywel was engaged in a long struggle with his
  uncle, Iago ab Idwal Foel, for control of Gwynedd, and was also in conflict with his

the activities of Welsh rulers impinged to any great extent upon their powerful counterparts in England: this is not surprising, particularly in the case of Æthelred the Unready, concerned as he was from the 980s with the serious problems presented by the Scandinavian pressure upon his own kingdom.

WALES AND ENGLAND IN THE EARLY ELEVENTH CENTURY

The most basic problem facing anyone wishing to look at Anglo-Welsh relations within this period is that of sources: there is not very much information bearing upon Wales in this period, and such as there is largely comprises *obits*. However, it is possible to identify a number of interesting incidents. These are listed below. Nor are any events known for the 1020s: however, it should be noted that there are relatively few notices for this period at all in Welsh chronicles and that all but one of these entries are very simple *obits*. (The exception is the comparatively long and detailed account of Llywelyn ap Seisyll's conflict with the 'Irish' pretender Rhain.) The known Anglo-Welsh contacts of this period are as follows.

992

Edwin ab Einion, with the help of 'Edelis' (*Annales Cambriae* [B]),[6] 'Eclis' *Brut y Tywysogion* (RB),[7] the Englishman, ravaged all the territories of Maredudd ab Owain ap Hywel Dda in Deheubarth. *Brenhinedd y Saesson*[8] does not name the English leader, simply stating that Edwin had English help. *Brut y Tywysogion* (RB) calls him a leader from the seas of the South.

1012

St Davids was ravaged by Eadric and Ubis the Englishmen.[9] The identity of this

---

distant kinsman, the south Welsh king, Einion ab Owain, in the period *ca* 974–*ca* 985. On several occasions Hywel had recourse to English aid according to the Welsh Annals, ravaging Clynnog Fawr with the English in *ca* 978, and attacking the lands of Einion ab Owain with an English leader in *ca* 983. This latter event is something of a crux: both versions of *AC* make it plain that the English leader 'Alfre' and Hywel were collaborating, the *Brutiau* seem to indicate that the English were attacking a joint force of Hywel and Einion. This interpretation, however, does seem to be more dependent upon the punctuation supplied to the *Brutiae* by Thomas Jones, than upon the actual syntax of the entries. It is worth noting that Lloyd considered Hywel to be acting with the English (*A History*, I.350). The alliance was not wholly to Hywel's benefit: he fell in *ca* 985 through English treachery.

6 *AC* (B) *s.a.* [993].
7 *ByT* (RB) *s.a.* 990 (*recte* 992).
8 *ByS* *s.a.* 991 (*recte* 992).
9 *AC* (B) *s.a.* [1011]; *AC* (C) *s.a.* [1013]; *ByT* (Pen. 20) *s.a.* 1011 (*recte* 1012); *ByT* (RB) *s.a.* 1010 (*recte* 1012); *ByS* *s.a.* 1011 (*recte* 1012). *ByS* differs from the other texts, reading 'y diffeithwyt Myniw y gan y Saesson. Ac y bu varw Vbis Haearddur, manach o Enlli.', omitting Eadric entirely and associating Ubis with the monk Haearddur,

pair is somewhat uncertain – Lloyd[10] identified Eadric with the notorious Eadric Streona, earl of Mercia from 1007, but could not identify Ubis. However, there is an 'Usic' (possibly a scribal error for 'Ufic'[11]) mentioned in a charter granted in Herefordshire in 1043 × 1046,[12] in which land is bought by one Leofwine from Eadric son of Ufic at Mansell. If this Usic/Ufic is our Ubis, then he might have been a tenant or thegn of Eadric Streona, and hence his involvment in the raid. It is, however, puzzling as to why the raid happened – perhaps the Welsh had become too enthusiastic on Eadric's borders? – and as to why St Davids was attacked. Could this have been a sea-attack? If the force had had to travel through all of south Wales, one might expect greater notice of its victims. Lloyd certainly was of this opinion, and considered indeed that one of the Danish ships which had entered English service in 1012 might have been involved.[13] In the vacuum of evidence, this incident can be explained only as another part of the Anglo-Welsh strife which had characterised Welsh history to this time.

1035

Caradog son of Rhydderch was slain by the English.[14] This Caradog was the son of Rhydderch ab Iestyn, who had been supreme in south Wales 1023–33, and a brother of the important south Welsh ruler Gruffudd ap Rhydderch, king of Deheubarth 1044–55/56. Almost nothing is known of Caradog – there is a brief mention of him in *Liber Landauensis*[15] as being one of the kings in whose lifetime Bishop Herewald was active: this however seems improbable, since Herewald's predecessor Joseph is known to have died in 1045, more than a decade after the end of Caradog's life.[16] He presumably was one of the sons of Rhydderch who were in conflict with the sons of Edwin ab Einion over the control of south Wales in 1034. His death is not noticed in English sources, however, and there is no known reason for his slaying at English hands. The dynasty descended from Rhydderch ab Iestyn was active in Glamorgan, however, and another of its members, Rhys ap Rhydderch, was to become a victim of the English in 1052. It is entirely conceivable that, given their position close to the English border, members of this family were known to be a threat to England, and thus were an object of enmity.

---

whose death is also noted by *ByT* (Pen. 20) and *ByT* (RB) at the end of the entries dealing with Eadric and Ubis.

10 Lloyd, *A History*, I.350.
11 This is the view of Robertson, *Anglo-Saxon Charters*, p. 435.
12 This is described in Sawyer, *Anglo-Saxon Charters*, no. 1469.
13 Lloyd, *A History*, I.350.
14 *AC* (B) *s.a.* [1034]; *AC* (C) *s.a.* [1036]; *ByT* (Pen. 20) *s.a.* 1033 (*recte* 1035); *ByT* (RB) [1035]; *ByS* *s.a.* 1033 (*recte* 1035).
15 *The Text of the Book of Llan Dâv*, edd. Evans and Rees, p. 278.
16 *AC* (B) *s.a.* [1044]; *ByT* (Pen. 20) *s.a.* 1043 (*recte* 1045); *ByT* (RB) *s.a.* [1045]; *ByS* *s.a.* 1043 (*recte* 1045).

These events constitute the whole of what is known of Anglo-Welsh political relations in the first third of the eleventh century. This sparseness must be, at least in part, a result of the thinness of our sources; nevertheless, it does seem that Wales was not a major English concern in this period. Nor can England have been very significant to the Welsh, for the first forty years or so of this century were turbulent in Wales, with many different rulers and conflicts occurring internally. Clearly both countries were largely concerned with their own affairs. No pattern is discernible in what little we know of their relations. Lloyd saw Eadric's raid as part of an English tendency in the later tenth and early eleventh centuries to leave Wales to the earls of Mercia, and indeed there is no clear reason to call this view into question: one of Eadric's tenth-century predecessors, Ælfhere, seems to have been capable of exploiting Welsh differences – by acting with the north Welsh Hywel ab Ieuaf against the south Welsh Einion ab Owain, he may have helped to distract the attention of both away from his own English domains.

The identity of the 'Edelis' of 992 is not clear. Lloyd, following Freeman, rendered the name as Æthelsig, but did not know who this person might have been.[17] Thomas Jones, in his editions of the *Brutiau*, transcribed it as 'Edylfi', but made no attempt at explanation. The statement of *Brut y Tywysogion* (RB) that he was a leader from the 'seas of the South' is particularly odd: could this mean he was a Continental Saxon, or perhaps a Scandinavian (the usual viking harassers of Wales appear to have been based in Ireland: this individual might just have come from one of the viking settlements in France). It is not possible to identify him: however, if he was English (and the annalist of *Annales Cambriae* claim that he was an English 'dux'), then this incident perhaps serves to illustrate the English habit of using internal Welsh hostilities to their own advantage, either for reward in plunder, or to distract from their own possessions, or both.

This is a thin picture, then, but one which does not differ to any great extent from that visible in the previous century, with the men of the two countries interacting predominantly on the battlefield, the English alternately punishing and exploiting Welsh activities.

WALES AND ENGLAND 1039–1071

This period marks a change in Anglo-Welsh relations, and I propose to begin by simply listing the evidence without comment or interpretation. It comes from a much wider range of sources than does the evidence for the earlier period: that for 992–1038 is found only in Welsh sources; that for 1039–1071 comes from English and Anglo-Norman texts as well as Welsh.

1039

The accession of Gruffudd ap Llywelyn, and his first victory against the English

17 Lloyd, *A History*, I.350, n. 110.

123

at Rhyd-y-Gors.[18] The Welsh slay Eadwine, the brother of Earl Leofric, and the king's nobles Thurkill and Ælfgeat son of *Elfi*, and many others.[19]

1046

Earl Swegn son of Earl Godwine ravaged in Wales with Gruffudd 'the Northern king', and took hostages.[20]

1049

Thirty-six Hiberno-Scandinavian ships came up the River Severn, and with the help of Gruffudd, 'the Southern king', ravaged in that area. Crossing the River Wye, they burnt *Duredham*, and threatened Worcestershire. Bishop Ealdred moved a force against them, with a few men from Gloucester and Hereford. But the Welsh whom they (the English) had with them warned Gruffudd, who attacked before the bishop's force was ready, and slew many of them, while the remainder fled.[21]

1052

Gruffudd 'the Welsh king' ravaged Herefordshire near Leominster and defeated a mixed force of 'French' and English, on the same day, thirteen years later, as Eadwine had been killed.[22]

1053

Rhys, 'the Welsh king's brother', was slain by the English.[23]

1055

Ælfgar son of Earl Leofric was exiled for the first time. He went to Ireland and Wales for aid and, having burnt Hereford with his allies, was reinstated. Gruffudd ap Llywelyn defeated Earl Ralf and ravaged and burnt Hereford. Punitive action was initially taken by Earl Harold, but a peace settlement was soon made.[24]

---

18 *AC* (B) *s.a.* [1038]; *AC* (C) *s.a.* [1040]; *ByT* (Pen. 20) *s.a.* 1037 (*recte* 1039); *ByT* (RB) *s.a.* [1039]; *ByS s.a.* 1037 (*recte* 1039).
19 ASC (C) *s.a.* 1039; JW *s.a.* 1039.
20 ASC (C) *s.a.* 1046.
21 JW *s.a.* 1049; ASC (D) *s.a.* 1050.
22 JW *s.a.* 1052; ASC (D) *s.a.* 1052; *HR*^{2}, *s.a.* 1052. The account in this text, for this year, and indeed for much of the eleventh century, is taken almost verbatim from JW.
23 ASC (C) *s.a.* 1052; ASC (D) *s.a.* 1053; JW *s.a.* 1053; *HR*^{2} *s.a.* 1053.
24 ASC (C) *s.a.* 1055; ASC (D) *s.a.* 1055; ASC (E) *s.a.* 1055; ASC (F) *s.a.* 1055; JW *s.a.* 1055; *HR*^{2} *s.a.* 1055; William of Malmesbury, *De Gestis Regum Anglorum*, ed. Stubbs, I.241–5; HH *s.a.* 1055. The Welsh chronicles omit all reference to Ælfgar, but note the raid: *AC* (B) *s.a.* [1055]; *AC* (C) *s.a.* [1058]; *ByT* (Pen. 20) *s.a.* 1054 (*recte* 1056); *ByT* (RB) *s.a.* [1056]; *ByS s.a.* 1054 (*recte* 1056).

1056

The new bishop of Hereford, Earl Harold's chaplain Leofgar, led a force against Gruffudd ap Llywelyn, which was heavily defeated, and Leofgar himself was slain. Peace was established by the intervention of Harold, Leofric, and Bishop Ealdred.[25]

1058

Earl Ælfgar was exiled for a second time, but gained reinstatement with the help of Gruffudd ap Llywelyn and an unexpected Norwegian fleet.[26] Gruffudd ap Llywelyn, assisting Magnus son of Harold, king of 'Germany', ravaged England.[27]

1063

Earl Harold led a force into Wales, and burnt Rhuddlan. Gruffudd ap Llywelyn narrowly eluded him. Later in the same year (the next year, according to John of Worcester) Harold with a sea-force, and Tostig with a land force made a joint assault on Wales, and extracted Welsh hostages. They received the submission of the Welsh, who promised to forswear Gruffudd. In August, Gruffudd was slain by his own men, and his head was sent to Harold. Harold sent it to Edward the Confessor who appointed new rulers for Wales, Gruffudd's half-brothers, Bleddyn and Rhiwallon, the sons of Cynfyn. These two promised allegiance to King Edward, and to Harold.[28] The Welsh annals omit most of this, noticing simply the death of Gruffudd at the hands of his own men.[29]

1065

Earl Harold attempted to build a hunting lodge at Portskewett in south Wales, but Caradog ap Gruffudd ap Rhydderch attacked and destroyed it. In the wake of the expulsion of Earl Tostig, Morkere son of Ælfgar was made earl of Northumbria. He journeyed North with the help of his brother, Eadwine earl of Mercia, and a large train including a number of Welshmen.[30]

25 ASC (C) s.a. 1056; ASC (D) s.a. 1056; JW s.a. 1056; HR² s.a. 1056.
26 ASC (D) s.a. 1058; JW s.a. 1058; HR² s.a. 1058.
27 AC (B) s.a. [1056]; AC (C) s.a. [1059]; ByT (Pen. 20) s.a. 1056 (recte 1058); ByT (RB) s.a. [1058]; ByS s.a. 1056 (recte 1058).
28 ASC (D) s.a. 1063; ASC (E) s.a. 1063; JW s.a. 1063 and s.a. 1064; HR² s.a. 1063 and s.a. 1064; William of Jumièges, Gesta Normannorum Ducum, pp. 191–2.
29 AC (B) s.a. [1061]; AC (C) s.a. [1064]; ByT (Pen. 20) s.a. 1061 (recte 1063); ByT (RB) s.a. 1060 (recte 1063); ByS s.a. 1061 (recte 1063). For a discussion of this event, see Maund, 'Cynan ab Iago'.
30 ASC (C) s.a. 1065; ASC (D) s.a. 1065; JW s.a. 1065; HR² s.a. 1065.

1067

Eadric *Cild*, a Shropshire thegn, resisting the Normans, ravaged Hereford with the assistance of the Welsh.[31]

1068

Bleddyn and his Welshmen supported the rebellion of Eadwine and Morkere against William the Conqueror.[32]

1070

William led a punitive expedition against the men of Cheshire and the Welsh, and received the submission of Eadric *Cild*.[33]

1071

Eadwine, in flight to Scotland, was slain by his own men; his brother Morkere was captured in the siege of Ely and imprisoned.[34]

This, then, is the framework of Anglo-Welsh political relations in the middle part of the eleventh century. Even a cursory glance reveals that there has been a change from the conflict-exploitation pattern of the tenth century and the early eleventh (excepting Rhyd-y-Gors [1039], and the slaying of Rhys ap Rhydderch [1053], which may belong to this older pattern). The sudden increase in notices of Welsh activities in English sources may itself be an indication of this change. I hope to demonstrate that this change was largely rooted in the policies and actions of one man, Gruffudd ap Llywelyn, king first of Gwynedd and then of all Wales. It was a policy with significant effects both in Wales and in England, and one which outlived the death in 1063 of its initiator.

The English connexions of Gruffudd and, later, of his half-brother and successor Bleddyn find no explicit mention in the native Welsh sources. In *Annales Cambriae* and the *Brutiau*, Gruffudd stands revealed only as the scourge of the English, never as an ally of any of them.[35] It is in the English texts that we can see him acting with, as well as against, the English, and in conjunction with particular Englishmen. Two English nobles can be identified acting with the support of Gruffudd, both within the reign of Edward the Confessor: Swegn, the eldest son of the powerful Godwine, earl of Wessex, and himself controlling

---

[31] ASC (D) *s.a.* 1067; JW *s.a.* 1067; Orderic Vitalis, *Historia Ecclesiastica*, Book IV: ed. & transl. Chibnall, II.228.

[32] Orderic Vitalis, *Historia Ecclesiastica*, Book IV: ed. & transl. Chibnall, II.214, 216.

[33] *Ibid.*, II.234.

[34] ASC (E) *s.a.* 1071; JW *s.a.* 1071; HH *s.a.* 1071; Orderic Vitalis, *Historia Ecclesiastica*, Book IV: ed. & transl. Chibnall, II.256–8. Orderic's account is very long and places Morkere's capture before Eadwine's death: Eadwine is said to have been slain while collecting an army to free his brother.

[35] *AC* (B) *s.a.* [1038]; *ByT* (Pen. 20) *s.a.* 1037 (*recte* 1039); *ByT* (RB) *s.a.* [1039]; *ByS s.a.* 1037 (*recte* 1039).

lands on the Welsh border, and Ælfgar, son of Leofric earl of Mercia. Both these two had somewhat chequered careers within England, and neither seems to have possessed an entirely stable or secure position within the English polity: despite the undoubted power held by both their fathers, these particular sons suffered periods of exile, dispossession, and disgrace. It is not possible to say from whom the initiative to alliance first came: in the case of Swegn, the joint Anglo-Welsh action undertaken was to the benefit of both Swegn himself and Gruffudd ap Llywelyn, since both were doubtless concerned by the growing power in southern Wales of Gruffudd ap Rhydderch. The relationship seems to have had no long-lasting effects. Indeed Swegn appears to have treated the whole affair in a freebooting spirit not dissimilar from that of a troop of Hiberno-Scandinavian mercenaries! The case of Ælfgar is more complex, and I propose to examine it in greater detail later in this chapter. As an initial proposition, however, I should contend that Gruffudd's relations with Ælfgar and his relations with Swegn differed in one very crucial way, as will be shown below, although it may be that the contact with Swegn was what gave Gruffudd the idea of forming a more permanent liaison with an English earl.

Relatively little is known about the relationship between Gruffudd and Swegn. Our knowledge of it comes from one source only, the C-text of the Anglo-Saxon Chronicle, *s.a.* 1046, written at Abingdon. This reads:[36]

Her on þysum geare for Swegn eorl into Wealan and Griffin se norþerne cyng forð mid him, and man him gisloda. Þa he hamwerdes wæs, þa het he feccan him to þa abbedessan on Leomynstre; and hæfde hi þa while þe him geliste and let hi syþþan faran ham.

The Welsh chronicles have nothing to say about this incident. However, it becomes relatively comprehensible once seen within its proper Welsh context. Gruffudd had become ruler of Gwynedd in 1039, on the death of Iago ab Idwal, and from the very beginning of his rule he displayed a forceful and aggressive attitude towards both the English and his fellow Welsh kings. In the year of his accession, he struck out strongly against both, inflicting a defeat upon the English at Rhyd-y-Gors on the River Severn, slaying Eadwine, the brother of the earl of Mercia, in the process, and driving his rival, Hywel ab Edwin, the king of South Wales from Deheubarth. Clearly Gruffudd was beginning as he meant to go on, and his expansionist policy is obvious throughout his twenty-four-year reign. He wished to establish his authority all through Wales, and out into those areas, once Welsh, which Englishmen now accounted part of England. He began at home, and the first fifteen years or so of his reign were dominated by his efforts to acquire supremacy over Deheubarth. The king in Deheubarth at the time of Gruffudd's accession in the North was Hywel ab Edwin (a grandson of Einion ab Owain) who had been ruling since 1033. Gruffudd lost no time in attempting to dislodge him, and for the next five years the two were in conflict, culminating in Hywel's death in battle at the mouth of the River Tywi. However, Gruffudd's victory was to prove short-lived; no sooner had he defeated one Southern rival than another appeared. In 1045 Gruffudd is found fighting the sons of Rhydderch ab Iestyn (king of south Wales 1023–1033) and from this time onwards he had to

36 See note 20.

contend with a particularly strong opponent, Gruffudd ap Rhydderch. It is in the early throes of this conflict that Swegn Godwinesson made his brief appearance upon the stage of eleventh century Wales, in 1046.

It is worth noting that, for this period, the chronology of the English sources (and their dependent Anglo-Norman cousins) is out of step with that of the Welsh texts. This unhappy situation is not, unfortunately, alleviated by the 'corrected' dates supplied to the *Brutiau* by their most recent editor, Thomas Jones. (The chronology of *Annales Cambriae*, at least in Williams's edition, is rendered totally obscure by his conflation of the B and C texts.) The dates as supplied by the texts of *Brut y Tywysogion* (Pen. 20) and *Brenhinedd y Saesson* (*Brut y Tywysogion* [RB] has none) would place events such as the attack on Hereford and defeat of Ralf, or the arrival of Magnus Haraldsson one or two years earlier than they are placed by the Anglo-Saxon Chronicle. Jones's revisions bring some, but not all, of these occurrences into step. Hence the *Brutiau* would give an uncorrected date of 1054, or a corrected one of 1056, to the raid on Hereford, as against 1055 in the Anglo-Saxon Chronicle; but give an uncorrected 1056 and a corrected 1058 for Magnus in comparison with the 1058 supplied by the D-text of the Anglo-Saxon Chronicle. As has been said above, the one witness to Swegn's involvement with Wales, ASC C, places the event in 1046. In *Annales Cambriae* and the *Brutiau*, there is recorded at (uncorrected) 1045, or (corrected) 1047, the slaughter in Ystrad Tywi of Gruffudd ap Llywelyn's warband, and Gruffudd's vengeful devastation of Ystrad Tywi and Dyfed in the same year. Lloyd[37] saw these two incidents as separate, the massacre perhaps resulting from Swegn's and Gruffudd's actions of the preceding year. However, I do not see the necessity for this. Given the uneven chronological relations of the Welsh and the English sources, it seems highly likely that the punitive attack on Dyfed and Ystrad Tywi of 1047, and the raid with English help of 1046, are one and the same. Angered by the massacre and, perhaps, unexpectedly short of manpower, Gruffudd had recourse to his English neighbour. Swegn's own earldom shared a border with the kingdom of Gruffudd ap Rhydderch in the South, and it is not inconceivable that he too was disturbed by the Southern ruler's activities (the English had already found it necessary to dispose of one member of this dynasty, Caradog ap Rhydderch, in 1035). The link with Gruffudd of north Wales had advantages for both participants. For Gruffudd it provided more military resources. For Swegn it no doubt proved a source of more financial resources, in the form of plunder, not to mention an outlet for his clearly belligerent nature. The relationship does not appear to have persisted beyond this raid: none of the recensions of the Anglo-Saxon Chronicle has much good to say of Swegn; if he had had extensive dealings with the Welsh, it might be expected that the anti-Godwinist texts at least might have made more of this. The situation appears to have been one of mutual use – Lloyd[38] viewed the combination of Gruffudd ap Llywelyn and Swegn as arising from the former's alarm at the rise of Gruffudd ap Rhydderch in Deheubarth:

So threatening was it that in 1046 Gruffydd ap Llywelyn had recourse to English help; the

[37] Lloyd, *A History*, II.361.
[38] *Ibid.*

intervention of Earl Swegen . . . was secured, and king and earl went together through South Wales, hoping no doubt to crush the movement in favour of the son of Rhydderch.

There may be something in this as an explanation, but such an assertion requires much more substantiation for it is perhaps to read too much into the brief statement of the C-text of the Anglo-Saxon Chronicle. Moreover, if the Welsh chronicles are any guide, Gruffudd in fact experienced as much, if not more, difficulty with Hywel ab Edwin as he did with Gruffudd ap Rhydderch. It is difficult while reading Lloyd's account not to feel that this fine historian felt something of a distaste for the son of Llywelyn, and he may have perhaps overstated the extent of the threat represented by Gruffudd ap Rhydderch. It is not possible fully to uncover the motives for the brief alliance of Gruffudd ap Llywelyn and Swegn. Both clearly stood to gain: Gruffudd had the hope of crushing a rival, Swegn may have sought money and adventure; more significantly, he may have hoped to achieve some balance against the rising power of his own brothers within England. Given what is known of the erratic character of Swegn,[39] I am inclined to think that the link was a Welsh initiative: Gruffudd in his struggle with Hywel ab Edwin had observed the latter making use of Hiberno-Scandinavian mercenaries as a back-up. In the wake of the loss of what may have been a considerable proportion of his warband (seven score), he may have seen the English earl as a useful supply of cannon-fodder. I am not convinced that he was as terrified as Lloyd implied. Whatever the cause of the link it was not to endure: during no recorded part of his periods of exile did Swegn seek aid from Wales. It is tempting to speculate what part this expedition to Wales in 1046 played in Swegn's expulsion from England in 1047, an exile normally explained as a consequence of Swegn's abduction of the abbess of Leominster in the wake of his Welsh raid.

The relationship of Gruffudd with Ælfgar is of a somewhat different type. Its importance has long been recognised. While (unlike Lloyd) I should hesitate to describe the link with Swegn as an alliance (at least in the full sense of the word), that word does seem to be the best description of the relationship between Gruffudd ap Llywelyn and Ælfgar, son of Earl Leofric and himself an earl, first of East Anglia and then of Mercia. While the connexion is made explicit in our sources on only two occasions (1055 and 1058), less obvious traces can still be found which show that the relationship was maintained over a long time, and in a serious manner.

According to English and some Anglo-Norman sources,[40] in 1055 Ælfgar was exiled from England and deprived of his earldom, for a reason unstated in any but the most general terms (the Godwinist author of the E-text of the Anglo-Saxon Chronicle accuses him of treason, but of an unspecified nature). His guilt, or guiltlessness, is also unknown to us: the pro-Godwinist E-text of the Anglo-Saxon Chronicle and F/F Lat. which derives from the same source as E, state Ælfgar's culpability, and his admission of it. The Abingdon chronicler whose work is found in the C-text of the Anglo-Saxon Chronicle, and the Mercian John

[39] On the character and behaviour of Swegn, see Barlow, *Edward the Confessor*, pp. 90–1 and 99–103.
[40] See note 24.

129

of Worcester both state his innocence. The compiler of D attempts to combine both viewpoints and manages to make his text somewhat ridiculous. It is probable that Ælfgar's guilt or innocence was then – and may still be – a matter of which viewpoint was taken at the time.

However, whatever opinion is adopted as to his guilt, what is clear from all the accounts is that during his exile Ælfgar sought and obtained assistance from Wales, returned to English territory and devastated Hereford.[41] The C- and E-texts of the Anglo-Saxon Chronicle, together with John of Worcester, Henry of Huntingdon and the second part of the *Historia Regum* name Gruffudd as his helper ('Griffine cinge' C, 'ond Ælfgar eorl gesohte Griffine's gehealdon on Norðwalum' E, 'Griffinum regem Walensium' JW [and the so-called *HR²*, following JW] 'Griffinum regem Nordwales' HH).[42] These sources also (with the exception of Henry of Huntingdon) state that, before going to Wales, Ælfgar went to Ireland and acquired the assistance of a fleet of pirates. While the fullest, most detailed accounts are those of the C-text of the Anglo-Saxon Chronicle and John of Worcester, the basic story seems to vary very little. Ælfgar, having got his Welsh and Irish allies, went with Gruffudd into Herefordshire where they defeated and put to flight a force commanded by Ralf the Timid whose territory this was. The victorious army then ravaged, plundered, and burnt the town of Hereford, including its minster. A large English force was gathered, which Harold Godwinesson led into north Wales: Gruffudd and Ælfgar evaded him by departing into south Wales. Dispersing much of his force, Harold went to Hereford and fortified it. Meanwhile messengers passed between the two parties, and a meeting occurred at Billingsley at which peace was made. Ælfgar's fleet departed for Chester to await payment, while he went to King Edward and was reinvested with his earldom. These events do not pass unnoticed in the Welsh chronicles: a victory by Gruffudd over Ralf is recorded in the Welsh texts, and the sacking of Hereford in both Welsh and Latin texts. No mention is made, however, of Ælfgar or his role in these events. *Brut y Tywysogion* (RB) reads:[43]

A gwedy hyny y kyffroes Gruffud ap Llywelyn lu yn erbyn y Saesson a ch[w]eiraw bydinoed yn Henford. Ac yn y erbyn y kyfodes y Saesson a diruawr lu gantunt, a Reinwlf yn dywyssawc arnunt. Ac ymgyfaruot ac ef a orugant a chweiraw bedinoed ac ymparatoi y ymlad. A'e kyrchu a wnaeth Gruffud yn dianot a bydinoed kyweir gantaw. A gwedy bot brwydyr chwerwdost, a'r Saesson heb allel godef kynwryf y Brytanyeit, yr ymchoelassant ar fo ac o diruawr ladua y dygwydassant. A'e hymlit yn lut a wnaeth Grufud y'r gaer; ac a mywn y doeth, a dibobli y gaer a wnaeth a'e thorri a llosgi y dref. Ac odyna gyt a diruawr anreith ac yspeil yr ymchoelawd o'e wlat yn hyfryt vudugawl.

And after that, Gruffudd ap Llywelyn moved a host against the Saxons, and he arrayed forces at Hereford. And against him rose up the Saxons and a mighty host with them, and Reinwlf as a leader over them. And they came up against him, and arrayed forces and prepared to fight. And Gruffudd without delay attacked them with well-ordered forces. And after a bitter-keen struggle, the Saxons, unable to withstand the assault of the Britons,

41 Except ASC (F) and ASC (F Lat) which note his exile and state that he was guilty, but give no account of his subsequent actions.
42 ASC (C) *s.a.* 1055; ASC (E) *s.a.* 1055; *HR²* *s.a.* 1055; HH *s.a.* 1055.
43 *ByT* (RB) *s.a.* [1056]. The translation is that of Jones. Compare *ByT* (Pen. 20) *s.a.* 1054 (*recte* 1056) and *ByS* *s.a.* 1054 (*recte* 1056).

turned to flight, and fell with great slaughter. And Gruffudd closely pursued them to the fortress; and he entered therein, and he pillaged the fortress and destroyed it and burned the town. And thereupon, with vast spoil and booty, he returned to his land happily victorious.

The event is given no explicit date in this text, or in either version of *Annales Cambriae*. *Brut y Tywysogion* (Pen. 20) and *Brenhinedd y Saesson* give 1054, however, corrected by Jones to 1056. But 1055 would seem to be the most probable date. The account given in the Welsh chronicles is clearly referring to the same event as that described in the English and Anglo-Norman texts mentioned above.

The second explicit conjunction of Ælfgar and Gruffudd occurs in the D-text of the Anglo-Saxon Chronicle and in John of Worcester (and the second part of the *Historia Regum*) at 1058.[44] John's account reads as follows:

Algarus Merciorum comes a rege Eadwardo secundo exlegatus est, sed regis Walanorum Griffini iuuamine et Norregiani classis adminiculo, quae ad illum uenerat ex improuiso, cito per uim suum comitatem recuperauit.

The D-text of the Anglo-Saxon Chronicle, however, while mentioning both the exile and the Norwegian fleet, makes no explicit connexion between the two, saying:

Her man ytte ut Ælfgar eorl; ac he com sona inn ongean mid strece þurh Gryffines fultum. And her com scyphere of Norwegan. Hit is langsum to atellanne eall hu hit gefaran wæs.

The Welsh sources note this event, but again omit Ælfgar. *Annales Cambriae* (B) reads, 'Magnus filio Haraldi uastauit regionem Anglorum auxiliante Grifino rege Britonum'.[45] The vernacular chronicles have substantially the same account, with the additional detail that this Magnus was son of the king of 'Germany'. *Brut y Tywysogion* (Pen. 20) has blundered, calling the Scandinavian leader 'Rhodri mawr', an error ascribed by Jones to a scribal miscomprehension of 'Magnus' as an epithet rather than a personal name.[46]

The connexion of the activities of Magnus with those of Gruffudd, and, by extension, those of Ælfgar, would appear to be reasonably reliable, especially in the face of the tendency of the compiler of the D-text of the Anglo-Saxon Chronicle to understate matters in his accounts of events.

What, then, was the context of this evident alliance, and how did it come to arise? In an examination of this question, the broader circumstances of the period are crucial. The early 1050s were a difficult time probably for the kingdom of England: in 1051 occurred the notorious 'English revolution' in which a decade of tension between the family of Earl Godwine and King Edward came to a head. In the wake of this confrontation, the whole of Godwine's family was dispossessed and fled into exile. Edward redistributed at least some of their lands, and

---

44 ASC (D) *s.a.* 1058; JW *s.a.* 1058; *HR*² *s.a.* 1058.
45 *AC* (B) *s.a.* [1056].
46 *ByT* (Pen. 20) *s.a.* 1056 (*recte* 1058). For Jones's comment, see *ByT* (Pen. 20), transl. Jones, p. 151, n. 14 35.

Ælfgar was one of the beneficiaries, receiving Harold's former earldom in East Anglia. In the following year, 1052, Godwine and his sons made their (ultimately successful) attempt to regain their lands and their status, landing in Southern England, and again confronting the king. In the same year, and seemingly much at the same time, the Welsh made a reappearance upon the English scene. The D-text of the Anglo-Saxon Chronicle records:[47]

On þam ilcan gere hergode Griffin se Wylisca cing on Herefordscire þæt he com swyþe neah to Leomynstre; and men gadorodon ongean ægðer ge landes men ge Frencisce men of ðam castele; and man þær ofsloh swyþe feola Engliscra godra manna and eac of þam Frenciscum; þæt wæs ylcan dæges on ðreotene geara þe man ær Eadwine ofsloh mid his geferum. And sona com Harold eorl of Irlande mid his scipum to Sæfern muðan.

This event is also noticed by John of Worcester and hence by *Historia Regum*. It is, I think, of importance for the relationship which developed beween Gruffudd ap Llywelyn and Ælfgar and therefore deserves examination. The raid itself is a clear piece of opportunism: given the troubles within the English polity, English attention was very probably directed away from the Welsh border, and Gruffudd seized his opportunity with both hands. The question is, which Gruffudd – Gruffudd ap Rhydderch, who as lord of south Wales had a common border with Herefordshire, or Gruffudd ap Llywelyn, the true extent of whose power at this time is unclear? (It is, for instance not known when he acquired ascendancy over Morgannwg: the tendency has been to assume that he achieved this when he overcame Gruffudd ap Rhydderch in 1055/56 – however, there is no hard and fast evidence either way.) David Walker has made out a strong case for the Southern Gruffudd based largely on geographical considerations:[48] he considered that the main area attacked was too far south for the attack to have originated in Gwynedd or Powys. His arguments are forceful but not, I think, conclusive. Gruffudd ap Llywelyn, from the very beginning of his reign, was capable of action within southern Wales – he drove Hywel ap Edwin out of Deheubarth in 1039, and pillaged Llanbadarn; he defeated Hywel at the mouth of the Tywi in 1044 (and in a context which suggests that Hywel, not Gruffudd, was the invader); and in 1047, as we have seen, he led a force through Ystrad Tywi and Dyfed. In 1055, he attacked Hereford again, and the tone of the account in the Anglo-Saxon Chronicle is such as to suggest that he brought his force initially from the North. Gruffudd ap Llywelyn clearly was capable of action within south Wales; moreover, while Gruffudd ap Rhydderch may have been holding Deheubarth, and even Glamorgan, we do not know which of these men was in power in, for instance, Buellt. However, there is a much stronger piece of evidence than that of geography to be brought forward here: it lies in the chronicle of John of Worcester. John, unlike almost all other English chroniclers, could tell his Gruffudds apart. It is not at all clear from the tone of the Anglo-Saxon Chronicle if the authors of the relevant recensions (CDE) were fully aware that there were two kings called Gruffudd in Wales at this time. John of Worcester, however, did know this, and he clearly knew which one did what and when. John always made

[47] ASC (D) *s.a.* 1052.
[48] Walker, 'A Note on Gruffudd ap Llywelyn'.

132

a distinction between the two Gruffudds: whenever he is writing of Gruffudd ap Llywelyn, he refers to him as *Griffinus rex Walensium*,[49] except on one occasion, in his annal for 1065, where he refers to him as *rex Nordwalanorum*. (This, however, is done to make a clear distinction: in his account of Caradog ap Gruffudd's raid on Portskewett, John has just been explaining that Caradog was the son of the south Welsh Gruffudd, who had been killed by the north Welsh Gruffudd.) In referring to Gruffudd ap Rhydderch, John always described him as 'Griffinus rex Australium Britonum/Suthwalanorum'.[50] John notices the raid on Hereford in 1052. He names the perpetrator as *Walensium rex Griffinus*,[51] the phrase used by him to denote Gruffudd ap Llywelyn. Of our sources for this period of Anglo-Welsh political relations, the *Chronicarum Chronica* of John of Worcester is one of the most reliable and careful: and in his opinion, the raid of 1052 was led by 'the Welsh king, Gruffudd' – Gruffudd ap Llywelyn. In view of this, I must disagree with Dr Walker, and consider that the incident in question was the work of Gruffudd ap Llywelyn.

This event more or less coincided with the return to power in England of Earl Godwine and his family, in the wake of which Ælfgar lost his newly acquired earldom of East Anglia to its original holder, Earl Harold. However, when Godwine died the next year, Harold came into possession of Wessex, and Ælfgar once more received East Anglia (that he did so, rather than the earldom passing into the hands of another son of Godwine, is interesting in itself, and may tell us something about the power of Leofric at this time, or of Edward's attitude to his newly restored in-laws). In 1055, the Northumbrian earl, Siward, died, and was replaced with Tostig Godwinesson; in the same year Ælfgar himself fell foul of royal authority and went into exile, as described above, combining with Gruffudd ap Llywelyn in his efforts to be reinstated. Historians have generally held that the link with Gruffudd was forged during this exile, perhaps as a matter of expediency, Ælfgar needing armed support, and Gruffudd having earlier in the same year succeeded in killing his rival Gruffudd ap Rhydderch. This was the view held by Lloyd.[52] I should like to question this, and to resurrect a suggestion originally made about a century ago by J. R. Green: Ælfgar's overtures to Gruffudd began before his first exile, and, indeed, it may well have been this attempt to establish a relationship between the heir to the earldom of Mercia, and a Welsh ruler of increasing power which constituted the treason of which Ælfgar stands accused in the E-Text of the Anglo-Saxon Chronicle and F/F Lat. Green's view of the situation was this:[53]

The death of Siward, the elevation of Tostig, could hardly fail to rouse to a new effort the one house that remained to vie with the house of Godwine. Girt in by Godwine's sons to north and to south, isolated in Mid-Britain, Leofric was too old and too sickly to renew single-handed and without help from the king the struggle of 1051. But his son Ælfgar of East Anglia was now practically master of Mid-Britain and in this emergency seems to have sought aid from his Welsh neighbours in the West. His alliance with Gruffudd of

49 JW *s.a.* 1055, 1058, 1063, and 1064.
50 JW *s.a.* 1049, 1053, and 1065.
51 JW *s.a.* 1052.
52 Lloyd, *A History*, II.364.
53 Green, *The Conquest*, II.291–3.

133

North Wales marks the establishment of new relations between England and the Welsh princes. No league of Englishmen with Welshmen with a view of influencing English politics had been seen since Penda's league with Cadwallon. The co-operation of Welshmen with the Danes had simply been a co-operation of two foes against the English themselves. But from the time of Ælfgar to the time of Earl Simon de Montfort the Welsh play a part in English history as allies of the English combatants. The danger was the greater that Gruffudd had just become master through the death of a rival of the whole of our modern Wales, and we can hardly doubt that it was tidings of a negotiation between earl and prince that drove Harold to a sudden stroke, in the banishment of Ælfgar by the witan in the spring of 1055.

I cannot accept the entirety of this argument, but nevertheless regard the core of it as sound. Green somewhat overstated Ælfgar's position in 1055: Leofric cannot have been so weak, as he is found negotiating with Gruffudd in tense circumstances in 1056 – a situation from which Ælfgar is conspicuous by his absence. However, in the reign of the Confessor, it was by no means unheard of for earls to interest themselves in other kingdoms: Siward had spent some time intervening in Scotland, and Tostig made a marriage-alliance in Flanders. The appointment of Tostig to the important Northumbrian earldom, however, was a significant step in the developing power of the sons of Godwine, and Green was surely correct in pointing to this as the cause of Ælfgar's bid to increase his own standing. (Indeed, it is worth wondering whether Ælfgar had had hopes of obtaining Northumbria for himself.) But why would an earl of East Anglia look to Wales for an ally? Partly, no doubt, on account of Ælfgar's expectations and family-background in Mercia. However, I should suggest that what Ælfgar was primarily seeking was an ally with power and military strength – and Gruffudd had only a few years earlier provided the English with an all too potent demonstration of his abilities, in the heavy raid on Hereford of 1052. Ælfgar's attention had been drawn to him, and, faced with an increasing Godwinist bloc, Gruffudd may have seemed an obvious ally. Both parties no doubt stood to gain: Ælfgar acquired strength to back up his own status, and Gruffudd acquired a voice and a protector at the English court.

When Green proposed this idea it did not go unchallenged and, indeed, a counter-argument by Lloyd seems to have caused Green's account to sink from historians' view. Dismissing him in a footnote, Lloyd wrote[54] '. . . the sources imply that Ælfgar and Gruffydd did not come to terms until the former had returned from Ireland, and so the view . . ., that their earlier relations had provoked the attack on Ælfgar, is to be rejected.' It is the case that those sources which mention Ælfgar's visit to Ireland place it before his arrival in Wales, but not all the sources include the trip to Ireland and, moreover, pace Lloyd, there is nothing in the phrasing of any of the sources, even those mentioning Ireland, which can be taken in any way as indicating whether or not Ælfgar and Gruffudd had had any prior contact. It might be objected that, to almost any English man of the time, consorting with the Welsh would have constituted treason – and yet the Anglo-Saxon Chronicle (C) speaks of Ælfgar as guiltless. However, when one is dealing with the Anglo-Saxon Chronicle for this period, it should always be

[54] Lloyd, A History, II.364, n. 19.

remembered that the three recensions of the Chronicle covering Edward's reign were greatly concerned with the activities of the house of Godwine, E supporting this family, and C disparaging it (D, being a later compilation, is a – not always successful – attempt to steer a middle course): it seems very probable that to the mid-eleventh century author of C, consorting with the Welsh was a far lesser sin than consorting with Godwine or his sons, and that, moreover, in the wish to blacken the latter family, the writer might well gloss over or deny faults in those whom he saw as opponents of Harold and his kin. Furthermore, in this period of English history, it was by no means a standard course of action to apply to Wales for aid. The Scandinavians of Ireland appear to have operated as mercenaries, acting with whoever could pay them or offer sufficient incentive – as with Hywel ab Edwin in 1044,[55] or Harold Godwinesson in 1052.[56] However, there is no clear evidence for the Welsh acting in such a manner: indeed as a general rule they seem to have provided a threat, at least on the borders, rather than a resource, to the English. I cannot see that, barring accidents of tide and weather,[57] an English exile (and one from a family which had lost at least one member to Gruffudd's aggression), even backed by a Hiberno-Scandinavian fleet, would have risked an encounter with the Welsh before attempting reclamation of his rights in England, unless he was either moderately sure of being received peacefully, or else felt that he could subdue the Welsh ruler into aiding him. The latter course seems unlikely for various reasons: (i) if Ælfgar had the potential to be able to antici-pate overcoming a notoriously powerful Welsh ruler, why did he need Welsh assistance at all? (ii) if he did not, or if he was unsure of his own strength, why take such a large gamble before confronting the English? (iii) if the connexion did begin in such a manner, what real incentive was there for Gruffudd to continue the relationship – especially when Ælfgar was again weakened by his second exile? Some degree of previous connexion does appear to be more prob-able. It might be asked what Gruffudd stood to gain by forming this alliance. Lloyd thought that Ælfgar became a protector to Gruffudd in some way:[58] given Ælfgar's rather equivocal position, this cannot really have been military protec-tion. However, as the son of a leading royal counsellor and later, as earl of Mercia, Ælfgar may have been able to confer protection in a political sense, as spokesman and perhaps mediator, at the English court (and it is the case that English royal attention was not properly turned to chastising Gruffudd until Ælfgar was dead). Also, it would seem probable that it was at this time that Gruffudd's gains in territory on the marches were made, including Ergyng, as Christopher Brooke has suggested[59] – and Ælfgar again may have been an influence upon the king in helping to bring about a recognition of Gruffudd's power in these areas.

From the English side, at least, the alliance must have been to some extent a move in the power-game between the English nobles; the house of Godwine had connexions with Flanders, Tostig having married Judith, the sister of Count

55 *ByT* (Pen. 20) *s.a.* 1042 (*recte* 1044).
56 ASC (C) *s.a.* 1052; ASC (D) *s.a.* 1052; ASC (E) *s.a.* 1052; JW *s.a.* 1052.
57 A happenstance which the phrasing of ASC does seem to discount.
58 Lloyd, *A History*, II.369.
59 Brooke, *The Church and the Welsh Border*, pp. 10–11.

Baldwin V,[60] and with Denmark. Siward had had influence in Scotland, involving himself in the conflict between MacBethad and Malcolm Canmore. Ælfgar, as was suggested above, probably sought friendship with Gruffudd to counterbalance the power and influence of the house of Godwine, and his choice of Gruffudd as an ally may have been influenced by the latter's demonstration of force at Hereford in 1052. The alliance may have been formed in 1053, when Godwine died, an event which may (for a time at least) have loosened the cohesion of the Godwinist bloc, and perhaps wrought a brief reduction in their power (this seems likely, since Edward was able to replace Harold in East Anglia by Ælfgar rather than by one of Harold's own brothers). Or, and more probably, the alliance may have begun in early 1055, when Tostig was made earl of Northumbria, an event which may have threatened and alarmed Ælfgar by placing a potentially hostile earl at his rear.

However, whatever the motives behind this alliance, we can still trace some of its ramifications. It was effective: the rapid reinstatement of Ælfgar in 1055 bears witness to that, as does Harold's recourse to negotiation rather than pitched battle in the aftermath of the sack of Hereford. Green considered that this course of action was adopted because Harold's '. . . cool sense preferred peace to a useless victory; and at the close of the year Ælfgar was suffered to return baffled to his earldom . . .'.[61] I do not concur. The devastation of Hereford had provoked the assembly of a very large army[62] which Harold led against the rebels into Wales itself: Ælfgar and Gruffudd were clearly perceived as a very serious threat. The movement into Wales was thwarted: disappearing into south Wales, the allies eluded Harold, and he let much of his force disperse while he returned to Hereford. Once there, he commenced fortifications – was he expecting another attack? – an action showing that he was aware of the danger presented by the rebel earl and his Welsh ally. Meanwhile, we are told, messengers passed between the two groups, resulting eventually in the meeting at Billingsley and the subsequent peace. Ælfgar, by his show of strength, achieved his aim, receiving his earldom back again from the king. This was no opportunity for Harold to gain a 'useless victory', this was a very serious threat to the English polity, to be met with action no less definite than that taken against the returning family of Godwine in 1052.

That the alliance was perceived as threatening is shown by the events of the following year, 1056, when Leofgar, the new bishop of Hereford, and a former chaplain of Harold's, initiated an attack upon, and was defeated by, Gruffudd.[63] Peace was again made, through the agency this time not only of Harold but also of Leofric and Bishop Ealdred – and Gruffudd swore to be an underking to Edward.[64] This incident shows not only Harold's recognition of Gruffudd as a threat, but also the recognition by all the English magnates of Gruffudd as a significant power. Gruffudd far from being treated simply as an enemy was being formally drawn into the English polity.

60 ASC (D) s.a. 1051.
61 Green, The Conquest, II.292.
62 ASC (D) s.a. 1055 'Ða gaderade man fyrde geond eall Engla land.'
63 See note 25.
64 ASC (C) s.a. 1056.

It is possible to trace further ramifications of Ælfgar's alliance with Gruffudd. Orderic Vitalis[65] records that Ælfgar's daughter Ealdgyth was married to Gruffudd – Lloyd[66] seems to have thought that the event occurred *ca* 1057, the year in which Leofric died and Ælfgar became earl of Mercia. By the testimony of Giraldus Cambrensis,[67] the Norman marcher lord Bernard of Neufmarché, the conqueror of Brycheiniog, was married to one Nest, herself the daughter of Nest ferch Gruffudd ap Llywelyn. This latter Nest has been taken to be Gruffudd's child by Ealdgyth, although Giraldus does not say so. Bernard was active in Wales *ca* 1090–*ca* 1125. His wife Nest was the daughter of Osbern fitz Richard (living 1086). If this Nest was a daughter of Ealdgyth, then on these grounds Lloyd's date for the marriage is as good as any. (She cannot, surely, have been the mother of Gruffudd's sons Owain [*ob.* 1059] Maredudd and Ithel [both *ob.* 1069].)

The so-called-foundation charter of Coventry Abbey[68] also has some interesting indications (see S.1000, 1226).[69] Amongst the estates to which the abbey laid claim in the foundation-charter (which is an early twelfth-century forgery, purporting to have been granted in 1043 by Earl Leofric) is *Eatun* – 'Eatun iuxta aminem que clicitur De in cestre prouincia'.[70] This place is identified in the charter as Eaton-on-Dee in Maelor Cymraeg Hundred.[71] According to the Cheshire Domesday,[72] this estate was owned *tempore regis Eadwardi* by St Chad's, Chester, but:

Rex E. dedit regi Griffino totam terram quae iacebat trans aquam quae De vocatur. Sed postquam ipse Griffin forisfecit ei, abstulit ab eo hanc terram, et reddidit episcopo de Cestre et omnibus suis hominibus qui antea ipsa tenebant.

This clearly reflects some part of one of the peace settlements with Gruffudd (whose influence over the border as revealed in Domesday book has long been recognised).[73] At the time of the Domesday survey this particular estate was part of the land of the bishop of Chester, and not a holding of Coventry Abbey. Lancaster suggested that Coventry made the claim as a result of the connexion which grew up early in the twelfth century between Coventry Abbey and the bishopric of Chester[74] (moved to Coventry in 1098 by Bishop Robert de Limesey), but, as none of the other estates claimed by Coventry was Chester episcopal land, I do not think that this argument fully explains the claim. I should rather suggest that it was the connexion with Gruffudd which prompted the claim:

65 Orderic Vitalis, *Historia Ecclesiastica*, Books III and IV: ed. & transl. Chibnall, II.138, 216. There is also a reference to this in Orderic's interpolations into the *Gesta Normannorum Ducum* of William of Jumièges, in chapter 31.
66 Lloyd, *A History*, II.369.
67 Gerald of Wales, *The Journey Through Wales*, transl. Thorpe, pp. 88–9.
68 S.1000, ed. & transl. Harmer, *Anglo-Saxon Writs*, no. 45, pp. 214–22; S.1226, ed. Lancaster, 'The Coventry Forged Charters', p. 141.
69 Sawyer, *Anglo-Saxon Charters*, pp. 298–99 and 358.
70 Lancaster, 'The Coventry Forged Charters', p. 141.
71 See note 70.
72 *Domesday Book*, Cheshire, fo 263ra, where the modern spelling is 'Eyton'.
73 Lloyd, *A History*, II.365–7.
74 Lancaster, 'The Coventry Forged Charters', p. 131.

Coventry was a foundation of Earl Leofric, and its first two abbots were members of his family, which in the persons of Ælfgar and his children was linked quite closely to the north Welsh ruler. Is it entirely surprising that the family-foundation should reflect this connexion? Further support for this hypothesis may be found in the Warwickshire Domesday, where, among the holdings of Coventry Abbey in 1086 is to be found an estate (unmentioned in the foundation-charter) at *Bilvaie* (Binley), which the abbot had bought from Osbern Fitz Richard (who was himself married to a daughter of Gruffudd). However, the Domesday entry also tells us the previous owner of the estate, namely,[75] *hanc terram tenuit Aldgid uxor Griffin.* The connexion between the family of Leofric and Gruffudd appears to have been well remembered in 1086, then. The above entry may also support the hypothesis that Nest the wife of Osbern Fitz Richard was the daughter of Ealdgyth as well as of Gruffudd, since Osbern may have acquired the land from his wife, who might have acquired it from her mother.

Gruffudd ap Llywelyn was killed in 1063, after a year of determined campaigns against him by the Godwinessons. Ælfgar, it is usually assumed, had died before this date – he disappears from our record in 1062, and it is possible that this circumstance provided a political climate within England which permitted Harold to launch another attack on Gruffudd. It is very likely that the earl of Wessex wished to prevent the Mercia-Gwynedd alliance from persisting into the lifetimes of Ælfgar's sons, Eadwine, the new earl of Mercia, and Morkere. It has to be said that in this aim at least he failed. I have discussed the circumstances attendant upon the death of Gruffudd ap Llywelyn elsewhere[76] and I do not propose to repeat my arguments in detail here. It is clear that Harold's expedition was intended to be punitive: it is not clear that it was intended to bring about the actual death of Gruffudd. What is known is that Gruffudd was killed after Harold's expedition, and by his own men, a circumstance which leads me to think that the actual killing may have been the result of an internal Welsh struggle, catalysed and aided by Harold's activities, but not actually ordered by Harold. What survives in tradition as to the character of Gruffudd ap Llywelyn is such as to suggest that he was a harsh man,[77] perhaps excessively so, and it is likely that the events of 1063 gave some of his opponents the necessary opportunity to strike back at him. His successors in north Wales were his own maternal half-brothers, Bleddyn and Rhiwallon sons of Cynfyn, who apparently made some kind of submission to Edward and Harold[78] on entering the kingship. In 1069 they fought at Mechain to keep it against their nephews, Gruffudd's sons Maredudd and Ithel. The Welsh chronicles are notably uninformative for the period between Gruffudd's death and the battle of Mechain. (Indeed their account of Gruffudd's death is very unelaborated: the *Brutiau* give an encomium on him, but neither they nor *Annales Cambriae* mention Harold at all, and both attribute the killing to Gruffudd's own men). While I should hesitate to point the finger directly at Bleddyn and Rhiwallon, their actions in 1063 and 1069 suggest that

---

75 *Domesday Book*, Worcestershire, fo 238vb.
76 Maund, 'Cynan ab Iago'.
77 Walter Map, *De Nugis Curialium*, chapters 22 and 23, pp. 186–96.
78 ASC (D) *s.a.* 1063; JW *s.a.* 1064; *HR²* *s.a.* 1064.

they were anxious to hold and enjoy the kingship – and kinslaying is not at all uncommon in early mediaeval Wales.

Whatever the immediate causes of Gruffudd's death, its effects upon the English polity are both obvious and very interesting. In the period after the death, Earl Harold can be seen making overtures to the house of Leofric. This speaks for the power still enjoyed by that family (if Harold was as all-powerful as some historians seem to have thought, need he have put himself out for two very young nobles?) and also for the political sense of Harold: if he was aiming at the English crown by this time, as is possible, he must have been aware of the need to build up support for himself within the English aristocracy – and he clearly recognised that his brother Tostig, far from being a useful supporter, was a dangerous rival. Harold exploited the events following Gruffudd's death: he seems to have associated himself with the accession of Bleddyn and Rhiwallon[79] (was he trying to build his own Welsh alliance?). And he tried very hard to placate the house of Leofric. Orderic Vitalis[80] tells us that Harold married Gruffudd's widow Ealdgyth, the sister of Eadwine and Morkere, thus binding the family to him by ties of kinship – and perhaps holding out the prospect of a second crown for Ealdgyth, and the accompanying political influence for her brothers. Furthermore, in 1065, Harold backed Morkere as the new earl of Northumbria, at the expense of his brother Tostig. The latter was his rival, but would Harold have promoted as his supplanter another enemy? It seems to me that Harold was aware of the Mercian house as a power, and he was aware that he had injured them in provoking the death of Gruffudd: his actions suggest a rapid and major attempt to placate them. Perhaps he also hoped to woo them away from Wales and into a closer link with himself. If he had succeeded in holding England in 1066, the degree to which he achieved this might be discernible. However, he had not succeeded fully by 1065, and the Welsh connexion with the house of Leofric persisted well after Harold's death.

Despite the deaths of Ælfgar and Gruffudd, the Welsh-Mercian connexion appears to have endured and continued through Ælfgar's sons and Gruffudd's half-brothers. In 1065, Welshmen made up part of the force with which Earl Eadwine marched north to assist his brother Morkere, on the latter's being chosen earl of Northumbria.[81] The source of this Welsh aid becomes more apparent in the post-Conquest period. Between 1066 and 1071 these last two earls of the line of Leofric constituted a thorn in the side of William the Conqueror. Neither had fought at Hastings, and both initially submitted to the Norman king. However, this submission was not long-lasting, and the two earls rapidly became rebels, for the period ca 1068–1071. Orderic Vitalis is the main witness to this, although Eadwine's death at the hands of his own men, and Morkere's surrender at Ely, both in 1071, are incidents also known from other sources.

Orderic[82] relates that, at some time after the arrival in England of Queen

79 See note 28.
80 Orderic Vitalis, *Historia Ecclesiastica*, Books III and IV: ed. & transl. Chibnall, II.138, 216.
81 See note 30.
82 Orderic Vitalis, *Historia Ecclesiastica*, Book IV: ed. & transl. Chibnall, II.214–16.

Matilda (1068), Eadwine and Morkere rebelled, with the help of a great part of the English and the Welsh

Tempore Normannicae cladis quae nimis oppressionibus Anglos immoderate conquassauit, Blidenus rex Gualorum ad auunculos suos suppetias uenit, secumque multitudinem Britonum adduxit.

Bleddyn was in fact not related to Eadwine and Morkere, except through his half-brother's marriage: in calling the Mercian earls the uncles of Bleddyn, Orderic is repeating his earlier error[83] of calling Bleddyn the son of Gruffudd and Ealdgyth. In fact, Bleddyn and Gruffudd shared the same mother, Angharad ferch Maredudd ab Owain. Nevertheless, it is clear that this error represents a memory of some kind of link between the family of Leofric and that of Gruffudd. Orderic does not seem to have known a great deal about Ælfgar, whom he has confused with Leofric; so it is possible that he was ignorant of the events of 1055 and 1058. But he did know that the two lines had some kind of relationship, more than a simple use of Welsh mercenaries. As their father had done before them, Eadwine and Morkere turned towards Wales to assist them in time of need.

Bleddyn ap Cynfyn was a king who left a favourable impression on his contemporaries, if the panegyrics on him found in the *Brutiau* are any kind of guide.[84] In addition, however, he appears to have inherited his predecessor's political sense. Bleddyn clearly continued Gruffudd's Mercian alliance, in the face of the Norman threat, which was probably already being noted within Wales. He did not restict his support to Eadwine and Morkere: in 1067 he and his brother Rhiwallon are to be found aiding Eadric *Cild* against Richard Fitz Scrob and William Fitz Osbern. Throughout the post-Conquest period, whenever there is a rebellion against the king of England, then there are Welsh aiding the rebels. Bleddyn in 1067 and 1068–71 could be seen as the originator of this policy, were we ignorant of the career of Gruffudd ap Llywelyn before him. A strong power in England was always a potential threat to the Welsh kingdoms, and Gruffudd found a way to mitigate this, by entering the English polity and attempting to influence it. Rather than raiding, he began to intervene in English affairs, and also found a voice on his behalf in the English political arena. He also never missed a chance to disrupt the English whenever an opportunity presented itself, raiding Hereford in 1052 when the king was engaged in conflict with the family of Godwine, and supporting the rebel earl Ælfgar against his peers in 1055 and 1058. Under the Norman kings, times of stress within England were increasingly to prove the opportunity for the Welsh, and Bleddyn, while adhering to the Mercian alliance, was perhaps beginning to exploit this in his support of Eadric in 1067. In 1071, the two earls of the Mercian house finally fell, one being murdered, the other imprisoned, and Gruffudd's alliance ended. Welsh intervention in English politics did not; Gruffudd had demonstrated that it was possible to do more than raid and ravage – his successors took notice of his lesson.

---

83 *Ibid.*, Book III, II.138.
84 *ByT* (Pen. 20) *s.a.* 1076 (*recte* 1078); *ByT* (RB) *s.a.* [1078]; *ByS s.a.* 1076 (*recte* 1078).

Most of the other incidents of this period fit into the raid and counter-raid pattern common in the tenth century and early eleventh century. In no case do the Welsh appear to be trying to influence or change the course of English politics, and there is only one instance of the English trying to affect Welsh affairs, the slaying of Rhys ap Rhydderch in 1053. Almost nothing is known of this Rhys, but from the habit of the Welsh annalists of referring to the 'sons of Rhydderch' rather than to 'Gruffudd ap Rhydderch' as a significant power in south Wales, it is possible that he was in some way associated with the south Welsh kingship. His killing is said to have occurred because he did harm to the English[85] and ravaged frequently: nothing more is known of this, unless it be supposed that he was involved in his brother's raid of 1049 with the Scandinavian fleet in Gloucestershire.

The attack in 1065 upon Earl Harold's hunting lodge at Portskewett is probably to be interpreted as an attempt by the southern Welsh Caradog ap Gruffudd ap Rhydderch to drive the English out of Wales, and was probably not a vengeance-action for Gruffudd ap Llywelyn. Caradog was to become a significant force in south Wales, but he was a ruler who confined his interest to Welsh politics, and on the one occasion when we find him leagued with the Normans, it was in an action which affected the Welsh polity, and Caradog's own power, far more than that of the Normans. The 1070 campaign of William the Conqueror was probably mainly directed at English rebels, especially Eadric *Cild*, rather than at the Welsh, who seem to have been involved only as auxiliaries. Our source for this incident, Orderic Vitalis,[86] does not imply either that William penetrated very far in Wales on this campaign, or that he actually encountered the rulers of the Welsh.

WALES AND THE NORMANS

The early incursions of the Normans into Wales (and especially south Wales), is a subject which has recieved much discussion and attention. In view of this, I do not intend to analyse in detail here the progression and development of the Norman conquest of Wales, a topic already examined for us by such scholars as R. R. Davies,[87] D. Crouch,[88] L. H. Nelson,[89] and Christopher Lewis,[90] as well as the earlier work of Lloyd[91] and J. G. Edwards.[92] I propose rather to examine the

---

85 See note 23.
86 Orderic Vitalis, *Historia Ecclesiastica*, Book IV: ed. & transl. Chibnall, II.234.
87 Davies, *Conquest, Coexistence and Change*. See also Davies, 'Kings, Lords and Liberties in the March of Wales 1066–1272'.
88 Crouch, 'The Slow Death of Kingship in Glamorgan 1067–1158'.
89 Nelson, *The Normans in South Wales*.
90 Lewis, 'English and Norman Government'.
91 Lloyd, *A History*, chapters 11 and 12, II.357–461, and also Lloyd, 'Wales and the coming'.
92 Edwards, 'The Normans and the Welsh March'. Other useful studies are: Rowlands,

Welsh response to this new threat. As such I shall not deal to any great extent with the material of the Domesday Book: those wishing to see a thorough account and explanation of Norman activities as revealed by this source are advised to turn to the excellent work of Lewis, who has analysed this evidence for the Welsh border both before and after the Norman Conquest.

Before turning to the Welsh reaction to their new neighbours, however, it is necessary to give a brief account of the Norman settlement in and around the Welsh border. Norman activity in this area began early, William I establishing trusted followers along the border in the persons of William FitzOsbern (earl of Hereford *ca* 1067–1071), Roger de Montgomery (earl of Shrewsbury 1071–1094) and Hugh d'Avranches (earl of Chester *ca* 1070–1101). Lewis has charted the activities of these men in Wales in this period, and shown how they each organised their border offences and defences.[93] The Welsh chronicles also demonstrate this progress to some degree, showing us a Norman presence in Morgannwg by 1072,[94] assaults on Dyfed and Ceredigion by 1073,[95] a Norman presence at Rhuddlan possibly by 1075,[96] (and certainly by 1086[97]). For south Wales, at least, the incursions were somewhat lulled in the 1080s: in 1081, in the wake of the important battle of Mynydd Carn, William I entered Wales, with an army according to the E-text of the Anglo-Saxon Chronicle,[98] and on a pilgrimage to St Davids according to *Annales Cambriae*[99] and the *Brutiau*.[100] During this period, Lloyd suggested, William met with the king of Deheubarth, Rhys ap Tewdwr, and made some kind of agreement with him.[101] While we do not know its exact terms, the relative calm enjoyed by south Wales in this time, and the Domesday record of the £40 render of Rhys for south Wales – as Lloyd pointed out – give us some indications of its nature.[102] It appears to have been a truce, which lasted the life-time of William I: it is not until after his death that we see renewed Norman attacks on southern Wales.

This truce cannot have extended to north Wales. We know from *Historia*

'The Making of the March: Aspects of the Norman Settlement of Dyfed'; Cathcart-King, 'The Defence of Wales 1066–1283: the Other Side of the Hill'; Smith, 'The Kingdom of Morgannwg and the Norman Conquest of Glamorgan'; Walker, *The Norman Conquerors* and 'The Norman Settlement in Wales'; Mason, 'Roger de Montgomery and His Sons'; Meisel, *Barons of the Welsh Frontier*; D'Haenens, *Les Invasions normandes*; Husain, *Cheshire under the Norman Earls*; Le Patourel, *The Norman Empire*; Körner, *The Battle of Hastings*.

93 Lewis, 'English and Norman Government', chapters 6–9.
94 *AC* (B) *s.a.* [1071]; *AC* (C) *s.a.* [1073]; *ByT* (Pen. 20) *s.a.* 1070 (*recte* 1072); *ByT* (RB) *s.a.* 1070 (*recte* 1072); *ByS s.a.* 1070 (*recte* 1072).
95 *AC* (C) *s.a.* [1074]; *ByT* (Pen. 20) *s.a.* 1071 (*recte* 1073); *ByT* (RB) *s.a.* [1071]; *ByS s.a.* 1071 (*recte* 1073).
96 *HGK*, ed. Evans, pp. 7 and 9–10.
97 *Domesday Book*, Cheshire, 269ra–rb. The holdings of the Normans in north Wales and especially those of Robert of Rhuddlan, are quite large. Robert was claiming all of north Wales, as well as Arwystli. Rhos and Rhufoniog were listed as separate fiefs.
98 *ASC* (E) *s.a.* 1081.
99 *AC* (B) *s.a.* [1081]; *AC* (C) *s.a.* [1082].
100 *ByT* (Pen. 20) *s.a.* 1079 (*recte* 1081); *ByT* (RB) *s.a.* [1081]; *ByS s.a.* 1079 (*recte* 1081).
101 Lloyd, *A History*, II.393–4.
102 *Domesday Book*, Herefordshire, fo 179rb.

Gruffud vab Kenan[103] and from Orderic[104] that Rhys's co-victor of Mynydd Carn, the would-be ruler of Gwynedd, Gruffudd ap Cynan, was captured soon after the battle in 1081 and imprisoned by either Hugh d'Avranches or Robert of Rhuddlan for an uncertain period. *Historia Gruffud vab Kenan* tells us that on Gruffudd's capture Earl Hugh overran Gwynedd and built castles in Arfon, Anglesey, Bangor and Meirionydd.[105] The agressive attitude of Hugh and of Robert of Rhuddlan to Wales has been shown also from the Domesday evidence by Lewis.[106] The *Brutiau* speak of castles in Gwynedd as existing by 1094 (although they give no account of their founding). It is clear that some of the Norman incursions into north Wales had already occurred before 1081 – Rhuddlan was seemingly held by Robert in 1075,[107] yet it had been a royal court of Gruffudd ap Llywelyn in 1063.[108]

Lewis suggested very convincingly that not all the Welsh lands described in Domesday as being in Anglo-Norman hands had been gained since 1065. In the case of Ergyng and some parts of Cheshire particularly, he pointed to the campaigns of Harold Godwinesson in 1063, suggesting that land (possibly formerly English and conquered by Gruffudd ap Llywelyn) returned to English hands just before the Norman Conquest, becoming a legacy for the new Norman lords.[109] Some of his north Welsh land may therefore have come to Hugh with his earldom. Hugh's attitude to Wales was aggressive: by 1086 he and his kinsman Robert of Rhuddlan were making substantial claims to lordship in Northern Wales (whether they actully possessed such lordship is another question), with Robert paying £40 to the king for north Wales,[110] the same sum rendered by Rhys for the South. The extent of their claims is not surprising, given the context. Rhys ap Tewdwr had already been established in Deheubarth when he defeated his rival Caradog ap Gruffudd at Mynydd Carn. This was not the case for Rhys's ally at the battle, Gruffudd ap Cynan. Since 1075, Gruffudd had been trying to establish himself in at least some part of Gwynedd, and meeting with little success (indeed, if *Historia Gruffud vab Kenan* is to be trusted at all, it seems Gruffudd met with considerable hostility from the local nobles).[111] His rival was Trahaearn ap Caradog, a member of an Arwstli dynasty, but who was recognised as king in at least some parts of Gwynedd. With the exception of a confused statement in *Historia Gruffud vab Kenan*,[112] and a line in Orderic's epitaph for Robert of Rhuddlan,[113] there is no clear evidence for Norman attacks on Trahaearn, or upon his predecessor Bleddyn ap Cynfyn. Indeed, what we know of the careers of these two seems to indicate that they took a strong interest in

103 *HGK*, ed. Evans, pp. 16–19.
104 Orderic Vitalis, *Historia Ecclesiastica*, Book VIII: ed. & transl. Chibnall, IV.144.
105 *HGK*, ed. Evans, p. 18.
106 Lewis, 'English and Norman Government', chapter 6.
107 See note 96.
108 ASC (D) *s.a.* 1063; JW *s.a.* 1063.
109 Lewis, 'English and Norman Government', chapter 5. This point was originally made by Brooke, *The Church and the Welsh Border*, pp. 10–11.
110 See notes 97 and 102.
111 *HGK*, ed. Evans, p. 10. His lack of success is also noted by Davies, *Conquest, Coexistence and Change*, p. 33.
112 *HGK*, ed. Evans, pp. 12–13. For a discussion of this see Maund, 'Trahaearn'.
113 Orderic Vitalis, *Historia Ecclesiastica*, Book VIII: ed. & transl. Chibnall, IV.144.

south Wales[114] (and England in the case of Bleddyn[115]). There are two implications to this: the first is that they seem to have inherited not only the kingship but also the ambitions of Gruffudd ap Llywelyn, the second is that they must have been reasonably secure in their own lands, or they would not have been readily able to lend support and mount expeditions in other areas. (I have argued elsewhere that Trahaearn was present at Mynydd Carn essentially as an ally of Caradog ap Gruffudd, and that the main issue provoking this battle was the lordship of south Wales, not that of Gwynedd.[116]) *Pace* the author of *Historia Gruffud vab Kenan*, I would suggest that Norman pressure on north Wales did not become very intense until after Mynydd Carn, as a result of which battle Gwynedd was deprived for some time of strong leadership. Ironically, the battle which brought Norman respect for the power of Rhys ap Tewdwr in the South laid the North open to Norman hostility.

The death in 1087 of William I brought about a similar change for south Wales. It has been suggested that William II was less interested in honouring the agreement with Rhys, and that on the death of William I it again became possible for the Normans to expand strongly into south Wales.[117] Rhys ap Tewdwr met his death in 1093 at the hands of the Normans of Brycheiniog,[118] an incident which suggests that the expansion had already begun, and that Rhys, feeling threatened, was seeking to check it. The consequences of his death were very serious for south Wales. *Brut y Tywysogion* (RB) records:[119]

[D]eg mlyned a phetwar ugeint a mil oed oet Crist pan [las] Rys uap Tewdwr, brenhin Deheubarth, y gann y Ffreinc a oed ynn presswylaw Brecheinawc. [Ac yna, y dygwydawd teyrnas y Brytanyeit] . . . Ac yna deu uis wedy hynny, amgylch Kalan Gorff[ennaf], y deuth y Ffreinc y Dyuet a Cheredigyawn, [y rei a'e kynhalassant] gantunt etwa ac y kadarnaassant o [kestyll]; a holl tir y Brytannyeit achubassant.

One thousand and ninety was the year of Christ when Rhys ap Tewdwr, king of Deheubarth, was slain by the French who were inhabiting Brycheiniog. And then fell the kingdom of the Britons . . . And two months after that, about the Calends of July, the French came to Dyfed and Ceredigion, which they have held to this day, and fortified them with castles, and they seized all the land of the Britons.

The removal of Rhys was an opportunity not only for the Normans but for the north Welsh; a point I shall return to. However, on his death, the Normans were able once more to penetrate Dyfed and Ceredigion, and to build fortifications therein: it was probably at this time that Arnulf de Montgomery commenced building Pembroke castle, which is mentioned by the *Brutiau* as being one of the two castles in Deheubarth which did not fall in the Welsh rebellion of 1094.

---

114 *AC* (B) s.a. [1075] and [1078]; *AC* (C) s.a. [1076] and [1079]; *ByT* (Pen. 20) s.a. 1073 (*recte* 1075) and 1076 (*recte* 1078); *ByT* (RB) s.a. [1075] and [1078]; *ByS* s.a. 1073 (*recte*1075) and 1076 (*recte* 1078).
115 Orderic Vitalis, *Historia Ecclesiastica*, Book IV: ed. & transl. Chibnall, II.216.
116 See Maund, 'Trahaearn'.
117 Lloyd, *A History*, II.396.
118 *AC* (B) s.a. [1093]; *AC* (C) s.a. [1093]; *ByT* (Pen. 20) s.a. 1091 (*recte* 1093); *ByT* (RB) s.a. 1090 (*recte* 1093); *ByS* s.a. 1091 (*recte* 1093).
119 *ByT* (RB), ed. & transl. Jones, pp. 32–3.

This rebellion helped to check the Norman progress to some extent (helped by the death around this time of Robert of Rhuddlan).[120] However, it was not conclusive. In 1095 the Normans ravaged Gower, Cydweli and Ystrad Tywi,[121] and in the autumn William II led an army into Wales.[122] In 1096, Brycheiniog, Gwent and Gwynllwg did homage to the Normans, but a second wave of Welsh rebellion brought about some checks on Norman activity in Gwent and Brycheiniog, and perhaps in Dyfed.[123] William II responded with another army in the following year, although he met with little success.[124] In 1098, however, an army lead by two earls, Hugh d'Avranches and Hugh de Montgomery, earl of Shrewsbury since the death of his father Roger in 1094, met with greater success. This force, with the co-operation of Owain ap Edwin of Tegeingl, was able to sweep the north Welsh back to Anglesey, where they besieged them. Expected help from the Hiberno-Scandinavians having failed to materialise, the two Welsh leaders fled to Ireland, leaving the Normans apparently in control. This history of Wales might have been very different had not the king of Norway, Magnus Bareleg, passed by Anglesey in the midst of an attempt on the Hebrides and Man. Seeing an army drawn up, he went to investigate, and meeting with hostility, opened fire. In the ensuing fight, Hugh of Shrewsbury was slain, apparently by Magnus himself, and the Normans retreated from Anglesey, taking their spoils and captives back to England. As perhaps the unkindest cut of all, their erstwhile ally, Owain ab Edwin, rose up against them with the men of Gwynedd.[125] The following year, the Welsh leaders returned from Ireland to the North. Norman power in Wales was by no means broken, but it was perhaps weakened a little: making their peace with the Normans, the Welsh leaders received portions of Wales from them.

This pattern of attack and counter-attack, conquest and resistence, was to continue on into the twelfth and thirteenth centuries, and from it was to grow the unique marcher society, a society whose beginnings are already visible in the late 1060s, when, as discussed above, Bleddyn ap Cynfyn lent his strength to the rebels Eadric *Cild*, Eadwine and Morkere against the king of England.

I should now like to turn away from the framework of events to the interplay of policy and attitude revealed therein, and to discuss the response of the Welsh in the last third of the eleventh century to the presence, activities and ambitions of their new Norman neighbours.

120 Orderic Vitalis, *Historia Ecclesiastica*, ed. & transl. Chibnall, IV.xxxiv–xxxviii.
121 *AC* (B) *s.a.* [1095]; *AC* (C) *s.a.* [1095]; *ByT* (Pen. 20) *s.a.* 1093 (*recte* 1095); *ByT* (RB) *s.a.* 1091 (*recte* 1095); *ByS s.a.* 1093 (*recte* 1095).
122 See note 121.
123 *AC* (B) *s.a.* [1096]; *AC* (C) *s.a.* [1096]; *ByT* (Pen. 20) *s.a.* 1094 (*recte* 1096); *ByT* (RB) *s.a.* 1092 (*recte* 1096); *ByS s.a.* 1094 (*recte* 1096). *AC* note the rebellion, but make no mention of the homage.
124 *AC* (B) *s.a.* 1097; *AC* (C) *s.a.* [1097]; *ByT* (Pen. 20) *s.a.* 1095 (*recte* 1097); *ByT* (RB) *s.a.* 1093 (*recte* 1097); *ByS s.a.* 1095 (*recte* 1097).
125 *ByT* (Pen. 20) *s.a.* 1096 (*recte* 1098); *ByT* (RB) *s.a.* 1094 (*recte* 1098); *ByS s.a.* 1096 (*recte* 1098).

(i) The early years: 1067–1081

The initial response of Welsh rulers to the Normans has already been discussed in the earlier part of this chapter. As Gruffudd ap Llywelyn had done with the rebel Ælfgar, Bleddyn ap Cynfyn made use of the troubles besetting the brand-new Anglo-Norman polity, and assisted the English rebels against the Norman king (an activity which may have distracted attention away from his own borders, at least for a while). The actions of the south Welsh in the period 1066–1071 are not as well recorded, but in so far as they go, it seems that the two men prominent in south Wales at this time, Caradog ap Gruffudd and Maredudd ab Owain ab Edwin, were more concerned with their internal struggle than with the Normans (although the Normans probably were showing an interest in at least some parts of south east Wales). The first definite statement of Norman activity in south Wales comes in 1072 – but it occurs within a Welsh political context.

As has been said, at this time there were two prominent rulers in the South. One was Caradog ap Gruffudd ap Rhydderch, who was active in south east Wales at least from the time of the death of Gruffudd ap Llywelyn, for it was he who ejected Harold Godwinesson from Portskewett in 1065.[126] The second was Maredudd ab Owain ab Edwin, nephew of the Hywel ab Owain who had ruled Deheubarth 1033–1044, and who, according to the *Brutiau*, became prominent in the South in 1069.[127] Caradog ap Gruffudd was both ambitious and able, and he seems to have made a policy of attacking and destroying his southern rivals: although there is no record of such strife in any of our sources, it seems likely that between 1069 and 1072 Caradog was occupied at least in part with harassing Maredudd. The Normans were present in south east Wales, but it would be hard to say how much of this presence was due to the acquisitions of Harold Godwinesson. (In addition to Caradog, there was another ruler active in south east Wales at this time, up till around 1075: this was Cadwgan ap Meurig, the last scion of the old dynasty of Morgannwg. Nothing at all is known about the career of this individual, apart from the fact that he apparently made a number of grants:[128] if the Normans bothered him, there is no full extant account of it, only a passing reference by Orderic.[129])

Lewis has taken what might be thought a rather harsh view of Caradog ap Gruffudd, seeing him almost as a collaborator with the Normans, who conceded much of his authority in Gwent to the Norman earls of Hereford, and whose various successes and failures can be attributed to the presence or absence of Normans supporting him. He built this theory on two pieces of evidence. The first is the statement in the *Brutiau* that Maredudd ab Owain was slain by a coalition of Normans and Caradog on the banks of the Rhymni in 1072;[130] the second is the absence of Caradog from charter 274 in *Liber Landauensis*, in which the grantor (who elsewhere in *Liber Landauensis* occurs in association with Caradog) has as his guarantor Roger FitzWilliam, earl of Hereford. This is a

---

126 ASC (C) *s.a.* 1065; ASC (D) *s.a.* 1065; JW *s.a.* 1065.
127 *ByT* (Pen. 20) *s.a.* 1068 (*recte* 1069); *ByT* (RB) *s.a.* [1069]; *ByS s.a.* 1068 (*recte* 1069).
128 *LL* charters 259, 260, 263, and 267. For a discussion of these, see chapter V below.
129 Orderic Vitalis, *Historia Ecclesiastica*, Book IV: ed. & transl. Chibnall, II.260.
130 *AC* (C) *s.a.* [1073]; *ByT* (Pen. 20) *s.a.* 1070 (*recte* 1072); *ByT* (RB) *s.a.* 1070 (*recte* 1072); *ByS s.a.* 1070 (*recte* 1072).

weak foundation for a theory. The Llandaff charter evidence begs a number of questions, not least whether Roger FitzWilliam is original to the grant in which his name is found (he could have been added by the compiler of *Liber Landauensis* in the mid-twelfth century). Moreover, it is not uncommon in *Liber Landauensis* for individuals to occur in association with different rulers: this does not necessarily imply a change of allegiance, however, for we simply do not know to what extent Welsh nobles were tied to any one lord in the eleventh century. Nor do we know if a charter received its guarantor at the behest of its grantor or of its benefitor. If the latter is the case, and if *LL* 274 was originally made to Llandaff – or, rather, to a church of Bishop Herewald, the so-called bishop of Llandaff – then using a Norman earl as guarantor was sensible: at least part of Herewald's territory seems to have lain in Herefordshire, at least since the death of Gruffudd ap Llywelyn, and it may have been English earlier in the century also, and gained by Gruffudd in the 1050s.[131]

Caradog ap Gruffudd is better understood in his Welsh context. Throughout his career he seems to have been seeking to take and control south Wales: this was his main interest. He paid attention to the Normans on his borders in much the same way as earlier rulers had paid attention to the English, or the Hiberno-Scandinavians: they were part enemy, part resource, but not as important to him as his native Welsh rivals in the South. The alliance with the Normans in 1072 should not be over-estimated: it seems to belong in the same category as the brief link between Gruffudd ap Llywelyn and Swegn Godwinesson in 1047,[132] or that between Edwin ab Einion and 'Edylfi' in 992.[133] In all these instances, we see a Welsh ruler making use of a force from outside his borders to help him in the pursuit of an essentially Welsh struggle. We do not know exactly who the allies of Caradog were: it has been assumed that they were the men of Roger Fittz-William, but, as has been observed by Lewis, this young earl was dissatisfied with his role in the Anglo-Norman polity, and looking for action. I should suggest that, like Swegn Godwinesson before him, he found some outlet for his adventurousness by joining in with a Welsh quarrel, perhaps in return for booty and excitement. The case for Caradog as a collaborator is not proved.

Norman attention in 1073 and 1074 seems to have been directed away from the South East: attacks were made, rather, on Dyfed and Ceredigion, and probably by the earls of Shrewsbury, not the earls of Hereford. That this was the direction of attack may speak for, rather than against, the power of Caradog ap Gruffudd. While he was probably quite secure in his hold on Morgannwg, the more westerly kingdoms of south Wales lacked leadership (the kingship fluctuated until 1081). The area was fought over for the next ten years by a variety of candidates, of whom Caradog was one, the others being the brothers of Maredudd ab Owain, Rhys and Hywel, and the cousins of Caradog, Rhydderch and Meirchion, and the sons of Cadwgan ab Elystan.[134] Caradog survived until 1081,

---

131 Brooke, *The Church and the Welsh Border*, pp. 10–11.
132 See the section on Wales and England 1039–1071 above.
133 See above, chapter II, *sub* Deheubarth.
134 *AC* (B) *s.a.* [1073], [1076], [1077], and [1078]; *AC* (C) *s.a.* [1076], [1077], [1078], and [1079]; *ByT* (Pen. 20) *s.a.* 1073 (*recte* 1075), 1074 (*recte* 1076), 1075 (*recte* 1077), and 1076 (*recte* 1078); *ByT* (RB) *s.a.* [1075], [1076], [1077], and [1078]; *ByS s.a.* 1073

removing a number of rivals en route: the others were less fortunate. A new rival appeared in 1079, Rhys ap Tewdwr, who was to be the ultimate victor in the struggle for Deheubarth. One side effect of this instability, however, was that Deheubarth was vulnerable to Norman incursions, and the Normans exploited this. The final victory of Rhys ap Tewdwr over Caradog (whose junior he probably was) has one clear effect: Norman hostility to Deheubarth was to some degree arrested, as Rhys's position was regularised by his recognition by William I in 1081.

I have already devoted some space to the relations of the Normans and north Wales at this period earlier in this section. Evidence for Norman interest in Gwynedd before 1081 is slender. On the statement of Orderic[135] and of *Historia Gruffud vab Kenan*,[136] Robert of Rhuddlan was active in the North by the mid 1070s: the details of his career are lost to us. In addition, Orderic hints at some strife between Robert and Trahaearn ap Caradog, but the context of this is unknown.[137] The Welsh chronicles do not speak of a Norman presence in the North until 1094, when they mention the existence in Gwynedd of castles: I should suggest that most of these were, however, established after 1081, when Gwynedd had been deprived of its king through death, and his would-be successor through captivity. I have argued elsewhere for the power of Trahaearn: possibly the swift seizure of Gruffudd ap Cynan in 1081 reflects a Norman desire to prevent another leader from establishing himself in the North, and to create a vacuum into which they might expand.

(ii) 1081–1102: Cadwgan ap Bleddyn and the Welsh resistance

As has been mentioned above, while the 1080s saw relative freedom from Norman attack in south Wales, north Wales at this time was heavily pressurised, a fact made possible at least in part by a lack of real leadership. In 1087, William I died, and with this south Welsh fortunes began to change. It was probably around this time that Robert FitzHamo was moving against Glamorgan, and Bernard of Neufmarché strengthened his move into Brycheiniog.

However, the initial effect of William I's death was a hopeful one for Wales. In 1088, there was a rebellion in England against William II, and its leaders included a number of leading marcher lords – Roger de Montgomery, Bernard of Neufmarché, Ralf Mortimer, Roger de Lacy and perhaps Osbern FitzRichard. These lords led an assault on Worcestershire, in which Welshmen participated,[138] as they had done in the days of Eadric *Cild* and the house of Leofric. Weakness in the English polity had always been the Welsh opportunity, and it is unsurprising that in the same year we see the first traces of what was to become a revival

---

(*recte* 1075), 1074 (*recte* 1076), 1075 (*recte* 1077), and 1076 (*recte* 1078). Bleddyn ap Cynfyn may also have interested himself in the struggle over this area: he was killed by treachery by the men of Ystrad Tywi in 1075.

135 Orderic Vitalis, *Historia Ecclesiastica*, Book VIII: ed. & transl. Chibnall, IV.138–44.
136 See note 96.
137 I omit from discussion here the evidence of *Historia Gruffud vab Kenan*, which I have examined elsewhere. See Maund, 'Trahaearn'.
138 ASC (E) *s.a.* 1087; JW *s.a.* 1088.

of leadership for north Wales. In 1088, Rhys ap Tewdwr was driven out of Deheubarth by the sons of Bleddyn ap Cynfyn, Madog, Rhirid and Cadwgan. They were probably operating from Powys, rather than from Gwynedd (their father had ruled both); nevertheless, in order to be able to attack – and attack successfully, at least at first – the south Welsh king, they must have developed a powerbase, and a reasonably secure one. I should suggest that in the confusion and conflict following the death of William I, Norman attention was drawn away from north Wales, at least temporarily, and the sons of Bleddyn were able to exploit this, and develop support for themselves.

Although he was able to fight back in 1088, Rhys ap Tewdwr's position was beginning to be eroded. In 1091, he suffered a local attack.[139] One of his nobles, Cedifor ap Gollwyn, died; and Cedifor's sons sent for a rival claimant to Deheubarth, Gruffudd ap Maredudd, son of the Maredudd ab Owain whom Caradog ap Gruffudd had killed in 1072. Rhys again proved the victor. However, we know from Domesday book that Gruffudd ap Maredudd held land in Herefordshire:[140] could he have had Norman backing for this attack on Rhys? Rhys no longer had royal protection: Gruffudd may have been sponsored not only by the sons of Cedifor but also by some marcher lord. At around the same time, Rhys was involved in a conflict with Bernard of Neufmarché:[141] could the two incidents be connected?

Bernard's men killed Rhys in 1093, and the Normans renewed the attack on south Wales. So, interestingly enough, did Cadwgan ap Bleddyn.[142] In Cadwgan's ravaging of Dyfed in 1093 we may trace a familiar pattern: the fall of one Welsh ruler, be it through Welshmen, vikings, Englishmen or Normans, is the opportunity of another. Cadwgan presumably had maintained his more northerly powerbase, but, like his father Bleddyn and his uncle, Gruffudd ap Llywelyn, he had ambitions *vis à vis* the South, or, at the very least, he bore a grudge against Rhys and the men of Deheubarth for the slaying of his brothers in 1088. Cadwgan was to continue to take an interest in south Wales, involving himself with the de Bellême family and with Gerald of Windsor. Between the death of Rhys ap Tewdwr, and the emergence of Gruffudd ap Rhys in 1115, there is no clear native south Welsh ruler. Cadwgan, whose roots seem to have lain in Powys and Ceredigion, was an important figure for both north and south Wales in the 1090s. It was Cadwgan who was named by the Anglo-Saxon Chronicle as the leader of the Welsh in the rebellions of the 1090s. It was Cadwgan and his brothers to whom the de Bellêmes turned for help in 1102.

The Welsh rebellion of 1094 began in Gwynedd. It was argued by Lloyd that this can be attributed partly to the escape from prison around this time of Gruffudd ap Cynan.[143] There are problems surrounding this view. For a start, we have no exact idea of the length of captivity of Gruffudd (unless his possible

---

139 *AC* (B) *s.a.* [1091]; *ByT* (Pen. 20) *s.a.* 1089 (*recte* 1091); *ByT* (RB) *s.a.* [1091]; *ByS s.a.* 1089 (*recte* 1091).
140 *Domesday Book*, Herefordshire, fo 187ra and 187va.
141 Orderic Vitalis, *Historia Ecclesiastica*, Book VI: ed. & transl. Chibnall, III.254.
142 See note 118.
143 Lloyd, *A History*, II.404.

association with Godfrey Meranach be considered a delimiting factor). Chibnall has argued for his involvement in the death *ca* 1093 of Robert of Rhuddlan.[144] I discuss this at the end of this chapter: suffice to say here that while I consider Gruffudd's involvement to be possible, I do not consider it to be proved. Gruffudd was free by 1098, and probably before that year. His role in the rebellions of 1094 and 1096 is, however, not at all clear. It is interesting that, in the Welsh chronicles, even in 1098 Cadwgan is named first as the leader of the Welsh.

Cadwgan's part in the Welsh resistance to the Normans seems clear. His status was noted by the Anglo-Saxon Chronicle,[145] and acknowledged by Lloyd.[146] In 1094, a rebellion began in north Wales: the men of Gwynedd destroyed Norman strongholds and when the Normans brought an army against them, it met with defeat in the battle of Coedysbys, at the hands of Cadwgan. Following upon this victory, the rebellion spread to Ceredigion (where Cadwgan probably already had influence) and Dyfed. The Norman response, when it came, was powerful. Ystrad Tywi, Gower and Cydweli were attacked in 1095 (to prevent them also rebelling?) and William II himself led an army into Wales.[147] He did not meet with success, defeated by the terrain. The Welsh, meanwhile, stormed Montgomery castle.[148]

In 1096, the rebellion was still continuing.[149] One of the two southern castles which had not fallen in 1094, Rhyd-y-Gors, now fell, owing to the death of its castellan, William FitzBaldwin, and the desertion of its garrison. Three Welsh regions did homage to the Normans (Gwent, Gwynllwg and Brycheiniog, all on the border), but the Normans still found it necesary to lead an army into Gwent. It met with no success, and on returning was defeated at Celli Garnant. The Normans then turned their attention to Brycheiniog: again with little success, and again their force was defeated, this time at Aber-Llech, by the Welsh led by Gruffudd and Ifor, sons of Idnerth ap Cadwgan.[150] These victories were not, however, conclusive: the castle remined intact. Pembroke castle was less fortunate: the warband of Cadwgan, together with Uchdryd ab Edwin, Cadwgan's cousin, and Hywel ap Goronwy, attacked and despoiled it in the same year.

The prominence of leaders from north and central Wales in this rebellion supports the statement of John of Worcester that the rebellion began in the North and then spread.[151] Cadwgan's father Bleddyn ap Cynfyn had been king of north Wales 1063–1075, and was the half-brother of Gruffudd ap Llywelyn. Uchdryd ab Edwin came from Tegeingl,[152] an area very vulnerable to Hugh d'Avranches and Robert of Rhuddlan – he was, furthermore, Cadwgan's first cousin, his mother Iwerydd having been Bleddyn's (half) sister. Hywel ap Goronwy was later lord of Cydweli, but his family seem to have been originally linked with

---

144 See note 120.
145 ASC (E) *s.a.* 1097.
146 Lloyd, *A History*, II.404.
147 See note 121.
148 ASC (E) *s.a.* 1095; JW *s.a.* 1095.
149 See note 123.
150 See note 123.
151 JW *s.a.* 1094.
152 Lloyd, *A History*, II.408.

Buellt and Rhwng Gwy a Hafren,[153] bordering on Cadwgan's family kingdom of Powys. Hywel was related to the sons of Idnerth ap Cadwgan who defeated the Normans in 1096 at Aber-Llech. Lewis took these sons of Idnerth ap Cadwgan to be descendants of Cadwgan ap Meurig of Glamorgan:[154] they were not. They came of the line of Elystan Glodrydd, associated with Buellt: Hywel ap Goronwy was their first cousin.

Up until the appearance in 1098 of Gruffudd ap Cynan, all the leaders of the rebellion not only came from the Powys area, but were interlinked as a group. This suggests that the Welsh rebellion was centred in and around the Powys dynasties, and may well have been headed by Cadwgan ap Bleddyn. Gruffudd, on his escape from prison, joined the rebellion: I am not convinced that his escape initiated it (indeed, it seems more likely that his escape was provoked by it). He first occurs as one of the Welsh leaders in the Anglesey siege in 1098, but Cadwgan's name is given before Gruffudd's in the Welsh chronicles, and it is Cadwgan who these texts (and the Anglo-Saxon Chronicle) name as the leader in the earlier 1090s. The role of Gruffudd in the rebellion may well have become over-estimated because of the biased testimony of *Historia Gruffud vab Kenan*.

The rebellion of the 1090s was not conclusive: the Normans remained a strong force in both north and south Wales. Nor was the Welsh attitude to them uniformly hostile: Owain ab Edwin, the brother of Uchdryd, may have been coerced into aiding the two earls in 1098 – his family held land in the vulnerable area of Tegeingl, which may have made it easy for Hugh d'Avranches to pressurise Owain. The latter's rebellion on Hugh's defeat lends support to this notion. On the other hand, the activities of Cadwgan and his brothers in 1102 does not suggest coercion.

In this year, the new earl of Shrewsbury, Robert de Bellême, rebelled against Henry I. Robert was a supporter of Robert Curthose, and had been fortifying his English possessions before 1102: Henry called him to account, and Robert launched a revolt, assisted by his younger brother Arnulf, lord of Pembroke. They enlisted Welsh help – as Ælfgar had done before them, and as the rebels of 1088 had also done. Three sons of Bleddyn joined Robert: Cadwgan, Maredudd and Iorwerth. By this time, it must have seemed likely that the Normans had arrived to stay: by involving themselves in this dispute, the sons of Bleddyn were probably hoping to gain advantages for themselves and for Wales at the expense of England. To a degree, they succeeded (although Robert failed, and he and Arnulf had to flee to Normandy). Iorwerth shifted allegiance, joining Henry I – perhaps he thought the king a more powerful friend, perhaps he coveted the lands which Henry offered him as a bribe. If we are to believe the *Brutiau*, the English king could at this time dispose of Powys, Ceredigion, half of Dyfed, Ystrad Tywi, Cydweli and Gower.[155] I have said in chapter two that I think it probable that part of Powys and Ceredigion were in the possession of Cadwgan at this time. What Henry may actually have been offering Iorwerth was the Welsh possessions of the de Bellêmes, together with, perhaps, official recognition for the position of

153 Bartrum, *Tracts*, p. 48; Lloyd, *A History*, II.406, n. 31.
154 Lewis, 'English and Norman Government', chapter 9.
155 *ByT* (Pen. 20) *s.a.* 1100 (*recte* 1102); *ByT* (RB) *s.a.* 1100 (*recte* 1102); *ByS s.a.* 1100 (*recte* 1102).

the sons of Bleddyn in some parts of Powys and Ceredigion. The latter perhaps involved the areas which Cadwgan was probably holding – he is said in the Welsh chronicles to have 'acquired' them (done homage for them?) from the Normans in 1099.[156] Alternatively, Henry may have been offering these lands to Iorwerth because Cadwgan was in rebellion. If so, the move was not entirely successful, as, according to the *Brutiau*, Iorwerth gave them to Cadwgan anyway. Powys and Ceredigion continued to be in Cadwgan's possession after the rebellion (though his position was never wholly secure). Iorwerth, who had joined the victorious Henry, gained not at all: Cydweli, Gower and Ystrad Tywi were given to Hywel ap Goromwy, Dyfed to one Saer,[157] while Iorwerth himself was imprisoned.[158]

Why did Henry reward his enemies (Hywel was one of the rebel leaders of the 1090s)? I suggest that he was attempting to buy them off: unable to conquer them outright, he tried to bind them to him with ties of homage. It has to be said that this policy did not succeed fully. Hywel remained a rebel till his death in 1106 (by Norman-instigated treachery). Cadwgan was more amenable, but became increasingly troubled by the antics of his son Owain, falling frequently into disgrace. The buying-off policy worked better with Gruffudd ap Cynan, who had received Anglesey from the Normans in 1099: while maintaining a hold on Gwynedd, Gruffudd apparently kept his head down. He was involved as a target in Henry's invasion of Wales in 1114, but while Henry seems mainly to have been seeking to punish Owain ap Cadwgan, the hostility towards Gruffudd came from his neighbour, the earl of Chester, who was probably hoping to expand westwards.[159] Gruffudd rapidly made peace and consolidated it by betraying Gruffudd ap Rhys ap Tewdwr to the Normans in 1115.[160]

It is not my purpose to examine Norman-Welsh relations after the end of the eleventh century. However, it must be said that despite the rebellion of the 1090s the Normans remained a strong presence in Wales, and the various rebel leaders adapted to this. Cadwgan did so by associating with a powerful earl, and later by keeping an uneasy fealty to the king. Hywel ap Goronwy would not compromise, and was murdered. Gruffudd ap Cynan was the best survivor, but perhaps the least honourable: he played the system, so to speak.

Two phases may be seen in the late eleventh century in Wales. In the first, Norman incursions have not yet grown too great, and the Welsh attitude to them appears to have been much like the Welsh attitude to the English: the Normans are sometimes enemies, sometimes allies, accorded a recognition in the way that Æthelstan was, or perhaps in the way that Gruffudd ap Llywelyn recognised Edward the Confessor, as nominal overlord. However, after Mynydd Carn, for

---

156 *AC* (C) *s.a.* [1099] (the territory is not named); *ByT* (Pen. 20) *s.a.* 1097 (*recte* 1099); *ByT* (RB) *s.a.* 1095 (*recte* 1099) (Cadwgan 'took' Ceredigion and part of Powys); *ByS* *s.a.* 1097 (*recte* 1099).

157 See note 155.

158 *AC* (B) *s.a.* 1103; *AC* (C) *s.a.* [1103]; *ByT* (Pen. 20) *s.a.* 1101 (*recte* 1103); *ByT* (RB) *s.a.* 1101 (*recte* 1103); *ByS* *s.a.* 1101 (*recte* 1103).

159 *ByT* (Pen. 20) *s.a.* 1111 (*recte* 1114); *ByT* (RB) *s.a.* 1111 (*recte* 1114); *ByS* *s.a.* 1111 (*recte* 1114).

160 *ByT* (Pen. 20) *s.a.* 1112 (*recte* 1115); *ByT* (RB) *s.a.* 1112 (*recte* 1115); *ByS* *s.a.* 1112 (*recte* 1115).

north Wales, and after the deaths of William I and Rhys ap Tewdwr for the South, the Normans materialised as a far more serious threat. Lacking a firm leadership, almost all of Wales was vulnerable, and the Normans exploited this. A backlash followed, led probably from Powys by Cadwgan ap Bleddyn and his allies and kin. They did not stem the tide, but they delayed it a little, winning some recognition for themselves and their status (though to a lesser degree than was accorded to Rhys ap Tewdwr). The rebellion of Robert de Bellême marked the opening of another phase, with the earliest signs of the development of marcher culture, wherein Welsh and Normans alike could play off each other and the king. What should be remembered is that, for the Welsh, this intervention in English politics was not new. In supporting Robert, Cadwgan and his brothers repeated the actions of Gruffudd ap Llywelyn with Earl Ælfgar, of Bleddyn ap Cynfyn with Eadric *Cild*, Eadwine and Morkere, and foreshadowed the actions of many subsequent Welsh leaders throughout the middle ages.

(iii) Gruffudd ap Cynan and the death of Robert of Rhuddlan

I have already discussed much of the evidence about the Norman period found in *Historia Gruffud vab Kenan*, both in this chapter and elsewhere.[161] I propose now to examine the evidence of this text which has been linked to the death of Robert of Rhuddlan.[162] Orderic Vitalis, in a passage following his account of the 1088 rebellion against William II, describes how Robert was killed.[163] According to Orderic, around the same time, the Welsh king Gruffudd invaded Robert's lands with an army, ravaging and burning around Rhuddlan, and seizing much plunder. Robert, hearing of this, was distressed and angered. Orderic then passes into a description of Robert's character and career: he was a commander under Hugh d'Avranches at a time when the Welsh were savagely attacking the king and his men, so a castle was built at Rhuddlan by royal command. Robert frequently fought with, and slew the Welsh, driving them back, and enlarging his lands, building a castle at Degannwy near the sea. These activities lasted some fifteen years. However, on the third of July in an unnamed year, King Gruffudd landed with three ships at 'Hormahede' and ravaged thereabouts. Robert rushed out unarmed to pursue the Welsh, with a few men. His companions refused to fight, so Robert attacked with the support of only one man, Osbern d'Orgères. Robert died in the battle, and the Welsh took his head. The Normans pursued the Welsh ships, and Gruffudd retaliated by throwing the head overboard, whereupon the pursuit was abandoned. Robert was taken for burial at Chester. Orderic then gives a poem on Robert, saying that he had ambushed and put to flight King Bleddyn (Bleddyn ap Cynfyn, king of Gwynedd 1063–1075: this implies Robert was active in north Wales before 1075), that he captured King Hywel (probably Hywel ab Ithel, who held land in Rhos and Rhufoniog in the early twelfth century) and also King Gruffudd (ap Cynan), and that he vanquished Trahaearn (Trahaearn ap Caradog, king of Gwynedd 1075–1081). At Robert's death, the poem continues, Owain proclaimed the news (Owain ab Edwin of Tegeingl) and

---

161 See Maund, 'Trahaearn'.
162 See note 120.
163 Orderic Vitalis, *Historia Ecclesiastica*, Book VIII: ed. & transl. Chibnall, IV.134–44.

King Hywel gloried. It strikes me as odd that the poem does not give Gruffudd's reaction: he was, after all, by Orderic's account, responsible for Robert's death.

Lloyd believed that Orderic was mistaken in associating Gruffudd with the death on two grounds.[164] The first was that Orderic seems to place the event in 1088, yet *Historia Gruffud vab Kenan* tells us that Gruffudd was in prison for twelve or sixteen years from 1081.[165] The second was that the death of Robert of Rhuddlan is not mentioned in *Historia Gruffud vab Kenan*, which Lloyd saw as an official panegyric, written in the reign of Owain Gwynedd ap Gruffudd, and which would have recorded such a major event, were it true. Marjorie Chibnall has challenged this view.[166] She suggested that Robert was killed, not in 1088 as has generally been computed from Orderic, but in 1093. Her argument is based on two points: firstly that a date of 1093 would accord with a twelve year imprisonment for Gruffudd, and secondly – and more convincingly – that Robert could not have been buried in St Werburh's, Chester, in 1088, as it was not founded until autumn 1092. By placing the event in 1093, Chibnall was able to accept all of Orderic's account except for the statement that Gruffudd raided Robert's lands during the 1088 rebellion against William I.[167]

Historia Gruffud vab Kenan does not record the killing of Robert. Chibnall explained this omission by equating the raid with a raid on Anglesey described in *Historia Gruffud vab Kenan*, in which Gruffudd's harpist Gellon was slain.[168] (This account in *Historia Gruffud vab Kenan* makes no reference to Robert at all.) She suggested that, Robert being unarmed, the Welsh did not recognise him, and that the loss of the harper may have deprived the Welsh of a full account of the event. While much of her argument for placing the death in 1093 is convincing, I cannot accept the latter part of it. To begin with, *Historia Gruffud vab Kenan* seems to place the Anglesey raid in the period of the Welsh uprising of 1094 (in so far as it is possible to tell anything about chronology from this text). Whichever of the statements in *Historia Gruffud vab Kenan* about the length of Gruffudd's captivity, twelve years or sixteen years, be accepted, the earliest possible date for his escape is 1093, as Chibnall noted, and after his escape, the author of *Historia Gruffud vab Kenan* describes a long period of wandering ('several months') in north and south Wales, as well as three trips across the Irish sea, before any of the raiding and ravaging activities described are said to have occurred. This is a lot to fit in before the third of July, even if Gruffudd escaped at the very beginning of the year. Gruffudd's enemy, and the target of his raids is, moreover, said to be Hugh d'Avranches. As to Welsh ignorance about Robert's identity at his death, this thesis is contradicted by Orderic himself, who states that the Welsh took Robert's head and used it to taunt the Norman pursuers. Moreover, there is no mention of the involvement of Gruffudd in Robert's death in the Elegy for Gruffudd written by his known bard and contemporary, Meilir

---

164 Lloyd, *A History*, II.390, n. 109.
165 *HGK*, ed. Evans, pp. 16–17 and 18.
166 See note 120.
167 *HGK*, ed. Evans, pp. 9–10. This might, in my opinion, be a misplaced reference to the attack that Gruffudd made on Robert in *ca* 1075, according to *Historia Gruffud vab Kenan*.
168 *Ibid.*, p. 21.

Brydydd, a poem which notes most, of not all, of Gruffudd's triumphs, and whose author would have been in a position to know if his patron was involved in the killing of so notorious an enemy of the Welsh as Robert of Rhuddlan.[169] On these grounds, while accepting 1093 as a probable death-date for Robert, I must agree with Lloyd and place a question-mark against the involvement of Gruffudd.

How did Orderic come to make the association? He records, as noted above, a raid by Gruffudd on Rhuddlan, which he attributes to the same year as the rebellion in England led by Odo of Bayeux, 1088. *Historia Gruffud vab Kenan* also mentions a raid by Gruffudd on Rhuddlan, placing it apparently in 1075. Neither source is always entirely clear in its chronolgy: Orderic had a tendency to relate events by association of persons, while *Historia Gruffud vab Kenan* can be charitably described as confused. However, it would seem that Gruffudd did raid Rhuddlan at some time between 1075 and his capture in 1088, but neither of our sources seems to have been completely certain as to the exact date of this. *Historia Gruffud vab Kenan*, as noted, put it in 1075, the same year that the author of this text believed that Robert had lent some help to Gruffudd. Orderic, discussing Robert, placed it around the same time as the events which had caused him to mention Robert in the first place, that is 1087–8. Conceding that this latter date is improbable (unless we assume that the length of Gruffudd's captivity is totally obscure), I should suggest that the raid happened *ca* 1081: this was a year of great change in Wales, and one in which the Normans can be seen coming to terms with the Welsh. After Mynydd Carn, two relatively new powers came to the fore, Rhys ap Tewdwr in the South (with whom William I rapidly made an agreement) and Gruffudd in the North. According to *Historia Gruffud vab Kenan*, Gruffudd's response to his new power was to plunder Powys and Arwystli.[170] It is more than likely that he would have paid attention to the Norman incursors in Gwynedd also, and it may even be that he raided Rhuddlan in this year, and was imprisoned as a direct result of such an action, Robert and Hugh wishing to remove this new threat before he grew too powerful or too entrenched.

169 French, 'Meilir's Elegy for Gruffudd ap Cynan'.
170 *HGK*, ed. Evans, p. 16.

IV

WALES AND THE HIBERNO-SCANDINAVIANS
IN THE ELEVENTH CENTURY

The activities of the Scandinavians in Wales in the early middle ages are some-thing of a grey area: academic attention has been turned to this issue,[1] but on nothing like the scale that it has been turned to England or Ireland, for instance. This in part is due to the nature of the evidence: Wales undoubtedly came in for its share of viking attention, but the sources describing this activity are simply less full for Wales than for many other areas. Nor is it possible to draw any firm conclusions about Scandinavian settlement in Wales in this period. Attempts have been made to develop a picture using place-name evidence,[2] but many of the conclusions thus reached are not wholly trustworthy and in the end the image of the Scandinavian settlements in Wales remains murky. All we can say is that there seem to have been coastal settlements in south Wales: the evidence points to trade, very probably with the Hiberno-Scandinavian settlements across the Irish sea, but evidence for agricultural settlement is sparse, with possible indica-tions in Flint, Pembrokeshire and perhaps Glamorgan.[3]

In so far as our evidence goes, it would seem to support the notion that many of the viking raids on Wales came not from directly from Scandinavia itself, but from Ireland and the Isles, with their colonies of vikings. The first known attack on Wales came around 852,[4] a little later than the first known incidents in England and Ireland, which were already beginning to be colonised by the Scandinavians. This attack on Wales would seem to have followed upon the plundering of the Norwegian settlement at Dublin by a party of Danes,[5] an incident which may have caused some of the defeated *Finngaill* to look across the sea to Wales. From this time onward, viking attacks seem to have been fairly frequent occurrences. Nevertheless, it does not appear that Wales was settled to the same extent as was elsewhere in the same period. The high incidence of coastal Scandinavian place-names suggests that Wales was important in matters of trade, and especially in terms of the routes to Bristol and Chester. This is

---

1   See, for example, Charles, *Old Norse Relations with Wales*; Loyn, *The Vikings in Wales*; Lloyd, *A History*, I.320–352.
2   Charles, *Old Norse Relations*; see also Jones, 'The Scandinavian Settlement in Ystrad Tywi'; Richards, 'Norse Place-Names in Wales'.
3   Richards, 'Norse Place-Names in Wales', pp. 57–8.
4   *AC* (A) *s.a.* 850; *AC* (B) *s.a.* [858]; *ByT* (Pen. 20) *s.a.* 850 (*recte* 852); *ByT* (RB) *s.a.* [852].
5   *AU s.a.* 850 (*recte* 851).

almost impossible to date, however: H. R. Loyn suggested a date of the first half of the tenth century for the emergence of Chester (in the wake of Scandinavian settlements in the Wirral, perhaps?), while Bristol and the route to it became important somewhat later, at the end of the tenth century, or early in the eleventh, although interest in Pembrokeshire may have begun earlier, perhaps in the early part of the tenth century.[6]

One thing should be made clear, however: in no Welsh source for the early mediaeval period is there any reference to a permanent Scandinavian settlement anywhere in Wales. Indeed, the vikings are often referred to as having arrived by sea for any particular raid. A second point to note is the crucial importance of the Hiberno-Scandinavians for Wales: many, if not most, of the vikings who came to Wales in the early eleventh century and before came there from Ireland – and were, indeed, often referred to as 'Irish' in the Welsh chronicles.

The scope of this chapter is not great enough to examine in any detail the whole of Scandinavian activity in Wales; I intend to confine my discussion to the eleventh century. Naturally, any argument is less valuable if its context is incomplete: the issue of the vikings in Wales in the ninth and tenth centuries is an important one, and overdue for renewed attention. However, until such time as this occurs, we may look to the work of Lloyd, Charles and Loyn for many insights into this important period of Welsh history, and to the works of such scholars as Ó Corráin, Sawyer, D'Haenens and Smyth for the activities (comparable at least to a degree) of the Norse speaking peoples elsewhere in Western Europe.[7]

Raids were made on Wales throughout the tenth century. The sons of Amhlaibh were active in north Wales *ca* 961,[8] and a viking force ravaged Tywyn *ca* 963,[9] and Aberffraw in *ca* 968.[10] In about 971, Penmon was ravaged by Magnus son of Harald,[11] and *ca* 972 Godfrey son of Harald ravaged Anglesey and took great plunder,[12] (while in the same year, according to the Annals of the Four Masters, his brother Magnus turned his attention to Ireland, plundering Inis Cathaig, and carrying off Imhar of Limerick[13]). These sons of Harald were from the Isles and Man rather than from Ireland, although their dynasty was active in Ireland. In 978 Wales suffered again when an otherwise unknown Gwrmid ravaged Llyn.[14] In 979 Iago ab Idwal Foel, of the Northern Branch of the line of Rhodri Mawr, was captured by vikings after having been defeated and deprived

---

6 Loyn, *The Vikings in Wales*, pp. 18–21.
7 Sawyer, *The Age of the Vikings* , 'The Vikings and the Irish Sea', and 'The Vikings and Ireland'; Ó Corráin, *Ireland before the Normans*; D'Haenens, *Les Invasions normandes en Belgique au neuvième siècle*; Smyth, *Scandinavian Kings in the British Isles 850–880* and *Scandinavian York and Dublin*.
8 *ByT* (Pen. 20) *s.a.* 959 (*recte* 961); *ByT* (RB) *s.a.* [961]; *ByS s.a.* 959 (*recte* 961); AFM *s.a.* 960. These must be sons of Olaf Cuaran, king of Dublin.
9 *ByT* (Pen. 20) *s.a.* 961 (*recte* 963); *ByT* (RB) *s.a.* [963]; *BS s.a.* 961 (*recte* 963).
10 *ByT* (RB) *s.a.* [968]; *ByS s.a.* 966 (*recte* 968).
11 *ByT* (RB) *s.a.* [969]; *ByS s.a.* 967 (*recte* 969).
12 *AC* (B) *s.a.* [971]; *ByT* (Pen. 20) *s.a.* 969 (*recte* 971); *ByT* (RB) *s.a.* [971]; *ByS s.a.* 969 (*recte* 971).
13 AFM *s.a.* 972.
14 *ByT* (Pen. 20) *s.a.* 977 (*recte* 978).

of the kingdom of Gwynedd by his nephew Hywel ab Ieuaf.[15] This incident may perhaps be linked to the defeat at Dublin of the Scandinavians of that place and of the Isles in the same year by the Irish king of Mide, Máelsechlainn II:[16] many were slain, and others went overseas (including the king of Dublin, Olaf Cuaran), so the abductors of Iago may have been in flight from Dublin. The following year saw an incident of a type which was to become increasingly common in the eleventh century: Custennin ab Iago, one of the numerous claimants to supremacy in Gwynedd, ravaged Llyn and Anglesey in company with Godfrey son of Harald, allying with the viking leader in an attempt to increase his own power. (The attempt failed: Custennin was slain in the same year by his rival, Hywel ab Ieuaf.[17]) Two years later, in 982, Godfrey's men ravaged Dyfed and St Davids.[18] In 987, the same leader, Godfrey Haraldsson, ravaged Anglesey with the 'Black Host', capturing two thousand men and causing the remainder to flee South under the protection of the king of Deheubarth, Maredudd ab Owain ap Hywel Dda.[19] The 'Black Host' implies that the compiler of this entry in the Welsh chronicles considered the raiders to have been ultimately of Danish rather than Norwegian extraction. Another raid followed in 988, when vikings ravaged Llanbadarn, St Davids, Llanilltud, Llandudoch and Llancarfan.[20] The next year saw the king of Deheubarth, Maredudd ab Owain, paying a tribute, or perhaps a ransom, of one penny per person to the Black Host.[21] The same year, the Welsh chronicles note the death of one of the notable leaders of Dublin, Gluniarn son of Amhlaibh. This individual did not die in Wales, but was slain by his slave, Colban, according to the Annals of the Four Masters, the Annals of Tigernach and Chronicum Scottorum.[22] That this was noticed in the Welsh chronicles suggests that he too may have been a raider of Wales (one of the sons of Amhlaibh of 961?). Also in 989 occurred the death of Godfrey son of Harald, described as king of the Isles, slain in Dál Riada.[23] It is possible to speculate that his death occurred later in the year than Maredudd's tribute, made apparently to Godfrey's men as a consequence of the raid of 987. 989 was something of a crux year, in fact, for it also saw the seizure by Máelsechlainn of Dublin,[24] as part of the

---

15 AC (C) *s.a.* [981]; *ByT* (Pen. 20) *s.a.* 978 (*recte* 979); *ByT* (RB) *s.a.* [979]; *ByS s.a.* 978 (*recte* 979). This latter text, however, claims Iago was captured by the men of Hywel ab Ieuaf, not by vikings.
16 AFM *s.a.* 977 (*recte* 979); *CS s.a.* 978.
17 *AC* (B) *s.a.* [982]; *AC* (C) *s.a.* 984; *ByT* (Pen. 20) *s.a.* 979 (*recte* 980); *ByT* (RB) *s.a.* [980]; *ByS s.a.* 979 (*recte* 980).
18 *ByT* (Pen. 20) *s.a.* 981 (*recte* 982); *ByT* (RB) *s.a.* 980 (*recte* 982); *ByS s.a.* 981 (*recte* 982).
19 *AC* (B) *s.a.* [987]; *AC* (C) *s.a.* [988] – the area ravaged is named as *Menevia* not Anglesey. *ByT* (Pen. 20) *s.a.* 986 (*recte* 987); *ByT* (RB) *s.a.* [987]; *ByS s.a.* 986 (*recte* 987).
20 *AC* (B) *s.a.* [988]; *AC* (C) *s.a.* [989]; *ByT* (Pen. 20) *s.a.* 987 (*recte* 988); *ByT* (RB) *s.a.* [988]; *ByS s.a.* 987 (*recte* 988).
21 *AC* (B) *s.a.* [989]; *AC* (C) *s.a.* [990]; *ByT* (Pen. 20) *s.a.* 988 (*recte* 989); *ByT* (RB) *s.a.* [989]; *ByS s.a.* 988 (*recte* 989).
22 AFM *s.a.* 988 (*recte* 989); *CS s.a.* 987; *AT s.a.* 989; *AClon. s.a.* 982.
23 See note 22.
24 See note 22.

increasing pressure put upon the Hiberno-Scandinavians in the later tenth century by Máelsechlainn and his part-time ally, Brian Boru of Munster.

In 992 Maredudd ab Owain, up till this time a victim of the vikings, had recourse to viking help, an event most readily comprehensible when it is put into its proper Welsh context. Earlier in the same year, Maredudd's nephew, Edwin ab Einion, had, in alliance with the English, ravaged all of Maredudd's lands in the South. Maredudd responded by hiring a force of viking mercenaries and laying waste Glamorgan, presumably Edwin's powerbase.[25] It is possible that this force had been raiding in Wales when Maredudd hired it: *Brenhinedd y Saesson* records for this year that St Davids was ravaged 'a third time'.[26] 994 also saw viking activity in Wales, this time in the North, for Anglesey was ravaged on Ascension Tuesday.[27] This raid may have had some political connexion with events in Gwynedd, for it is preceded in the Welsh chronicles by a notice of the ravaging of Gwynedd by another group of claimants to power there, the sons of Meurig:[28] it is thus not inconceivable that the two groups were acting in loose alliance to cause trouble for the kingdom's ruler of the time (although the exact ruler is not known for this period). However, it is equally possible that the two events were coincidental, the vikings perhaps exploiting a tense and unstable situation in Gwynedd to their own advantage. It is not hard to find a motive for this raid for in this year (or perhaps the year before) – one of the leaders of the Hiberno-Scandinavians, Imhar, had been expelled from Dublin by a rival, Sihtric son of Amhlaibh, and had fled overseas with three ships.[29] Anglesey would be an obvious target for such a force. This Imhar remained a contender for Dublin for a few years after this, and achieved control in 995, only to be expelled almost immediately.[30]

There were no more raids on Wales from Ireland for a period of around six years, although the Welsh chonicles note the harrying of Man in 995 by Sweyn son of Harald.[31] This period saw fairly intense activity by the vikings within Ireland, which may explain the brief respite for Wales.

The next notice for viking raids in Wales come not from the Welsh chronicles, but from an English source, the Anglo-Saxon Chronicle (versions CDE), together with John of Worcester and *Historia Regum*[2]. This is not surprising under the circumstances, for the raid that is noted in 997 by these texts was an action not of Wales's usual oppressors, the Hiberno-Scandinavians, but of the *here*, one of the viking armies that had been active in England since the 980s. This force sailed around Wessex, up the River Severn and plundered in 'North' Wales, Cornwall and Devon.[32] The description 'North' Wales is probably not to be taken literally as Gwynedd and Anglesey, but rather being an attempt by the old English

25 *ByT* (Pen. 20) *s.a.* 991 (*recte* 992); *ByT* (RB) *s.a.* 990 (*recte* 992).
26 *ByS* *s.a.* 991 (*recte* 992).
27 *ByT* (Pen. 20) *s.a.* 992 (*recte* 993); *ByT* (RB) *s.a.* [993]; *ByS* *s.a.* 992 (*recte* 993).
28 See note 27. *ByT* (Pen. 20) differs slightly, reading that hostages from the sons of Meurig were in Gwynedd.
29 AFM *s.a.* 992; AI *s.a.* 993.
30 AFM *s.a.* 994; AI *s.a.* 995.
31 *AC* (B) *s.a.* [995]; *ByT* (Pen. 20) *s.a.* 994 (*recte* 995); *ByT* (RB) *s.a.* [995]; *ByS* *s.a.* 994 (*recte* 995).
32 ASC (C) *s.a.* 997; ASC (D) *s.a.* 997; ASC (E) *s.a.* 997; JW *s.a.* 997; *HR*[2] *s.a.* 997.

chronicler whose work underlies these texts to make a clear distinction between two Celtic areas, *Cornwealas* and its more Northern neighbour, *Nordwealas*. The area ravaged was in fact likely to have been modern south Wales, given the importance of the River Severn in this attack. The following year this force moved away from Wales into Dorset and renewed its attacks upon England.

In 999 the Hiberno-Scandinavians returned to Wales: St Davids was harried and its bishop, Morgenau, was slain.[33] This incident may be connected with the expulsion of Sihtric son of Amhlaibh from Dublin which occurred around this time.[34] The ravaging of Dublin is recorded by the Welsh chronicles, in fact, but in the subsequent year to the slaying of the bishop: this may suggest either that this attack on St Davids preceded the expulsion, or, to my mind my probably, that the news of the expulsion (which the Irish annals place in 998 or 999) did not reach Wales until after the raid on St Davids, although it may well have preceded the latter event. The Welsh chronicles note various Irish events, but these are often placed later than the notices of the same events in the Irish annals: for instance, the Welsh chronicles record the death of Imhar of Waterford *s.a.* 1000 (*recte* 1001), an occurrence which most of the sets of Irish annals place in 999.[35] In 1001, there was another raid on Wales, in Dyfed, which may again be a consequence of the plundering of Dublin: at least some of the Hiberno-Scandinavian had returned to Dublin in 1000, but this attack may represent the stragglers.

No further attacks on Wales from Ireland are recorded in any of our sources until 1022, although the battle of Clontarf is noted in the Welsh Chronicles, and some versions of the Irish annals claim 'Britons' formed part of the Dublin/Leinster force in that battle.[36] It seems probable, however, that this would refer not to the Welsh of our Wales, but to the men of Strathclyde, if any Britons were present at all. The incident in 1022 cannot be properly described as a viking attack: the event in question is the appearance and defeat in south Wales of Rhain 'the Irishman', a pretender to rule in Deheubarth, who claimed to be the son of Maredudd ab Owain ap Hywel Dda. This person (whose real identity is completely obscure) achieved some recognition in the South, but was defeated and driven out by the ruler of Gwynedd, Llywelyn ap Seisyll.[37] This Rhain is said in the *Brutiau* to have lead a host in the Irish fashion, which may suggest an Irish (or Hiberno-Scandinavian) element in his army. It is difficult to decide his nationality: he seems to have a Welsh name. yet is described as an Irishman – and it has to be remembered that in the eleventh century, the Welsh chronicles frequently use 'Irish' to describe men who seem otherwise to be Hiberno-Scandinavian.[38] It is most probable that Rhain – like the later Gruffudd ap Cynan – was of mixed blood, Welsh, Irish and Hiberno-Scandinavian.

---

33 *AC* (B) *s.a.* [999]; *AC* (C) *s.a.* [1002]; *ByT* (Pen. 20) *s.a.* 998 (*recte* 999); *ByT* (RB) *s.a.* [999]; *ByS s.a.* 998 (*recte* 999).
34 AFM *s.a.* 998; AI *s.a.* 999; AT *s.a.* 999; AU *s.a.* 998 (*recte* 999).
35 *CS s.a.* 998; AFM *s.a.* 999; AU *s.a.* 999 (*recte* 1000); AT *s.a.* 1000.
36 ALC *s.a.* 1014.
37 *AC* (B) *s.a.* [1021]; *AC* (C) *s.a.* [1023]; *ByT* (Pen. 20) *s.a.* 1020 (*recte* 1022); *ByT* (RB) *s.a.* [1022]; *ByS s.a.* 1020 (*recte* 1022).
38 For example, Rhydderch ab Iestyn was killed by the 'Irish' ('Yscotteit', *ByT* [RB]; 'Scotis' *AC* [B]); Hywel ab Edwin led a fleet of the 'folk of Ireland', also Irish ('genedyl Iwerdon', 'Gwydyl', *ByT* [RB]; where AC [B] has 'classis gentilium').

In the same year, but apparently after Rhain's defeat, there was a renewed Scandinavian threat to Wales from England, with the arrival of *Eilaf*, who ravaged Dyfed and plundered St Davids.[39] Although no subsequent raids by this individual are noted, he was clearly regarded as a serious problem, for his departure from England in 1035 at the death of Cnut is also noted by the Welsh chronicles.[40] He can be identified as the viking leader Eglaf, who was made an earl by Cnut, and who fought against the king of Denmark in 1026. He witnessed many of Cnut's charters in the period 1081–1024. He held land in Gloucestershire, which may explain his interest in Wales.[41]

There were no further attacks on Wales by Scandinavians until 1033. The long period of relative calm 1001–1033 (with the exception of 1022) can be attributed to a number of factors. Firstly, the nature of the sources at this time: the Welsh chronicles in the eleventh century are never very full, but they are particularly sparse for its early years,[42] and it is possible that there were raids in this period which were not recorded. Secondly, the viking groups in Ireland, at least in the first part of this period, seem to have been busy with conflicts within that country, and particularly with the various campaigns of Brian Boru and Máelsechlainn, and after Clontarf it is possible that some time was necessary to rebuild strength. Thirdly, much Scandinavian attention in the first two decades of the eleventh century was being focussed on England and this may have contributed to the apparent respite enjoyed by Wales. After 1018 many members of the original viking forces in England were probably involved in the various campaigns of Cnut, and with the affairs of Denmark and Norway. A fourth reason may lie within the politics of Wales at the time: certainly from 1018, (and probably before then), and until 1023, north Wales was ruled by, and south Wales at least influenced by, the powerful king Llywelyn ap Seisyll. As with his even more powerful son Gruffudd, Llywelyn could have possessed sufficient strength to deter conflict and harassment within his borders. He was known in Ireland:

Gruffudd ap Cynan was helped in the battle of Mynydd Carn by 'Irish' ('Yscotteit', *ByT* [RB]); 'Scots and Irish' helped Rhys ap Tewdwr in 1088 ('Scotteit a Gwydyl' *ByT* [RB]; 'ex Hibernia classis', *AC* [B]). This latter usage may perhaps indicate that 'Irish' could be used to indicate Hiberno-Scandinavians, and the phrase suggests that Rhys's force consisted of a mixture of Irishmen and vikings.

39 *AC* (B) *s.a.* [1021]; *AC* (C) *s.a.* [1023]; *ByT* (Pen. 20) *s.a.* 1020 (*recte* 1022); *ByT* (RB) *s.a.* [1022]; *ByS s.a.* 1020 (*recte* 1022).

40 *ByT* (Pen. 20) *s.a.* 1033 (*recte* 1035); *ByT* (RB) *s.a.* [1035].

41 Stenton, *Anglo-Saxon England*, pp. 403–4 and 416.

42 For this period, *AC* (B) has twelve annals with entries, including six obits and two notices of English affairs. *AC* (C) has ten annals with entries, including four obits and three notices of English matters, plus one on Ireland. *ByT* (Pen. 20) has seventeen entries. Of these seven consist simply of obits, two are concerned with England alone, and one with Ireland alone. A further two (which may be duplicates) record a *decemnoualis* and nothing else. *ByT* (RB) has fifteen entries, seven being solely obits, two being English and one Irish. *ByS*, if the material drawn from an English chronicle be ignored, has fifteen entries, including seven simple obits, one Irish event and the *decemnoualis*. It is difficult to assess which of the entries on England belong to the original Welsh text, given the amount of English chronicle material included in this text.

that is made clear by the Irish annals, several versions of which record his death.[43] This fact suggests that his power was realised and recognised by the Irish and probably by the Hiberno-Scandinavians, and Wales may owe some of her freedom from viking attack to the strength of Llywelyn.

The next definite incident of Hiberno-Scandinavian aggression in Wales occurred in 1033, when the 'Irish' slew Rhydderch ab Iestyn, ruler of south Wales.[44] As mentioned above, 'Irish' in the Welsh chronicles may be taken at least to include the Hiberno-Scandinavian in this period. The context of the killing is not given: it would seem likely that it occurred during a raid from Ireland upon south Wales – in the next ten years or so such attacks are a notable feature of south Welsh history. The date 1033 is the 'corrected' date for the death: *Annales Cambriae* (B) give [1032], *Annales Cambriae* (C) give [1034]; *Brut y Tywysogion* (Pen. 20) notes it *s.a.* 1031, *Brut y Tywysogion* (RB) *s.a.* 1030, and *Brenhinedd y Saesson s.a.* 1031. The Irish Annals of Tigernach have *ca* 1030 a notice concerning Wales which may be of interest for the death, however:[45]

Orguin Bretan o Saxonaib agus o Gallaib Atha Cliath

Plundering of Wales by Saxons and Dublin vikings.

This notice is not found in any other of the Irish annal texts. Within the Annals of Tigernach, it occurs within a very long annal containing material that is found in other versions of the Irish Annals, and the date of *ca* 1030 is supplied by comparison with the dates supplied for these other events by these other texts. I should like to suggest that this notice in the Annals of Tigernach, and the *obit* for Rhydderch ab Iestyn in the Welsh Chronicles are pieces of the same event, a plundering expedition by the Hiberno-Scandinavians in the course of which the south Welsh king met his death, and which occurred at some point in the period *ca* 1030–*ca* 1033. (the date 1033 appears to derive from the fact that the *Brutiau* state that the death of Cnut occurred two years later, an event which can be fairly firmly assigned to 1035.)

From some point in the second quarter of the eleventh century, viking interest in Wales seems to have been renewed. Following the relative peace of the first thirty or so years, there is a succession of new onslaughts on Wales, largely from Ireland. The first of these occurred around 1036: again, our sole witness is the Annals of Tigernach, which record that one viking leader, the son of Gluniarn, slew another, Godfrey son of Sihtric, in Wales. There is no notice of a Scandinavian presence in Wales at this time in the Welsh sources: there are no notices at all in the Welsh chronicles for 1035 to 1039.

Why should a renewed interest develop at about this time? The answer appears to lie within Irish events. In the 1020s and early 1030s, the various Hiberno-Scandinavians groups were very active in the Irish polity, and with some success. Máelsechlainn II had died in 1022, and no single Irish ruler managed to

---

43 *CS s.a.* 1021; ALC *s.a.* 1023; A.Clon. *s.a.* 1023; AU *s.a.* 1023.
44 *AC* (B) *s.a.* [1032]; *AC* (C) *s.a.* [1034] – this text does not mention the vikings; *ByT* (Pen. 20) *s.a.* 1031 (*recte* 1033); *ByT* (RB) *s.a.* 1030 (*recte* 1033); *ByS s.a.* 1031 (*recte* 1033).
45 AT, ed. & transl. Stokes, *Revue Celtique*, 17 (1896) 370.

achieve the strength or prominence that he (and his deceased ally Brian) had enjoyed. However, the 1030s saw the rise of Diarmait mac Máel na mBó of Leinster. In 1037, he plundered Waterford. Although he did not achieve supremacy in Leinster until 1046,[46] he was already a force to reckon with in the later 1030s, and the reappearance of the Hiberno-Scandinavians in Wales in the 1030s and 1040s may be attributed at least in part to the pressure he represented in Ireland. Moreover, the vikings of Waterford in particular seem to have been undergoing an internal struggle at this time, if the rapid turnover of their kings in the 1030s is anything to go by, and some of the raiders in Wales may represent supporters of unsuccessful contenders.

In 1039, a member of the ruling dynasty of Morgannwg, Meurig ap Hywel, was captured by vikings.[47] In the same year, a king of north Wales, Iago ab Idwal, died, an event noticed by the Irish annals.[48] Iago was an obscure king in many ways: although we know his pedigree we know nothing about his career, and this combined with his death at the hands of his own men suggests that he may not have beeen an overwhelmingly powerful ruler. Yet the Irish annals notice his death. There are various possible explanations for this: it could be argued that the Irish annals were interested in him because of his grandson Gruffudd ap Cynan, who reputedly had Irish connexions, and it is the case that a 'son of Iago' is mentioned by the Annals of Ulster and the Annals of Loch Ce as the slayer of Iago's successor, Gruffudd ap Llywelyn. However, there is no definite reason to believe that this 'son of Iago' was a son of Iago ab Idwal, let alone that he was Cynan, the father of Gruffudd[49] and, furthermore, the Irish annals show no interest in Gruffudd ap Cynan, despite his supposed connexions both to Dublin and to various Irish rulers. However, the Irish annals do show an interest in the kings of Gwynedd in the central eleventh century, noticing the deaths of Llywelyn ap Seisyll and Gruffudd ap Llywelyn as well as that of Iago. I should suggest that this is due at least in part to the renewed Hiberno-Scandinavian interest in Wales in the central decades of the eleventh century, and the obits of these kings may reflect information acquired from Hiberno-Scandinavian men who had fought in Wales.

It seems fairly clear that viking interest in Wales was reviving at this point. In 1042, the ruler of south Wales, Hywel ab Edwin, defeated a Scandinavian force which had been ravaging Dyfed in the battle of Pwlldyfach.[50] In the same year, Hywel's major rival, the north Welsh king Gruffudd ap Llywelyn, was captured by the vikings of Dublin. It is not clear from the Welsh chronicles that the two viking bands involved were identical, but this is not improbable: a force defeated in south Wales might well turn its attention northwards as a result. The nature of Gruffudd's captivity is unknown: no ransom is recorded, nor is it known whether he was taken out of Wales. He was free by 1044, and probably before that year,

46 For Diarmait, see Ó Corráin, *Ireland before the Normans*, pp. 13–17.
47 *AC* (C) *s.a.* [1040]; *ByT* (Pen. 20) *s.a.* 1037 (*recte* 1039); *ByT* (RB) *s.a.* [1039]; *ByS s.a.* 1037 (*recte* 1039).
48 *CS s.a.* 1037; *AT s.a.* 1039; *ALC s.a.* 1039; *AU s.a.* 1039.
49 See Maund, 'Cynan ab Iago'.
50 *AC* (B) *s.a.* [1042]; *ByT* (Pen. 20) *s.a.* 1040 (*recte* 1042); *ByT* (RB) *s.a.* 1040 (*recte* 1042); *ByS s.a.* 1040 (*recte* 1042).

for when the Welsh chronicles next mention him, he had achieved a position of considerable strength. In 1044, Hywel ab Edwin, having been expelled from his kingdom, gathered a fleet of Hiberno-Scandinavians with the intention of ravaging 'the whole kingdom', presumably Deheubarth, from the site of the ensuing battle. On his arrival, he met Gruffudd ap Llywelyn and an army at the mouth of the Tywi: battle followed and Hywel was slain.[51] This event clearly shows the developing power of the north Welsh king: he seems to have been established in the South, and its former ruler was having recourse to the vikings in an attempt to regain the territory. To have gained such a position, it is unlikely that Gruffudd's captivity had been of long duration.

This direct involvement of the Hiberno-Scandinavians in the Welsh polity was to be a feature of the central eleventh century, and indeed was to extend to England also. Although raids did still occur, increasingly the Hiberno-Scandinavians were to become a resource for exiles and for individuals seeking to establish or re-establish themselves, a process that was to reach a climax in the career of Gruffudd ap Cynan.

In 1049, a fleet of thirty six ships came up the River Usk from Ireland and ravaged in the adjoining areas. Their initial attention seems to have been focussed on Deheubarth,[52] but they then turned to England. They had the assistance of Gruffudd ap Rhydderch, Hywel's succesor as king of Deheubarth, who may have taken the opportunity to harass his neighbour, Meurig ap Hywel, king of Gwent and perhaps other parts of Morgannwg,[53] in addition to the English. The effect on England was noticeable: the D-text of the Anglo-Saxon Chronicle and John of Worcester record that Tidenham was ravaged, and the bishop of Worcester, Ealdred, summoned the levies of Herefordshire and Gloucestershore to combat the threat. However, the Welsh element in these levies warned Gruffudd, and he and his Hiberno-Scandinavian allies took the English force by surprise and defeated it heavily.[54] He would then seem to have returned to Wales, but his family remained active on the border – his brother Rhys was killed by the English in 1053 on account of his raiding,[55] and a Welsh raid was made on Westbury, perhaps in reprisal.[56] The fleet of 1049 had probably come to Wales on its own account, but the south Welsh king rapidly turned its presence to his own advantage, using this new force to help him achieve his own aims.

This treatment of the Hiberno-Scandinavians as a military resource passed into England also: it is well known that in the wake of the English revolution of 1051 Harold Godwinesson went to Ireland and, indeed, on his return to England in 1052 he was accompanied by an Irish fleet.[57] The E-text of the Anglo-Saxon Chronicle claims that Harold spent the winter in Ireland with 'the king', probably

---

51 *AC* (B) *s.a.* [1043]; *AC* (C) *s.a.* [1045]; *ByT* (Pen. 20) *s.a.* 1042 (*recte* 1044); *ByT* (RB) *s.a.* [1044]; *ByS s.a.* 1042 (*recte* 1044).
52 *AC* (B) *s.a.* [1048]; *AC* (C) *s.a.* [1050]; *ByT* (Pen. 20) *s.a.* 1047 (*recte* 1049); *ByT* (RB) *s.a.* [1049]; *ByS s.a.* 1047 (*recte* 1049).
53 Lloyd, *A History*, II.362.
54 ASC (D) *s.a.* 1050 (*recte* 1049); JW *s.a.* 1049.
55 ASC (D) *s.a.* 1053; JW *s.a.* 1053.
56 ASC (C) *s.a.* 1053.
57 ASC (C) *s.a.* 1052; ASC (D) *s.a.* 1052; ASC (E) *s.a.* 1052.

Diarmait mac Máel na mBó of Leinster.[58] In 1052, Diarmait marched on Dublin in a successful campaign which culminated in the flight of its king, Eachmarcach son of Ragnall, and the assumption of rule by Diarmait himself.[59] Did Harold benefit as a result of this campaign, either through receiving a fleet from a newly victorious Diarmait, or through finding a readily-hired fleet amongst the Dublin refugees? Either hypothesis is possible, and whatever is the truth, the fall of Dublin was to the advantage of both Diarmait and of Harold ultimately. This incident also illustrates that the Dublin vikings had been taking an interest in Wales at this time. The Irish annals tell us that Eachmarcach fled overseas; the Welsh chronicles finish the tale, for in 1052 they record a fleet coming from Ireland that foundered in Deheubarth.[60] This fleet must represent some of the refugees from Dublin, perhaps some of Eachmarcach's supporters. (Not all the Dublin vikings left; they were to form a part of Diarmait's forces in Ireland in subsequent years.)

In 1055 another English earl, Ælfgar son of Leofric, became an outlaw, as was described in chapter three. Like Harold before him, Ælfgar found his way to Ireland and gathered a force of 'pirates' – eighteen ships – before returning to England, via Wales, to join his ally Gruffudd ap Llywelyn. This fleet was probably a major part of Gruffudd and Ælfgar's force, and was with them throughout the plundering of Hereford and subsequent evasion of Harold Godwinesson's forces, for upon the making of peace at Billingsley, Ælfgar sent his Hiberno-Scandinavian allies to Chester to await payment.[61] It is likely that, like Harold, Ælfgar had found his way to Diarmait mac Maíl na mBó, and had been supplied with a fleet from Dublin: the Irish annals in this period make several references to the 'vikings of Diarmait' as a force in Ireland, suggesting that the king of Leinster was well aware of their usefulness as a military resource.[62]

The 1055 campaign resulted in Ælfgar's reinstatement, and in 1057 he became earl of Mercia. In 1058 he underwent another change of fortune and was again exiled. The events of this second exile and the circumstances surrounding it are not completely clear. But what is clear is that he made his way once again to Gruffudd ap Llywelyn and that the two of them formed an alliance with a viking fleet.[63] This fleet was not of Hiberno-Scandinavian origin, but was led by Magnus, the son of Harald Hardrada, king of Norway. The presence of this force in the Irish sea at this time is connected to other matters than the exile of Ælfgar, and, indeed, in the account of the fleet given in the Welsh and Irish sources, Ælfgar is not mentioned at all. The Annals of Tigernach read:[64]

---

58 Barlow, *Edward the Confessor*, p. 120.
59 AT *s.a.* 1052; AFM *s.a.* 1052.
60 *AC* (B) *s.a.* [1051]; *AC* (C) *s.a.* [1053]; *ByT* (Pen. 20) *s.a.* 1050 (*recte* 1052); *ByT* (RB) *s.a.* 1050 (*recte* 1052); *ByS* *s.a.* 1050 (*recte* 1052).
61 ASC (C) *s.a.* 1055; ASC (D) *s.a.* 1055; ASC (E) *s.a.* 1055; JW *s.a.* 1055.
62 Diarmait's vikings are with him in AT *s.a.* 1054 and 1067; AFM *s.a.* 1054 and 1061; AI *s.a.* 1067; CS *s.a.* 1064.
63 ASC (D) *s.a.* 1058; JW *s.a.* 1058; *AC* (B) *s.a.* [1056]; *AC* (C) *s.a.* [1059]; *ByT* (Pen. 20) *s.a.* 1056 (*recte* 1058); *ByT* (RB) *s.a.* [1058]; *ByS* *s.a.* 1056 (*recte* 1058).
64 AT *s.a.* 1058.

Longes la maic ríg Lochland, co nGallaib Indsi Orcc agus Innsi Gall agus Átha Cliath, do gabail rigi Saxan, acht nocor deonaig Dia sin.

A fleet [led] by the son of the king of Norway, with the Foreigners of the Orkenys and the Hebrides and Dublin, to seize the kingdom of England; but to this God consented not.

Magnusson and Pálsson, in their translation of King Harold's Saga, suggest that this incident may be connected with the treaty made by Magnus the Good of Norway (the cousin of Magnus Haraldsson) and Hardacnut about the disposition of their various kingdoms, to which treaty Magnus's father, Harald Hardrada, considered himself to some extent the heir, and which caused him to have designs on England.[65] However, it must be said that if this fleet had intentions simply on England, then the Irish sea is a very odd starting place, and I should suggest that, while raiding England may well have been on the agenda, Magnus was also trying to to enforce Norwegian control in Orkney and the Hebrides. The meeting with Gruffudd and Ælfgar must have provided a good opportunity for acquiring plunder in England.[66]

There are no further recorded raids on Wales, or even mercenary fleets in Wales, until 1073. This may to some extent be attributed to events in Ireland – Diarmait mac Máel na mBó continued to dominate Irish politics until 1072, and the Irish annals have several notices of vikings accompanying him or his son Murchadh on expeditions.[67] It may also be due to deficiencies in our sources, always a possibility with the Welsh chronicles. However, I wish to draw attention to the fact that apparently no viking force raided in Wales between 1050 and 1073, and more particularly, 1055 and 1063. There were Hiberno-Scandinavian fleets active at this time: they helped Harold Godwinesson in 1052 and Ælfgar in 1055. However, Wales was not raided. I should like to attribute this in part to the power of Gruffudd ap Llywelyn: it is noticeable that for the nine years of his supremacy in Wales there were no conflicts recorded of any kind other than Gruffudd's own attacks on England in 1055/6 and 1058. It is true that the Welsh chronicles are sparse in this period, but I should like to suggest that this extraordinary absence of conflict has its roots not in a deficiency in our evidence, but in the control exerted by Gruffudd. There was no conflict and no raids in part at least because the power of Gruffudd ap Llywelyn prevented them. That Gruffudd influenced Irish action is hinted at in the Irish annals, where his death is noted,[68] clearly, he was of sufficient importance to warrant annalistic attention in Ireland. That the absence of viking activity continued until 1073 must be due to Irish affairs, however: it is significant that the first raid occurs in the year after the death of Diarmait mac Maíl na mBó. Between them, he and Gruffudd dominated

---

65 *King Harald's Saga*, transl. Magnusson and Pálsson, p. 137, n. 1.
66 This Magnus should not be confused with the King Magnus who slew Hugh de Montgomery in 1098. This latter Magnus was Magnus 'Barelegs' Olafsson, king of Norway 1093–1103, and was a nephew of Magnus Haraldsson. Magnus Haraldsson was himself king in Norway for a short time, together with his brother Olaf (1066–69). Olaf then ruled alone until 1093. This family were interested in the affairs of the Orkneys and Hebrides, if the evidence of Orkneyinga Saga can be trusted.
67 AFM *s.a.* 1061 and 1069; *CS s.a.* 1064 and 1066; AI *s.a.* 1067; AT *s.a.* 1067.
68 ALC *s.a.* 1064; AU *s.a.* 1064.

the political affairs of Ireland and Wales, and influenced those of England, throughout the central years of the eleventh century.

While Wales remained undisturbed until 1073, England did not. In the wake of the Norman Conquest, the sons of Harold Godwinesson fled to Ireland, to the protection of Diarmait.[69] In 1068 they returned to England with a fleet and ravaged in Somerset. A force was dispatched to meet them, led by Eadnoð the Staller, but this was defeated, its leader slain and the sons of Harold returned to Ireland.[70] The following year they returned, again with a fleet, numbering forty-four ships acording to John of Worcester, sixty-four according to the D-text of the Anglo-Saxon Chronicle, and sixty-six according to William of Jumièges. They ravaged in south west England. This time a large force was sent against them, led by Brian, son of Eudo, count of Brittany. This defeated the sons of Harold in two battles on one day, leaving a few survivors who fled to Ireland.[71] It is of interest to note the timing of these raids: the first occurred in the year in which William I was occupied with the harrying of the North, while the second coincided with the attempted invasion of England by Swein Estrithsson of Denmark. It is possible that in 1069 at least these events were connected, for William of Malmesbury tells us that the sons of Harold had been to Denmark as well as Ireland.[72] Following this, the sons of Harold disappear from our record, although Harold Haroldsson may have accompanied Magnus Bareleg of Norway on an expedition in 1098.[73]

In 1070, Murchadh mac Diarmait, who had been appointed by his father to be king of Dublin, died, probably as a consequence of injuries received in a raid in Mide.[74] In 1072, his father died, an event noticed in Welsh sources as well as Irish,[75] which is testimony to his status. According to the Annals of Inisfallen, after Diarmait's death his ally and protegé, Toirdhelbhach Ua Briain of Munster, led an expedition into Osraige and Leister, receiving the submission of the Uí Neill king of Tara, the king of Osraige and the king of Dublin, named as Godfrey grandson of Ragnall, and imprisoning Domnall mac Diarmait at Dublin.[76] The same annal claims that Toirdhelbhach was given the kingship of Dublin, but this probably means that he was recognised as its overlord, rather than that he acquired direct rule. His influence was not longlasting, however. In 1073, the Welsh chronicles record the ravaging of St Davids and Bangor by vikings,[77] the

---

69 Orderic Vitalis, *Historia Ecclesiastica*, Book IV: ed. & transl. Chibnall, II.224; William of Jumièges, *Gesta Normannorum Ducum*, p. 141.

70 ASC (D) *s.a.* 1068; JW *s.a.* 1068; William of Malmesbury, *De Gestis Regum Anglorum*, ed. Stubbs, II.312–3.

71 ASC (D) *s.a.* 1069; JW *s.a.* 1069.

72 William of Malmesbury, ed. Stubbs, II.318.

73 Hudson, 'The Family of Harold Godwinesson and the Irish Sea Province', p. 100.

74 AT *s.a.* 1069, 1070; AFM *s.a.* 1069, 1070; AClon. *s.a.* 1069; *CS s.a.* 1066; ALC *s.a.* 1070; AU *s.a.* 1070.

75 *AC* (C) *s.a.* [1073]; *ByT* (Pen. 20) *s.a.* 1070 (*recte* 1072); *ByT* (RB) *s.a.* 1070 (*recte* 1072); *ByS s.a.* 1070 (*recte* 1072).

76 AI *s.a.* 1072.

77 *AC* (B) *s.a.* [1072]; *AC* (C) *s.a.* [1074]; *ByT* (Pen. 20) *s.a.* 1071 (*recte* 1073); *ByT* (RB) *s.a.* [1073]; *ByS s.a.* 1071 (*recte* 1073).

first such raid in more than twenty years. By 1075, Godfrey had freed himself from Toirdhelbhach and was banished for his pains.[78] Godfrey died overseas while preparing a host to re-take Dublin. Meanwhile, Domnall mac Murchadha mac Diarmait had taken the kingship of Dublin, and he also died within the year. On his death, Toirdhelbhach appointed his own son Muirchertach to rule Dublin,[79] a position which he probably enjoyed for a while thereafter,[80] though Donnchadh mac Domnall mac Diarmait was active there in 1089 according to the Annals of Tigernach.

In 1080, a Hiberno-Scandinavian fleet again ravaged St Davids, an event which may be linked to Irish happenings.[81] The Annals of Inisfallen record that in this year, Diarmait Ua Briain, another son of Toirdhelbhach, brought a fleet to Wales and took great spoil,[82] which is probably a reference to the same event. In the following year occurred the battle of Mynydd Carn, a conflict that was to be a turning point for Wales, and amongst the armies was a Hiberno-Scandinavian contingent led by Gruffudd ap Cynan and supplied to him by his Hiberno-Scandinavian connexions.[83] The case of Gruffudd ap Cynan is very important in any analysis of Cambro-Scandinavian relations in the later eleventh century, and I propose to discuss it separately below.

In 1088, the king of Deheubarth, Rhys ap Tewdwr, suffered a reverse of fortune, being expelled from his kingdom by the sons of Bleddyn ap Cynfyn. Following in the footsteps of his predecessor Hywel ab Edwin, as well as those of his one-time ally Gruffudd ap Cynan, Rhys turned to Ireland for assistance. Having gathered a fleet, he returned to Wales and defeated the sons of Bleddyn at Llech-y-Crau, giving a large reward to his helpers.[84] The record of this event in the Welsh chronicles is interesting for it provides us with an indication of the mixed nature of these mercenary fleets: Rhys is said to have hired 'Scotteit a Gwyddyl'.[85] The fleet may have proved, however, to be something of a liability: in the next year, St Davids was again plundered, and it is possible that this was the work of Rhys's erstwhile followers, returning to Ireland.[86] The same church suffered in 1091, this time at the hands of the vikings of the Isles.[87] In the same year, Godfrey Meranach seized control of Dublin[88] (he was also lord of the Isles). The attack on St Davids may have been a preliminary raid to gather resources.

Rhys ap Tewdwr died in 1093, an event which was crucial in the history of the

---

78 AI *s.a.* 1075; AT *s.a.* 1075; ALC *s.a.* 1075; AFM *s.a.* 1075.
79 AI *s.a.* 1075; AClon. *s.a.* 1074.
80 Ó Corráin, *Ireland before the Normans*, p. 138.
81 *AC* (B) *s.a.* [1080]; *AC* (C) *s.a.* [1081]; *ByT* (Pen. 20) *s.a.* 1078 (*recte* 1080); *ByT* (RB) *s.a.* [1080]; *ByS s.a.* 1078 (*recte* 1080).
82 AI *s.a.* 1080.
83 *ByT* (Pen. 20) *s.a.* 1079 (*recte* 1081); *ByT* (RB) *s.a.* [1081]; *ByS s.a.* 1079 (*recte* 1081). See also the long account of this battle in *HGK*, ed. Evans, pp. 14–16.
84 *AC* (B) *s.a.* [1088]; *AC* (C) *s.a.* [1088]; *ByT* (Pen. 20) *s.a.* 1086 (*recte* 1088); *ByT* (RB) *s.a.* [1088]; *ByS s.a.* 1087 (*recte* 1088).
85 *ByT* (RB) *s.a.* [1088].
86 *AC* (B) *s.a.* [1089]; *AC* (C) *s.a.* [1089]; *ByT* (Pen. 20) *s.a.* 1087 (*recte* 1089); *ByT* (RB) *s.a.* [1089]; *ByS s.a.* 1088 (*recte* 1089).
87 *AC* (B) *s.a.* [1091]; *AC* (C) *s.a.* [1091]; *ByT* (Pen. 20) *s.a.* 1089 (*recte* 1091); *ByT* (RB) *s.a.* [1091]; *ByS s.a.* 1089 (*recte* 1091).
88 AT *s.a.* 1091.

Norman incursions into Wales. His death earns a mention in the Annals of Inisfallen, which record that an individual with a Norse name, Turcaill son of Eola, fell with Rhys.[89] Could this person have been a remnant of the mercenary fleet of 1088, or perhaps a representative of one of the Scandinavian-influenced settlements in Pembrokeshire?

In 1098 north Wales endured a massive Norman invasion led by Hugh d'Avranches, earl of Chester and Hugh de Montgomery, earl of Shrewsbury, with the guidance of a local magnate, Owain ab Edwin of Tegeingl. The north Welsh leaders, Cadwgan ap Bleddyn and Gruffudd ap Cynan, retreated with their supporters to Anglesey where they awaited help in the form of a fleet from Ireland. The fleet duly arrived and accepted the bribes of the Norman earls, deserting the Welsh. Cadwgan and Gruffudd fled to Ireland, leaving Gwynedd at the Normans' mercy. However, as was described in chapter three, Magnus Bareleg, king of Norway arrived unexpectedly with a small fleet. The Norwegian king had been enforcing his control of the Orkneys and Hebrides, and may have had intentions towards Ireland also. Seeing the forces drawn up on Anglesey, he investigated, was attacked by the Normans, and opened fire. Hugh of Shrewsbury was slain in the fight, whereupon the Norman force retreated.[90] Magnus then departed himself. This king continued to show an interest in the Irish sea province until his death in 1103: his appearance in 1098 must have, however, seemed like providence to the beleaguered Welsh.

Gruffudd and Cadwgan returned from Ireland in 1099 and made peace with the Normans. In the same year, Hywel ab Ithel (later a force in Rhos and Rhufoniog) departed to Ireland.[91] It is not possible to discover his motives, unless he was seeking Irish help against Norman pressure on his lands, nor is it known when he returned: the Welsh chronicles are entirely silent about him until he fell in conflict with the sons of Owain ab Edwin in 1118.[92]

The Irish and the Hiberno-Scandinavians had become a resource for Welsh rulers and for English exiles in the eleventh century. Very early in the twelfth century, a Norman magnate with a powerbase in south Wales turned his eyes to Ireland in search of support, foreshadowing by seventy years the action of Richard de Clare. This was Arnulf de Bellême, a younger son of the de Montgomery family, and brother of the current earl of Shrewsbury, Robert, who had succeeded to the earldom after the death of Hugh in 1098. Arnulf's base was in Pembrokeshire, a holding which he acquired at some time after the death of Rhys ap Tewdwr in 1093, probably in the Norman invasion of Dyfed and Ceredigion in that year,[93] and he was responsible for the initial building of Pembroke castle. The de Bellême family had extensive and important holdings in both Normandy and England: on the death of Roger de Montgomery in 1093/4 these holdings

---

89 AI *s.a.* 1093.
90 *AC* (B) *s.a.* 1098; *AC* (C) *s.a.* [1098]; *ByT* (Pen. 20) *s.a.* 1096 (*recte* 1098); *ByT* (RB) *s.a.* 1094 (*recte* 1098); *ByS s.a.* 1096 (*recte* 1098).
91 *AC* (B) *s.a.* 1099; *AC* (C) *s.a.* [1099]; *ByT* (Pen. 20) *s.a.* 1097 (*recte* 1099); *ByT* (RB) *s.a.* 1095 (*recte* 1099); *ByS s.a.* 1097 (*recte* 1099).
92 *AC* (B) *s.a.* 1118; *AC* (C) *s.a.* [1118]; *ByT* (Pen. 20) *s.a.* 1115 (*recte* 1118); *ByT* (RB) *s.a.* 1115 (*recte* 1118); *ByS s.a.* 1115 (*recte* 1118).
93 *AC* (B) *s.a.* [1093]; *AC* (C) *s.a.* [1093]; *ByT* (Pen. 20) *s.a.* 1091 (*recte* 1093); *ByT* (RB) *s.a.* 1090 (*recte* 1093); *ByS s.a.* 1091 (*recte* 1093).

were split between his two oldest sons, the Norman lands passing to Robert, the English ones to Hugh. On Hugh's death, Robert acquired the English lands also. In 1100 William II died and was succeeded by Henry I. Robert de Bellême, a supporter of Robert Curthose, prepared himself and his lands for rebellion, strengthening and building castles at Arundel, Tickhill, Bridgnorth and Shrewsbury. In 1102 he was called to account for his activities by the king, and openly rebelled. Arnulf joined him, as did three sons of Bleddyn ap Cynfyn, Iorwerth, Cadwgan and Maredudd. While Robert strengthened his castles – and particularly those in the March area, according to the *Brutiau*,[94] Arnulf was searching for allies. Like native Welsh magnates before him, he looked to Ireland and he dispatched his steward, Gerald of Windsor, to King Muirchertach Ua Briain, the most important Irish ruler since the death of his father Toirdhelbhach in 1086. Gerald requested, and received, a daughter of Muirchertach as a wife for Arnulf, and with her came a fleet.[95] In the same year, Magnus Bareleg reappeared in the Irish sea area, also seeking a daughter of Muirchertach as a wife for his son[96] (whom he installed as the king of Man). Despite the Irish and Welsh assistance, the de Bellême revolt was not succeeding: Henry I had taken Tickhill and Arundell, and suborned Iorwerth ap Bleddyn, leaving Robert hard-pressed, while his brother went to meet his new bride. Hearing of the presence of Magnus, who had come to Anglesey for timber before returning to Man, and who was now a relation by marriage, Robert sent messengers to the Norwegian king, begging for help. Magnus refused, an action which seems to have been the last straw for Robert: surrendering Bridgnorth to the king, he fled to Normandy. This being heard by Arnulf, he too surrendered his possessions in England and Wales, and joined his brother in Normandy. Unlike Rhys ap Tewdwr or Gruffudd ap Cynan, his Irish alliance had not brought him success. The connexion seems to have endured, however (*pace* Orderic Vitalis[97]), for in 1103, Muirchertach wrote to Archbishop Anselm, thanking him for his intervention on Arnulf's behalf.[98] The rest of Arnulf's career is largely obscure: on the evidence of Orderic he spent some time in Normandy;[99] he may also have spent some time in Ireland. Lloyd thought that Arnulf's fall was in part due to the presence of Magnus in the Irish sea:[100] pre-occupied with a possible threat from the Norwegian king, Muirchertach was unable to help Arnulf. However, the evidence of the *Brutiau* seems to make this explanation unnecessary – Muirchertach does seem to have dispatched a fleet to Arnulf's help, but it apparently arrived too late to be of any real use. Magnus himself had little benefit from the Irish marriage alliance: in 1102 he

---

94 *ByT* (Pen. 20) *s.a.* 1100 (*recte* 1102); *ByT* (RB) *s.a.* 1100 (*recte* 1102); *ByS s.a.* 1100 (*recte* 1102).
95 See note 94, and also Orderic Vitalis, *Historia Ecclesiastica*, Book XI: ed. & transl. Chibnall, VI.32.
96 AFM *s.a.* 1101 and 1102; AT *s.a.* 1102; AI *s.a.* 1102; ALC *s.a.* 1102 and 1103; AU *s.a.* 1102.
97 Orderic Vitalis, *Historia Ecclesiastica*, Book XI: ed. & transl. Chibnall, VI.50.
98 Migne, *Patrologia Latina*, CC IV.85.
99 See note 97.
100 Lloyd, *A History*, II.413–14.

made a year's peace with Muirchertach,[101] and in 1103, he was killed while raiding in Ulster.[102]

Before concluding this chapter, it is necessary to turn our attention to one final source. This is *Historia Gruffud vab Kenan*,[103] a text which has already received some attention above.[104] This text was written after the death of Gruffudd ap Cynan in 1137, and probably after the accession of Henry II in England (1154) at the earliest. It is a biography of Gruffudd ap Cynan, the north Welsh king, and contains a fair amount of material referring to Ireland.

According to the *Historia*, Gruffudd himself was partly Hiberno-Scandinavian, through his mother, named as:[105]

Ragnell, verch Avloed, vrenhin Dinas Dulyn a phymhetran Ywerdon ac enys Vanav, a hanoed gynt o deyrnas Prydein. A brenhin oed ar lawer o enyssed ereill, Denmarc, a Galwei, a Renneu, a Mon, a Gvyned, en e lle y gwnaeth Avloed castell cadarn a'e dom a'e fos etwar en amlvc, ac a elwit castell Avloed vrenhin; yg Kymraec, hagen, y gelwir Bon y Dom.

Ragnaillt the daughter of Olaf, king of the city of Dublin and a fifth part of Ireland, and of the Isle of Man which was formerly part of the kingdom of Britain. Moreover, he was king over many other islands, Denmark and Galloway, and the Rinns, and Anglesey, and Gwynedd where Olaf built a strong castle with its mound and ditch still visible, and called 'The castle of King Olaf'. In Welsh, however, it is called *Bon y Dom*.[106]

Historia Gruffud vab Kenan is a very strange text in a number of ways, and it was written with a very clear purpose: to promote the legitimacy of Gruffudd's rule in Gwynedd. Indeed, the ferocity with which its unknown author pursues this goal is such as to raise the very strongly the question as to just how far this apparently precious legitimacy was recognised by Gruffudd's Welsh contemporaries. It is a fact that upon his first appearance the Welsh annalist found it necessary to identify him as 'Gruffudd the grandson of Iago',[107] rather than by a patronym, as was usual. This suggests that when he arrived upon the political scene in 1075 he was somewhat obscure to his contemporaries – far from being the 'rightful lord' presented in *Historia Gruffud vab Kenan*. It must also be admitted that historical material in the text is scanty: much of the biography is filled with pedigrees, legends and biblical parallels. Even more surprising, while it is relatively full for the early years of Gruffudd's career (1075–1098), a period in which its hero's progress was less than triumphant,[108] it is thin concerning the years of his undisputed reign in the North (1100–1137). There is no overt attempt to establish a chronology within the text: it contains no dates. Attempts to relate it to the external framework of the Welsh chronicles rapidly demonstrate that the author

---

101 See note 96.
102 AU *s.a.* 1103; AI *s.a.* 1103; AT *s.a.* 1103; AFM *s.a.* 1103; ALC *s.a.* 1103; CS *s.a.* 1099.
103 *HGK*, ed. Evans. For an English translation, it is still necessary to use *The History of Gruffudd ap Cynan*, ed. & transl. Jones.
104 See chapters II and III.
105 *HGK*, ed. Evans, p. 2.
106 *HGK*, transl. Jones, p. 105.
107 *AC* (C) *s.a.* [1076]; *ByT* (Pen. 20) *s.a.* 1073 (*recte* 1075); *ByT* (RB) *s.a.* [1075]; *ByS s.a.* 1073 (*recte* 1075).
108 Davies, *Conflict, Coexistence and Change*, pp. 33.

had only a shaky conception of the chronology of his hero's life. There is, however, some unique material in *Historia Gruffud vab Kenan*, but it must be said that much of the text relates matter which could easily have been taken from the Welsh chronicles and from Meilir Brydydd's elegy on Gruffudd. I should like to focus attention upon the Irish and Hiberno-Scandinavian elements of the text.

A. G. Van Hamel gave it as his opinion that the author of the *Historia* visited Ireland to research his biography, and acquired information from both Irish and Scandinavian alike.[109] Other scholars have been less certain as to the accuracy of the *Historia*, but have tended to treat it as a source of reasonable reliability[110] – as recently as 1985, Lewis described it as 'near contemporary',[111] implying that it might be treated as a reliable source for the later eleventh century in Wales. With all due respect to other students of mediaeval Wales, past and present, this opinion will not do. Many of the ills besetting modern scholarship about eleventh-century Wales – and particularly the endless issue of 'legitimate' and 'intrusive' rulers – may be laid squarely at the door of the anonymous author of *Historia Gruffud vab Kenan*. At the most generous estimate, it was composed at least sixty years after the earliest events (those of 1075) which it describes – that is to say, barely within living memory. The Wales in which its author dwelt was a Wales different from that of 1075–1098, when the Welsh rulers were still operating largely outside the Norman polity and when the Marcher barons were only just beginning to be powerful. Legitimacy and dynastic connexions cannot be shown to have been as important in the eleventh century as they were to become in the twelfth century and later.

I should like to put forward another view of *Historia Gruffud vab Kenan*, suggesting that the text is not nearly contemporary. I should suggest that its historical conformity to the late eleventh century, such as it is, results from the author's awareness of earlier records of the events, and that where it deviates from or adds to our material for the period, these deviations and additions should not be treated as reliable, unless they may be supported from another source which is independent of *Historia Gruffud vab Kenan*.

Arthur Jones, attempting to establish the date of the text, observed that it was free from anachronisms or casual irrelevancies which might help one to discover its age. It also omits several important events of Gruffudd's career: Jones felt that these two things made probable the theory that it was originally composed soon after the death of Gruffudd, before the fame of his contemporary princes had spread and before legends about Gruffudd himself had become common knowledge in Wales.[112] Lloyd appears to have thought that it was composed with the consent of Gruffudd's son Owain Gwynedd:[113] Jones, noticing the absence of reference to Owain's deeds, considered the text to have been a product inde-

109 Van Hamel, 'Norse History in *Hanes Gruffudd ap Cynan*', p. 343.
110 Consider Lloyd, *A History*, II.379: 'Despite some inaccuracies and the inevitable disposition to magnify the deeds of its hero, the Ancient History of Gruffydd ap Cynan ap Iago tells s story which is in general conformity with what is known of the history of the time, and in the following pages the evidence yielded by it is used without hesitation.'
111 Lewis, 'English and Norman Government'.
112 *HGK*, transl. Jones, pp. 17–18.
113 Lloyd, *A History*, II.379.

pendent of court-influence.[114] The latter must be correct for, regardless of the prominence or otherwise of Owain, it seems very unlikely that anyone who had access to Gruffudd's immediate circle would have created quite as many errors and confusions. Also it seems that the text cannot have followed very quickly upon Gruffudd's death: its narrative is definitely unbalanced in favour of the early part of Gruffudd's life, and it says little of his later activities. This is rather strange: after all his emphasis on Gruffudd's 'legitimacy' one would think that the biographer might go on to describe his hero's behaviour once he was securely king. Moreover, had it been written very soon after his death, it would have been these achievements which would have been foremost on most people's minds. *Historia Gruffud vab Kenan* is not a royal biography in the sense that it is not an account of Gruffudd the king: it is a biography of the young Gruffudd – Gruffudd the adventurer. It is the story of a young royal exile who in pursuit of his legitimate rights must overcome the illegitimate possessors of his rightful property. He has many obstacles to surmount, including the initial unreliability of those who should pay allegiance to him, but he survives, to become a respected ruler with the friendship – as an equal – of the neighbouring kings. His accession means happiness and peace for all, and prosperity for Gwynedd. The point is not to tell the story of his life, but it is rather to demonstrate the inevitable triumph of legitimate blood. It is tempting to point to a parallel – a context? – for this paradigm of righteousness triumphant, in the early career of Llywelyn ap Iorwerth. Like Gruffudd, Llywelyn was the grandson of a well-known king, but the son of a somewhat overshadowed father; like Gruffudd, he probably grew up away from his patrimony which meanwhile fell into illegitimate hands. Could *Historia Gruffud vab Kenan* belong to the early years of the struggle of Llywelyn ap Iorwerth? The lack of any reliable dating indications in the text means that this idea must remain very speculative; however, there are perhaps a few points in its favour. If *Historia Gruffud vab Kenan* belongs to this period – the very end of the twelfth century, or the early thirteenth when Llywelyn was still striving to gain power, or just afterwards, perhaps, then this might explain the lack of detail in the *Historia* about Gruffudd's later years, or his sons: the text was designed as a panegyric on legitimate blood, not on Gruffudd himself. There is, moreover, one tiny scrap of positive evidence to suggest a late date for the *Historia*: the use of the name 'Guilim gleddyf hir', 'William Longsword', for William Rufus. This is usually explained as an error arising from an association with William Longsword the son of Rollo of Normandy; and indeed the first occurence of the name follows on an account of Rollo.[115] however, the mistake is reiterated later in the text, in the account of William Rufus's campaigns in Wales in the 1090s.[116] As it happens, early in the twelfth century there was a William Longsword who led expeditions into Wales: this was William Longespée, earl of Salisbury and illegitimate son of Henry II, warden of the Welsh march from 1208 and commander in King John's Welsh and Irish expeditions of 1210–1212.[117] It is just possible that a

114 *HGK* transl. Jones, pp. 17–18, and n. 2.
115 *HGK*, ed. Evans, p. 4.
116 *Ibid.*, pp. 22–3.
117 On William Longsword, see the article by Hunt in *The Dictionary of National Biography*, vol. 34, pp. 116–18.

confusion with the early Norman duke was reinforced by the activities of yet another invading William in the early part of the thirteenth century. This in itself does not prove a late date for the *Historia* – it may, for instance, suggest that an error crept in, not in the original of *Historia Gruffud vab Kenan* but in the translation into Welsh from which all our knowledge descends (and which had been made by the mid-thirteenth century, the date of our earliest manuscript of *Historia Gruffud vab Kenan*). However, this may open up a little the question of the date of *Historia Gruffud vab Kenan* and make its 'contemporary' nature perhaps less generally assumed.

Whatever its date, the Irish material in the *Historia* is of a highly dubious character on the whole. It consists partly of pedigree and legendary matter, and partly of a number of references to Gruffudd's relationships with several Irish rulers and the help which they gave him, as follows.

Gruffudd was born in Dublin in the days of Edward, king of England, and Toirdhelbhach, king of Ireland. He was reared at Swords, near Dublin. His father was 'Kenan vrenhin Gwyned' and his mother was Ragnaillt, daughter of Olaf, king of Dublin and of one-fifth of Ireland. A pedigree is given for Ragnaillt (see figure 1) on her father's side, and Olaf's titles are given (king of Dublin, a province of Ireland, Man, Galloway, the Rinns, Denmark, Anglesey and Gwynedd). The pedigree goes back – impossibly – to Harald Harfagr, son of the king of Denmark. An account of Harald and his brothers is then given (including the odd story of Alyn and Thurkil[118]) and their exploits throughout Europe. Harald is said to have founded the Hiberno-Scandinavian settlements in Ireland, while his brother Rollo settled in Normandy. Although Rollo in this account is supposedly a Dane, the settlement of Normandy is said by the author to have been made by Norwegians. This Rollo was the ancestor of William the Conqueror, his sons William 'Longsword' and Henry, and his nephew, Stephen. This section concludes with the remark that 'in this wise was King Gruffudd noble on his mother's side, on the part of his mother's father'.[119] The author then describes Gruffudd's pedigree through his maternal grandmother (figures 2, 3, and 4), which seems to be designed to show that Gruffudd was a kinsman of most of the prominent Irish ruling families. It includes a very short – and probably spurious – account of his supposed uterine half-brothers, Ragnall and Áed sons of Mathagamain, kings of Ulster.

During his childhood in Ireland, Gruffudd's mother told him of his patrimony and that tyrants dwelt therein. Gruffudd, learning of this (and having grown up, one assumes), went to the court of 'Murchath vrenhin' and complained to him and to the other kings of Ireland that a 'strange race' was ruling his paternal kingdom. The Irish kings took pity on him, and promised help. Gruffudd then left for Gwynedd.[120] Once there he expelled his rival, Trahaearn, and attacked and burnt Rhuddlan castle. The news reached the king of Ireland and his barons, who rejoiced at the good fortune of their kinsman and foster-son. However, Gruffudd's new Welsh supporters betrayed him and killed two hundred and twenty Irish men of the knights of Gruffudd's household. Trahaearn returned and de-

---

[118] For a discussion of this, see Van Hamel, 'Norse History in *Hanes Gruffudd ap Cynan*'.
[119] *HGK*, transl. Jones, p. 109.
[120] On this, see appendix 2.

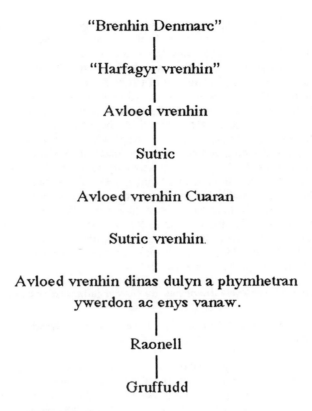

"Brenhin Denmarc"
|
"Harfagyr vrenhin"
|
Avloed vrenhin
|
Sutric
|
Avloed vrenhin Cuaran
|
Sutric vrenhin.
|
Avloed vrenhin dinas dulyn a phymhetran
ywerdon ac enys vanaw.
|
Raonell
|
Gruffudd

Figure 1

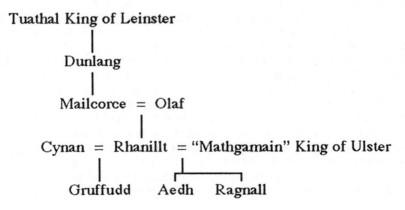

Tuathal King of Leinster
|
Dunlang
|
Mailcorce = Olaf
|
Cynan = Rhanillt = "Mathgamain" King of Ulster
|
Gruffudd   Aedh   Ragnall

Figure 2

175

feated Gruffudd in battle, Gruffudd being supported by the men of Anglesey and Arfon and a few Danes and Irishmen. In the battle, many fell, including Gruffudd's foster-father 'Cerit' and 'Varudri', leader of the Irish and lord of Cruc Brenan. Gruffudd was forced to flee and took ship first to the Isle of 'Adron' and thence to Wexford. Once in Ireland, Gruffudd complained grievously to the king and his chieftains. They considered his situation to be intolerable and urged him to return swiftly with a well-prepared fleet which they had given him, of thirty ships of Irishmen and Danes. He returned to Gwynedd and Trahaearn fled in terror. Gruffudd occupied Llyn, Arfon and Anglesey. However, the Danes of his household became discontented because they had not received their custom of plundering as promised. They ravaged Anglesey in spite of Gruffudd, and returned to Ireland with the spoil, taking Gruffudd with them against his will.

Gruffudd then remained in Ireland for a year as the guest of 'Diermit vrenhin' and other noblemen. The king gave him a fleet from Waterford of Danes, Irishmen and Britons, and Gruffudd sailed to Wales. Arriving at St Davids, he encountered Rhys ap Tewdwr, king of Deheubarth, and formed an alliance with him. The battle of Mynydd Carn then followed: the Hiberno-Scandinavian element in Gruffudd's force is described as follows.

. . . gvyr Denmarc ac eu bwyeill deuvinyauc a'r Guydyl gaflachauc ac eu peleu haearnaul kyllellauc.[121]

. . . the men of Denmark and their two-edged axes, and the spear-armed Irishmen with their sharp iron *pila*.[122]

An Irishman, 'Gucharki', slew Trahaearn and Gruffudd and Rhys were victorious. The *Historia* then goes on to describe Gruffudd's ravaging in mid-Wales and his captivity. The Irish material resumes once Gruffudd has escaped from prison. On his escape, he at once embarked for Ireland, but was blown off course, to Porth Hodni in Deheubarth. For some months he wandered, collecting companions until he came to Ardudwy. Seeing the Normans in Gwynedd, he went to Ireland in a skiff belonging to the church of Aberdaron. At the end of a month he returned, and at once set off for Ireland again. From there, he sailed to the Isles of Denmark, to his friend King Guthrie, to ask for ships. He obtained help and returned to Anglesey with the men of the Isles in sixty ships. After winning a battle against the Normans, the vessels returned to the Isles: Gruffudd, however, stayed with one ship on the Isle of Ron (like *Adron* earlier, this place is described as the isle of seals) and indulged in piracy before returning to Llyn. He drove the Normans from Gwynedd, and reigned peaceably for two years. Of this period, the author remarks that he is unequal to the task of relating the combats of Gruffudd and the Welsh and the Irish and the men of the Isles of Denmark, and many other nations. After two years occured the famous incident on Anglesey involving Hugh of Chester and Hugh of Shrewsbury. Gruffudd and Cadwgan ap Bleddyn retreated before this Noman force to Anglesey to await help. Sixteen long keeled ships came from Ireland to Gruffudd, but the Normans succeeded in suborning them. Gruffudd and Cadwgan fled to Ireland, leaving the Normans to

121 *HGK*, ed. Evans, p. 15.
122 *HGK*, transl. Jones, p. 109.

Figure 3

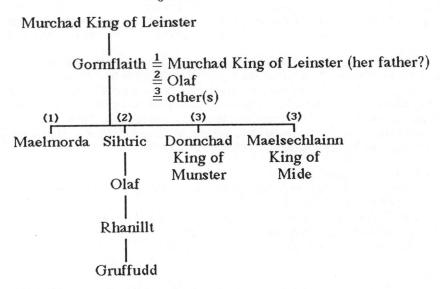

Figure 4

ravage Anglesey, and to be defeated by Magnus Bareleg. The Normans then retreated, having tricked Gruffudd's disloyal Hiberno-Scandinavian fleet, giving them not the promised reward of young maidens and strong male slaves, but rather all the old and deformed captives. The fleet returned to Ireland where the unnamed king punished them with mutilation and exile.

Gruffudd then returned from Ireland to find Gwynedd deserted: he lived there in poverty for some years. (This incident is reminiscent of the fortunes of Manawyddan in the third branch of the Mabinogi.) Eventually, he achieved prosperity, and reigned for many years in friendship with the kings nearest to him, Henry of England, 'Mwrchath' king of Ireland, and the king of the Isles of

177

Denmark. Nearing death, he gave money to Christ church, Dublin, and other unnamed chief churches of Ireland (in addition to a number of Welsh ones). His death was lamented by Welshmen, Irishmen and Danes.

If the material about the spurious exploits of Harald Harfagr and his brothers be omitted, it can be seen that the evidence of *Historia Gruffud vab Kenan* about Cambro-Irish relations falls largely into two parts, genealogical and 'historical'. I shall consider the genealogical material first.

Peter Bartrum, in his collection of early Welsh pedigree-material, expressed reservations about all the pedigrees, Welsh and Irish, contained in the *Historia*.[123] Most significantly, he thought that one of the pedigrees (that of Rhodri Mawr, going back to God) shows signs of having been influenced by the *Historia Regum Britanniae* of Geoffrey of Monmouth, a work which appeared *ca* 1135 × 1138. Bartrum considered it possible but improbable that Geoffrey's work would be so swiftly adapted to the needs of royal pedigrees (using Arthur Jones's date for *Historia Gruffud vab Kenan* of 1137 × 1170), especially since the version of *Historia Regum Britanniae* used would have had to have been in Welsh. He thus suggested that it is unlikely that the present form of the pedigree was composed as early as 1170 (which may be another small scrap of evidence to suggest a late date for *HGK*).

He noted many errors in the Hiberno-Scandinavian pedigrees, and Jones was also aware of these.[124] As far as the pedigree in the male line of the house of Dublin is concerned, Harald Harfagr was king of Norway, not Denmark, nor was his father king of Denmark. The chronology of these pedigrees is also suspicious. Many of the Hiberno-Scandinavians and Irish who appear therein are also known to us from Irish chronicles and as such may be assigned at least approximate dates, with a few exceptions. These are given below.

(1) Hiberno-Scandinavians
   Sihtric 'Caech', the great-great-great-grandfather of Gruffudd: living 919, died young in 927.
   Olaf Cuaran, great-great-grandfather, died on Iona in *ca* 980.
   Sihtirc Silkenbeard, great-grandfather, died 1042.
   Olaf 'Arnaid', grandfather, died in battle in 1013.

(2) Irish
   Murchad, king of Leinster, great-great-great-grandfather = Murchad mac Finn, died in 972.
   Gormflaith, great-great-grandmother, *ob.* 1030.
   Maelmorda, half-brother of Gruffudd's great-grandfather = Maelmorda mac Murchada meic Finn, *ob.* 1014.
   Donnchad of Munster, another half-brother of Gruffudd's great-grandfather – Donnchad Ua Briain, *ob.* 1064.
   Maelsechlainn of Mide, another half-brother of Gruffudd's great-grandfather, = Maelsechlainn II mac Domnall Uí Néill, *ob.* 1022.
   Brian of Munster, great-great-grandfather = Brian Boru, *ob.* 1014.

---

[123] Bartrum, *Tracts*, pp. 35 and 134–6.
[124] *HGK*, transl. Jones, pp. 39–47.

Mathgamain of Ulster (?stepfather) = Mathgamain mac Dubhgall, *ob*. 1014.
Tuathal of Leinster, great-great-grandfather – Tuathal mac Augaire, *ob*. 958.
Aed and Ragnall, putative half-brothers. I have not been able to identify
these two, unless Aed = Eochaid ua Mathgamna of Ulster, *ob*. 1127.

It is fairly clear from this that *Historia Gruffud vab Kenan* has made a number of
errors. Maelmorda was a brother of Gormflaith, not a son. Máelsechlainn II, far
from being a half-brother of Donnchad Ua Briain, was the contemporary and ally
of Donnchad's father Brian. Some of the persons who the *Historia* would make
contemporaries were patently not: hence Sihtric Caech and Murchad mac Finn
are supposedly great-great-great-grandfathers of Gruffudd, yet the former died in
927, the latter in 972 – even allowing for the fact that Sihtric is said to have died
young, this is a large gap.

Much of the pedigree is correct to a degree within its Irish context (apart from
the confusion of the husbands and sons of Gormflaith). Nevertheless, I cannot
accept most of it as accurate as regards Gruffudd. These pedigrees look like an
attempt by someone to glorify Gruffudd by connecting him with famous Irish
figures. Too many of the crucial links – and particularly that to Brian via Slani –
depend on *Historia Gruffud vab Kenan* alone. I should suggest that, while Gruffudd may have been related to the Hiberno-Scandinavian kings of Dublin, he
was not kin to the Irish royal dynasties (except in so far as some intermarriage
had already occurred). Slani, his putative great-great-grandmother, is the most
suspicious link, since it was through her that Gruffudd was connected to the
prestigious Muirchertach Ua Briain.

The historical evidence of the *Historia* is concerned mostly with Gruffudd's
relations with Irish kings and with the presence in his armies of Hiberno-
Scandinavian contingents. To summarise:

ca 1075, Gruffudd, having acquired a force from 'Murchath', king of Ireland,
takes and loses Gwynedd in one year.
ca 1076 × *ca* 1081 Gruffudd with a fleet takes Llyn, Arfon and Anglesey: his
Hiberno-Scandinavians allies plunder there and carry him off to Ireland.
ca 1081 After a year as the guest of 'Diermit', king of Ireland, Gruffudd assem-
bles a fleet. The battle of Mynydd Carn, his triumph and capture.
ca 1093 × *ca* 1097 He escapes and eventually makes his way to Ireland and the
Isles of Denmark, where King 'Guthrie' helps him. He returns to Wales, drives
out the Normans and reigns for two years.
ca 1098 The Anglesey incident. Gruffudd is betrayed by his Hiberno-Scandinavian allies and flees; Magnus Bareleg intervenes to the benefit of the Welsh.
ca 1099 Gruffudd returns and finds Gwynedd deserted. Eventually he prospers
and lives in peace and harmony with King Henry and King 'Mwrchath' until
his death.

In fact, there is very little information about Ireland in *Historia Gruffud vab
Kenan*, and almost nothing that could not have been found from the Welsh
chronicles. These tell us of Gruffudd's arrival in 1075, his presence on Anglesey
and of one of the battles of that year with Trahaearn, Bron-y-Erw. The other,
Gwaet-Erw, which need not belong to 1075 anyway, is noted in Meilir's elegy for

Gruffudd[125] and this poem could have supplied the author of the *Historia* with the name, upon which he then embroidered.[126] The presence of the Irish in his force in this year is not stated by the Welsh chronicles, but could easily have been extrapolated backwards from their accounts of Mynydd Carn in 1081 and Anglesey in 1098. The very long account of Mynydd Carn in *Historia Gruffud vab Kenan* is mostly embroidery – the speeches of Rhys and Gruffudd are designed to imply the superiority of the north Welsh king to his south Welsh contemporary. As I have argued above, in chapter two, this battle was primarily a Southern battle, and the presence of Gruffudd and Trahaearn should not be overemphasised. The account of the Anglesey incident adds nothing to that found in the Welsh chronicles and is, in fact, less detailed than that of John of Worcester.

The raid some time between 1075 and 1081 is unique to the *Historia*, however. It cannot be firmly dated – the *Historia* puts it soon after Gruffudd's return to Ireland after Bron-y-Erw, and places Mynydd Carn a year after it, which makes nonsense of the chronology. The implication is that it occurred some time in the later 1070s. It has previously been noticed that the 1070s marked a renewal of Hiberno-Scandinavian interest in Wales (St Davids and Bangor ravaged 1073, St Davids alone 1080). I should suggest that this raid of Gruffudd's – the main incident in which is the plundering of Anglesey – is a memory of a viking attack on that island at around the time of Bron-y-Erw and Mynydd Carn, and that Gruffudd's name was attached to it by the author of the *Historia*, finding himself short of information about his hero in this period.

What of the various Irish kings mentioned? There are between four and six: four if one simply takes the two occurrences of the name 'Murchath' as meaning the same man, six if one separates them and also includes the nameless 'man who was ruling' in 1098 who punished Gruffudd's errant fleet. The names given are 'Theredelach', ruling at the time of Gruffudd's birth; 'Murchath', who helped Gruffudd in 1075; 'Diermit', who sheltered him for a year before Mynydd Carn (which occurred in 1081); 'Guthrie', king of the isles of Denmark, who gave him a fleet at some point in the mid-1090s; and 'Mwrchath' again, his royal friend.

There are two contenders for 'Murchath'. Murchad mac Diarmait mac Máel na mBó, and Muirchertach Ua Briain. While it is possible, and indeed probable, that the author of the *Historia* intended Murchad mac Diarmait as the helper of 1075, and Muirchertach Ua Briain as the royal friend, I am not at all sure that he himself was aware that there were two different men involved. He simply knew of a 'Murchath', king of Dublin in the 1070s, and of a 'Mwrchath', king of Ireland and contemporary of Gruffudd and Henry I, and equated the two. From the chronological discrepancies in the *Historia*, I do not think its author knew a great deal about the dating of Gruffudd's career (witness the shortfall of years between Bron-y-Erw and Mynydd Carn). The Irish kings in the text support this notion. Toirdhelbhach Ua Briain is described as a contemporary as king of Ireland of Edward the Confessor: Edward died in 1066, but Toirdhelbhach was not in a position to be described as 'king of Ireland' until 1072, although he first appears in our records in 1053. The Murchath of 1075 is probably meant to be Murchad mac Diarmait, yet Murchad died in 1070. It is true that the Annals of

125 French, ed. & transl., 'Meilir's Elegy for Gruffudd ap Cynan'.
126 See appendix 2.

180

Inisfallen say that Muirchertach Ua Briain took rule of Dublin in 1075,[127] but it is not clear that this was in anything other than name (that is, as overlord), and besides there were two other kings of Dublin active in the same year, Gofraid grandson of Ragnall, and a son of Murchad mac Diarmait, Domnall. My main reason for holding that Murchad is intended, however, is that the next named reference in *Historia Gruffud vab Kenan* to a king of Ireland is to 'Diermit', and this accords with our knowledge of Dublin in the early 1070s. 'Diermit' can only be Diarmait mac Máel na mBó, who took over the control of Dublin on his son's death: 'Murchath' to 'Diermit' is a logical progression. It is still chronologically impossible, however. Gruffudd supposedly sheltered with Diarmait for a year immediately before Mynydd Carn. Mynydd Carn occurred in 1081. Diarmait, unfortunately, died in 1072. We have only the word of *Historia Gruffud vab Kenan* that Gruffudd was associated with either of these kings. The author of the *Historia* knew the names of some kings of Dublin in the later eleventh century. I suggest he associated them with Gruffudd in order to increase the prestige of his hero, but he did so in a chronological haze. Our author was not a near contemporary: he knew a few major facts about Gruffudd and he knew they occurred roughly in the time of Diarmait mac Máel na mBó and of Trahaearn ap Caradog. By embroidering on these facts, he created his text, but he did not check his chronology.

'Guthrie', however, may be a different matter. This name must refer to Godfrey Meranach, king of Dublin and the isles in the early 1090s. In chapter three, I discussed the death-date of Robert of Rhuddlan, and the association of Gruffudd with this event. While I doubt Gruffudd's involvement in Robert's death, I should suggest that the occurrence of Godfrey might lend a certain amount of support to the notion of a twelve year captivity for Gruffudd rather than a sixteen year one. We have several examples of Welsh and English men turning to the Hiberno-Scandinavians for aid (Ælfgar in 1055, Rhys ap Tewdwr in 1088, for instance). Gruffudd's very brief association with Godfrey has the ring of truth. The connexion is not lauded by the author of *Historia Gruffud vab Kenan*, it is not longlasting, no kinship is claimed. It looks like simple expediency. Moreover, Godfrey is known to have been in the isles in 1094 – he had been driven out of Dublin by Muirchertach Ua Briain that year. By 1095, he was again in Dublin, where he died.[128] If Gruffudd met Godfrey in the isles in 1094, then he would have been captive for twelve years. This connexion with Godfrey may be reasonably reliable. (It would still not permit of Gruffudd's participation in Robert's death, however: that event occurred in 1093, yet Gruffudd is said to have had a fleet by Orderic Vitalis.[129])

On the whole, *Historia Gruffud vab Kenan* tell us little about relations between Wales and the Hiberno-Scandinavians that we do not already know. Ireland was a refuge for exiles: Harold Godwinesson in 1051, Ælfgar in 1055, Hywel ab Edwin probably in 1044, Rhys ap Tewdwr in 1088, Gruffud ap Rhys in 1093, Gruffudd ap Cynan and Cadwgan ap Bleddyn in 1098, Hywel ab Ithel, perhaps, in 1099, and it is not difficult to accept the addition of Cynan ap Iago to

127 AI *s.a.* 1075.
128 AI *s.a.* 1094 and 1095.
129 Orderic Vitalis, *Historia Ecclesiastica*, Book VIII: ed. & transl. Chibnall, IV.140–42.

this list. Ireland was a source of military support: Hywel ab Edwin in 1044, Ælfgar in 1055, Gruffudd ap Cynan at Mynydd Carn in 1081, Rhys ap Tewdwr in 1088. The Hiberno-Scandinavians were raiders and ravagers, but they were not entirely inimical: the Welsh rulers exploited the presence of these marauders in their own and each others' kingdoms, and employed them as necessary. It is the same attitude with which they initially greeted the Normans, the same attitude with which Hywel ab Ieuaf treated the English in the 970s. As allies, they were not wholly reliable: they could be suborned with higher payment. The relationship between the Welsh and the vikings never achieved the sophistication of that between Gruffudd ap Llywelyn and Earl Ælfgar, for instance. But there was a relationship, nevertheless. The Hiberno-Scandinavians do not seem to have settled extensively in Wales, although they used her coastline as trading and staging posts. They were not uninterested in Wales, however, and a reversal of their fortunes in Ireland often resulted in renewed attacks on Wales. But as was the case with the English, the Welsh terrain may have proved difficult, and the power of Gruffudd ap Llywelyn in the central years of the eleventh century put a halt to raiding, just as it did to internal Welsh conflicts. Llywelyn ap Seisyll may have had a similar effect. The Hiberno-Scandinavians may have begun as an external threat: by the end of the eleventh century they were a resource to be exploited, to be turned to the ends of individual Welsh kings. Our sources tell us nothing of their impact upon ordinary Welshmen, but they show clearly the behaviour of the Welsh rulers: survive, exploit, absorb. The earlier kings – Rhodri Mawr and his sons – had the strength to survive; their descendants in the later tenth century, and even more so in the eleventh, learnt to exploit. Gruffudd ap Cynan was a logical product of this pattern; an Irish Welshman who used the resources of his motherland to acquire those of the land of his father.

V

THE ELEVENTH-CENTURY CHARTERS IN
THE BOOK OF LLANDAFF

The twelfth century document, *Liber Landauensis*, has long been a source of contention among the historians of early medieval Wales, and there has long been a dispute over the reliability, usefulness, and, indeed, historical role of the text. Professor Wendy Davies has published a number of works upon this subject[1] and has drawn many interesting conclusions about the nature of Glamorgan between the sixth and the twelfth centuries from the testimony of *Liber Landauensis*. Her valuable studies have yielded much fascinating information, and have proved very important for subsequent writers. Nevertheless, her conclusions cannot go entirely unchallenged: in particular her use of the material contained within the Narrations of the Llandaff charters. I do not intend to discuss the nature of the Narrations in detail here, but shall consider only the material relating to the eleventh century. The charters which appear to belong to the eleventh century are twenty in number: 246, 249a, 249b, 251, 253, 255, 257, 258, 259, 260, 261, 262, 263, 264a, 264b, 267, 269, 271, 272, and 274. Of these, two are admitted to be spurious, 253 and 260.[2] There are Narrations attached to 249b, 255, 257, 259, 261, 263, 264b, 267, 271, 272. 253 and 269 both purport to be confirmations of the church of Llandaff in its property. I intend to consider all of the charters separately, but for convenience I shall divide them up acccording to the bishops to whom they are supposed to have been made.

---

[1] In particular, by Davies, *Llandaff Charters*, *Microcosm*, 'The Consecration of Bishops', '*Liber Landavensis*: its Construction and Credibility', 'The Orthography of Personal Names in the charters of *Liber Landavensis*', 'Unciae: Land Measurement in the *Liber Landavensis*', and 'St. Mary's, Worcester, and the *Liber Landavensis*'. Other valuable works on this text are: Anscombe, 'Landauensium Ordo Chartarum'; Bartrum, 'Some Studies in Early Welsh History'; and Jones, 'The Book of Llandaff'. For the history of Llandaff in the wider historical context, see: Conway Davies, *Episcopal Acts*; Brooke, *The Church and the Welsh Border*; and Cowley, *The Monastic Order in South Wales 1066–1349*.

[2] Davies, *Llandaff Charters* pp. 126 and 127; *Microcosm*, pp. 186–7.

(1) CHARTERS OF BISHOP BLEDDRI

Charter 246

This charter, attributed to a date of *ca* 1020 by Davies,[3] records the gift of *Lannguronui* by the four *alumni* Elfoen, Nudd, Melwas and Arwystl, to Saints Dyfrig, Teilo and Euddogwy, and Bishop Bleddri, with the guarantee and consent of King Rhys ab Owain.

Within the charter itself, there are no obvious indications of date. *Liber Landauensis*[4] records that Bleddri was reputedly consecrated in 983 with the consent of Kings Owain, Idwallon, Cadell and Cynfyn, sons of Morgan Hen, who were all ruling in Morgannwg, and of Rhodri and Gruffudd sons of Elise. Bleddri's consecration supposedly took place at the hands of Ælfric, archbishop of Canterbury (995–1005) and in the presence of King Æthelred the Unready (978–1016). The account goes on to say that Bleddri died thirty nine years after his consecration, that is *ca* 1022.

Davies[5] has pointed out, however, that Ælfric was not made archbishop of Canterbury until 995; so either the date of Bleddri's consecration as supplied by *Liber Landauensis* is wrong, or, even more probably, the association with Canterbury is false, and originates not in any historical fact, but in the policy pursued by Bishop Urban in the twelfth century of placating the see of Canterbury.

If any reliability at all can be placed on the date of consecration, this would provide a *terminus ante quem* of 1022 for *LL* 246. However, as there is no record of Bleddri extant outside *Liber Landauensis*, there are no independent checks on this date, and it cannot thus be accepted unconditionally.

None of the other individuals named within the charter are of use with this problem either. The king, Rhys ab Owain, is not known from any other source, and this is his only charter-attestation. Apparently he was a grandson of Morgan Hen who, according to the *Brutiau* and *Annales Cambriae*, died *ca* 974. If the consecration-record of Bleddri can be used, then it would suggest that Rhys's father Owain was alive *ca* 983. Owain also features in charter 240, in association with his father and brothers.

Of the witnesses, only two occur in any other charter. One of the lay witnesses, Gwrgan ap Meirchion, is found as a lay witness in charter 243, a charter of Bishop Gwgan. This charter is dated *ca* 980 by Davies, but she comments that it is atypical[6] (although she still regards it as genuine). She does however consider the adult presence of Gwrgan (the grant was made by his father Meirchion) as very unlikely. Gwrgan also occurs in *LL* 262, a charter of Bishop Joseph, dated *ca* 1022 by Davies,[7] which Gwrgan granted in association with his father. This association with Joseph may tend to support an eleventh-century date for *LL* 246. The other witness who recurs is 'Ioseb' *presbiter* and deacon of Llandaff, who is

---

3   Davies, *Llandaff Charters*, p. 126; *Microcosm*, p. 185.
4   *The Text of the Book of Llan Dâv*, edd. Evans & Rhys.
5   Davies, 'The Consecration of Bishops', pp. 63 and 67.
6   Davies, *Llandaff Charters*, p. 125; *Microcosm*, p. 185.
7   Davies, *Llandaff Charters*, p. 128; *Microcosm*, p. 187.

presumably to be identified with the later Bishop Joseph (ob. *ca* 1045[8]). It is presumably his presence which has led Davies to consider *LL* 246 as the latest of the three Bleddri charters.

I can see no obvious means of refining the date of the text as it stands, beyond saying that it is probably not later than *ca* 1022, the alleged date of Bleddri's death. I do not, however, see why it has to be as late as 1020: in theory it could be earlier, as there is no obvious other way of pinpointing its date. The presence of Gwrgan in the earlier *LL* 243 may suggest a slightly earlier date for *LL* 246.

Davies identifies *Lannguronui* as Rockfield (formerly Llanoronui) in Monmouthshire. Gwent was for at least part of the early medieval period considered to be a part of Morgannwg; Rhys ab Owain as king of Morgannwg could presumably consent to a grant made in that area. However, by Davies's own reckoning, one Edwin ap Gwriad was supposedly the ruler of Gwent *ca* 1015–*ca* 1035.[9]

Charter 249b

This charter has been assigned a date of *ca* 1015 by Davies.[10] It records the grant of *Uilla Iunuhuc* by King Edwin ap Gwriad of Gwent to Saints Dyrig, Teilo and Euddogwy, and to Bishop Bleddri. The charter further purports to record the circumstances of the grant: the *familia* of King Edwin quarrelled with that of the bishop, and a fight ensued in which blood was shed in the presence of the bishop. Bleddri intervened and was injured. He then went to Llandaff and summoned a full synod which excommunicated the king. On discovering this, Edwin sought pardon from the bishop, and handed over to him the men who had caused the injury. Pardon was granted to him, and the king responded with the gift of *Uilla Iunuhuc*. Davies doubts the full authenticity of this tale, yet suggests that it may embody the memory of such a dispute.[11] This seems improbable. The story found here is one which, with slight variations, occurs attached to a number of the Llandaff charters (*LL* 216b, 225, 233, 257, and 267). While these accounts are not completely identical, they are in their essence very similar indeed – a quarrel between the *familia* of the bishop and that of a layman, the synod, the excommunication and the reparation with land. Given the repetition of this story over a number of charters, and in association with a number of bishops, I can see no reason to consider it even slightly factual in *LL* 249b; it seems to have all the hallmarks of a conventionalised story designed to give a semblance of rationale to the claim of Llandaff to possession of a given territory. There are a number of such stories which are repeated over and over again in *Liber Landauensis*: this one is no more or less credible than any of the others, and I do not consider the account in *LL* 249b to have any historical weight for the eleventh century at all.

The dating of this charter is again uncertain. The presence of Bleddri might give a *terminus ante quem* of *ca* 1022 (although it must always be remembered in dealing with the Llandaff charters that, if they have any core of genuine material

8 *AC* (B) *s.a.* [1044]; *ByT* (Pen. 20) *s.a.* 1043 (*recte* 1045); *ByT* (RB) *s.a.* [1045]; *ByS s.a.* 1043 (*recte* 1045).
9 Davies, *Microcosm*, pp. 72, 84, 87 and 96.
10 Davies, *Llandaff Charters*, p. 126; *Microcosm*, p. 185.
11 See note 10.

185

at all, the bishop may not be a part of it, but may simply be a later Llandaff accretion). Edwin ap Gwriad is not known from either the Welsh chronicles or the pedigrees, but *LL* 255 makes him a contemporary of King Meurig ap Hywel (who is known from the Welsh chronicles to have been living *ca* 1039[12]) and also of Meurig's father Hywel ab Owain (*ob. ca* 1043[13]). Davies has attempted to date Edwin in terms of the lifespan of his supposed son Hywel ab Edwin,[14] king of Deheubarth 1033–1044. This argument is not reliable: the weight of evidence suggests that Hywel was actually the son of Edwin ab Einion ab Owain of the Southern Branch of the dynasty of Rhodri Mawr. This Edwin ab Einion was living *ca* 992,[15] and not related to Edwin ap Gwriad at all. Hywel ab Edwin's activities therefore cannot be used to date Edwin ap Gwriad.

Of the other witnesses to this charter, one occurs in other charters. This is the clerical witness Cyfeiliog, who seems to be identical with the person found attesting charters of Bishop Joseph (264b, 264a, 255, 258, 263). This might indicate that this charter belongs to the later years of Bleddri's episcopate. Amongst the lay witnesses is one 'Gurhi', while a 'Gurci' occurs in 251 (also a Bleddri charter). Davies, however does not consider these two to be the same person.[16]

She has identified *Uilla Iunuhuc* as possibly being Undy, Gwent. It is thus credible as the gift of a ruler of Gwent.[17]

Charter 251

This charter has been dated *ca* 1005 by Davies.[18] It records the gift by Rhodri and Gruffudd sons of Elise, kings of Gwent, of *Penn Celli Guennhuc*, to Saints Dyfrig, Teilo and Euddogwy, and to Bishop Bleddri.

Again, one could suppose a *terminus ante quem* of *ca* 1022 based on Bleddri's alleged obit. Nothing is known in the annals or the genealogies of Rhodri and Gruffudd, who were apparently descendants of an earlier king also known from *Liber Landauensis*, Arthfael ap Nowy. They are mentioned in association with the consecration of Bleddri which is claimed to have occurred *ca* 983. This might just possibly be a reason for assigning this charter to the later tenth century rather than to the eleventh. Of the witnesses only one, a layman, Gwrgi, is known elsewhere: Davies[19] has tentatively identified him with Gurci filius Gurcimanu who witnessed *LL* 243 (dated *ca* 980 by Davies,[20] a charter of Bishop Gwgon). He might equally be identified with the *Gurhi* of *LL* 249b.

---

12 *AC* (C) *s.a.* [1040]; *ByT* (Pen. 20) *s.a.* 1037 (*recte* 1039); *ByT* (RB) *s.a.* [1039]; *ByS s.a.* 1037 (*recte* 1039).
13 *AC* (C) *s.a.* [1042]; *ByT* (Pen. 20) *s.a.* 1041 (*recte* 1043); *ByT* (RB) *s.a.* [1043]; *ByS s.a.* 1041 (*recte* 1043).
14 Davies, 'The Consecration of Bishops', pp. 63–4.
15 *AC* (B) *s.a.* [993], 'Guyn filius Eynaun'; *AC* (C) *s.a.* [992], 'Owein filius Eyniaun'; *ByT* (Pen. 20) *s.a.* 991 (*recte* 992); *ByT* (RB) *s.a.* 990 (*recte* 992); *ByS s.a.* 991 (*recte* 992).
16 Davies, *Llandaff Charters*, pp. 67, 170 and 171.
17 See note 10.
18 Davies, *Llandaff Charters*, p. 126; *Microcosm*, p. 185.
19 Davies, *Llandaff Charters*, pp. 67 and 170.
20 See note 6.

Davies identifies *Penn Celli Guennhuc* as being near Llangwern in Gwent Is Coed, again a region that fits with the presence of supposed rulers of Gwent.

CONCLUSION TO THE CHARTERS OF BISHOP BLEDDRI

Very little can be said about these three charters. Davies places them in the chronological order 251, 249b, 246,[21] which seems reasonable given the presence in 246 of Joseph, and that of his supposed contemporary Cyfeiliog in 249b, and the presence of the apparently late tenth century rulers Rhodri and Gruffudd sons of Elise in 251. As said above, I wonder whether 251 might not be of late tenth century date, especially if *Gurci* is the Gurci son of Gurcimanu of *LL* 243, and is not identical with the *Gurhi* of 249b. I do find it slightly odd that Davies has attributed all three of Bleddri's charters to the eleventh century (and hence to the second half of his episcopate). As explained in my discussion of it, I find the Narration of 249b unconvincing as historical fact, and would see it as a product of twelfth-century Llandaff convention, added to an actual grant and witness list (if these are genuine) in order to add credibility and weight to the grant.

None of these charters seems to contain anything which particularly illuminates our knowledge of eleventh-century Glamorgan, especially once the Narration of 249b is rejected. The grants themselves are very short (which may be a point in their favour) and very unelaborate aside from the conventional formulae which were probably written into them at Llandaff in the early twelfth century – if there is any original material present. In their current form, they present no trustworthy evidence, however, since we lack real knowledge of their provenance, and their original beneficiaries.

(2) CHARTERS OF BISHOP JOSEPH

Charter 249a

This charter records the gift of *Uilla Elcu* by Meurig ap Hywel, king of Glamorgan, to Saints Dyfrig, Teilo and Euddogwy, and to Bishop Joseph. It has been assigned the date *ca* 1040 by Davies.[22]

As far as attempting to date this charter goes, there is once again relatively little evidence. The grantor, Meurig ap Hywel, is known to have been alive *ca* 1039.[23] He appears in several other Llandaff charters (255, 259, 260, and 261). In 257 and 255 he occurs in association with his father Hywel ab Owain, Hywel being called king in 257, but Meurig being the named king in 255. This suggests that Meurig had some power in the lifetime of his father. The absence of Hywel from 249a may either reflect separate spheres of influence, or, more probably, suggest that this charter postdates Hywel's death. (The latter is more likely

---

21 Davies, *Llandaff Charters*, pp. 67 and 72.
22 Davies, *Llandaff Charters*, p. 126; *Microcosm*, p. 185.
23 See note 12.

because Meurig bears the title 'king of Glamorgan' in 249a.) Hywel died *ca* 1043,[24] which may provide a *terminus post quem* for this charter.

Bishop Joseph appeared as a priest in the witness-list of the Bleddri charter 246. According to *Liber Landauensis*[25] he was Bleddri's successor, consecrated in 1022 by Æthelnoð, archbishop of Canterbury, in the presence of King Cnut, and with the consent of two Welsh rulers, Rhydderch ab Iesyn and Hwyel ab Owain. This date is not impossible: according to *Annales Cambriae*[26] and the *Brutiau*,[27] Rhydderch was active *ca* 1022–*ca* 1033. Hywel, as mentioned above, died *ca* 1043 in advanced old age. Æthelnoð held Canterbury 1020–1038, and Cnut reigned 1016–35, which gives a range for the consecration of 1020 × 1035. However, that the dates are possible does not seem to me to prove that Canterbury was in any way involved in the consecration: the association may have arisen from twelfth-century political expediency rather than from eleventh-century fact – indeed, given the desire of Bishop Urban in the early twelfth century to placate Canterbury, the latter seems the more probable.

Joseph is mentioned in *Annales Cambriae* (as 'episcopus Landauensis')[28] and in the *Brutiau* (as 'Teilo's bishop'),[29] as having died in Rome *ca* 1045. This accords with the statement of *Liber Landauensis* that he died in the twenty-fourth year of his episcopate (supposing this to have begun in 1022).[30] It is thus likely that we have a *terminus ante quem* of *ca* 1045 for this charter.

Of the witnesses, *Ruid sacerdos* also occurs in other Joseph charters (255, 257, 258, 259, 263, 264a, 264b), and the clerical witness Bleinguid is found in 261. Tegwared priest of Saint Docgwin also occurs in 257. Of the lay witnesses, Meurig ap Hywel is found in 255, 257, 259, 260 and 261, all Joseph charters. Tewdwr ab Edwin occurs in 259 (together with Meurig) and 263. Atrit ab Elffin is also found in 258; while he cannot be identified with the Eithin ab Elffin who attests 267, a charter of Bishop Herewald, it is not impossible that there may be a family connection here. Atrit and Eithin could conceivably have been brothers. *Dissaith* is also a witness in 263. With the possible exception of the ?sons of Elffin, then, there is no overlap with the charters of either the preceding bishop, Bleddri (save for Joseph himself) or the following bishop, Herewald.

Davies[31] has identified *Uilla Elcu* as being near Llandaff. It is thus within the relevant area for a king of Glamorgan.

Charter 253

Davies[32] has assigned this charter to *ca* 1025, while admitting that it is probably spurious. It purports to be a confirmation of Llandaff and of Bishop Joseph in

24 See note 13.
25 *The Text of the Book of Llan Dâv*, edd. Evans & Rhys, p. 252.
26 *AC* (B) *s.a.* [1022] and [1033]; *AC* (C) *s.a.* [1024] and [1034].
27 *ByT* (Pen. 20) *s.a.* 1021 (*recte* 1023) and *s.a.* 1031 (*recte* 1033); *ByT* (RB) *s.a.* [1023] and *s.a.* 1030 (*recte* 1033); *ByS s.a.* 1021 (*recte* 1023) and *s.a.* 1031 (*recte* 1033).
28 *AC* (B) *s.a.* [1044], 'Ioseph episcopus Landauensis'.
29 *ByT* (Pen. 20) *s.a.* 1043 (*recte* 1045), 'Joseph escog Teilaw'; *ByT* (RB) *s.a.* [1045], 'Josef, esgob Teilaw'; *ByS s.a.* 1043 (*recte* 1045), 'Joseph, escob Teiliau'.
30 *The Text of the Book of Llan Dâv*, edd. Evans & Rhys, p. 252.
31 See note 22.
32 Davies, *Llandaff Charters*, p. 126; *Microcosm*, p. 186.

possession of all their churches and territories, including those within the diocese of St Davids, made by Rhydderch ab Iestyn, king of Morgannwg. It is supposedly supported by Archbishop Æthelnoð and King Cnut. It makes a passing reference to Iago ab Idwal whom it calls king of Anglesey. The charter states that Rhydderch was king of all Wales except for Anglesey. This claim seems exaggerated, to say the least: while Rhydderch was undeniably powerful in South Wales, there is nothing in the annalistic evidence to suggest that he was ever powerful (or even active) in north Wales – all references to him in the Welsh annals indicate that the South was his sphere of influence.[33] It is of some interest to note that the twelfth-century fabricator of this charter considered Rhydderch and Iago to have been contemporaries, a state of affairs that is not made entirely clear by the Welsh annals: in none of these texts is Iago referred to before the death of Rhydderch in 1033. However, the *Brutiau* state that Iago had been king of Gwynedd since the death of Llywelyn ap Seisyll in 1022.[34]

Davies has attempted to salvage this text to some degree: she suggests that since it has clearly undergone whar she considers interpolation (the insertion of stock formulae), the charter may ultimately derive from a note of this event made during Joseph's episcopate.[35] I can see no justification for this view at all. To begin with, a text of this type has a clear political purpose within the twelfth-century context of *Liber Landauensis*: a charter seemingly re-affirming Llandaff's 'rights', and in the names of two powerful rulers, would be of use to lend an air of authority to Llandaff's claims, particularly in its dispute with St Davids.[36] It is by no means the sole document of its type in *Liber Landauensis*: there is a very elaborate charter, in the name of King Morgan, *LL* 152, with a long narration, which purports to confirm to Bishop Euddogwy, and to the congregations of Cadog, Docgwin and Illtud, all their privilges and rights as against royal control, and which Davies dates *ca* 670[37] although it appears very unreliable. There is also a confirmation-charter of Morgan Hen, supposedly suported by Archbishop Dunstan and King Edgar, *LL* 240,[38] which contains a clear error, making Edgar and Hywel Dda contemporaries (Edgar was not king until 957, Hywel died *ca* 950). The charter again specifically mentions the confirmation of Llandaff's possessions in the diocese of St Davids, and again has all the hallmarks of belonging to the twelfth-century political context. Finally there is the confirmation-charter of Gruffudd ap Llywelyn, *LL* 269, which will be discussed below. None of these charters appears to be other than a twelfth-century forgery,[39] and I see no sign of any original eleventh-century elements in 253. To assign it to any other date than that of the composition of *Liber Landauensis* itself seems to be unnecessary, and I do not consider this text to be of any use for the eleventh-century history of Morgannwg, or of any other part of Wales.

33 See notes 26 and 27.
34 *AC* (B) *s.a.* [1022]; *AC* (C) *s.a.* [1024]; *ByT* (Pen. 20) *s.a.* 1021 (*recte* 1023); *ByT* (RB) *s.a.* [1023]; *ByS s.a.* 1021 (*recte* 1023).
35 See note 32.
36 See Brooke, *The Church and the Welsh Border*, pp. 6–49.
37 Davies, *Llandaff Charters*, p. 101; *Microcosm*, p. 169.
38 Davies, *Llandaff Charters*, p. 125; *Microcosm*, pp. 184–5.
39 Although some of the information in *LL* 269 may be original, this is not part of the Confirmation section.

This charter is dated by Davies *ca* 1035.[40] It records a grant made by the king of Glamorgan, Meurig ap Hywel, to Bishop Joseph and Saints Dyfrig, Teilo and Euddogwy of *Uilla Penn i Prisc*, also called *Difrinn Anouid*, *Uilla Tref Eliau in Senghenydd*, also called *Uilla filiorum Quichtrit*, and *Lann Tiuauc*. It has a Narration, recounting that King Meurig, having sworn an oath of peace with King Edwin ap Gwriad of Gwent, on holy relics, and in the presence of the bishop, broke his vow and seized and blinded Edwin. Bishop Joseph then called a synod, and excommunicated Meurig, who sought his pardon and made reparation with the aforementioned gift.

This is one of the commonest types of Narration found in *Liber Landauensis*: even Davies admits that it is a standard type.[41] The same story is told of King Meurig and Cynfeddw (*LL* 147), Kings Morgan and Ffriog (*LL* 152), Kings Tewdwr ap Rhun and Elgystyl ab Awst (*LL* 167), and Kings Clydri and Idwallon (*LL* 176b). There is very little variation between these. Unlike Davies, I can see no reason for considering any part of the Narration to be reliable: it would seem to have been attached in the twelfth century with the purpose of lending extra credibility to the grant, and of emphasizing the power and influence that the so-called bishops of Llandaff had been able to wield in the past century. Having said this, it is not inconceivable that the actual grant itself may be genuine, at least in part (although it would be almost impossible to say how much of it is genuine, once all the obvious Llandaff additions are removed: any genuine material must have been heavily rewritten in the twelfth century).

As far as the date of this charter goes, Hywel ab Owain, father of King Meurig, is present in the witness-list. He is known from the Welsh annals to have died *ca* 1043.[42] This charter is therefore probably no later than that date. Bishop Joseph, moreover, is said by the Welsh annals to have died *ca* 1045;[43] so the charter would appear to have a *terminus ante quem* of *ca* 1045, even if the presence of Hywel be discounted.

The Narration makes a curious reference to the common enemies of Meurig's and Edwin's kingdoms (Glamorgan and Gwent respectively). These are named as the men of Brycheiniog, the English and the South Welsh (presumably Deheubarth). The mention of Brycheiniog and Deheubarth would seem to point more to the twelfth century than to the eleventh (the activities of Bernard of Neufmarché were threatening this area from at least 1093). There is no record now extant of hostility to South East Wales from Brycheiniog or Deheubarth at about such time as this charter may be supposed to have originated (ie before 1045, and probably before 1043). It is worth noting, however, that there is a record of English aggression around this time: Caradog ap Rhydderch, son of Rhydderch ab Iestyn, who we know to have been active in Morgannwg, was killed by the English in 1035.[44] The Narration is of very dubious worth, but if we can make anything at

---

40 Davies, *Llandaff Charters*, p. 127; *Microcosm*, p. 186.
41 See note 40.
42 See note 13.
43 See note 8.
44 *AC* (B) *s.a.* [1034]; *AC* (C) *s.a.* [1036]; *ByT* (Pen. 20) *s.a.* 1033 (*recte* 1035); *ByT* (RB) *s.a.* [1035]; *ByS s.a.* 1033 (*recte* 1035).

all out of this reference to the English, it might suggest a date for *LL* 255 of the later 1030s, or the early 1040s, and probably not later than 1043.

Of the clerical witnesses, Rhuryth occurs in 249a, 257, 258, 259, 263, 264a, and 264b, all Joseph-charters. Cyfeiliog is found in the Joseph-chartes 258, 263, 264a and 264b, and also in one Bleddri charter, 249b. Joseph priest of Illtud occurs in 259. Of the lay witnesses, Meurig ap Hywel is mentioned in 249a, 259, 260, and 261, all Joseph-charters. Hywel ab Owain appears as king in the Joseph-charter 257. Cyngen *map Guebric* occurs in 257. There thus is no overlap with the charters of Bishop Herewald, but Cyfeiliog provides one with those of Bleddri.

Davies has identified these lands as Cwm Nofydd and ?Splott, which are situated within the area of influence of a king claiming rule over Morgannwg.[45]

Charter 257

This charter, dated by Davies *ca* 1023,[46] records the grant by Rhiwallon ap Rhun of his hereditary land, *Riubrein*, plus one third of the wood, *Ynys Prithan*, to Saints Dyfrig, Teilo and Euddogwy, and to Bishop Joseph. There is a short Narration which purports to provide the reason for the grant: Rhiwallon fought with the bishop's *familia* and injured one of the bishop's friends. He was therefore expelled from the country and excommunicated. However, at length he made an agreement with the bishop, and with his own parents, and received pardon, making the above-named grant. This is another common story, of the same type as that found in 249b, discussed above, and similarly in *LL* 125a, 257, 263, and 267. Given the conventional nature of the Narration, I see no reason to accept it as genuine: like that of 249b it may simply be a twelfth-century rationalisation, designed to enhance the status and power of the bishops, and to give apparent believability to the grant. The grant is made with the consent of King Hywel ab Owain and his son Meurig.

The status of Hywel as king and his precedence over Meurig probably indicates that this charter is earlier than 249a or 259 in which Meurig appears alone as king, and also earlier than 255 where Hywel occurs but does not take precedence. Hywel died in advanced old age in 1043,[47] and 255 may be attributed to his last years, he being incapacitated or senile. 257 must be earlier: Hywel is apparently still relatively competent, at least sufficiently so to be still considered king (unlike 255 which reads 'King Meurig and his father Hywel'). Bishop Joseph died in 1045, and may have been consecrated in 1022. However, I am unable to refine the date beyond this. The grantor, Rhiwallon ap Rhun, is known from neither annals nor genealogies.

Of the clerical witnesses, Rhuryth occurs in several other charters of Bishop Joseph. Tegwared, priest of Docgwin is found in 249a. Sed, *presbiter* of Cadog is unique to this text. Of the lay witnesses, Hywel (as noted above) also occurs in 255, and Meurig in 249a, 255 and 259. Cyngen ap Gwefrig is also found in 255

---

45 See note 40.
46 Davies, *Llandaff Charters*, p. 127; *Microcosm*, p. 186.
47 See note 13.

(which may suggest he was more a contemporary of Hywel than of Meurig). There is no link to either the previous or the following episcopates.

Davies identifies *Riubrein* as being near Whitechurch, by which I take her to mean Whitechurch, Glamorgan, rather than Whitechurch, Ergyng.[48]

Charter 258

This charter records the grant by Gwrgan ab Ithel of *Uilla Tref Ginhill*, to Saints Dyfrig, Teilo and Euddogwy, and to Bishop Joseph, for Gwrgan's soul. It is dated by Davies *ca* 1038.[49] There is no mention of royal consent, but neither is Gwrgan called a king – however, it is possible that he was the local holder of royal power (his son Iestyn exercised similar royal power, without a title stated in the charters, in the later eleventh century).

Gwrgan ab Ithel, while not mentioned in the Welsh chronicles, seems to have been a significant person. His son Iestyn also features in *Liber Landauensis*, and both of them occur in the genealogies *ABT* 15[50] and MP 3.[51] *ABT* 15 is entitled *Gwehelyth Morgannwg*, perhaps an indication of the status of this family. The pedigree, taken back to legendary figures, is that of Morgan ap Caradog, active in the twelfth century. The text suggests that this line were, like Hywel ab Owain and Meurig ap Hywel, descendants of Morgan Hen (*ob.* 974), king and eponym of Morgannwg. Gwrgan's line would have been cousins of the branch of the family which claimed the kingship in the eleventh century, as the following diagram shows: MP 3 is a pedigree of Caradog ab Iestyn ap Gwrgan, and is thus one generation shorter than *ABT* 15. It is titled *Brenhin Llwyth Morganwc*, which may be further evidence for the royal, or semi-royal status of this family, at least by the twelfth century.

There is no royal consent to *LL* 258. However, King Meurig does give his consent to the other charter in which Gwrgan appears, 263. In this, Gwrgan is found not only in the witness list but in the main text, as one of those present. While one should not read too much into this, it may be an indication of his status.

Gwrgan is of little help for dating purposes. Bishop Joseph, if he is part of the original record, might provide a *terminus ante quem* of *ca* 1045, the date of his death. There are no other dating indications.

Of the clerical witnesses, Rhuryth is found in most Joseph charters. Cyfeiliog occurs in four charters of Joseph (255, 263, 264a, 264b) and one of Bleddri (249a). This latter circumstance may indicate that 258 belongs to the early or middle part of Joseph's episcopate rather than the later part. On the other hand, Benedictus is found in no other charters of Joseph, but does occur in two of Bishop Herewald, 269 and 272. It seems probable therefore that 258 belongs to the middle part of Joseph's episcopate. Of the lay witnesses, Gwrgan, as said above, appears in 263. Atrit occurs in another Joseph charter, 249a.

Davies identifies *Uilla Tref Ginhill* as being on the River Ely in Glamorgan.[52]

---

48 See note 46.
49 Davies, *Llandaff Charters*, p. 127; *Microcosm*, p. 186.
50 *ABT* 15, ed. Bartrum, *Tracts*, p. 105.
51 MP 3, ed. Bartrum, *Tracts*, p. 122.
52 See note 49.

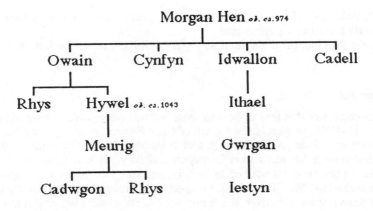

Morgan Hen *ob. ca.974*

Owain   Cynfyn   Idwallon   Cadell

Rhys   Hywel *ob. ca.1043*   Ithael

Meurig   Gwrgan

Cadwgon   Rhys   Iestyn

Figure 1

Charter 259

This charter has been dated by Davies *ca* 1040.[53] It records the return by King Meurig, to Saints Dyfrig, Teilo and Euddogwy of *Uilla Tref Gulich*, which had been the property of these saints since the time of King Ithel ab Arthwys and Bishop Euddogwy. There is a Narration explaining the circumstances of the grant: Meurig, having quarrelled with one of his men, Seisyll ap Gistlerth, violated Llandaff's sanctuary by seizing from thence Seisyll's wife, and wounding one of the bishop's *familia*. Joseph called a synod and excommunicated the king, who sought pardon, restored the woman, and made this grant. Davies is of the opinion that while this Narration contains standard formulae, details of its story may have been recorded soon after the transaction.[54] However, the violation of sanctuary is a conventional story repeated in various of the Llandaff charters, including *LL* 125a, 217, 218, 239, and 271. There are strong similarities between all these, and all have the apperance of being conventionalised explanations designed to strengthen Llandaff's twelfth-century claims. The name Seisyll ap Gistlerth appears in the witness list of 258, and may have been taken thence to embroider this grant. The same event is used as the rationale for *LL* 260 and *LL* 261 also.

There is no mention of Hywel ab Owain in this text, which may suggest that it was granted after his death which occurred *ca* 1043. Joseph died *ca* 1045; this date may thus provide a *terminus ante quem* (always supposing Joseph was an original part of the text).

Of the clerical witnesses, Rhuryth occurs in most Joseph charters. Joseph *sacerdos* is found in 255. Of the lay witnesses, Meurig ap Hywel occurs in 249a, 255, 257 and 261, all Joseph charters. Tewdwr ab Edwin is found in 249a, and 263. Seisyll ap Gistlerth occurs in 264a. Caradog ap Gwlfrid attests several charters – possibly one more charter of Bishop Joseph, 261, and four of Here-

---

53 Davies, *Llandaff Charters*, p. 127; *Microcosm*, p. 186.
54 See note 53.

wald's, 267, 269, 271, and 272. This may suggest that the charter is later rather than earlier in Joseph's episcopate.

Davies has identified the land as Dyffryn Golych, now Worlton, in Glamorgan.[55]

Charter 260

Davies considers this text to be spurious, but has nevertheless assigned to it a date *ca* 1040.[56] It purports to be a grant of *Uilla Fratris*, given by King Meurig to Saints Dyfrig, Teilo and Euddogwy, and to Bishop Joseph. The grant is made in association with Meurig's sons Cadwgan and Rhys. It was suposedly granted because of the events described in 260. Davies suggests that it was originally a note attached to 259.[57] This, if it is the case, may explain how it became attached to the Seisyll story. However, the document has no witness list, and it is equally possible that the compilers of *Liber Landauensis* simply added a claim to this terrritory to the saga which they had already generated to substantiate their claims to *Uilla Tref Gulich*. If this latter is the case, then this text has no relevance to the eleventh century at all. Such internal evidence as it contains concerning dating is identical to that of 259 (probably its source) and this suggests a date *ca* 1043 × *ca* 1045. However, I see no grounds for considering this document as having had a pre-twelfth-century origin; this date should not be taken seriously, therefore.

Davies identifies *Uilla Fratris* as being on the River Thaw in the Vale of Glamorgan.[58]

Charter 261

This charter has been assigned a date of *ca* 1045 by Davies.[59] It records a grant by Caradog ap Rhiwallon, *comes* of King Meurig of Morgannwg, of *Lannpetyr in Hennriu* to Saints Dyfrig, Teilo and Euddogwy, and to Bishop Joseph. The charter is guaranteed by Cadwgan ap Meurig king of Gwent. It purports to have been made as a penance for Caradog's part in the saga of Seisyll (as descibed in 259). Davies considered the Narration to contain standard interpolations, but that its essence was noted probably about the same time as the grant itself.[60] In discussing 259, I have discussed the inherent conventionality – and improbability – of the story of Seisyll; and I do not consider it to be anything more than a conventional embroidery here in 261. It is possible that this grant was drawn into the tale simply through documentary proximity. Moreover, I find it odd that Meurig ap Hywel is mentioned in the Narration of 261, given that his son Cadwgan is both guarantor and chief witness in the basic charter. Meurig is absent save for the *comes* clause: this may well suggest that he was interpolated

55 See note 53.
56 Davies, *Llandaff Charters*, p. 127; *Microcosm*, p. 186.
57 See note 56.
58 See note 56.
59 Davies, *Llandaff Charters*, pp. 127–8; *Microcosm*, pp. 186–7.
60 See note 59.

into the charter along with the Seisyll material, in which he is a principal character. The grantor of 261, Caradog ap Rhiwallon, is mentioned neither in the body nor in the witness-list of 259, which may further suggest that the Narration is not original to 261.

In so far as the dating of this text goes, if Meurig's association with the grant is accepted, then the absence of his father Hywel may give a *terminus post quem* of 1043. The death of Joseph might give a *terminus ante quem* of 1045. However, Meurig and Joseph may not be original to the text, in which case it would be impossible to assign this charter any date more certain than the central eleventh century, since Cadwgan appears to have been active until some point probably in the 1070s.

Of the clerical witnesses, *Bleinguid* occurs in 249a. Bishop Joseph's frequent associate Rhuryth is absent (he was, however, present in 259), which might be an indication that this text does not belong with 259. Of the lay witnesses, Cadwgan ap Meurig was mentioned in the spurious 260, and occurs as king in 267, a charter of Bishop Herewald. The witness list confusingly reads 'Caratauc et Riguallaun filii Gulfrit', and does not appear to mention the grantor, Caradog ap Rhiwallon. There was a Caradog ap Gwlfrid – he is found attesting 259, 267, 271 and 272, while Caradog ap Rhiwallon witnessed 269, 272 and 274. The confusion in the witness list may suggest that both were present, and that a scribe then ran their names together.

Davies has identified *Lannpetyr* as Langstone, Llanbedr, in Monmouthshire, appropriate to a grant guaranteed by a king of Gwent.[61]

Charter 262

This text has been dated *ca* 1022 by Davies.[62] It records a grant by Meirchion ap Rhydderch and his son Gwrgan of *Uilla Carnou* and *Uilla Crucou*, to Saints Dyfrig, Teilo and Euddogwy, and to Bishop Joseph, with the consent of an unnamed king (for whom no kingdom is stated).

Apart from the apparent dates of Joseph's episcopate – *ca* 1022–*ca* 1045 – there is no evidence for dating in this text.

Of the clerical witnesses, Nobis may be the same person who attests 269, a grant of Bishop Herewald (and would thus be long-lived!). Gwrgan ap Dunna, on the other hand, could be the 'Gurcant' who witnesses 249b, a charter of Bishop Bleddri. Of the lay witnesses, Meirchion ap Rhydderch attested two charters of Bleddri's predecessor Gwgan, 243 and 244, while Gwrgan ap Meirchion attested one of Bleddri's charters, 246, and one of Bishop Gwgan's, 243.[63] *Gurcinnif map Gurci* is found in 251, another of Bleddri's charters. This would all tend to indicate a date for 262 of early rather than late in Joseph's episcopate – or, alternatively, may suggest that 'Joseph' is an error for 'Bleddri' (always supposing that either of these bishops had any original connection with the document).

Davies considers these places to be near Crick, in Gwent Is Coed.[64]

---

61 See note 59.
62 Davies, *Llandaff Charters*, p. 128; *Microcosm*, p. 187.
63 On this family, see Davies, *Llandaff Charters*, p. 85, n. 26; *Microcosm*, p. 115.
64 See note 62.

This charter has been dated *ca* 1040 by Davies.[65] It records a grant by Cadwallon ap Gwriad, with the guarantee of his father Gwriad and the consent of Meurig king of Morgannwg, of *Lann Sant Breit in Mainaur Crucmarc*, to Saints Dyfrig, Teilo and Euddogwy. The grant is accompanied by a Narration describing how Cadwallon quarreled with, and struck, Rhiwallon ap Beli in the bishop's court. The bishop arrested and imprisoned Cadwallon in the presence of his kin, that is, his father, his cousin Gwrgan ab Ithel, and others. In prison, Cadwallon sought pardon and in compensation made this grant to Bishop Joseph. He also compensated Joseph's attendant, presumably Rhiwallon ap Beli. Davies considers this Narration to be unusually detailed and precise, and despite the evidence of standard interpolations, she thinks that the greater part of it was probably recorded soon after the grant was made.[66] However, it must be pointed out that slaying or injuring some-one (usually a member of the bishop's retinue) in the bishop's presence is a story found as a rationale in several other Llandaff charters: 125a, 216b, 218, 225, 233 249b, 257 and 267. While none of these are identical to 263 in detail, the theme is very much the same in all of them. The Narration here seem to be serving a double purpose: to justify a claim by Llandaff to ownership of this territory, and to claim jurisdictional powers for the bishop over the nobility of the area. As it stands I am not happy to accept this Narration as original.

The presence in the body of the text (though not in the witness-list) of King Meurig ap Hywel without his father Hywel may suggest that this charter is later than *ca* 1043, the date of Hywel's death, although (as neither of them appears in the witness list), this need not be the case: Meurig could have been interpolated into the record later at Llandaff, perhaps. Joseph's obit would give a *terminus ante quem ca* 1045. That Gwrgan ab Ithel heads the witness list may both reflect his status (he may have been a descendant of Morgan Hen, a cousin of King Meurig, and possibly himself a ruler) and also cast doubt on the original involvement of Meurig – could Gwrgan have been the original guarantor?

Of the clerical witnesses, Rhuryth appears in most of Bishop Joseph's charters. Cyfeiliog is found in 255, 258, 264a and 264b, and also 249a, a charter of Bishop Bleddri. Of the lay witnesses, Gwrgan ab Ithel occurs in 258. Dissaith and Tewdwr sons of Edwin both occur in 249a. The presence of Cyfeiliog might just place this charter earlier rather than later in Joseph's episcopate, but this would be hard to prove beyond reasonable doubt.

Davies has identified the place granted as being St Bride's-super-Ely in Glamorgan.[67]

[65] Davies, *Llandaff Charters*, p. 128; *Microcosm*, p. 187.
[66] See note 65.
[67] See note 65.

This charter has been dated *ca* 1030 by Davies.[68] It is a grant by Seisyll ap Gistlerth of *Cecin Penn Ros* on the Monnow on the other side of Llangynfyl, to Saints Dyfrig, Teilo and Euddogwy, to Bishop Joseph, and to the church of Llangynfyl, with the guarantee of King Gruffudd.

Several problems are presented by this charter. To begin with, the date assigned by Davies is surely too early. The period of activity of Gruffudd ap Rhydderch, the guarantor, is not definitely known, but placing him *ca* 1030 would allow him to overlap with his father Rhydderch ab Iestyn (although it is not entirely inconceivable that Gruffudd was a sub-king). South Wales seems to have been dominated by Hywel ab Edwin ab Einion 1033–44, while Glamorgan was ruled until 1043 by Hywel ab Owain, with his son Meurig, who succeeded him. I should prefer to place 264a within the known period of activity of Gruffudd ap Rhydderch, that is 1044–1055/6. The main drawback of this dating might seem to be the mention of Bishop Joseph, who died in 1045. Moreover, the grantor, Seisyll ap Gistlerth, appeared in 259 as a man of King Meurig ap Hywel. However, neither of these problems is insurmountable. As far as Seisyll is concerned, I have already stated that the Narration of 259 (wherein he is described as one of Meurig's men) is of very conventional form, and probably is not original. Without the Narration, Seisyll would simply be a witness to 259, which is not improbable: it is likely that he was a local nobleman of some kind – and may have been less one of Meurig's men than a local figure whose support was sought by different kings. The problem of Joseph also has a solution: this charter within its text makes it clear that the grant was being made to the church of Llangynfyl, and two of the witnesses, Clemens and Idmab, are explicitly linked to Llangynfyl in the witness-list ('Clemens presbiter Lann Cinfall' and 'Idmab de Lan Cinnfall prepositus episcopi'). From this, it appears very probable that what we have here is a charter made to Llangynfyl, into which Joseph and Llandaff were later interpolated, probably by the compilers of *Liber Landauensis*.

Llangynfyl seems to have been in Ergyng. This is of interest since Gruffudd ap Rhydderch is known, from the D-Text of the Anglo-Saxon Chronicle, to have ravaged the border area with Danish help and defeated a force from Worcester in 1049.[69] Gruffudd may also have been responsible for the attack on Westbury recorded by the C-text of the Anglo-Saxon Chronicle in 1053.[70] This shows that he was active in the Ergyng area, and it is not impossible that this charter is connected with one of these raids, probably that of 1049 – a thanksgiving for victory, perhaps? – which would suggest a date for the charter in the later part of 1049, or early 1050 (the battle against the Worcester forces occurred on 26th July 1049).

The reason for Davies's early dating of this charter lies in the witness-list, and probably particularly in the presence therein of the cleric Cyfeiliog. This character appears in several of the earlier charters of Bishop Joseph, and in one of Bleddri. However, it seems possible that he, like Joseph, may be a Llandaff

68 Davies, *Llandaff Charters*, p. 128; *Microcosm*, p. 187.
69 ASC (D) *s.a.* 1050 (*recte* 1049).
70 ASC (C) *s.a.* 1053.

accretion to this text. This may also be the case with another of the clerical witnesses, Rhuryth, who witnesses almost all of Joseph's charters. The other clerical witness, Clemens, is explicitly linked with Llangynfyl, and is unique to this charter. Of the lay witnesses, Seisyll ap Gistlerth occurs in 259, and Rhydderch ab Eivid in 272, a charter of Bishop Herewald.

This, then, is *not* a 'Llandaff' charter in origin: it is a grant to the church of Llangynfyl, made *ca* 1044 × *ca* 1055/6, possibly in 1049 or 1050.

Charter 264b

This charter has been assigned a date of *ca* 1025 by Davies.[71] It records a grant made by Rhiwallon ap Tudfwlch of his hereditary land, *Cecin Pennicgelli*, to Saints Dyfrig, Teilo and Euddogwy, and to Bishop Joseph, in penance for his raid on St Maughans (Llanmocha). In the Narration, he is said to have plundered this church, and left with his spoils: however, as he came to to Ffynnon Oer, his horse shied and he was thrown, breaking an arm. He at once summoned his household and ordered the plunder returned, and moreover made this grant. Davies considered this Narration to have few interpolations and probably to have been recorded soon after the event.[72] However, it has similarities to *LL* 157, and to *LL* 222. While the story in 264b is less obviously conventional within *Liber Landauensis* than are some others, it nevertheless is not unique, and it does have the air of a rationale. I must therefore diagree with Davies and consider the Narration to have little or no historical basis.

However, what does seem very likely is that this text was originally connected with St Maughans. That St Maughans features in the Narration suggests that it was mentioned in the original text; moreover, the land granted is situated near St Maughans. (The brook, Ffynnon Oer, mentioned in the Narration, also occurs quite prominently in the Welsh boundary clause.) Furthermore, the witness-list includes a unique clerical witness, Elgu, priest of St Maughans (the other clerical witnesses are the usual trio, Bishop Joseph, Cyfeiliog and Rhuryth). I should suggest that this text was originally a grant to St Maughans, later adapted to Llandaff's purposes.

As far as dating goes, if the document was indeed adapted to Llandaff's purposes, we cannot use Joseph as a dating indicator. However, the witness-list includes King Rhydderch ab Iestyn, dateable by reference to *Annales Cambriae* and the *Brutiau* to *ca* 1023–*ca* 1033, and who is found in one other Llandaff charter, the spurious *LL* 253. All the other lay witnesses are unique to this text, which may be further support for its being originally a St Maughan's document.

Davies has identified the land granted as being near St Maughans, in Monmouthshire.[73]

---

71 Davies, *Llandaff Charters*, p. 128; *Microcosm*, p. 187.
72 See note 71.
73 See note 71.

Davies gives the following order to the charters which include Joseph: 262, 264b, (253), 264a, 267, 255, 258, 263, 259, (260), 261.[74] I do not entirely agree with this, and should order them as follows:

Davies's Dates

ca 1022   *262* Certainly quite early, but no clear evidence as to dating, other than Joseph's episcopal dates *ca* 1022 × *ca* 1045.

ca 1025   *264b* between 1023 and 1033.

ca 1025   *(253)* Spurious, and dating probably to the early twelfth century. But by appearances, it would belong to 1023 × 1033.

ca 1030   *264a ca* 1044 × *ca* 1055/6, with a preference for late 1049 or 1050. 261 may postdate this charter.

ca 1038   *258* No later than *ca* 1045, and probably belonging to the middle years of Joseph's episcopate.

ca 1033   *257* No later than *ca* 1043, and definitely earlier than 259 and 249a, and probably earlier than 255, since in the latter, Hywel ab Owain appears after his son Meurig, while he is first in 257.

ca 1035   *255* In the lifetime of Hywel ab Owain, so before *ca* 1043, but later rather than earlier in his life (he died in advanced old age, and his son Meurig may have deputised for him).

ca 1040   *249a* Possibly not before *ca* 1043, and not later than *ca* 1045.

ca 1040   *263* Possibly before *ca* 1045, perhaps close to 249a, since Dissaith and Tewdwr sons of Edwin witness both.

ca 1040   *259 ca* 1043 × *ca* 1045.

ca 1040   *(260)* Spurious, with an apparent eleventh-century date of *ca* 1043 × *ca* 1045.

ca 1045   *261 ca* 1043 × *ca* 1045, if Joseph is part of the original record. Otherwise undateable, other than to say that it is probably no later than *ca* 1070 when King Cadwgan ap Meurig seems to have vanished from view.

I should thus agree with Davies in placing 262 early in the sequence. 264b on the other hand could be a few years later than she suggests, although I remain very dubious about its connection with Llandaff. 264a, however, is very much later than Davies thought, and must have been originally a Llangynfyl document. 253 is without any eleventh-century value and probably no effort should be expended on trying to give it such a date. 257 must be reasonably early by virtue of the primacy in it of Hywel ab Owain, and 255 probably postdates it since in the latter Hywel is no longer king. 258 might be a little later – after Hywel's death *ca* 1043, and perhaps limited by Joseph's death *ca* 1045. 263 has no indications as to date other than Joseph's obit, but on the evidence of its witness-list, it may be close to 249a: this might place both of them *ca* 1043 × *ca* 1045. 259 and the spurious 260 should probably also be placed in this period. 261 seems to belong to the reign of

---

[74] Davies, *Llandaff Charters*, pp. 67–8 and 72.

Cadwgan ap Meurig, a king who unfortunately is undateable save by reference to Llandaff material. I consider it unlikely that Joseph is original to this charter, and should therefore simply date it as mid-eleventh century. 264a was obviously not originally connected with Llandaff, and belongs to *ca* 1044 × *ca* 1055/6.

Both 264a and 264b show signs of originating in churches other than Llandaff. 264a shows every sign of belonging originally to Llangynfyl in Ergyng, while 264b may be a St Maughans text. This is significant, and is a valuable indication of the archival compilation-process at twelfth-century Llandaff.

CHARTERS OF BISHOP HEREWALD

Charter 267

Davies has assigned a date of *ca* 1070 to this charter.[75] It records a grant by Cadwgan ap Meurig, king of Morgannwg, of *Henriugunua* to Saints Dyfrig, Teilo and Euddogwy and to Bishop Herewald. There is a Narration, which claims that the grant was made in penance: the *familia* of King Cadwgan visited Llandaff at Christmas, and being drunk attacked and slew one of the inhabitants, the bishop's grandson Berthutis. The bishop called a synod and excommunicated the king's *familia*. The king then gathered his nobles, and sought pardon, making this grant. The grant itself is in the first person, presented as the king's speech. Davies notes few interpolations in the Narration, and considers it to have been recorded at the same time as the grant.[76] The story, however, is one of the standard ones found in *Liber Landauensis*, and the motif of slaying/injuring one of the bishop's *familia* is also found in *LL* 216b, 225, 233, 249b, and 257, with variations of detail, but the same basic structure. The tale is of a type designed to show the power of Llandaff's bishops and their effect on kings, and it seems impossible to credit that it has any detectable foundation in truth either here or in any of the other charters.

There is little within this charter which is helpful in respect of dating. Cadwgan ap Meurig is not known outside *Liber Landauensis*. Bishop Herewald is mostly known from *Liber Landauensis* also, although he is mentioned in the related bishop-list in Canterbury, Cathedral Library, MS *Cartae Antiquae* C.117. As Davies has shown, there is confusion over Herewald's consecration date.[77] According to *Liber Landauensis*, he was consecrated in 1059, with the consent of Gruffudd, king of Wales (presumably meant to be Gruffudd ap Llywelyn), and of Meurig ap Hywel, by the hand of Cynesige, archbishop of York, in the presence of Edward King of England.[78] The consecration of bishops of 'Llandaff' by English archbishops is something of a problem: it is possible that this is an element which entered *Liber Landauensis* as a part of Llandaff's attempt to prove their independence of St Davids in the twelfth century, and it is a moot point whether any of these bishops were consecrated under the auspices of York or

---

75 Davies, *Llandaff Charters*, p. 129; *Microcosm*, p. 187.
76 See note 75.
77 Davies, 'The Consecration of Bishops', pp. 64–6; *Llandaff Charters*, p. 78.
78 *The Text of the Book of Llan Dâv*, edd. Evans & Rhys, pp. 265–6.

Canterbury before the late eleventh or early twelfth century. There is some confusion within *Liber Landauensis* about Herewald's consecration: it states that he died in the time of Archbishop Anselm and King William I.[79] His death date is given as 1104, and he is said to have died in the forty-eighth year after his consecration. This implies that he was consecrated in 1056.[80] As regards the 1050s consecration, Gruffudd ap Llywelyn was active in South Wales 1055/6–1063, and Meurig ap Hywel was certainly still living in the 1040s, and probably the 1050s (although this cannot be proved). If Cynesige and Edward were involved, they would supply dates of *ca* 1051–*ca* 1060 in the case of Cynesige, and 1042–1066 in that of Edward. It is probably reasonable to suppose that Herewald was consecrated in the later 1050s.[81]

Of the clerical witnesses, Morfarch also attests 269, 271 and 272, all of which are charters of Bishop Herewald, as does Merchfyw. Tudnerth also attests 269 and 271. Joseph, lector of Cadog, occurs in 272. *Aidan*, priest of Cadog, is found in 271 and 272. None of these connects with any earlier charter (unless Joseph is identical with the Joseph, priest of Illtud, of 255, which seems improbable). Of the lay witnesses, Cadwgan ap Meurig occurs in two charters of Bishop Joseph, 260 and 261 (as king in the latter). His brother, Rhys, is found in 260 – however, 260 is spurious, and therefore cannot be relied upon for purposes even of internal chronology. Caradog ap Gwlfrid occurs in two charters of Bishop Joseph, 249 and 261, and in three of Bishop Herewald (269, 271 and 272). It should, however, be remembered that 261 may not belong to Bishop Joseph's lifetime, but the link to 259 might conceivably suggest a date earlier than 1070 for this document.

The place granted has not been identified, although Davies thought that it might be near Llandaff.[82] The repetition of St Cadog in the witness-list may indicate that this text was originally connected with Llancarfan.[83]

79 *Ibid.*, p. 280.
80 On the relationships between *Cart. Ant.* C.177, *LL* and Ralph Diceto, see Davies, 'The Consecration of Bishops'; Brooke, *The Church and the Welsh Border*, p. 19, n. 15; and Conway Davies, *Episcopal Acts*, I.57–66.
81 Brooke suggested that this may be connected with Gruffudd ap Llywelyn's acquisition of lands in Ergyng in the later 1050s, which is believable, and may perhaps explain the involvement of an English king and archbishop. Brooke, *The Church and the Welsh Border*, pp. 10–11, 92–3. R. R. Davies also considered Herewald to have been consecrated in England: Davies, *Conquest, Coexistence and Change*, p. 189.
82 See note 75.
83 On Llancarfan and Llandaff, see Brooke, *The Church and the Welsh Border*, pp. 30–44; and Conway Davies, *Episcopal Acts*, II.506–37.

This charter is dated *ca* 1060 by Davies.[84] The charter is apparently a confirmation, made by Gruffudd, king of all Wales, of Llandaff in all its property, including that in Brycheiniog (and thus in the jurisdiction of St Davids). The only places named are Llandeilo Fawr and *Penn Alun*, which seem to have been regarded as subdivisions of Llandaff itself. The king also made a grant of *Uilla Pennros* to Bishop Herewald. Wendy Davies has commented that the preamble to this charter recalls tenth-century English charters, and that the terms of the confirmation resemble *LL* 253 (which is spurious).[85] Notwithstanding this, she considered 269 contemporary.

The 'confirmation charter', it must be said, is a standard type within *Liber Landauensis*. Other examples are *LL* 152, 240 and 253. 269 does not appear more reputable than any other. The type as a whole most probably belongs to the early twelfth-century context of the dispute over territory in which Llandaff was engaged with both St Davids and Hereford.

This said, there is nonetheless one possible eleventh-century element within 269, the grant of *Uilla Pennros*. We may have here a charter of Gruffudd ap Llywelyn, granting this place, onto which has been grafted the confirmatory element – Gruffudd as an important ruler would be an obvious candidate for this role (as were at least two of the earlier 'confirmers', Morgan Hen and Rhydderch ab Iestyn).

It should be noted, however, that apart from the title 'king of all Wales' (also borne by Rhydderch ab Iestyn in *LL* 253), the only reason to identify the 'Gruffudd' here with Gruffudd ap Llywelyn is the mention in the witness-list of Maredudd, a son of Gruffudd ap Llywelyn, not of Gruffudd ap Rhydderch. It occurs to me to wonder whether the compilers of *Liber Landauensis* thought 'Gruffudd' ap Rhydderch of 264a and 'Gruffudd' of 269 were the same person.

If the *Uilla Pennros* grant be accepted, it is possible that this text represents a sweetener to a Southern Welsh church (the identity of which seems irrecoverable) offered by Gruffudd after his take-over of the South in 1055/6 (if it can be assumed that he had not already acquired ascendency in Glamorgan before this date). This would allow us to give the charter an approximate date of 1055 × 1063 (1063 being the death-date of Gruffudd). The uncertain consecration-date of Herewald need not be a problem: either one could assume that he is a later accretion to the text, along with the confirmatory material, or one could accept the presence at his consecration of Gruffudd, and see this grant as perhaps a gift from the king to his new bishop.

Of the clerical witnesses, Morfarch and Merchfyw are regular companions of Herewald, occurring in 267, 271 and 272. Tudnerth occurs in 267 and 271. Benedictus is found in 272, and also in a charter of Bishop Joseph, 258, which might suggest that 269 belongs to the earlier part of Herewald's episcopate (which would fit with the presence of Gruffudd ap Llywelyn). Nobis appears also in a charter of Bishop Joseph (262). Elynwy occurs in another charter of Herewald, 274. Of the lay witnesses, Caradog ap Gwlfrid occurs in 267, 271, and 272

---

[84] Davies, *Llandaff Charters*, p. 129; *Microcosm*, pp. 187–8.
[85] See note 84.

(all Herewald) and 259 and 261 (Joseph – although 261 might not in fact belong to the lifetime of this bishop). Caradog ap Rhiwallon is found in 272 and 274, and also in 261. Ithel ap Tewdos and Berddig of Gwent both occur in 272.

Uilla Pennros has not been identified.

Charter 271

Davies has dated this charter *ca* 1075.[86] It records a grant by Iestyn ap Gwrgan of *Uilla Meluc* to Saints Dyfrig, Teilo and Euddogwy, and to Bishop Herewald. It includes a Narration describing how Iestyn sent his household to Llandaff, lead by *Turguert* and Einion (this latter being Iestyn's nephew), who violated the refuge, and took away and raped Eurddilad ferch Cynwal, who had fled there for protection. However, having done this, the 'young man' (Einion?) became deranged. Bishop Herewald then cursed Iestyn, and excommunicated him and his retinue. In penance, Iestyn made this grant. Neither of the named culprits is found in the witness-list. Davies has seen few interpolations in the Narration and considered that it is a record of the event noted down soon after the grant was made.[87]

I do not agree with her conclusion. The use of a supposed violation of refuge as justification for a grant is found in several of the Llandaff charters: 125a, 217b, 239, and 259. 259 in particular has strong similarities to 271 since, in addition to the element of violation of refuge, it also contains the seizure and rape of a woman who had fled there. I should suggest that the formulaic elements are not simply a matter of phraseology (as Davies seems to assume), but also a matter of theme: and this charter, 271, is clearly in its Narration a variation on a common Landauensian theme, not a historical narrative at all.

There is little helpful material in this charter as far as dating is concerned. Iestyn ap Gwrgan appears in two genealogical texts, *ABT* 15[88] and MP 3,[89] but is not mentioned in any known chronicle. According to the *Brutiau*, his grandson Morgan ap Caradog was alive in 1179, but this is little help beyond making it possible that Iestyn could have been alive in the late eleventh century. Bishop Herewald may have been consecrated in the later 1050s; and he died *ca* 1104.[90]

Of the clerical witnesses, Morfarch and Merchfyw occur in 267, 269 and 272, and Tudnerth in 267 and 269. Lifris (son of the bishop), archdeacon and *magister* of St Cadog occurs in 272 and 274: this presumably is the Lifris who wrote a Life of St Cadog.[91] Gwrgi also occurs in 272. *Aidan* is found in 267 and 272. Of the lay witnesses, Iestyn ap Gwrgan appears in 272, as do Selyf ap Cynnor, Meurig ap Goronwy and Mei son of the bishop. Caradog ap Gwlfrid occurs in 267, 269 and 272, as well as two charters of Bishop Joseph, 259 and 261 (if the latter is correctly linked to Joseph).

---

86 Davies, *Llandaff Charters*, p. 129; *Microcosm*, p. 188.
87 See note 86.
88 See note 50.
89 See note 51.
90 *The Text of the Book of Llan Dâv*, edd. Evans & Rhys, p. 280.
91 Lifris's Life of St Cadog, ed. and transl. Wade-Evans, *Vitae Sanctorum Britanniae et Genealogiae*, pp. 24–141.

Davies has dated this charter *ca* 1072.[92] It records a grant by Caradog, king of Morgannwg, of *Uilla Tref Rita* near Llandegfedd, to Saints Dyfrig, Teilo and Euddogwy, and to Bishop Herewald. He supposedly did so in penance for having sent his retinue to St Maughans, where they forcibly partook of the bishop's foodrent, without the consent of the bishop's guest Rhydderch ab Egwyd, and then stayed the night, drunk, also without permission. The bishop sent messengers to the king to demand recompense, which was immediately forthcoming.

Davies has seen few interpolations in this text, and considers the Narration to be reasonably historically true. However, the same story (with minor variations of detail) occurs in *LL* 237b. I should see this as a variation of the violation of refuge/seizure of church property theme, a tale designed to demonstrate not only ownership by the church of Llandaff but also the rights, privileges and judicial powers of the church and the bishop.

It is clear that King Caradog is Caradog ap Gruffudd ap Rhydderch, who is known from English and Welsh sources to have been active in South Wales from 1064, and who died in the battle of Mynydd Carn in 1081.[93] 272 is therefore datable not later than 1081; it may however be later than *LL* 267. This latter was a charter of King Cadwgan ap Meurig, who may no longer have been living by the time when Caradog was able to make grants in Morgannwg.

Of the clerical witnesses, Morfarch and Merchfyw appear (here as priests of Teilo). Lifris, son of the bishop also occurred in 271 (with considerably more titles: could this indicate that 272 is older than 271?). Joseph, lector (here doctor) of Cadog, occurs in 267. Benedictus is found in 269, and in a charter of Bishop Joseph, 262. Gwrgi occurs in 271. Of the lay witnesses, Caradog ap Gwlfrid is found in 267, 269, 271 and two Joseph charters, 259 and 261. Caradog ap Rhiwallon occurs in 269, 274, as well as 261, a charter of Bishop Joseph. Ithel ap Tewdos occurs in 269, as does Berddig of Gwent. Iestyn ap Gwrgan occurs in 271, as do Selyf ap Cynnor, Meurig ap Goronwy and Mei son of the bishop. 271 was granted by Iestyn, who seems to have had at least the status, if not the title, of a king – this may further suggest that 271 is later than 272. The overlaps in 272 with charters of Bishop Joseph may indicate that this chater is a little later than Davies thought.

Davies has identified the place as being near Llanddegfedd, in Gwent.[94] The mention of St Maughans as the object of Caradog's wickedness may suggest that this document originally belonged to that church.

92 Davies, *Llandaff Charters*, p. 129; *Microcosm*, p. 188.
93 ASC (C) *s.a.* 1065; JW *s.a.* 1065; *AC* (B) *s.a.* [1081]; *AC* (C) *s.a.* [1073], [1079], and [1082]; *ByT* (Pen. 20) *s.a.* 1070 (*recte* 1072), 1073 (*recte* 1075), 1076 (*recte* 1078), and 1079 (*recte* 1081); *ByT* (RB) *s.a.* 1070 (*recte* 1072), [1075], [1078], and [1081]; *ByS* *s.a.* 1070 (*recte* 1072), 1073 (*recte* 1075), 1076 (*recte* 1078), and 1079 (*recte* 1081).
94 See note 92.

This charter has been assigned a date of *ca* 1075 by Davies.[95] It records a grant made by Caradog ap Rhiwallon to the four saints of Llangwm, and to Bishop Herewald, made on his deathbed in remembrance of his slaying of his brother Cynan, of *Uilla Gunnuc* in *Guarthaf Cwmm*. It is guaranteed by Roger Fitz William Fitz Osbern, count of Hereford and lord of Gwent, during the reign of William the 'father', presumably William I.

The text seems to be reasonably acceptable, especially if the presence of Herewald be discounted. It is noticeable that none of his usual companions – Morfarch, Merchfyw and Tudnerth – is present in the witness-list. (His son Lifris is a witness, but this is not surprising: given his later renown, he is an obvious candidate for addition, along with his father.) Another witness had appeared in Herewald's company in 269: this is Abraham, but given his rank of 'archdeacon of Gwent', his involvment is not incredible. Elynwy, monk of Llangwm, occurs in 269: his presence in 274 is reasonable since this charter was probably originally made to Llangwm. I suggest that Herewald, Llandaff, Saints Dyfrig, Teilo and Euddogwy, and perhaps Lifris are all later additions to its text, probably together with the brief Narration about Caradog's brother, and Caradog's seven pilgrimages.

Some attempt at dating this charter may be made by reference to Roger Fitz William, also known as Roger de Breteuil. He had succeeded to the earldom of Hereford in 1071, on the death of his father William Fitz Osbern. In 1075 he rebelled against the king and was imprisoned: it is thus possible that this text is a year or two earlier than Davies suggests, as Roger, who was acting in concord with the earl of East Anglia, may not have had very much time to spare for the Welsh in this year (although it is possible that Caradog was an ally also). The charter can be ascribed to 1071 × 1075.

Uilla Gunnuc in *Guarthaf Cwm* has been identified by Davies as Llangwm Isaf, in Gwent Is Coed.

CONCLUSION TO THE CHARTERS OF BISHOP HEREWALD

As with the charters of Bishop Bleddri, there is not a great deal to be said about these, although on the whole I should tend to place all of them a few years earlier than Davies has been inclined to do. She ordered them 269, 267, 272, 271, 274,[96] which is reasonable, although it should be remembered that 267 is internally undatable other than as 'mid-eleventh century'. Given the presence in this charter of Cadwgan ap Meurig and of Caradog ap Gwlfrid, I wonder if it might not be related in some way to the 'Joseph' charter, 261 (also undatable beyond 'mid-eleventh century'). The internal evidence of 267 suggests that it may originally have come from Llancarfan. 269 as it stands is largely spurious, a so-called confirmation-charter, grafted on to a short grant made by Gruffudd ap Llywelyn,

95 Davies, *Llandaff Charters*, p. 129; *Microcosm*, p. 188.
96 Davies, *Llandaff Charters*, pp. 69 and 72–3.

perhaps actually to Herewald. The known period of activity in South Wales of Gruffudd allows us to place this charter 1055 × 1063, or perhaps 1059 × 1063 (if 1059 be accepted as the consecration-date of Herewald, and if Herewald is original to the grant). 271 is very hard to date; however, the powerful status within it of Iestyn ap Gwrgan may suggest that it is later than 272, for in that charter Iestyn witnesses after a named king, Caradog ap Gruffudd (*ob.* 1081). 272 may be dated *ca* 1064 × 1081, these limitations being imposed by the known career of Caradog ap Gruffudd, its grantor. The mention in its text of St Maughans (as the object of violation) may indicate that that church was the first home of this charter. 274, while showing signs of later rewriting, would seem to belong to 1071 × 1075. Llandaff, Herewald, and perhaps Lifris may not be original to this charter: it was probably a grant made to Llangwm, appropriated and reshaped to Llandaff's purposes.

While on the whole I should follow Davies's order for these charters, I am not convinced that 274 is necessarily later than 271 and 272: both Caradog ap Gruffudd and Iestyn ap Gwrgan (as well as their descendants) managed to co-exist with Norman lords, as D. Crouch[97] has recently shown. It is not therefore impossible that one (271) or both these charters may be of about the same period as, or later than, 274.

[97] Crouch, 'The Slow Death of Kingship in Glamorgan 1067–1158'.

VI

CONCLUSION

A complex network of political ties links together Wales, England and Ireland in the eleventh century, such that it is not easy to consider one country without taking into account the events within the others. In this study, I hope that I have shown at least some of this network in operation.

The internal politics of the Welsh kingdoms were never simple, and the eleventh-century period of so-called 'intrusive' rulers was perhaps especially complicated. On the surface, kings rise and fall in a seemingly unconnected way: closer examination shows that they were frequently linked together by kindred or political ties. Very few of the prominent men of the period came from what are now wholly obscure backgrounds. The interactions of kings of different kingdoms were very complex. Some rulers – Gruffudd ap Llywelyn, for instance – seem to have been consistently aggressive towards their royal contemporaries in Wales, while others may be seen making alliances, sometimes for immediate ends (as with Rhys ap Tewdwr and Gruffudd ap Cynan in 1081), sometimes on an apparently longer-term basis (as with Trahaearn ap Caradog and Caradog ap Gruffudd). The century opened with a period of apparent confusion, with no readily identifiable rulers emerging until the third decade. From this confusion developed the hegemony of Gruffudd ap Llywelyn, foreshadowed, perhaps, by his father, Llywelyn ap Seisyll, and succeeded by a half-brother, Bleddyn ap Cynfyn, who possibly inherited Gruffudd's ambitions, as well as the Northern part of his kingdom. Bleddyn certainly inherited Gruffudd's wider political interests, and may have passed them on to his sons. The century ended with the Welsh in a difficult position, hard-pressed by the Normans, although resistance ran strong. In the early decades of the twelfth century, Welshmen were to fight back, and powerful Welsh rulers once more dominated the political scene. Even in the difficult 1090s, Welsh leadership did not collapse completely: Cadwgan ap Bleddyn succeeded in instigating a nationwide rebellion. The success of this ploy may in part be attributable to the lessons learnt under Gruffudd ap Llywelyn who looked outside Wales and exploited the troubles of his English neighbours to his own benefit.

The internal politics of eleventh-century Wales cannot be properly comprehended without reference to Ireland and England. In the late tenth century and the early eleventh, English and Hiberno-Scandinavians alike seem to have been seen mainly as a threat, occasionally exploited for Welsh ends, but not readily influenced by the Welsh. During the course of the century, this changed.

Welsh-English alliances were not unheard of: the later tenth century saw the North Welsh Hywel ab Ieuaf joining with English forces to harass neighbouring

Welsh kingdoms. The alliance was probably very loose, and it does not seem that either side put much faith in it: the English ultimately slew Hywel. But, while it lasted, it allowed Hywel to make gains at the expense of his neighbours, and no doubt provided plunder and adventure for the English. A similar sort of situation arose in the eleventh century, when Gruffudd ap Llywelyn joined with Swegn Godwinesson to attack Gruffudd ap Rhydderch of Deheubarth. The connection was brief and designed to provide aid and gain for both parties without any lasting responsibility.

Weakness in the English polity had long been to Welsh advantage, turning English attention away from the borders, and providing the opportunity for raiding. Gruffudd ap Llywelyn, however, seems to have seen beyond this – to have realised that it was possible to go beyond exploiting English politics, and to begin to influence their course. By the mid-1050s he was supreme in Wales. English attention had already been drawn to him by his raid of 1051. It seems to have occurred to him to find an ear and a voice in the English court. At the same time, Ælfgar, probable heir to the Mercian earldom and already earl of East Anglia, was facing the growing power of the house of Godwine. By combining, he and Gruffudd had the makings of a significant power-bloc. The undertaking was not without risk: Ælfgar twice endured exile, and Gruffudd became a target for the family of Godwine in 1056 and 1063. But in fact the alliance seems to have been successful: Ælfgar was not excluded from political influence by Godwine's sons, and Gruffudd had support, protection and influence in English affairs. The alliance was strengthened by the marriage of Gruffudd to Ælfgar's daughter and, while Ælfgar's death opened the way for a major invasion of Wales, provoking Gruffudd's fall, the deaths of the two allies did not destroy the alliance. Bleddyn ap Cynfyn, Gruffudd's half-brother, continued as a supporter of the Mercian house until its fall in 1072.

The Normans were a new threat, but the Welsh were not unaccustomed to invaders, even if the scale was now greater. Initially, at least, they reacted to the Normans as they had to the English, making use of them to further Welsh ends (as did Caradog ap Gruffudd in 1072, when he employed a Norman force to destroy his rival Maredudd ab Owain ab Edwin) and exploiting Norman political turbulence in order to gain plunder and freedom from interference. As pressure intensified, resistance increased, with Cadwgan ap Bleddyn leader against the invasions of the 1090s. However, the Welsh were already adapting to the new situation. Alliances formed and kindred-links grew up: the conqueror of Brycheiniog, Bernard of Neufmarché, married a granddaughter of Gruffudd ap Llywelyn, and Cadwgan ap Bleddyn numbered among his wives the daughter of the Norman Picot. The end of the eleventh century and the early part of the twelfth show the beginnings of the complex Cambro-Norman society which was to grow, dominating the Marches for many years to come.

By the eleventh century, Hiberno-Scandinavian raiders were already a familiar event in Wales, particularly of course on the coast. The pattern of their raiding can to some degree be linked with their fortunes in Ireland, with interest in Wales increasing when Irish events went against them, and decreasing when Irish politics favoured them, or required their presence. Similarly, at times of particular Welsh strength, (as in the reign of Gruffudd ap Llywelyn), Hiberno-Scandinavian interest decreased. The Welsh response to these marauders was not as complex as that to the English, perhaps because the Hiberno-Scandinavians were a less organised and more distant threat. The Welsh do not seem to have sought to influence the viking polity. Vikings in Wales were either fought, or employed as mercenaries. After a while, this use of them as a resource became quite widespread, and Ireland itself became a refuge for exiles (a practice found used by the English also). Short-term employment of viking-bands as a support against Welsh rivals is seen from the 1040s at least, when Hywel ab Edwin made use of a viking-fleet against Gruffudd ap Llywelyn. Most exiles fled to Ireland to return within the year (as was the case with Harold Godwinesson, Ælfgar and Rhys ap Tewdwr). However, this was not always the case. Gruffudd ap Rhys was to spend much of his childhood in Ireland, having been sent there on the death of his father. His Northern contemporary, Gruffudd ap Cynan, was partly Hiberno-Scandinavian by blood: his father, probably one of the earliest Welsh exiles of this period, had married a Hiberno-Scandinavian princess. Gruffudd's career was to reflect this Hiberno-Scandinavian connexion strongly, and he drew heavily on Ireland to support his attempts to gain power in Wales.

The three areas in question were interlinked in the eleventh century: the Welsh both helped to create the connexions and exploited them. Some kings, such as Caradog ap Gruffudd or Hywel ab Edwin, were interested largely in Wales and used external forces to make Welsh gains. Others, like Gruffudd ap Llywelyn or Bleddyn ap Cynfyn, sought to influence affairs outside Wales and intervened in non-Welsh politics, even becoming part of them by virtue of kin-ship-links, producing individuals like Gruffudd ap Cynan. The background thus created, of exploitation, alliance and intervention, probably helped in the Welsh response to the Normans and sowed the seeds which were to grow into Marcher society in the twelfth century and beyond.

209

BIBLIOGRAPHY

ANSCOMBE, A. 'Indexes to Old Welsh genealogies', *Archiv für celtische Lexicographie* 1 (1898–1900) 187–212 *and* 513–49; 2 (1901–4) 147–96; 3 (1905–7) 57–103

ANSCOMBE, A. 'Landavensium ordo chartarum', *Celtic Review* 6 (1909/10) 123–9, 272–7, 289–95, *and* 7 (1911/12), 63–7

ARNOLD, Thomas (ed.) *Henrici Archidiaconi Huntendunensis Historia Anglorum: The History of the English by Henry, Archdeacon of Huntingdon, from A.C. 55 to A.D. 1154, in Eight Books* (London 1879)

ARNOLD, Thomas (ed.) *Symeonis Monachi Opera Omnia* (2 vols, London 1882/5)

BARLOW, Frank *Edward the Confessor* (London 1970)

BARTLETT, Robert *Gerald of Wales 1146–1223* (Oxford 1982)

BARTRUM, P. C. (ed.) 'Achau Brenhinoedd a Thywysogion Cymru', *Bulletin of the Board of Celtic Studies* 19 (1960–2) 201–24

BARTRUM, P. C. (ed.) 'Bonedd yr Arwyr', *Bulletin of the Board of Celtic Studies* 18 (1958–60) 229–52

BARTRUM, P. C. (ed.) *Early Welsh Genealogical Tracts* (Cardiff 1966)

BARTRUM, P. C. 'Further Notes on the Welsh genealogical manuscripts', *Transactions of the Honourable Society of Cymmrodorion* (1976) 102–18

BARTRUM, P. C. (ed.) 'Hen Lwythau Gwynedd a'r Mars', *National Library of Wales Journal* 12 (1961/2) 201–29

BARTRUM, P. C. 'Notes on the Welsh genealogical manuscripts', *Transactions of the Honourable Society of Cymmrodorion* (1968) 63–98

BARTRUM, P. C. (ed.) 'Pedigrees of the Welsh Tribal Patriarchs', *National Library of Wales Journal* 13 (1963/4), 93–146 *and* 15 (1967/8) 157–66

BARTRUM, P. C. (ed.) 'Plant yr Arglwydd Rhys', *National Library of Wales Journal* 14 (1965/6) 97–104

BARTRUM, P. C. (ed.) 'Rhandiroedd Powys', *National Library of Wales Journal* 18 (1973/4) 231–7

BARTRUM, P. C. 'Some Studies in Early Welsh History', *Transactions of the Honourable Society of Cymmrodorion* (1948) 279–302

BARTRUM, P. C. *Welsh Genealogies A.D. 300–1400* (8 vols, Cardiff 1974, and supplement, Cardiff 1980)

BEST, R. I., and MACNEILL, E. (facs. edd.) *The Annals of Inisfallen reproduced in Facsimile from the Original Manuscript, Rawlinson B.503* (Dublin 1933)

BEST, R. I. 'Palaeographical Notes, I: The Rawlinson B.502 Tigernach', *Ériu* 7 (1913/14) 114–20

BINCHY, D. A. 'Irish History and Irish Law', *Studia Hibernica* 15 (1975) 7–36 *and* 16 (1976) 7–45

BOWEN, E. G. *Wales: A Study in Geography and History* (2nd edn, Cardiff 1947)

BRETT, M. 'John of Worcester and his Contemporaries', in *The Writing of History in the Middle Ages: Essays Presented to Richard William Southern*, edd. R. H. C. Davis *et al.* (Oxford 1981), pp. 101–26

BREWER, J. S., DIMOCK, J. F. and WARNER, G. F. (edd.) *Giraldi Cambrensis Opera* (8 vols, London 1861–91)

BROOKE, Christopher N. L. *The Church and the Welsh Border in the Central Middle Ages* (Woodbridge 1986)

BU'LOCK, J. D. *Pre-Conquest Cheshire, 383–1066* (Chester 1972)

CATHCART-KING, D. J. 'The Defence of Wales 1067–1283: the Other Side of the Hill', *Archaeologia Cambrensis* 126 (1977) 1–16

CHADWICK, Nora K. (ed.) *Celt and Saxon: Studies in the Early British Border* (Cambridge 1963; revised impression, 1964)

CHARLES, B. G. *Old Norse Relations with Wales* (Cardiff 1934)

CHARLES-EDWARDS, T. M. 'Some Celtic Kinship Terms', *Bulletin of the Board of Celtic Studies* 24 (1970–2) 105–22

CHIBNALL, Marjorie (ed. & transl.) *The Ecclesiastical History of Orderic Vitalis* (6 vols, Oxford 1969–80)

CHIBNALL, Marjorie 'Feudal Society in Orderic Vitalis', *Proceedings of the Battle Conference on Anglo-Norman Studies* 1 (1978) 35–48 *and* 199–202

CLASSEN, E., and HARMER, F. E. (edd.) *An Anglo-Saxon Chronicle from British Museum, Cotton MS., Tiberius B.iv* (Manchester 1926)

COWLEY, F. G. *The Monastic Order in South Wales, 1066–1349* (Cardiff 1977)

CROUCH, D. 'The Slow Death of Kingship in Glamorgan, 1067–1158', *Morgannwg* 29 (1985) 20–41

CURTIS, E. 'Muirchertach O'Brien, High King of Ireland, and his Norman Son-in-Law, Arnulf de Montgomery, *circa* 1100', *Journal of the Royal Society of Antiquaries of Ireland*, 6th series, 11 (1921) 116–24

DARLINGTON, R. R. *Anglo-Norman Historians* (London 1947)

DARLINGTON, R. R., and MCGURK, P. 'The *Chronicon ex Chronicis* of "Florence" of Worcester and its Use of Sources for English History before 1066', *Anglo-Norman Studies* 5 (1982) 185–96

DAVIES, James Conway *Episcopal Acts and Cognate Documents relating to Welsh Dioceses 1066–1272* (2 vols, Cardiff 1946/8)

DAVIES, R. R. *Conquest, Coexistence and Change: Wales 1063–1415* (Oxford 1987)

DAVIES, R. R. 'Kings, Lords and Liberties in the March of Wales, 1066–1272', *Transactions of the Royal Historical Society*, fifth series, 29 (1979) 41–61

DAVIES, W. 'The Consecration of Bishops of Llandaff in the Tenth and Eleventh Centuries', *Bulletin of the Board of Celtic Studies* 26 (1974–6) 53–73

DAVIES, Wendy *An Early Welsh Microcosm: Studies in the Llandaff Charters* (London 1978)

DAVIES, W. 'Land and Power in Early Medieval Wales', *Past and Present* 81 (1978) 3–23

DAVIES, W. 'The Latin Charter Tradition in Western Britain, Brittany and Ireland in the Early Mediaeval Period', in *Ireland in Early Mediaeval Europe: Studies in Memory of Kathleen Hughes*, edd. D. Whitelock *et al.* (Cambridge 1982) pp. 258–80

DAVIES, W. '*Liber Landavensis*: its Construction and Credibility', *English Historical Review* 88 (1973) 335–51

DAVIES, Wendy *The Llandaff Charters* (Aberystwyth 1979)

DAVIES, W. 'The Orthography of Personal Names in the Charters of *Liber Landavensis*', *Bulletin of the Board of Celtic Studies*, 28 (1978–80) 553–7

DAVIES, W. 'St Mary's, Worcester, and the *Liber Landavensis*', *Journal of the Society of Archivists* 4 (1970–3) 459–85

DAVIES, W. '*Unciae*: Land Measurement in the *Liber Landavensis*', *Agricultural History Review* 21 (1973) 111–21

DAVIES, Wendy *Wales in the Early Middle Ages* (Leicester 1982)

DAVIS, R. H. C., *et al.* (edd.) *The Writing of History in the Middle Ages: Essays Presented to Richard William Southern* (Oxford 1981)

DOUBLEDAY, H. Arthur (ed.) *The Victoria History of the County of Worcester* (4 vols, London 1901–24)

DOUGLAS, D. C. *William the Conqueror* (London 1964)

DUGDALE, William (ed.) *Monasticon Anglicanum* (revised edition by J. Caley, H. Ellis and B. Bandinel, 6 vols in 8, London 1817–30)

DUMVILLE, D. N. [review of K. Hughes, *The Welsh Latin Chronicles: Annales Cambriae and Related Texts* (1974)], *Studia Celtica* 12/13 (1977/8) 461–7

DUMVILLE, D. N. 'The "Six" Sons of Rhodri Mawr: a Problem in Asser's *Life of King Alfred*', *Cambridge Medieval Celtic Studies* 4 (1982) 5–18

DUMVILLE, D. N. 'Brittany and "Armes Prydein Vawr" ', *Études celtiques* 20 (1983) 145–59

EARLE, John, and PLUMMER, C. (edd.) *Two of the Saxon Chronicles Parallel with supplementary extracts from the others* (2 vols, Oxford 1892/9; revised impression, by D. Whitelock, 1952)

EDWARDS, J. G. 'The Normans and the Welsh March', *Proceedings of the British Academy* 42 (1956) 155–77

ELLIS, T. P. *Welsh Tribal Law and Custom in the Middle Ages* (2 vols, Oxford 1926)

ELRINGTON, C. R. (ed.) *A History of the County of Cheshire*, Victoria History of the Counties of England (Oxford 1979–)

EVANS, D. Simon (ed.) *Historia Gruffud vab Kenan* (Cardiff 1977)

EVANS, J. G., and RHYS, J. (edd.) *The Text of the Book of Llan Dâv reproduced from the Gwysaney Manuscript* (Oxford 1893)

FARMER, H. 'William of Malmesbury's Life and Works', *Journal of Ecclesiastical History* 13 (1962) 39–54

FORESTER, Thomas (transl.) *The Chronicle of Henry of Huntingdon* (London 1853)

FOREVILLE, Raymonde (ed. & transl.) *Gesta Guillelmi Ducis Normannorum et Regis Anglorum* (Paris 1952)

FRENCH, A. (transl.) 'Meilir's Elegy for Gruffudd ap Cynan', *Études celtiques* 16 (1979) 263–81

213

GRABOWSKI, K., and DUMVILLE, D. *Chronicles and Annals of Mediaeval Ireland and Wales: The Clonmacnoise-group Texts* (Woodbridge 1984)

GREEN, J. R. *The Conquest of England* (3rd edn, 2 vols, London 1899)

GWYNN, A. 'Were the Annals of Inisfallen written at Killaloe?', *North Munster Antiquarian Journal* 8 (1958–61) 20–33

D'HAENENS, Albert *Les Invasions normandes en Belgique au neuvième siècle* (Louvain 1967)

HARMER, F. E. (ed. & transl.) *Anglo-Saxon Writs* (Manchester 1952)

HARRISON, K. 'Epacts in Irish Chronicles', *Studia Celtica* 12/13 (1977/8) 17–32

HENNESSY, William M. (ed. & transl.) *The Annals of Loch Cé: A Chronicle of Irish Affairs from A.D. 1014 to A.D. 1590* (2 vols, London 1871)

HENNESSY, William M. (ed. and transl.) *Chronicum Scottorum. A Chronicle of Irish Affairs, from the Earliest Times to A.D. 1135; with a Supplement containing the Events from 1141 to 1150* (London 1866)

HENNESSY, William M., and MACCARTHY, B. (edd. & transl.) *Annala Uladh: Annals of Ulster; otherwise Annala Senait, Annals of Senat; a Chronicle of Irish Affairs from A.D. 431, to A.D. 1540* (4 vols, Dublin 1887–1901)

HOWARD, William (ed.) *Florentius Wigornensis, Chronica ex Chronicis ab Initio Mundi usque ad Annum 1141* (London 1592)

HOWORTH, H. 'The Chronicle of John of Worcester, previously assigned to Florence of Worcester', *Archaeological Journal* 73 (1916) 1–170

HUDSON, B. 'The Family of Harold Godwinsson and the Irish Sea Province', *Journal of the Royal Society of the Antiquaries of Ireland* 109 (1979) 92–100

HUGHES, Kathleen *Celtic Britain in the Early Middle Ages. Studies in Scottish and Welsh Sources* (Woodbridge 1980)

HUGHES, Kathleen *Early Christian Ireland: Introduction to the Sources* (London 1972)

HUNT, W. 'William Longespée', in *Dictionary of National Biography*, edd. L. Stephen and S. Lee, vol. 34 (London 1893), pp. 115–18

HUNTER BLAIR, Peter 'Some Observations on the *Historia Regum* attributed to Symeon of Durham', in *Celt and Saxon: Studies in the Early British Border*, ed. N. K. Chadwick (Cambridge 1963; revised impression, 1964), pp. 63–118

HUSAIN, B. M. C. *Cheshire under the Norman Earls, 1066–1237* (Chester 1973)

JAMES, J. W. 'Fresh Light on the Death of Gruffudd ap Llywelyn', *Bulletin of the Board of Celtic Studies* 30 (1982/3) 147

JAMES, M. R., BROOKE, C. N. L., and MYNORS, R. A. B. (edd. & transl.) *Walter Map: De Nugis Curialium, Courtiers' Trifles* (Oxford 1983)

JONES, Arthur (ed. & transl.) *The History of Gruffudd ap Cynan* (Manchester 1910)

JONES, E. D. 'The Book of Llandaff', *National Library of Wales Journal* 4 (1945/6) 123–57

JONES, F. 'An Approach to Welsh Genealogy', *Transactions of the Honourable Society of Cymmrodorion* (1948) 303–466

JONES, F. 'The Dynasty of Powys', *Transactions of the Honourable Society of Cymmrodorion* (1958) 23–32

JONES, G. P.   'The Scandinavian Settlement in Ystrad Tywi', *Y Cymmrodor* 35 (1925) 117–56

JONES, Thomas (ed. & transl.)   *Brenhinedd y Saesson, or The Kings of the Saxons: BM Cotton MS. Cleopatra B.v and The Black Book of Basingwerk, NLW MS.7006* (Cardiff 1971)

JONES, Thomas (ed.)   *Brut y Tywysogyon, Peniarth MS. 20* (Cardiff 1941)

JONES, Thomas (transl.)   *Brut y Tywysogyon, or the Chronicle of the Princes: Peniarth MS. 20 Version* (Cardiff 1952)

JONES, Thomas (ed. & transl.)   *Brut y Tywysogyon, or the Chronicle of the Princes: Red Book of Hergest Version* (2nd edn, Cardiff 1973)

JONES, T. G.   'Bardism and Romance: a Study of the Welsh Literary Tradition', *Transactions of the Honourable Society of Cymmrodorion* (1913/14) 205–310

KELLEHER, J. V.   'Early Irish History and Pseudo-history', *Studia Hibernica* 3 (1963) 113–27

KER, N. R.   'William of Malmesbury's Handwriting', *English Historical Review* 59 (1944) 371–6

KIRBY, D. P.   'British Dynastic History in the Pre-viking Period', *Bulletin of the Board of Celtic Studies* 27 (1976–8) 81–113

KIRBY, D. P.   'Hywel Dda: Anglophil?', *Welsh History Review* 8 (1976/7) 1–13

KIRBY, D. P.   'The Place of Ceredigion in the Early History of Wales, c. 400–1170', *Ceredigion* 6 (1968–71) 265–84

KÖRNER, Sten   *The Battle of Hastings, England, and Europe 1035–1066* (Lund 1964)

LAPIDGE, M.   'Byrhtferth of Ramsey and the Early Sections of the *Historia Regum* attributed to Symeon of Durham', *Anglo-Saxon England* 10 (1982) 97–122

LANCASTER, J. G.   'The Coventry Forged Charters: a Re-appraisal', *Bulletin of the Institute of Historical Research* 27 (1954) 113–40

LE PATOUREL, J.   *The Norman Empire* (Oxford 1976)

LEWIS, C. P.   'English and Norman Government in the Welsh Borders 1039–1087' (unpublished D.Phil. dissertation, University of Oxford, 1985)

LEWIS, C. P.   'The Norman Settlement of Herefordshire under William I', *Anglo-Norman Studies* 7 (1984) 195–213

LLOYD, J. E.   *A History of Wales From the Earliest Times to the Edwardian Conquest* (3rd edn, 2 vols, London 1939)

LLOYD, J. E.   'Wales and the Coming of the Normans (1039–1093)', *Transactions of the Honourable Society of Cymmrodorion* (1899/1900) 122–79

LLOYD, J. E.   'The Welsh Chronicles', *Proceedings of the British Academy* 14 (1928) 369–91

LOYN, H. R.   'Domesday Book', *Proceedings of the Battle Conference on Anglo-Norman Studies* 1 (1978) 121–30 *and* 220–2

LOYN, H. R.   *The Vikings in Wales* (London 1976)

LOYN, H. R.   'Wales and England in the Tenth Century: the Context of he Athelstan Charters', *Welsh History Review* 10 (1980/1) 283–301

MAC AIRT, Seán (ed. & transl.)   *The Annals of Inisfallen (MS. Rawlinson B.503)* (Dublin 1951)

MAC AIRT, Seán, and MAC NIOCAILL, G. (edd. & transl.)   *The Annals of Ulster (to A.D. 1131)*, Part 1 (Dublin 1983)

MACALISTER, R. A. S. 'The Sources of the Preface of the "Tigernach" Annals', *Irish Historical Studies* 4 (1944/5) 38–57

MAC NEILL, E. 'The Authorship and Structure of the "Annals of Tigernach" ', *Ériu* 7 (1913/14) 30–113

MAC NIOCAILL, Gearóid *The Medieval Irish Annals* (Dublin 1975)

MAGNUSSON, Magnus, and PÁLSSON, H. (transl.) *King Harald's Saga* (Harmondsworth 1966)

MAGOUN, F. P. (ed.) '*Annales Domitiani Latini*: an Edition', *Mediaeval Studies* 9 (1947) 235–95

MAGOUN, F. P. (ed.) 'The Domitian Bilingual of the Old English Annals: the Latin Preface', *Speculum* 20 (1945) 65–72

MARX, Jean (ed.) *Guillaume de Jumièges, Gesta Normannorum Ducum* (Rouen 1914)

MASON, J. F. A. 'Roger de Montgomery and his Sons', *Transactions of the Royal Historical Society*, fifth series, 13 (1963) 1–28

MAUND, K. L. 'Cynan ab Iago and the Killing of Gruffudd ap Llywelyn', *Cambridge Medieval Celtic Studies* 10 (1985) 57–65

MAUND, K. L. 'The Welsh Alliances of Earl Ælfgar of Mercia and his Family in the Mid-eleventh Century', *Anglo-Norman Studies* 11 (1988) 181–90

MAUND, K. L. 'Trahaearn ap Caradog: Legitimate Usurper?', *Welsh History Review* 13 (1986/7) 468–76

MEISEL, Janet *Barons of the Welsh Frontier: the Corbet, Pantulf and Fitz-warin Families, 1066–1272* (Lincoln, Nebraska 1980)

MILLER, M. 'Date-Guessing and Dyfed', *Studia Celtica* 12/13 (1977/8) 33–61

MILLER, M. 'Date-Guessing and Pedigrees', *Studia Celtica* 10/11 (1975/6) 96–109

MILLER, M. 'Forms and Uses of Pedigrees', *Transactions of the Honourable Society of Cymmrodorion* (1978) 195–206

MOORE, Donald (ed.) *The Irish Sea Province in Archaeology and History* (Cardiff 1970)

MORRIS, John (gen. ed.) *Domesday Book* (35 vols in 40, Chichester 1975–86)

MURPHY, Denis (ed.) *The Annals of Clonmacnoise, being Annals of Ireland from the Earliest Period to A.D. 1408, translated into English by Conell Mageoghagan* (Dublin 1896)

NELSON, L. H. *The Normans in South Wales 1070–1171* (Austin, Texas 1966)

Ó CORRÁIN, Donncha *Ireland before the Normans* (Dublin 1972)

Ó CUÍV, Brian (ed.) *The Impact of the Scandinavian Invasions on the Celtic-speaking Peoples, c. 800–1100 A.D.* (Dublin 1975)

O'DONOVAN, John (ed. & transl.) *Annála Ríoghachta Éireann: Annals of the Kingdom of Ireland, by the Four Masters, from the Earliest Period to the Year 1616* (2nd edn, 7 vols, Dublin 1856)

O'DWYER, B. W. 'The Annals of Connacht and Loch Cé, and the Monasteries of Boyle and Holy Trinity', *Proceedings of the Royal Irish Academy* 72 C (1972) 83–101

OLESON, Tryggvi J. *The Witenagemot in the Reign of Edward the Confessor* (Toronto 1955)

O'RAHILLY, Cecile *Ireland and Wales: Their Historical and Literary Relations* (London 1924)

PAGE, William (ed.) *The Victoria History of the County of Hereford* (London 1908–)

PAGE, William (ed.) *The Victoria History of the County of Shropshire* (London 1908–)

PARKES, M. B., and WATSON, A. G. (edd.) *Medieval Scribes, Manuscripts and Libraries* (London 1978)

PHILLIMORE, E. (ed.) 'The *Annales Cambriæ* and Old Welsh Genealogies from *Harleian MS.* 3859', *Y Cymmrodor* 9 (1888) 141–83

PHILLIMORE, E. 'The Publication of Welsh Historical Records', *Y Cymmrodor* 11 (1890/1) 133–75

PRINGLE, K. D. 'The Kings of Demetia', *Transactions of the Honourable Society of Cymmrodorion* (1970) 70–6 *and* (1971) 140–4

PUGH, T. B. (ed.) *The Glamorgan County History, III, The Middle Ages* (Cardiff 1971)

REES, W. J. (ed. & transl.) *The Liber Landavensis* (Llandovery 1840)

RICHARDS, Melville *Welsh Administrative and Territorial Units, Medieval and Modern* (Cardiff 1969)

RICHTER, Michael *Giraldus Cambrensis: the Growth of the Welsh Nation* (2nd edn, Aberystwyth 1976)

RITCHIE, R. L. Graeme *The Normans in England before Edward the Confessor* (Exeter 1948)

ROBERTSON, A. J. (ed. & transl.) *Anglo-Saxon Charters* (2nd edn, Cambridge, 1956)

RODERICK, A. J. 'The Feudal Relationship between the English Crown and the Welsh Princes', *History*, new series, 37 (1952) 201–12

ROSITZKE, H. A. (ed.) *The C Text of the Old English Chronicles* (Bochum-Langendreer 1940)

ROWLANDS, I. W. 'The Making of the March: Aspects of the Norman Settlement in Dyfed', *Proceedings of the Battle Conference on Anglo-Norman Studies* 3 (1980) 142–57 *and* 221–5

SAWYER, P. H. *The Age of the Vikings* (2nd edn, London 1971)

SAWYER, P. H. *Anglo-Saxon Charters: An Annotated List and Bibliography* (London 1968)

SAWYER, P. H. (ed.) *Domesday Book: A Re-assessment* (London 1985)

SAWYER, P. H. 'The Vikings and Ireland', in *Ireland in Early Mediaeval Europe: Studies in Memory of Kathleen Hughes*, edd. D. Whitelock *et al.* (Cambridge 1982), pp. 345–61

SAWYER, P. H. 'The Vikings and the Irish Sea', in *The Irish Sea Province in Archaeology and History*, ed. Donald Moore (Cardiff 1970), pp. 86–92

SIMS-WILLIAMS, P. [Review of Wendy Davies, *The Llandaff Charters* (Aberystwyth 1979) and *An Early Welsh Microcosm* (London 1978)], *Journal of Ecclesiastical History* 33 (1983) 124–9

SMITH, J. B. 'The Kingdom of Morgannwg and the Norman Conquest of Glamorgan', in *The Glamorgan County History, III, The Middle Ages*, ed. T. B. Pugh (Cardiff 1971), pp. 1–44

SMYTH, Alfred P. *Scandinavian Kings in the British Isles 850–880* (Oxford 1977)

217

SMYTH, Alfred P. *Scandinavian York and Dublin: The History and Archaeology of Two Related Viking Kingdoms* (2 vols, Dublin 1975/9)

STENTON, F. M. *Anglo-Saxon England* (3rd edn, Oxford 1971)

STEPHEN, Leslie, and LEE, Sidney (edd.) *Dictionary of National Biography* (63 vols, London 1885–1900)

STOKES, W. (ed. & transl.) 'The Annals of Tigernach', *Revue celtique* 16 (1895) 374–419; 17 (1896) 6–33, 119–263, 337–420; 18 (1897) 9–59, 150–97, 267–303

STUBBS, William (ed.) *Willelmi Malmesbiriensis Monachi De Gestis Regum Anglorum Libri Quinque; Historiae Novellae Libri Tres* (2 vols, London 1887/9)

THOMSON, R. M. 'The "Scriptoria" of William of Malmesbury', in *Medieval Scribes, Manuscripts and Libraries*, edd. M. B. Parkes and A. G. Watson (London 1978), pp. 117–42

THOMSON, R. M. 'William of Malmesbury as Historian and Man of Letters', *Journal of Ecclesiastical History* 29 (1978) 387–413

THORPE, Benjamin (ed. & transl.) *The Anglo-Saxon Chronicle, according to the Several Original Authorities* (2 vols, London 1861)

THORPE, Lewis (transl.) *Gerald of Wales: The Journey Through Wales and The Description of Wales* (Harmondsworth 1978)

VAN HAMEL, A. G. 'Norse History in *Hanes Gruffudd ap Cynan*', *Revue celtique* 42 (1925) 336–44

VAN HOUTS, E. M. C. 'The *Gesta Normannorum Ducum*: a History without an End', *Proceedings of the Battle Conference on Anglo-Norman Studies* 3 (1980) 106–18 *and* 215–20

WADE EVANS, A. W. (ed. & transl.) *Vitae Sanctorum Britanniae et Genealogiae* (Cardiff 1944)

WALKER, David *The Norman Conquerors* (Swansea 1977)

WALKER, D. 'The Norman Settlement in Wales', *Proceedings of the Battle Conference on Anglo-Norman Studies* 1 (1978) 131–43 *and* 222–4

WALKER, D. 'A Note on Gruffudd ap Llywelyn (1039–1063)', *Welsh History Review* 1 (1960–3) 83–94

WALSH, A. *Scandinavian Relations with Ireland during the Viking Period* (Dublin 1922)

WALSH, P. 'The Annals of Loch Cé', *Irish Ecclesiastical Record*, fifth series, 56 (1940) 113–22

WALSH, P. 'The Dating of the Irish Annals', *Irish Historical Studies* 2 (1940/1) 355–75

WALSH, Paul *The Four Masters and Their Work* (Dublin 1944)

WALSH, Paul *Irish Men of Learning* (Dublin 1947)

WARREN, W. L. *Henry II* (London 1973)

WHITELOCK, Dorothy, *et al.* (transl.) *The Anglo-Saxon Chronicle: A Revised Translation* (London 1961; revised impression, 1965)

WHITELOCK, Dorothy, *et al.* (edd.) *Ireland in Early Mediaeval Europe: Studies in Memory of Kathleen Hughes* (Cambridge 1982)

WILLIAMS, A. H. *An Introduction to the History of Wales* (2 vols, Cardiff 1941/8)

WILLIAMS, A. 'Land and Power in the Eleventh Century: the Estates of Harold Godwineson', *Proceedings of the Battle Conference on Anglo-Norman Studies* 3 (1980) 171–87 *and* 230–4

WILLIAMS, Ifor   *The Beginnings of Welsh Poetry* (2nd edn, Cardiff 1980)

WILLIAMS, J. E. C.   'Beirdd y Tywysogion: Arolwg', *Llên Cymru* 11 (1970/1) 3–94

WILLIAMS (AB ITHEL), John (ed.)   *Annales Cambriæ* (London 1860)

INDEX

(ch) refers to a genealogical chart appearing on the page cited.

222

Einion ap Cadwaladr 91 (ch); 105; 109 (ch)
Einion ap Cadwgan (ab Bleddyn) 107 (ch)
Einion ap Gwalchmai 74
Einion Clud ap Madog 49 (ch); 50 (ch)
Einion ab Owain ap Hywel Dda 5; 8; 10; 11; 12; 13; 14–17; 18; 19 (ch); 20; 21 (ch); 23; 24 (ch); 25 (ch); 28 (line of); 29; 31; 36; 37 (ch); 38; 39 (ch); 40; 42; 43 (ch); 51 (ch); 52 (descendants of); 53 (line of); 54; 56; 57 (ch); 63 (ch); 69 (ch); 70 (ch); 77 (ch); 80; 116 (line of); 120(–1) n. 5; 123; 127
Einion, nephew of Iestyn ap Gwrgan 203
Eithin ab Elffin 188
Elen ferch Meirchion ap Rhys 31; 33 (ch)
Elen ferch Tewdwr 37 (ch)
Elfoen, *alumnus* 184
Elgan Weflhwch ap Cynan 41 (ch)
Elgu, priest of St Maughans 198
'Elgystyl' ab Awst 190
Elidir ap Llywarch 47 (ch)
Elidir Lydanwyn ap Meirchion 18; 72
Elise ab Anarawd 25 (ch); 61 (ch); 63 (ch); 69 (ch); 101 (ch)
Elise ap Gruffudd 104
Elise ap Madog 72; 75 (ch); 109 (ch)
Elizabeth, daughter of Sir Richard Grey 104
Ellylw ferch Cydifor 39; 40 (ch); 107 (ch)
Ellylw ferch Elidir 46; 47 (ch); 50 (ch); 60
Ely 126 (siege of); 139
Ely River, Glamorgan 192
Elynwy 202; 205
Elystan Glodrydd ap Cuhelyn 45 (ch); 47 (ch); 49 (ch); 50 (ch); 81 (ch)
Elystan Glodrydd, dynasty of 45–8; 51; 54; 82; 106; 118; 151
England 1; 4; 27; 65; 98; 120–55; 156; 159; 160; 161; 164; 165; 166; 167; 169; 170; 177; 207–9
English 1; 2; 3; 4; 11; 12; 14; 18; 25; 26; 27; 31; 42; 55; 64; 65; 93; 107; 120–55; 156; 159; 165; 181; 182; 190; 200; 207–9
English chronicles 3; 64; 126; 128; 129; 131; 204
Eochaid ua Mathgamna of Ulster 179
Ergyng 27; 135; 143; 197
Esyllt, mother of Rhodri Mawr 85
Eurddilad ferch Cynwal 203
Euddogwy, St 183–206

Euron ferch Hoedlyw ap Cadwgan 48; 50 (ch); 107 (ch)
Ewias 111

Ffriog, King 190
Ffynnon Oer 198
FitzBaldwin, William 150
FitzHamo, Robert 148
FitzOsbern, William 29; 34; 140; 142; 205
FitzPons, Richard 32
FitzRichard, Gilbert 104
FitzRichard, Osbern 69 (ch); 137; 138; 148
FitzScrob, Richard 140
FitzWilliam, Roger (Roger de Breteuil) 111; 146–7; 205
Flanders 134; 135
Flint 156
France 123 (viking-settlements in)
French: see Normans

Galloway 171; 174
Gellon, a harper 154
Genilles ferch Gwrgenau ab Ednywain 74 (ch)
Genilles ferch Hoedlyw 97 (ch)
Geoffrey of Monmouth 86; 178
Gerald of Windsor 11; 37 (ch); 38; 51; 73 (ch); 149; 170
Giraldus Cambrensis 7; 68; 137
Glamorgan 8; 13; 20; 42; 53; 65; 106–11; 113; 122; 132; 148; 151; 156; 159; 183–206
'Glinaru': see Glúniairn, son of Olaf Cuarán
Gloucester 27; 124; 161 (lands of Eglaf in); 164 (levy of)
Gloyw Gwlad Lydan ap Tynefan 71 (ch)
Glúniairn, son of 162
Glúniairn, son of Olaf Cuarán 86; 158
Godfrey or Gofraid grandson of Ragnall 167; 181
Godfrey Haraldsson 12; 55; 57; 157; 158
Godfrey Meranach 150; 168; 176; 179; 181
Godfrey son of Sihtric 162
Godwine, earl of Wessex 126; 131 (and family of); 133; 135; 136; 208
Godwine, house of 131; 133; 134; 135; 136; 140; 208
Gollwyn ab Ednywain 81 (ch)

Gwent Uchaf 27
Gwent Uch Coed 111
Gwenwen ferch Idnerth 45 (ch); 48; 49 (ch); 50 (Gwenwyn ap Idnerth, ch)
Gwenwyn ab Idnerth (see Gwenwen ferch Idnerth) 81 (ch)
Gwenwynwyn ab Owain Cyfeiliog 8; 9 (ch); 48; 50 (ch); 72; 75 (ch); 80; 81 (ch); 88; 89; 91 (ch); 105; 109 (ch)
Gwerystan ap Gwaithfoed 70 (and instability of name of); 71 (ch); 74 (ch); 81 (ch); 94; 95 (ch); 97 (ch); 101 (ch)
'Gwerystan ap Gwyn' (error for Gwerystan ap Gwaithfoed, q.v.) 71 (ch)
Gweunotyll, battle of 29; 30
Gweurfyl ferch Gwrgenau 9 (ch); 50 (ch); 75 (ch); 91 (ch); 109 (ch)
Gweurfyl ferch Owain Cyfeiliog 23 (ch); 32 (ch)
Gwgan, king of Ceredigion 10
Gwgan ap Meurig, foster-father of Hywel ap Goronwy 6; 52
Gwgan Cenau menrudd ap Pasgen 46; 47 (ch); 60
Gwgan, bishop of Llandaff 184; 186; 195
Gwineu Deufreuddwyd 48; 49 (ch); 71 (ch)
Gwladus ferch Aldud ab Owain 96; 99 (ch)
Gwladus ferch Gruffudd ap Rhys 37 (ch)
Gwladus ferch Llywarch 9 (ch); 81 (ch); 91 (ch)
Gwladus ferch Rhiwallon 6; 36; 37 (ch); 39 (ch); 73 (ch); 77 (ch)
Gwlfach 5
Gwrgan ap Dunna (cf. 'Gurcant') 195
Gwrgan ab Ithel 192; 196
Gwrgan ap Meirchion 184; 195
Gwrgenau ab Ednywain 74 (ch)
Gwrgenau ap Hywel 50 (ch)
Gwrgenau ap Seisyll 6; 55; 81 (ch); 90; 93; 94–5; 101 (ch); 102; 104; 118
Gwrgi, witness to LL 251 186
Gwrgi, witness to LL 271 203; 204
Gwrhydr ap Caradog 71 (ch)
Gwriad, father of Cadwallon 196
Gwrmid 3; 5; 12; 55; 157
Gwrwst (pedigree of, in Brut y Brenhinedd) 86
Gwyn ap Gollwyn 81 (ch)
Gwyn ap Gruffudd 6; 112; 113–14
Gwyn ap Gwaithfoed 71 (ch); 72 n. 139

Gwyn ap Rhydderch 41 (ch)
Gwynedd 1; 7; 8; 12; 17; 18; 28; 31; 42; 43; 52; 54–101; 102; 105; 106; 112; 115; 116 (rulers of); 117 (kings of); 120 n. 5; 126; 127; 132; 138; 143; 144; 145; 148; 149; 150; 152; 153; 155; 158; 159; 160; 169; 171; 173; 174; 176; 177; 179
Gwynllŵg 145; 150
Gwynnan ap Gwynnog Farfsych 71 (ch); 72 n. 139; 81 (ch)
Gwynnog Farfsych ap Ceidio 71 (ch)
Gwynnog Farfsych ap Lles Llawddeog 71 (ch); 72 n. 139; 81 (ch)

Haearddur, monk of Enlli 121(–2) n. 9
Haer ferch Cillyn y Blaidd Rudd 75 (ch); 107 (ch)
Hanesyn Hen 8
Harald Hardrada 165
Harald Harfagr 85 (ch: 'King Harfagr'); 86; 174; 175 (ch); 178 (and brothers)
Harald, sons of, vikings 157
Harold Godwinesson 4; 27; 28; 44; 66; 124; 125; 130; 132; 133; 134; 135; 136; 138; 139; 141; 143; 146; 164; 166 (and sons of); 167; 181; 209
Harold, son of Harold Godwinesson 167
Harthacnut, king of England 166
Hastings, battle of 139
Hebrides 145; 166 and n. 66; 168
Heimskringla 86
Hen Lwythau Gwynedd a'r Mars 67; 74; 81 (ch); 88; 93; 94; 96; 114
'Henriugunua', estate granted in LL 267 200–1
Henry I, king of England 11; 12; 13; 36; 44; 46; 51; 103; 104; 151; 152; 170; 174; 177; 179; 180
Henry II, king of England 171; 173
Henry ap Cadwgan 7; 107 (ch)
Henry of Huntingdon 130
Hereford 25; 27; 65; 111 (earl of); 122 (charter in); 124; 125; 128; 130; 132; 133; 134; 136; 140; 142; 146 (earls of); 149 (land in); 164 (levy of); 165; 202; 205
Herewald, bishop of Llandaff 110; 111; 122; 147; 188; 191; 192; 193–4; 198; 200–6
Hiberno-Scandinavians 1; 13; 22 (fleet of); 23; 33 (fleet of); 55; 65 (fleet of); 66 (activity of); 83 (fleet of); 85

(Dublin royal line); 86 (and Dublin royal line); 107 (force of); 124 (ships of); 127; 129 (mercenaries); 135; 141 (fleet of); 145; 147; 183–206; 207–10

Hirbarwch, battle of 55; 57

Historia Gruffud vab Kenan 33; 35; 59; 64; 77 (account of Trahaearn ap Caradog); 78 (account of Trahaearn ap Caradog); 79; 82; 83; 84; 85; 86; 93; 94; 100; 118; 142; 143; 144; 148; 151; 153–5; 171–81

Historia Regum Anglorum (attributed to Symeon of Durham) 130; 131; 132; 156

Historia Regum Britanniae of Geoffrey of Monmouth 178

Hoedlyw ap Cadwgan ab Elystan 50 (ch)

Hopkin, Walter 31

'Hormahede', place mentioned by Orderic Vitalis 153

Howdeg ap Rhun Rhuddbaladr (see also Bywdeg) 71 (ch)

Howyr Lew ap Howdeg (see also Pywyr Lew ab Bywdeg) 71 (ch)

Hugh d'Avranches, earl of Chester 83; 95; 142; 143; 145; 150; 153; 154; 155; 169; 176

Hugh de Montgomery, earl of Shrewsbury 83; 95; 145; 169; 170; 176

Hugh Donkey 40

Hunydd ferch Bleddyn 73 (ch); 75 (ch)

Hunydd ferch Einudd 75 (ch); 109 (ch)

Hwfa ab Ithel Felyn o Iâl 88; 91 (ch)

Hywel Dda ap Cadell 10; 14; 15 (ch); 16 (ch); 18; 22; 23 (ch); 25 (ch); 37 (ch); 42; 43 (ch); 46 (ch); 48; 50 (ch); 51 (ch); 52; 57 (ch); 63 (ch); 69 (ch); 77 (ch); 79 (ch); 92; 97 (ch); 101 (ch); 189

Hywel Dda, sons of (see also Owain, etc.) 10; 53

Hywel ab Edwin ab Einion 5; 8; 10; 11; 14; 17; 19 (ch); 21 (ch); 22–5 (ch, 24); 26; 27; 28; 36; 39 (ch); 42; 52; 53; 63 (ch); 64; 65; 66; 69 (ch); 70 (ch); 80; 114; 115; 127; 129; 132; 135; 146; 160 n. 38; 163; 164; 168; 181; 186; 197; 209

Hywel ab Edwin, wife of 5; 22; 64; 68

Hywel ab Idnerth 32 (ch)

Hywel ap Goronwy ap Cadwgan 6; 11; 12; 14; 40; 44; 46; 49 (ch); 50 (ch); 51–2; 54; 60; 67; 103; 114; 118; 150; 151; 152

Hywel ap Goronwy ap Rhydderch 33 (ch)

Hywel ab Ieuaf ap Cadwgan ab Elystan 50 (ch)

Hywel ab Ieuaf ab Idwal Foel 5; 11; 12; 13; 40; 41–2; 43 (ch); 54; 55–7 (ch); 58; 63 (ch); 100; 101 (ch); 120(–1) n. 5; 123; 158; 182; 207; 208

Hywel ab Ieuaf ab Owain 80; 81 (ch); 88; 91 (ch)

Hywel ab Iorwerth 23 (ch)

Hywel ab Ithel 6; 112; 113; 117; 153; 169; 181

Hywel ap Madog 49 (ch); 50 (ch)

Hywel ap Maredudd ab Bleddyn 75 (ch); 109 (ch)

Hywel ap Maredudd ap Rhydderch 33 (ch)

Hywel ab Owain ab Edwin 6; 17; 19 (ch); 21 (ch); 29–31; 36; 39 (ch); 43; 63 (ch); 69 (ch); 114; 115; 147

Hywel ab Owain ap Morgan 6; 13; 20; 53; 107; 108; 110; 111; 112; 113 (ch); 116; 186; 187; 188; 190; 191; 192; 193; 195; 196; 197; 198

Hywel ap Seisyll 47 (ch); 50 (ch)

Iago ap Gruffudd ap Cynan 88; 91 (ch)

Iago ab Idwal Foel ab Anarawd 5; 10; 13; 40; 41–2; 43 (ch); 55; 56; 57 (ch); 63 (ch); 101 (ch); 120(–1) n. 5; 157

Iago ab Idwal ap Meurig 6; 12; 20; 36; 54; 60; 62–4; 65 (ch); 69 (ch); 76; 78 (as grandfather of Gruffudd ap Cynan); 85 (ch); 89 (ch); 90; 92; 98; 99; 101 (ch); 114; 115; 116; 127; 163; 171; 189

Iago, son of 163

'Idmab' of Llangynfyl 197

Idnerth ap Cadwgan ab Elystan Glodrydd 49 (ch); 50 (ch); 51 (ch)

Idnerth ap Cadwgan ab Elystan Glodrydd, sons of (see also Gruffudd ab Idnerth and Ifor ab Idnerth) 45–8; 52; 150; 151

Idnerth ab Iorwerth Hirflawdd 45 (ch); 49 (ch); 50 (ch); 81 (ch)

Idnerth ab Owain 23 (ch); 32 (ch)

Idwal Foel ab Anarawd 10; 22; 43 (ch); 55; 56 (descendants of); 57 (ch); 59 (and family of); 63 (ch); 65 (ch); 69 (ch); 85 (ch); 89 (ch); 90 (family of); 98 (line of); 100; 101 (ch); 105 (line of)

Idwal ap Gruffudd ap Cynan o Benmon 88; 91 (ch)

Idwal Fychan ab Idwal Foel 5; 43 (ch); 55; 57 (ch); 63 (ch); 101 (ch)

'Lann Sant Breit in Mainaur Crucmarc' 196
'Lann Tiuauc' 190
'legitimate' rulers 7; 78; 79; 83; 171; 172; 173
Leinster 85; 86; 87 (ch); 160; 163; 165; 167; 175 (ch); 177 (ch); 178; 179
Leofgar, bishop of Hereford 125; 136
Leofric, earl of Mercia 124; 125; 127; 129; 133; 134; 136; 137; 138; 139 (house of); 148 (house of)
Leofwine 122
Leominster 124; 127 (abbess of); 129 (abbess of); 132
Lewys ab Edward 103
Lewys Morgannwg 103
Liber Landauensis 2; 7; 10; 13; 18; 20; 26; 27; 52; 92; 106; 108; 110; 111; 115; 122; 146; 147; 183–206
Lifris, archdeacon and *magister* of St Cadog 203; 204; 205
Limerick 157
Limesey, Robert de, bishop of Chester/Coventry 137

Llanbadarn 132; 158
Llancarfan 158; 201; 205
Llandaff 20; 110; 111; 147; 183–206
Llandaff bishop-list (Canterbury, Cathedral Library, MS. C.117) 200
Llandaff charters 2; 34; 110; 111; 147; 183–206
Llandaff charters, narrations in 183; 185; 187; 190; 191; 193; 194; 196; 197; 198; 200; 203; 204; 205
LL125a 191; 193; 196; 203
LL147 190
LL152 189; 190; 202
LL157 198
LL167 190
LL173 18
LL176b 190
LL216b 185; 196; 200
LL217 193; 203
LL218 193; 196
LL222 198
LL225 185; 198; 200
LL233 185; 198; 200
LL237b 204
LL239 193; 203
LL240 189; 202
LL243 185; 186; 195
LL244 195

LL246 183; 184–5; 195
LL249a 13; 183; 187–8; 191; 192; 193; 195; 196; 199
LL249b 183; 185–6; 191; 196; 200
LL251 183; 186–7; 195
LL253 13; 20; 108; 183; 188–9; 199; 202
LL255 13; 108; 183; 186; 187; 188; 190–1; 192; 193; 196; 199; 201
LL257 183; 185; 187; 188; 191–2; 193; 196; 199; 200
LL258 183; 186; 188; 191; 192; 196; 199; 202
LL259 13; 110; 111; 183; 187; 188; 191; 193–4; 195; 197; 198; 199; 201; 203; 204
LL260 111; 183; 187; 188; 191; 193; 194; 195; 199; 201
LL261 13; 111; 183; 187; 188; 191; 193; 194–5; 199; 201; 203; 204; 205
LL262 183; 186; 195; 199; 202; 204
LL263 13; 111; 183; 186; 188; 191; 192; 193; 196; 199
LL264a 20; 23; 110; 183; 186; 188; 191; 192; 193; 196; 199; 200; 202
LL264b 20; 108; 183; 186; 188; 191; 192; 196; 198; 199; 200
LL265a 13
LL267 15; 111; 183; 185; 188; 191; 194; 195; 196; 199; 200–1; 202; 203; 204; 205
LL269 111; 183; 189; 194; 195; 201; 202–3; 204; 205
LL271 22; 111; 183; 193; 194; 195; 201; 202; 203; 204; 205; 206
LL272 13; 111; 183; 194; 195; 198; 201; 202; 203; 204; 205; 206
LL274 18; 111; 146–7; 183; 195; 203; 204; 205; 206
Llanddegfedd, Gwent 204
Llandeilo Fawr 202
Llandudoch 11; 158
Llangwern, Gwent Is Coed 187
Llangwm 16 (battle near, in A.D. 994); 18 (location of); 20; 58 (battle near); 205 (saints of); 206
Llangwm Dinmael, Denbigh 18
Llangwm Isaf 18; 205
Llangwm, Monmouthshire 18
Llangwm, near Llanycefn, Pembrokeshire 18
Llangwm, Rhos, Pembrokeshire 18
Llangynfyl 110; 197–8; 199–200

232

Peniarth 132 103
Canterbury, Cathedral Library,
  Cartae Antiquae C.117 200–1
London, British Library,
  Additional 14919 103
  Additional 14967 103
  Harley 2300 31
  Harley 2414 43
  Harley 5835 22; 31
Oxford, Jesus College, 20 15; 16; 18;
  19; 37; 45 (ch); 46 (ch); 47 (ch); 48;
  49 (ch); 52; 59; 60; 64; 67; 72; 82;
  86; 105
Mared (Marared) ferch Gruffudd ap
  Cynan 81 (ch); 88; 91 (ch); 99 (ch)
Mared (Marared/Marued) ferch Madog ap
  Maredudd 71 (ch); 75 (ch); 109 (ch)
Maredudd ab Bleddyn 7; 9 (ch); 39 (ch);
  44; 53 (ch); 67; 71 (ch); 72 (and
  mother of); 75 (ch); 89; 98; 101 (ch);
  102; 103–5; 107 (ch); 109 (ch); 113;
  118; 151; 170
Maredudd Goch ap Cadwaladr 91 (ch);
  105; 109 (ch)
Maredudd ap Cadwgan ab Bleddyn 48;
  50 (ch); 107 (ch)
Maredudd ab Edwin ab Einion 5; 10; 14;
  17; 19 (ch); 21 (ch); 22–5; 36; 39 (ch);
  42; 53; 63 (ch); 69 (ch); 92; 114; 115
Maredudd ap Griffri ap Trahaearn 81 (ch)
Maredudd ap Gruffudd ap Llywelyn 6;
  55; 63 (ch); 67; 68; 69 (ch); 90; 92–3;
  98; 101 (ch); 137; 138; 202
Maredudd ap Llywarch 81 (ch)
Maredudd ab Owain ab Edwin 6; 10; 14;
  17; 19 (ch); 21 (ch); 28–9; 30; 34; 36;
  37–8; 39 (ch); 40; 43; 52; 53; 63 (ch);
  69 (ch); 70; 100; 111; 114; 115 (and
  brothers); 118; 146; 147 (brothers of);
  149 (son of); 208
Maredudd ab Owain ap Hywel Dda 5; 10;
  11; 12; 13; 14; 16 (ch); 17–20; 21 (ch);
  24 (ch); 25 (ch); 26; 42; 43 (ch); 46
  (ch); 51 (ch); 52; 53; 54; 57 (ch); 57–8;
  59; 60; 61; 62; 63 (ch); 67; 70 (ch); 79
  (ch); 97 (ch); 100; 101 (ch); 102;
  107–8; 114; 121; 158–9; 160
Maredudd ap Rhydderch ab Bleddri 41
  (ch)
Maredudd ap Rhydderch ap Caradog 6;
  32; 33 (ch)
Maredudd ap Rhydderch ap Tewdwr 73
  (ch); 75 (ch)

Maredudd ap Robert 48; 50 (ch); 80; 81
  (ch)
Margred ferch Hywel 33 (ch)
Mathgamain mac Dubgaill, king of Ulster
  87 (ch); 89 (ch); 175 (ch); 179
Matilda of Flanders 140
Mechain, battle of 28; 68; 92; 93; 138
Mei, son of the bishop 203; 204
Meilir Brydydd ap Mabon 154–5; 172;
  179
Meilir ab Owain ab Edwin o Degeingl 53
  (ch); 99 (ch)
Meilir ap Rhiwallon 6; 34; 35; 36; 55; 77;
  94; 116
Meilir ap Seisyll 47 (ch); 50 (ch)
Meirchion ap Rhydderch 184; 195
Meirchion ap Rhys 6; 22; 24 (ch); 30; 31;
  32 (ch); 33 (ch); 147
Meirionydd 13; 48; 102; 143
Melwas, *alumnus* 184
Merchfyw 201; 202; 203; 204; 205
Merchider ab Anor 49 (ch)
Mercia 70 (earls of); 123 (earls of); 129;
  133; 134; 135; 137; 138; 139 (house
  of); 140; 165; 208
Merfyn Frych ap Gwriad, king of
  Gwynedd 15 (ch); 37 (ch); 38; 85; 88
Meurig ab Arthfael 5; 112; 113
Meurig ap Goronwy 203; 204
Meurig ap Hywel 5; 13; 107; 108; 110;
  111; 113 (ch); 116; 163; 164; 186;
  187–8; 190; 191; 192; 193; 194; 195;
  196; 197; 199; 200; 201
Meurig ab Idwal Foel 43 (ch); 56; 57
  (ch); 58; 59; 63 (ch); 65 (ch); 69 (ch);
  85 (ch); 89 (ch); 90; 101 (ch); 112
Meurig ab Idwal Foel, sons of 5; 18; 54;
  58–9; 112; 115; 159
Meurig ap Meurig ap Trahaearn 81 (ch)
Meurig ap Trahaearn 6; 81 (ch)
Meurig, King 190
Mide 85; 87 (ch); 158; 167; 177 (ch); 178
'Miscellaneous Pedigrees' (MP) 192; 203
Môn: see Anglesey
Monmouthshire 18; 185; 195; 198
Monnow, River 197
Montfort, Simon de 134
Montgomery, Roger de 142; 145; 148;
  169 (and family of)
Montgomery castle 150
Môr ap Gwyn 5; 112
Môr ap Llywarch 47 (ch)
Morfarch 201; 202; 203; 204; 205

233

Morgan ap Cadwgan ab Bleddyn 39; 40 (ch); 107 (ch)
Morgan ap Caradog 37 (ch); 192; 203
Morgan ap Hywel 23 (ch); 32 (ch)
Morgan Hen ab Owain 113 (ch); 184; 189; 192; 193 (ch); 196; 202
Morgan, king of Glamorgan 189; 190
Morgenau, bishop of St Davids 160
Morgannwg 13; 20; 26; 106–11; 115–16; 117; 132; 142; 146; 147; 163; 164; 183–206
Morkere, earl of Northumbria 28; 70; 120; 125; 126; 138–40; 145; 153
Morwyl ferch Ednywain Bendew 97 (ch)
Muirchertach Ua Briain 168; 170; 171; 174; 177; 179; 180; 181
Munster (Mumu) 85; 86; 87 (ch); 167; 177 (ch); 178
Murchad son of Diarmait mac Maíl na mBó 166; 167; 180
Murchad mac Finn, king of Leinster 87 (ch); 177 (ch); 178
Murchath, Mwrchath: see Muirchertach, Murchad
Mynydd Carn, battle of 33; 34–6; 43; 77; 79; 80; 83; 84; 94; 117; 142; 143; 152; 155; 160(–1) n. 38; 168; 176; 179; 180; 181; 204

Nant Carno 42 (battle at)
Nest, daughter of Osbern FitzRichard 68; 69 (ch); 137
Nest ferch Cynfyn 74 (ch)
Nest ferch Gruffudd ap Llywelyn 69 (ch); 137; 138
Nest ferch Gruffudd ap Rhys 37 (ch)
Nest ferch Rhys ap Tewdwr 5; 6; 37 (ch); 38; 51; 73 (ch)
N.N. ap Meurig ap Trahaearn 81 (ch)
N.N. ferch Brochfael ap Moelwyn 75 (ch); 107 (ch)
N.N. ferch Gwerystan 101 (ch)
N.N. ferch Gwyn Ddistain 91 (ch)
N.N. ferch Llychwy o Lanbeulan 91 (ch)
N.N. ferch Madog ap Maredudd ab Bleddyn 109 (ch)
N.N. ferch Picot 107 (ch)
'Nobis' 195; 202
Norman conquest 4; 120 (of Wales); 143
Normandy 151; 169; 170; 173; 174
Normans 1; 2; 3; 4; 11; 12; 14; 28; 32; 33 (of Brycheiniog); 36; 40; 44; 45; 46; 48; 51–2; 54; 55; 70; 78; 84; 89; 95; 100; 103; 105; 107 (ch); 111; 114; 116; 118; 124; 126; 132 ('French' of Herefordshire); 137; 139; 140; 141–55; 169; 172; 176; 177; 179; 182; 206; 207–9
Northumbria 125; 133; 134; 136; 139
North Wales 2; 7; 18; 26; 28; 33; 35; 36; 41; 42; 48; 52; 54–101; 103; 105; 106; 114; 115; 117; 123; 127; 128; 130; 132; 133; 138; 142; 143; 144; 145; 148; 149; 150; 151; 153; 154; 155; 157; 159; 160; 163; 164; 169; 171; 180; 189; 207; 209
Norway 85 (king of); 86; 125 (fleet from); 131 (fleet from); 145 (king of); 161; 166; 167; 169; 178
Norwegians 156; 158; 174
Nudd, *alumnus* 184

Odo of Bayeux 155
Olaf Haraldsson 166 n. 66
Olaf son of 'King Harfagr' 85 (ch); 89 (ch); 175 (ch)
Olaf Cuarán son of Sitric Caech 85 (ch); 89 (ch); 175 (ch); 177 (ch); 178
Olaf Arnaid son of Sitric son of Olaf Cuarán 85 (ch); 87 (ch); 89 (ch); 171; 174; 175 (ch); 177 (ch); 178
Orderic Vitalis, historian 2; 29; 34; 65; 68–9; 78; 84; 137; 139; 140; 141; 142; 146; 148; 153–5; 170; 181
Orkneyinga saga 166 n. 66
Orkneys 166 and n. 66; 169
Osbern d'Orgères 153
Osraige 167
Owain Fychan ap Cadwaladr 91 (ch)
Owain ap Cadwgan ab Bleddyn 4; 6; 31; 39 (and brothers); 51; 73 (ch); 104; 105; 107 (ch); 152
Owain ap Caradog ap Gruffudd 23 (ch); 24 (ch); 31; 32 (ch); 44; 73 (ch); 75 (ch)
Owain ap Caradog ap Rhydderch 31; 33 (ch)
Owain Fraisg ap Cyndeyrn (Cyndrwyn/Cymdwr) Fendigaid 41 (ch)
Owain ap Dyfnwal 5; 112; 113
Owain ab Edwin ab Einion 17; 19 (ch); 21 (ch); 39 (ch); 51 (ch); 53 (sons of); 63 (ch); 66 (sons of); 69 (ch)
Owain ab Edwin ap Goronwy o Degeingl 6; 31; 49 (and sons of); 53 (ch); 55; 73 (ch); 76; 79 (ch); 84; 90; 95–6; 97 (ch);

99 (ch); 100; 101 (ch); 113 (sons of); 115; 118; 145; 151; 153; 169 (sons of)
Owain Cyfeiliog ap Gruffudd 8; 9 (ch); 50 (ch); 75 (ch); 81 (ch); 109 (ch)
Owain Gwynedd ap Gruffudd ap Cynan 9 (ch); 53 (ch); 76; 79 (ch); 80–2 and n. 157; 81 (ch); 86; 89; 91 (ch); 96; 97 (ch); 99 (ch); 154; 172–3
Owain ap Gruffudd ap Llywelyn 6; 63 (ch); 67; 68; 69 (ch); 137
'Owain ap Gruffudd' (error for Gwyn ap Gruffudd, *q.v.*) 113
Owain ap Hywel Dda 5; 10; 15 (ch); 16 (ch); 21 (ch); 22; 23 (ch); 24 (ch); 25 (ch); 37 (ch); 39 (ch); 43 (ch); 46 (ch); 51 (ch); 57 (ch); 62 (ch); 63 (ch); 69 (ch); 70 (ch); 77 (ch); 79 (ch); 97 (ch); 101 (ch); 112
Owain Fychan ap Madog 72; 75 (ch); 109 (ch)
Owain ap Morgan Hen 113 (ch); 184; 193 (ch)
Owain ap Rhydderch ap Tewdwr 73 (ch); 75 (ch)
Owain ap Trahaearn 81 (ch)

Pembroke castle 11; 44; 48; 51; 144; 150; 169
Pembrokeshire 18; 151 (lord of); 156; 157; 169
Penalun 202
Pencadair, battle of 11; 22; 65
Penda, king of Mercia 134
Penllyn 96; 99 (ch)
Penmon 157
'Penn Celli Guennhuc' (see also Llangwern) 186–7
Perrot family 31
Perrot, Sir Andrew 33 (ch)
Perrot, Steven 33 (ch)
Philip (Ffilip/Phylib) ap Seisyll 47 (ch); 50 (ch)
Picot, a father-in-law of Cadwgan ab Bleddyn 107 (ch); 208
Porth Hodni 176
Portskewett 28; 44; 125; 133; 141; 146
Powys 10; 11; 12–13; 36; 37; 44; 54; 70; 71; 74; 81 (ch); 94; 95; 102–6; 115; 116; 132; 149; 151; 152; 155
Powys Fadog 104
Powys Wenwynwyn 104
Prawst ferch Elise 24 (ch); 25; 61; 62; 63 (ch); 64; 69 (ch); 92; 96; 100; 101 (ch)

Pwlldyfach, battle of 11; 163
Pwllgwdig, battle of 29; 43
Pywyr Lew ab Bywdeg (see also Howyr Lew ap Howdeg) 71 (ch)

Ragnall son of Mathgamain, king of Ulster 87 (ch); 89 (ch); 174; 175 (ch); 179
Ralf the timid, earl of Hereford 124; 128; 130
Ralf Mortimer 148
Rhael (Rhuel) ferch Goronwy ab Owain 96; 99 (ch)
Rhain the Irishman 52; 60; 62; 90; 91; 118; 121; 160–1
Rhandiroedd Powys 72; 102; 103; 104
Rhandwlff ap Cadwaladr 91 (ch)
Rhanillt ferch Gruffudd ap Cynan 88; 91 (ch); 99 (ch)
Rhanillt, daughter of Olaf 85 (ch); 87 (ch); 89 (ch); 101 (ch); 171; 174; 175 (ch); 177 (ch)
Rhicart ap Cadwaladr 88; 91 (ch)
Rhicart ap Maredudd 40; 41 (ch)
Rhiddid ap Seisyll: see Rhirid ap Seisyll
Rhirid Mawr ab Amadanw 68 (ch)
Rhirid ab Bleddyn 6; 38; 39 (ch); 44; 51; 53 (ch); 63 (ch); 75 (ch); 103–5; 107 (ch); 149
Rhirid Flaidd ap Gwrgenau o Benllyn 99 (ch)
Rhirid ab Owain ab Edwin o Degeingl 53 (ch); 99 (ch)
Rhirid (Rhiddid) ap Seisyll 47 (ch); 50 (ch)
Rhiwallon ab Beli 196
Rhiwallon ap Cynfyn 6; 19; 21 (ch); 36; 39 (ch); 53 (ch); 54; 61 (ch); 63 (ch); 68–76; 77 (ch); 92; 93; 94; 95 (ch); 96; 97; 98; 101 (ch); 106; 115; 116; 125; 138; 140
Rhiwallon ap Gwlfrid 195
Rhiwallon ap Gwrydr 95 (ch)
Rhiwallon ap Rhun 191
Rhiwallon ap Tudfwlch 198
Rhodri ab Elise 184; 186; 187
Rhodri ab Idwal Foel 57 (ch); 63 (ch); 101 (ch)
Rhodri Mawr ap Merfyn Frych 7; 8; 9; 10; 15 (ch); 16; 19; 25 (ch); 26; 37 (ch); 38; 43 (ch); 57 (ch); 59; 63 (ch); 64; 65 (ch); 68; 69 (ch); 77 (ch); 79 (ch); 83; 85; 85 (ch); 86; 88; 89 (ch);

96; 97 (ch); 101 (ch); 114; 178; 182 (and sons)

Rhodri Mawr, dynasty of 7; 8; 9; 10; 16; 17; 22; 26; 36; 52; 56; 58; 60–1; 64; 68; 72; 83; 90; 96; 100; 105; 114; 116; 117

Rhodri Mawr, dynasty of, Northern branch 10; 18; 23; 36; 41; 42; 52; 59; 61; 96; 98; 100; 118; 157

Rhodri Mawr, dynasty of, Southern branch 7; 8; 26; 33; 36; 38; 42; 52; 53; 56; 62; 96; 100; 116–17; 186

Rhodri Mawr, sons of 7

Rhodri ab Owain Gwynedd 79 (ch); 97 (ch); 99 (ch)

Rhos, Gwynedd 113; 117; 142 n. 97; 153; 169

Rhos, Pembrokeshire 18

Rhotbert ap Llywarch 50 (ch); 81 (ch)

Rhuddlan 125; 142–3; 153–5; 174

Rhuel (Rhael) ferch Gruffudd ap Cynan 75 (ch); 91 (ch); 107 (ch); 120

Rhufoniog 113; 142 n. 97; 153; 169

Rhun Rhuddbaladr ap Llara/Llary 71 (ch)

'Rhuryth' 191; 192; 193; 195; 196; 198

Rhwng Gwy a Hafren 151

Rhyd-y-Gors 51 (castle at); 64; 124; 126; 127; 150 (castle at)

Rhydderch ab Bleddri 41 (ch)

Rhydderch ap Caradog 6; 10; 14; 22; 24 (ch); 28; 29; 30; 31–3; 43; 53; 70; 111; 115; 117; 147

Rhydderch ab 'Egwyd' 204

Rhydderch ab 'Eivid' 198

Rhydderch ab Elgan Weflhwch 41 (ch)

Rhydderch ab Iestyn 5; 8; 10; 13; 14; 20–2; 23 (ch); 24 (ch); 27; 32 (ch); 33 (ch); 43; 52; 59; 60; 62; 70 (ch); 92; 107; 108; 109; 111; 114; 115; 116; 117; 122; 128 (sons of); 160 n. 38; 162; 188; 189; 190; 197; 198; 202

Rhydderch ab Iestyn, dynasty of 8; 25 (sons of); 26; 27; 28; 29; 30; 31; 32; 53; 54; 66; 111; 114; 117; 118; 122

Rhydderch ap Tewdwr 37 (ch); 73 (ch); 75 (ch)

Rhymni, River 146

Rhys Mwynfawr ap Gruffudd ap Rhys 15 (ch); 16 (and mother of); 37 (ch); 38; 64; 76; 77 (ch); 88; 91 (ch); 117

Rhys ap Meurig ap Hywel 111; 113 (ch); 193 (ch); 194; 201

Rhys ab Owain ab Edwin 6; 8; 10; 14; 17;

19 (ch); 21 (ch); 28; 29–31; 36; 38; 39 (ch); 43; 45; 48; 51 (ch); 52; 53; 63 (ch); 68; 69 (ch); 76; 80; 100; 114; 115; 116; 117; 147

Rhys ab Owain Gwynedd ap Gruffudd 91 (ch)

Rhys ab Owain ap Morgan Hen 113 (ch); 184; 185; 193 (ch)

Rhys ap Rhydderch 6; 20; 22; 24 (ch); 25–7; 31; 32 (ch); 33 (ch); 65; 122; 124; 127; 141; 164

Rhys Gryg ap Rhys Mwynfawr 15; 37 (ch); 38; 59; 60; 64; 67; 72; 86; 89; 105; 106; 109 (ch); 117

Rhys ap Tewdwr 6; 10; 11; 14; 15 (ch); 16 (and wife of); 19 (ch); 31; 33–8 (ch–37); 39 (ch); 40; 43; 44; 46; 52; 53; 54; 56; 63 (ch); 69 (ch); 73 (ch); 77 (and ch); 79; 80; 83; 89; 100; 103; 105; 114; 115; 116; 117; 118; 142; 143; 144; 148; 149; 153; 155; 160(–1) n. 38; 168; 169; 170; 176; 180; 181; 207; 209

Rhys Sais, sons of 4; 6; 93; 94

Richard de Clare 169

Richard FitzBaldwin 52

Richard: see also Rhicart

'Riguallaun filius Gulfrit': see Rhiwallon ap Gwlfrid

Rinns, the 171; 174

'Riubrein' (see also Whitechurch) 191–2

Robert Curthose, duke of Normandy 151; 170

Robert of Rhuddlan 78; 84; 143; 145; 148; 150; 153–5; 181

Robert: see also Rhotbert

Rockfield, Monmouthshire (see also 'Languronui') 185

Rollo of Normandy 173; 174

Rome 28; 188

'Ron, Isle of' 178

'Ruid', *sacerdos* 188

Saer, knight 11; 44; 103; 152

St Bride's-super-Ely 196

St Chad's, Chester 137

St Davids 17; 28; 108; 121; 122; 142; 158; 159; 160; 161; 167; 168; 176; 180; 189; 200; 202

St Maughans 198; 200; 204; 206

St Werburh's, Chester 154

Salisbury 173 (earl of)

Sanan ferch Dyfnwal 107 (ch)

Scandinavia 156

237

Tywi, River 11; 22 (battle at mouth of); 65 (battle at mouth of); 127; 132; 164 (battle at mouth of)
Tywyn 157

'Ubiad' 5
Ubis/Ufic/Usic 121–2
Uchdryd ab Edwin 6; 11; 14; 40; 48–51; 53 (ch); 73 (ch); 76; 95; 115; 118; 150; 151
Uchdryd ab Edwin, sons of 7; 53 (ch)
uchelwyr 8
Uí Briain dynasty of Munster 1
Uí Néill kings 167
Uilla: places named in *Liber Landauensis*
Uilla Carnou 195
Uilla Crucou 195
Uilla Elcu 187; 188
Uilla Filiorum Quichtrit: see Uilla Tref Eliau in Senghenydd
Uilla Fratris 194
Uilla Gunnuc in Guarthaf Cwm 205
Uilla Iunuhuc (see also Undy) 185; 186
Uilla Meluc 203
Uilla Penn i Prisc, Difrinn Anouid (see also Cwm Nofydd) 190
Uilla Pennros 202; 203
Uilla Tref Eliau in Senghenydd, Uilla Filiorum Quichtrit (see also Splott) 190
Uilla Tref Ginhill 192
Uilla Tref Gulich (see also Dyffryn Golych, Worlton) 193; 194
Uilla Tref Rita (see also Llanddegfedd) 204
Ulster 85; 87 (ch); 171; 174; 179
Undy, Gwent 186
Urban, bishop of Llandaff 184; 188
Usk, River 164

'Varudri', lord of 'Cruc Brenan' in Ireland 176
Vaughan, Robert, of Hengwrt 103
vikings (see also Hiberno-Scandinavians) 1; 2; 3; 11; 12; 18; 64; 106; 108; 110; 123; 149; 156–82; 207–9

Walter Map 65; 66
Waterford (Port Lairge) 160; 163; 176

Welsh annalists 26; 60; 78; 141; 171
Welsh chronicles 2; 3; 28; 36; 38; 42; 48; 56; 62; 65; 66; 68; 70; 74; 76; 77; 78; 80; 82; 83; 84; 90; 93; 96; 97–8; 100; 106; 108; 110; 111; 112; 113; 114; 115; 117; 118; 120–1 (and n. 5); 125; 127; 128; 130; 131; 138; 142; 148; 150; 151; 152; 157; 158; 159; 160; 161 (and n. 42); 162; 163; 164; 165; 166; 167; 168; 169; 171; 180; 186; 189; 190; 191; 204
Welsh genealogies and pedigrees 2; 3–119; 186; 191
Welsh Marches 78; 170; 172; 173 (warden of); 208; 209
'Wenedocia': see Gwynedd
Wessex 133; 138; 159
Westbury 164; 197
Wexford 176
Whitechurch, Ergyng 192
Whitechurch, Glamorgan 192
William I the Conqueror, king of England 28; 34; 38; 40; 70; 93; 126; 139; 141; 142; 144; 148; 149; 153; 154; 155; 167; 174; 201; 205
William II Rufus, king of England 144; 145; 148; 150; 153; 170; 173
William Longespee, earl of Salisbury 173
William Longsword, 'Gwilym gleddyf hir' 173; 174
William of Jumièges 167
William of Malmesbury 2; 27; 65; 70; 167
'Wilsceaxan' 27
Wirral 157
witan 134
Worcester 197
Worcestershire 124; 148
Worlton 194
Wye, River 124

'Ynis Peithan' 191
York 200
Yslani: see Slani
Ystrad Tywi 11; 29; 44; 51; 65; 68 (men of); 70 (men of); 103; 111; 115; 128; 132; 145; 146; 151; 152

238